HOME-PSYCH

HOME-PSYCH

THE SOCIAL PSYCHOLOGY OF HOME AND DECORATION

JOAN KRON

DESIGN BY WALTER BERNARD

Clarkson N. Potter, Inc./Publishers NEW YORK

DISTRIBUTED BY CROWN PUBLISHERS, INC.

Grateful acknowledgment is hereby made to the following for
permission to reprint materials from their publications:

Excerpts from the March 17, 1977, and April 7, 1977, issues of
The New York Times, copyright © 1977 by The New York Times
Company. Reprinted by permission.

Excerpts from ABOUT THE HOUSE by W. H. Auden,
copyright © 1965, 1964, 1963, 1962, 1959 by W. H. Auden.
Reprinted by permission of Random House, Inc.

The 1933 Social Status Report from CONTEMPORARY
AMERICAN INSTITUTIONS: A SOCIOLOGICAL ANALYSIS
by F. Stewart Chapin, copyright 1935 by Harper
& Brothers. Used by permission.

Published by Clarkson N. Potter, Inc.,
One Park Avenue, New York, New York 10016 and simultaneously in
Canada by General Publishing Company Limited

Manufactured in the United States of America

Library of Congress Cataloging in Publication Data
Kron, Joan.
Home-psych: the social psychology of home and
decoration.

Bibliography: p.
Includes index.
1. Interior decoration—Psychological aspects.
I. Title.
NK2113.K76 1983   747'.01'9   83-17617
ISBN 0-517-54182-3

Spot illustrations by Marc Rosenthal
10 9 8 7 6 5 4 3 2 1
First Edition

to the memories of

Jane West,
who encouraged me to write this book

my father, Bernard Feldman,
who taught me to be house proud

and my daughter, Leslie Kron,
who wanted a house with a white picket fence

CONTENTS

ACKNOWLEDGMENTS

IT IS HARD TO SAY when an idea for a book such as this is conceived. Certainly my personal history has something to do with it. I have always joked that my earliest memories were of my parents quarreling over the furniture arrangement. Years of working as a designer before I became a journalist gave me insight into the highly charged emotional issues in furnishing a home. In 1973, when Nancy Newhouse (now of the *New York Times*) gave me my first assignment for *New York* magazine to write about the psychology of the bedroom, the idea began to take form. I realized after doing that article how complex the meanings of our habitats could be—and how much more there was to learn. Several subsequent discussions with the late sociologist Erving Goffman about the social pressures in interior decorating further opened up the possibilities of the subject to me. I regret that he did not live to see what he inspired.

All these threads came together when I tried to convince Mercedes Lopez-Morgan that costly crystal stemware was a waste of money since it would surely end up being broken. Her explanation of the significance of Baccarat glassware to her family, emigrées from Castro's Cuba, affirmed for me that there was much more to furnishing a home than functionality and good design, and I decided then to dig deeper. But where do you start? There was no taxonomy of the subject, no theory of home furnishings.

Without the enthusiasm and absolute faith in the idea of Jane West, the late editor-in-chief and publisher of Clarkson N. Potter, Inc., and the support she was able to marshal from Nat Wartels, Alan Mirken, and Bruce Harris of Crown Publishers, Inc., the idea would have remained "the book I will write one day." With only a title and an outline that was to be amended frequently, I began my quest. My two-pronged approach was to find theories that would explain our relationships to our homes and homemakers whose lives the theories would elucidate.

While the process has been lengthy and often lonely, it has opened up a whole world of ideas and people to me. Books and printed matter were the point of entry into the topic, and I am grateful to the libraries that made these so available to me. I want to especially thank the Research Library of the New York Public Library; the Graduate School of City University of New York library and the CUNY Environmental Psychology Department Library and Dean Harold Proshansky and Professor Leanne Rivlin there; the Berkeley Publications department and Berkeley's Environmental Design Library, and library aides Charles Shain and John Johnson there; the Regenstein Library at the University of Chicago; Harvard's Loeb Library; and the libraries of Columbia University and Barnard College, the New York Academy of Medicine, and the New York Psychoanalytic Institute. Special thanks to Henry Grunwald and Murray Gart of Time, Inc., for allowing me to use the Time, Inc., library in the first phase of this project.

In the course of my readings, I identified those key social scientists who might provide me with some answers and direction, and I set out to meet them. They all generously shared their opinions and knowledge and referred me to others in what came to be a model of networking. I am especially indebted to Irwin Altman, Dean of Behavioral Science at the University of Utah, not only for his books and articles which have been a great resource, but also for our discussions on environmental psychology. Sociologists Eugene Rochberg-Halton, formerly of the University of Chicago and now of Notre Dame, and Barry Schwartz of the University of Georgia, supplied me with grounding in their specialities, outlined my reading assignments, were always willing to talk to me, and kindly reviewed some early drafts. Their appreciation of what I was writing gave me the courage to keep going ever deeper into sociological waters. Geographers James Duncan of the University of British Columbia and Nancy Duncan of Syracuse University and psychologists Brian Little of Canada's Carleton University and Perla Korosec-Serfaty of Strasbourg, France's Université Louis Pasteur, all read parts of the text and were extraordinarily generous with their time and ideas which I found inspiring. Special thanks also to Kimberly Dovey and Clare Cooper Marcus of Berkeley, David Peretz of Columbia University, Jerome Tognoli of C.W. Post College, MIT's Rosalind Williams, Mike Brill of B.O.S.T.I., Cornell's Franklin Becker, Craig Zimring of the Georgia Institute of Technology, Columbia's Herbert Gans, Mihaly Csikszentmihalyi of the University of Chicago, Rikard Küller of Sweden's Lund University, Amos Rapoport of the University of Wisconsin, and CUNY's Harold Proshansky who had long discussions with me on a variety of subjects; and not the least to Mary Douglas of Northwestern University for her advice and insights and for allowing me to sit in on her seminars.

In addition, the following social scientists granted me interviews and referred me to colleagues, recommended further reading, supplied me with papers, helped me locate esoteric sources, and discussed sticky questions, among other kindnesses: John Archea, Robert Bechtel, Judith Blau, Sidney Brower, Anne Buttimer, Theodore Caplow, David Canter, Jan Cohn, James A. Davis, Sheila de Bretteville, Paul DiMaggio, Paul Douglas, Carla Dumesnil, Nicholas Feimer, Arnold Friedmann, Lita Furby, Marjorie Gelfond, Charlan Graff, Edward Guy, Jay Haley, David Halle, D. Geoffrey Hayward, David Henrich, Basil Honikman, Jaime Horwitz, Sandra Howell, William Ittelson, Laura Johnson, Rachel Kaplan, Morley Kare, Robert Kastenbaum, Suzanne Keller, Stephan Marc Klein, Florence Ladd, Jon Lang, Judith Langer, Myra Bluebond-Langner, Roderick Lawrence, Daniel J. Levinson, Lynn Lofland, Bonnie Loyd, Alfred Messer, Norbett L. Mintz, Gary Moore, Jerome Motto, Maria Nordstrom of the National Swedish Institute for Building Research, Emilie O'Mara, Martie Oury, Peggy Papp, Rebecca Peterson, Gerry Pratt, Milton Sapirstein, Edwin Shneidman, Jerome E. Singer, Robert Sommer, Fred Steele, Judy Stern, Dan Stokols, Anselm Strauss, Francoise Szigeti, Henry N. Tobey, Victoria Jane Willis, and Paul Windley. I am particularly indebted to EDRA, the Environmental Design Research Association, whose conferences exposed me to so many ideas and researchers, and to Willo White, EDRA's executive director. Special thanks also to the Facilities Management Institute's Cecil Williams and Mary Jane Whitaker; SRI's Gloria Esdale and Arnold Mitchell, and Yankelovich, Skelly and White's Barbara Caplan.

One group of people who helped me enormously I am unable to thank by name because they were promised anonymity. These are the dozens of homemakers I interviewed in their homes in various parts of the country. Many more were interviewed in group sessions or on the telephone. To protect the identities of these men and women, I have referred to them in the book by fictitious first names and no last names, and I have changed certain details of their stories. (Where first and last names are both used the people are real and the stories are unchanged.) My great appreciation to Joan Baeder, Dawn Bennett, Martin Davidson, Diane Gingles, Dolph Gotelli, Bruce Keiser, Blair Sabol and Lillian and Teddy Williams, for allowing me to use their names and experiences. All of my interviews with homemakers were moving and proved to me over and over again that the home is invested with enormous meaning.

In addition to these primary sources, I had assistance on small points of accuracy from a wide variety of experts: historians, designers, furniture retailers, market researchers, and others including Susan Gray Detweiler, Jane Nylander of Old Sturbridge Village, Edgard De N. Mayhew, Nory Miller, Suzanne Stephens, the American Association for the Blind, Nat Hendricks of the Brooklyn Brownstoners, Carole Edlin and Abbot Lutz of the Collectors Club, Robert Strickland of the Lowe's Co., Brad Farnsworth of the Do-It-Yourself Research Institute, Wallace Epperson of Wheat First Securities who supplied me with his proprietary market statistics, Glenn Goodwin of Seidman and Seidman who also supplied statistical information, Eckert Guethe of Condé Nast, Barbara Tober of *Bride's* magazine, Kay Anderson of *Furniture Today*, Hugh Curley of *Better Homes and Gardens*, Duane Garrison and Karen Laufler of Tiffany's, the Public Relations Department of General Mills, Donald Moe of the Irvine Co., and Linda Foa, Judy Gura, and Gilda Mintz who helped with special problems.

For additional ideas, comments, and leads, my thanks to Peter Aaron, Bob Anderson, Jaime Ardiles-Arce, Roberta Ashley, Robin Ashley, William Ayers, Ted Bakewell III, Pat Braun, Denise Scott Brown, Anne Cicero, Meg Coles, David Crane, Pat Crane, Marian Donnelly, Helen Drutt, Marilyn Evins, Barbara Feigen, Edward Feigen, Barbara Feldman, Jonathan Feldman, Barbara Flood, Tonny Foy, Susan S. Freedman, Judith Friedman, Alan Halpern, Dee Harget, Jim Hedrich, Marjorie Horwitz, Steven Izenour, JoAnne Jacobs, Janet Kardon, Matthew Klein, Carl Levine, Joy Lewis, Robert K. Lewis, Nancy Love, Karl Mann, John Mariani, Robert Metzger, Charles Morgan, Jerry Moskowitz, Richard Ohrbach, Elizabeth Paris, Robert Patino, Hank Plant, Richard Proctor, RB Industries, John Reid, Robin Roberts, Roma Furniture, Barbara Ross and Barbara Schwartz of Dexter Design, Arlene Rudykoff, Carl Ruff, John Saladino, Michael Schaible, Lila Schneider, Susan Shins, Mark Simon, Suzanne Slesin, Holly Solomon, Jay Spectre, Susan Subtle, University Microfilms, the Wallpaper Manufacturers Institute, Acey Wolgin, Hillary Wordell, and C. DeWayne Youts. Mario Buatta, Alan Buchsbaum, John Montorio, and Harriet Weintraub were a great cheering squad and never deserted me.

For shelter and hospitality in my travels, I am indebted to Judi Skalsky and Anne Gilbar in Los Angeles; Henry and Jean May in Berkeley; Clarissa and George Dyer in San Francisco; Bruce Schimberg, the late Sonia Cicero Schimberg, and Myrna and Don Lord in Chicago; and Joan Marie Ryan in Honolulu.

Most of the transcribing of recorded interviews was done by Rosemary Nicholson who was not only accurate but discreet as well. She gave me my first confirmation that others would find the material as interesting as I did. Debra Weiss, Rae Barlow, Larry Heiman, and Ann Goldstein were able library researchers; and Jonathan Marder, for the brief period he was on the job, was a positive whirlwind, racing from uptown libraries to downtown libraries, finding the unfindable books and dissertations, and creatively uncovering material that wasn't even on his list. He was also an enthusiastic reader of the manuscript and offered valuable suggestions.

This book was written on a Lexitron VT 1202 word processor and it was a steadfast assistant. My appreciation to Jerry Osley of Lexitron and its able technicians including Bobby Gronert, Richie Davis, Joe Jordan, and Tony Spinella; my thanks also to Ted Powell for his consultation on word processing, to Erica Stevens for her help in translating French sources, and to Judy Migliaccio, Lucy Mattimore, Sylvester Lloyd, Ruth and Max Lee of New World Books, Kathe Telingator, and Frank Lugo, for assistance in special areas. I am indebted to Judith Wright for helping me keep my own household intact while I wrote about others.

My agent Lucy Kroll was dedicated to the idea of the book from the start and carried the message to others. Her enthusiasm has never diminished and she has been there for me at every difficult pass giving emotional support and counsel.

My appreciation to the staffs of Clarkson N. Potter, Inc., and Crown Publishers, Inc., is boundless. Carol Southern stepped in as editorial director in midstream with her own brand of enthusiasm and commitment; her observations and suggestions have been invaluable in shaping the book. Nancy Novogrod, my editor, has been with the project since its inception and the relationship has been one that writers only dream of. Whatever faults there are in the book are my own. Despite coping with a series of special events including a family addition, a move, and a difficult loss, she has been an anchor for me, working overtime, discussing, reading and rereading, offering sound suggestions in content and style, checking my insights against her own, and giving her unstinting support and encouragement. My thanks to her spill over to her husband John Novogrod and their children Jamie and Caroline for bearing with this intrusion on their time and to Elvira Bocanegra who assisted them at home. Thanks also to Clarkson N. Potter, Inc., director of operations Michael Fragnito, a strong advocate of the book who created a schedule to aspire to and cheered us on to the wire; to Laurie Stark, managing editor of Crown, for her dedicated and sensitive supervision of copy editing and production; to Lynne Arany and David Bauer for diligent assistance in the production process; and to Gael Dillon for her judgment in art direction with which I always concur.

Walter Bernard was absolutely too busy to design this book, but I am delighted that he did; thanks also to Mark Rosenthal who did the book jacket and inside illustrations, Chris Callis who photographed the eyes, Jay Harper who retouched them, and to Milton Glaser for sidewalk superintendence. I am also pleased for both esthetic and sentimental reasons that Daniel Kron took my jacket photo.

My family helped in a crucial way. I am grateful to my husband Jerry Marder, my son Daniel, my stepchildren Jonathan, Susan, and Jane, my mother Rose Feldman, for their endurance—for handling so many things for me and without me, for excusing me from important events, and carrying on without me so often. They allowed me to pursue my obsession. Without their love, understanding, support, and indulgence I would never have been able to complete this book.

And last, I want to thank someone whose story is not in the book but whose life fascinates me still. That is Klaus Pfeffer, a 68-year-old San Francisco man to whom I was introduced because of his immaculately organized closets. When I interviewed him he was reaching the end of his trust funds and was planning to kill himself in six months. He had never worked a day in his life and had no family, no skills, and no desire to live on welfare. I checked in with him a few times during the following months and, finally, alarmed that he was absolutely serious, arranged for a suicidologist to consult with him. But, Klaus could not be deterred. He slipped off to a motel and killed himself with the pills he had been saving.

I regret I could not find a proper place for Klaus in this book, so atypical and bizarre was his story. I know that would disappoint him. If he is "on a cloud somewhere, looking down" as he assured me he would be when the book came out, I hope he will forgive me.

J. K.
July 17, 1983

PREFACE

Beyond Style

IT WAS A DARK and muggy midnight in July 1977. New York City was in the midst of a massive power outage and blackout. In the City Room of the *New York Times* the staff was working by the light of battery-powered lanterns trying to get an edition out. When a photo editor from the "hard news" side of the paper encountered a "home" reporter in the shadowy newsroom, he dumped some bitterness he might have been embarrassed to voice in better light. "How is the Home Section going to cover the blackout?" he asked her snidely. "Do a story about decorating with candles?"

The editor's remark wasn't merely the *Front Page* macho of an old-timer miffed at the growing importance of life-style sections to the newspaper's circulation; it was indicative of a widespread bias against decorating and style, which ranks even lower on the seriousness scale than gossip and fashion. Compared to hunger, crime, unemployment, and "the bomb," the home beat appears to be the lightweight champion of the news.

Gloria Emerson, the Vietnam war correspondent, put style in its place in a 1980 *Savvy* column in which she laced into women for reading the frivolous style sections of the newspaper before reading the front page. To big thinkers, decorating is style without content, empty calories—like the comics and coffee-table books and "Dallas." If you care about it, you had better apologize for it. And people do.

"I read . . . all those frivolous sections in the *New York Times*—the Home Section and the Living Section—all the things that appeal to one's basest instincts," confessed Susan Sheehan, known for her *New Yorker* articles on prisons, welfare mothers, schizophrenia, and Vietnam. Her ambivalence—her attraction to those newspaper sections and her embarrassment about it—points up the double bind we are in when it comes to decorating.

On the one hand, we tend to glorify and sentimentalize the beautiful home and the good life led in it. According to a recent history of the American home, there are "more house-shrines in America than in any other country in the world." We also subscribe to the notion that "living well is the best revenge." We worship good taste. We are advised ad infinitum in women's magazines to express ourselves in our homes—let the "me" come through. We are bombarded with ads and commercials about products that will improve our lives and our sacroiliacs and demonstrate our discrimination. No doubt about it, we are expected to be proficient in homemaking. We're not sure why and often not sure how to. We just know we must do it.

On the other hand, decorating is loaded with bad connotations. A preoccupation with it is considered trivial, narcissistic, materialistic, superficial. It smacks of status-seeking. It has been known to cause nervous breakdowns, bankruptcy, and divorce. And it is doubly suspect because it tends to be woman's work. Even many men who have been reeducated to give a hand with the housework expect a woman to make the decorating decisions.

This is a conundrum. If home is significant, why is home improvement insignificant? Does anyone have the answer?

Although the mass media keep us up-to-date on the psychology of everything from belly-button anxiety to animal's emotional lives, it has been struck nearly dumb on the psychology of home and decoration. Certainly you won't find many explanations in "shelter" magazines, where decorating is treated like fashion with the emphasis on "ins" and "outs." The burning question in these publications is "What's next?" Is elegance here to stay or is it here on a temporary visa? Will sofas be fat or slim? What's next after

Eclectic and Minimal and pastels and country? And which country is the one to watch? The more sophisticated shelter magazines treat "design," as they call decorating, as fine art—tableaux for esthetic contemplation, which may be nice to look at but are not always pleasant to inhabit.

It seems to me that treating the furnishing of the home as Fashion or Art, disconnected from human needs and social function, is like trying to eat plaster reproductions of food. But what other criteria do most of us have by which to judge an interior? Expertise in homemaking is built up out of the common stock of knowledge in a society—"this is how it's done"—and disseminated through custom and imitation. In our culture, the craft of homemaking is often taught in the media, where the curriculum has been *low* on theory and *heavy* on example, perhaps because examples are more photogenic.

Three years ago I set out to discover the meaning and purpose of this activity we call decorating. Why do we do it? I wanted to know. Is it just a ruffle on reality—a way to escape the bad news on the front page? Or is it an important human activity with redeeming social value? I admit I wasn't entirely unbiased. I was hoping to find significance in this endeavor.

One of my objectives was to learn what research had been done or was being done that could give the average homemaker insight into her or his own place-making. The search led me into a variety of disciplines: anthropology, sociology, geography, economics, popular culture, market research, and the relatively new field of environmental psychology. I thought I would be lucky if I found five to ten relevant studies. But to my amazement I found dozens of people nationwide and worldwide doing research that is related to the home and its decoration. Not that you will encounter the word "decoration" in the academic lexicon. To find anything out about the subject, you must look under such allied topics as "behavior settings," "consumption finesse," "human engineering," "impression management," "material environment," "place attachment," "ritual trappings," "spatial cognition," "appropriation of space," and "transitional objects."

The activity you and I call decorating social scientists call "marking" or "personalization," and it is not considered a trifling, inconsequential activity that appeals to "our basest instincts." In fact, personalization is probably as close as one can get to a universal human activity—as significant and meaningful a human endeavor as mating or food gathering or economic exchange.

Most people believe they are acting independently when they choose objects for their homes, but it became apparent to me as I went deeper into this subject that decorating is not a private matter between consenting individuals and their favorite styles. Decorating, like dressing, is as much a social act as an individual one. How we decorate our homes corresponds to social class, values, sex roles, and stage of life as much as it does to personal preferences. Certain styles become the rallying flags of group membership. And certain people prefer to express their membership in a group rather than their own personalities. Recent research tells us that a major concern when a man furnishes is fear of appearing feminine; the fondness for sentimental objects increases with age; the desire to own art increases with upward social mobility; counterculture families organize their spaces differently from conventional families and status-seeking is as natural as breathing and definitely has survival value.

To that perennial question "What's next in decorating?," I would answer, what's next is not a style, or a color, or a look, but *a way of looking* at the home. I call it "home-psych," short for the social psychology of home and decoration—and that is what this book is about.

Home-Psych is beyond style. It's not a prescription or a how-to diagram but rather an exploration of how we shape our environments and how they shape us. While it's not a decorating *idea* book in the traditional sense, it should open up a dialogue and get you thinking about such things as your relationship to your home and possessions, your conflicting needs for privacy and sociability, your ambivalence about standing out or conforming. These are "a thousand and one decorating ideas" of a different sort.

INTRODUCTION

Guilt and Desire
on the Home Front

Ⓞ N JUNE 7, 1979, Martin J. Davidson entered the materialism hall of fame. That morning the thirty-four-year-old New York graphic design entrepreneur went to his local newsstand and bought fifty copies of the *New York Times* expecting to read an article about himself in the Home Section that would portray him as a man of taste and discrimination. Instead, his loft and his life style, which he shared with singer Dawn Bennett, were given the tongue-in-cheek treatment under the headline: "When Nothing but the Best Will Do."

Davidson, who spent no more money renovating his living quarters than many of the well-to-do folks whose homes are lionized in the *Times*'s Thursday and Sunday design pages—the running ethnographic record of contemporary upper-middle-class life style—made the unpardonable error of telling reporter Jane Geniesse how much he had paid for his stereo system, among other things. Like many people who have not been on intimate terms with affluence for very long, Davidson is in the habit of price-tagging his possessions. His 69 cent per bottle bargain Perrier, his $700 Armani suits from Barney's, his $27,000 cooperative loft and its $150,000 renovation, his sixteen $350-per-section sectionals, and his $11,000 best-of-class stereo. Martin J. Davidson wants the world to know how well he's done. "I live the American dream," he told Mrs. Geniesse, which includes, "being known as one of Barney's best customers."

Davidson even wants the U.S. Census Bureau's computer to know how well he has done. He is furious, in fact, that the 1980 census form did not have a box to check for people who live in cooperatives. "If someone looks at my census form they'll think I must be at the poverty level or lower." No one who read the *Times* article about Martin Davidson would surmise that.

It is hard to remember when a "design" story provoked more outrage. Letters to the editor poured in. Andy Warhol once said that in our fast-paced media world no one could count on being a celebrity for more than fifteen minutes. Martin Davidson was notorious for weeks. "All the Martin Davidsons in New York," wrote one irate reader, "will sit home listening to their $11,000 stereos, while downtown, people go to jail because they ate a meal they couldn't pay for." "How can one man embody so many of the ills afflicting our society today?" asked another offended reader. "Thank you for your clever spoof," wrote a third reader. "I was almost convinced that two people as crass as Martin Davidson and Dawn Bennett could exist." Davidson's consumption largesse was even memorialized by Russell Baker, the *Times*'s Pulitzer Prize-winning humorist, who devoted a whole column to him: "While simultaneously consuming yesterday's newspaper," wrote Baker, "I consumed an article about one Martin Davidson, a veritable Ajax of consumption. A man who wants to consume nothing but the best and does." Counting, as usual, Davidson would later tell people, "I was mentioned in the *Times* on three different days."

Davidson, a self-made man whose motto is "I'm not taking it with me and while I'm here I'm going to spend every stinking penny I make," couldn't understand why the *Times* had chosen to make fun of him rather than to glorify his 4,000-square-foot loft complete with bidet, Jacuzzi, professional exercise gear, pool table, pinball machine, sauna, two black-tile bathrooms, circular white Formica cooking island, status-stuffed collections of Steiff animals, pop art (including eleven Warhols), a sound system that could weaken the building's foundations if turned up full blast, and an air-conditioning system that can turn cigarette smoke, which both Davidson and Bennett abhor, into mountain dew—a loft that has everything Martin Davidson ever wanted in a home except a swimming pool and a squash court.

"People were objecting to my life style," said Davidson. "It's almost as if there were a correlation between the fact that we spend so much on ourselves and other people are starving. No one yells when someone spends $250,000 for a chest of drawers at an auction," he complained. "I just read in the paper that someone paid $650,000 for a stupid stamp. Now it'll be put away in a vault and no one will ever see it."

But Dawn Bennett understood what made Davidson's consumption different. "It's not very fashionable to be an overt consumer and admit it," she said.

On December 21, 1980, when their well-maintained visages were on the cover of the *New York Times Magazine* under the headline "Living Well Is the Best Revenge," Françoise and Oscar de la Renta joined Martin Davidson in the materialism hall of fame.

"He designs dresses, she runs the house," began the article by Francesca Stanfill about the well-known dress designer and his French wife, a former fashion editor (who died in June 1983) and a mega-hostess with flair, panache, charisma, social savvy, power-heavy dinner party guests, and more flowered chintz per square inch than a Vuillard. The houses she runs are "sumptuous" with "infallibly fashionable interiors," including "flocked red velvet walls edged in green *faux marbre*, silk-upholstered Second Empire chairs, mother-of-pearl cabinets . . . windows swagged in heavy fringed silk. . . . Many see the couple's house-consciousness as a near mania," continued the article. "Rooms are constantly rearranged; wallpaper is replaced; new paintings and objects are added."

Sounding every bit as materialistic as Martin J. Davidson, Françoise de la Renta waxed enthusiastic about her bed and table linens. In Bordeaux, where she hailed from, she said, "A great thing is made about linen. I have a passion for linen. You don't know the joy I get, looking at my linen closets."

Do the de la Rentas consider themselves excessive spenders? "By my book I'm not extravagant," said Mr. de la Renta, "although by a lot of other people's standards, I suppose I am."

The angry letters poured in. Calvin Trillin did a satirical "tap dance" in the *Nation* about why he had never been invited to dine at the de la Rentas. Monday morning quarterbacks at the *Times* argued among themselves whether enshrining the values of the *nouvelle société à succès* was really all the news fit to print. Like Martin Davidson, the de la Rentas had committed the cardinal sin. They had no guilt, no remorse. But, then, as the *Times* article noted, the de la Rentas had "no fear of ostentation, nor are they inhibited by the pressure of discretion that often characterizes those with old fortunes."

The to-do over the de la Rentas was just a warm-up for the Reagans. In January 1981 newly inaugurated president Ronald Reagan put a freeze on all unnecessary furniture expenditures for his administration's offices but gave his wife carte blanche to refurbish their private living quarters in the White House. The big trivia question *before* they moved in—would they or wouldn't they keep the controversial family dining-room wallpaper with the Revolutionary War scenes that Jacqueline Kennedy had put up, Betty Ford had taken down, and Rosalynn Carter had put back up—was all but forgotten when the scope of Nancy Reagan's decorating plans became known. Returning the customary presidential decorating allotment of $50,000 to the Treasury, Mrs. Reagan raised eyebrows by raising contributions to her refurbishing fund from a long list of industrial fat cats.

By November of the same year, everything was in place upstairs. In less time than it takes a civilian client to get delivery on one made-to-order settee, first decorator Ted Graber of Los Angeles had installed close to a million dollars' worth of carpeting, swag draperies, marble sinks, silk lampshades, handpainted wallpaper, framed prints and photos (including an autographed one from England's Queen Mother), and down-filled upholstery, and had thirty-three mahogany doors refinished.

In the meantime, while the president was cutting back on federal support for school lunches, the "bride" of the White House was registering for 220 nineteen-piece place settings of ivory bone china bordered in her favorite red and imperial gold with a gold presidential seal in the center—incentive, perhaps, for guests to clean their plates.

This bride did not have to wait very long to complete her set. The $290,000 tab for the china was picked up graciously by a foundation—a fact that did not make the public any less critical of the expenditure. The china purchase attracted enough flack to shatter every piece in the first china cabinet. Embodied in the purchase were issues of taste, morality, values, national pride, and appropriateness. "The new White House china has become the single most controversial aspect of the domestic side of Reagan's short tenure," wrote critic Martin Filler in *Skyline*, the highbrow architectural journal. He also took issue with Mrs. Reagan's decorating taste. In a *Times* op-ed piece, MIT's Rosalind Williams, a social historian, accused Reagan of being as callous as French nobility before the Revolution—"heedless of the plight of the ragged peasants they glimpsed from gilded carriages."

The "My" Generation

Although they traveled in different circles, Martin Davidson, the de la Rentas, and the Reagans were in the visible vanguard of a nationwide trend. A 1979 Yankelovich, Skelly and White study for the Food Institute found "a rise in materialism amid economic gloom." Not only were Americans shifting from "self-denial" to "focus on self," as Tom Wolfe detailed in "The 'Me' Decade"—finding self-fulfillment in the human potential movement—but now they were reacquainting themselves with the potential of possessions. Enter the "My" Generation. After being locked in for *est* sessions without being allowed to go to the bathroom, they raised their hands to go to sybaritic bathrooms. One of the overflows from the rebirthing experience was the desire for soaking tubs; and the taste for pot gave way to an addiction to jogging, aerobic dancing, and Nautilus machines. People were cutting calories, but they were not cutting the fat out of their custom kitchens, sofas, and stereo systems. They wanted more. "For the overwhelming majority of Americans, an important part of living the good life simply means 'more,'" wrote Daniel Yankelovich in *New Rules*.

In 1975 people said a good job and a good marriage were the ingredients of a good life. By 1978 color TVs, money, and clothes moved to the top of the list, and a car became more important than children. "The egalitarian spirit is gone," Yankelovich's partner, Florence Skelly, told the American Society of Interior Decorators in 1980. There was a return to conspicuous consumption. People were making more money, especially the burgeoning group of two-earner families. "They want to demonstrate their upward mobility through material goods." In September 1981 the untrendy *U.S. News & World Report* did a cover story titled "Flaunting Wealth: It's Back in Style." The next month the *Times* heralded "The Success of Luxury"; the following month *Language of Clothes* author Alison Lurie was quoted as saying, "It is now acceptable to show off one's wealth."

The recession didn't dampen desire. It accelerated it. When people realized that the good life which had once seemed so available could no longer be taken for granted, they respected it more. To be bourgeois was "in" again, *New York* magazine told us in 1982. "It's no longer chic to be poor," said a twenty-six-year-old artist speaking for his generation. "I don't want to be a dirt farmer. I want goods, products, services."

By mid-1983 overt materialism seemed to have reached the highest watermark since Woodstock. In its own ads *Fortune* was advising "You don't have to hide your ambition anymore. 'If you've got it, go get it.'" Detroit noticed *big* cars were inching back in popularity. And Mitsubishi was pushing its television sets with an ad that read: "Even If You Can't Have the Best of Everything, You Can Have the Best of Something. It's only human nature to want the best. Rolls-Royces, chinchilla coats, villas on the Riviera, Renoirs on the wall." And a Park Avenue condominium with only fifty-six apartments for "fifty-six very special families," was proclaimed by its developers to be "the most expensive apartment house ever built in New York City." Were there really people who would want their home to be identified in such a way? People without modesty, with no fear of envy? "A lot of people would be very proud to live there," said the marketing consultant to the project. "They would see it as a benefit. But please," he requested, "don't say I'm responsible for that slogan."

That's odd. If it was such a good sales pitch, why did he want to dissociate himself from it?

Who Me? I'm Not Materialistic

Why? Because most of us are extremely ambivalent about materialism. We cringe when we read about object worshipers— kissing their things in public, so to speak. They make us uneasy.

We see what we consider to be the worst aspects of ourselves in them. They are flaunting the desires we are trying to repress. Yet we are drawn to them. We want to read about them. We binge on articles about celebrity homes as if they were chocolate truffles. Some of us, like self-appointed pornography watchdogs, avidly monitor reports of acquisitive life styles before denouncing them. And we are quick to condemn the materialistic ways of others, as we deny our own.

Call people anything, but don't call them materialistic—a thirteen-letter four-letter word. In the black-white, heaven-hell dialectic world of *Roget's Thesaurus,* where words reside in either positive or negative columns, "materialism" lives on the wrong side of the page under the heading of Selfishness, side by side with Greed, Self-interest, Acquisitiveness, and Self-indulgence. Materialism has a second home in this synonym-antonym book under Impiety, where its neighbors are Profaneness, Unholiness, and Worldliness.

Webster's Dictionary is no less judgmental. Materialism, "the tendency to be more concerned with material than with spiritual or intellectual goals," has been in bad repute with one group or another ever since Jesus renounced worldly goods. Moses, Mohammed, Buddha, Lao Tzu, St. Francis, Lenin, Marx, the Moslem sufis, the Hindu rishis, the Hebrew prophets, the Amish, the Quakers, Thomas Merton, and Gandhi, whose only possessions were his sheet, his sandals, and his glasses, all had one thing in common—their affection for the simple, possession-free life.

Almost every generation, every country, has had its denouncers of luxury. Religious, moral, political. Eighteenth-century Calvinist Jean-Jacques Rousseau said the luxuries people think they need are "chains binding them." The Protestant ethic promised eternal salvation in return for thrift, hard work, and efficiency; amassing wealth was God's work, but spending on luxury and worldly pleasure was the Devil's work. Thoreau advocated "voluntary poverty." Emerson preached plain living and high thinking. Thorstein Veblen, the American sociologist, in his 1899 polemic, *The Theory of the Leisure Class,* castigated the new rich millionaires of Newport and Saratoga—the Astors, Morgans, Goulds, Vanderbilts, et al.—for their "conspicuous consumption," "pecuniary emulation," and "keeping up with the Joneses."

In 1936, grass-roots philosopher Richard Gregg, inspired by

Gandhi and Eastern philosophy, preached *The Value of Voluntary Simplicity*, a combination of plain living and social responsibility. His ideas later inspired the generation of baby boomers who were raised in America's period of greatest material welfare and therefore felt freer than any generation before them to be idealistic. Down on religion, patriotism, and authority, they became active in the human potential, environmental, and consumer movements.

By 1977 it was estimated that 3 percent of the population—4 to 5 million Americans, mostly single, white, well-educated, politically independent young adults, "fully and wholeheartedly live a life of Voluntary Simplicity," while another third of the population, and perhaps more, were VS sympathizers. And, contrary to the Yankelovich forecast of rising materialism, there were those who thought the prognosis of the VS life style seemed good. In an article in *CoEvolution Quarterly*, Marvin Harris, a respected social scientist, cited evidence that Americans were becoming *less* materialistic; one of his studies showed that 63 percent of Americans felt it would be better if "emphasis were put on *learning to appreciate human values more than material values.*"

It sounded like a genuine revolution in human nature, but as Harris and experienced researchers know, respondents in opinion surveys don't always tell the whole truth—especially if they're a bit self-conscious about their opinions. With this in mind, a candid editorial assistant wrote a footnote to the Harris study: "I like this stuff," said Anne Herbert. "It makes me feel warm and wonderful." She'd vote for human values, too, she said. But she also confessed to having an expensive wish list: "I want a car, I want a stereo and a TV, I want to travel a lot first class, I want to make more money." Even in that altruistic corner of the world, there was guilt and desire.

Guilt and Desire

"People are conflicted," explained home and life-style trend analyst Barbara Caplan, a Yankelovich, Skelly and White vice-president. "They deplore cuts in social services. There was moral outrage over the White House china, but, still, people are out there buying ambience and drooling over elaborate decorating schemes in home magazines. And Lady Di had them glued to their sets."

Even Maine homesteaders Scott and Helen Nearing, vegetarians and authors of *Living the Good Life,* who have no television set, went over to a neighbor's house to catch the royal wedding.

Conflicted about our desire for possessions and our guilt in having or wanting them, many of us recite mea culpas. We confess. We atone by cleaning house. We opt for austerity. But we can't seem to reform. "I went through my pure period in the 1960s," said a Philadelphia woman. "I gave almost all my furniture away. My ideal person didn't clutter her life with maintenance of possessions. But little by little, I realized that was an absolute lie. I love furniture, I love pictures, I love gardens filled with everything." The lust for goods seems as difficult to curb as the craving for sexual gratification. The sexual revolution has gone a long way toward relieving sexual guilt. What about consumer guilt? Lectured repeatedly about the immorality of materialism, people are struggling with the guilt and shame caused by their covetous ways.

"A part of me feels guilty for caring enormously for objects," said Kitty, a successful advertising copywriter whose copy has sold everything from denture polish to eye shadow. She and her husband and their two children live in a modest Manhattan apartment; they weekend in an old farmhouse in the Catskills which they have been restoring for ten years—not what you would call ostentatious—yet she admits to a secret vice. "I have a habit of sitting in my living room in either of our homes and endlessly looking at each object or piece of furniture and remembering where I got it. I remember the day I got that chair from a certain antiques dealer. And the lace curtains . . . this must be very sick. I keep thinking my mind should be focused on more important things. I've been brainwashed by our society—possessions aren't supposed to be that important. So it bothers me that I care so much. It's like being caught playing with yourself."

How Much Is Too Much?

What is the proper level of consumption? Tolstoy said there were only two questions in life—how to live and what to live for. We all have to deal with these questions every day—how to allocate our resources. How much for education, for vacations, for charity? How costly a sofa or stereo system? What grade of mattress and coffee and beef? We like to think these decisions are matters of personal choice, but they are also matters between each person and the "state."

Every society has ways of controlling consumption. It can regulate income, production, possession, or desire. Americans abhor restraint on income, but they have learned to live with taxes on earnings and inherited wealth. These have never been steep enough, however, to erase class differences. If Americans were really committed to material equality, they would equalize income. But that does not seem imminent. One study showed that only a small percentage of people want to take substantial amounts of money away from the wealthy. The possibility of striking it rich is one of our inalienable rights, and few people begrudge the $5 million Bernice and Louis Eisenberg won in the New York lottery—or their trip to Hawaii, their move to a seventeenth-floor coop with terrace and ocean view, and their $8,000 marble bedroom set. "Sweetness here wanted it," said Mr. Eisenberg. "How could I say no?"

Luxury can also be controlled by limiting production of nonessentials, which is always done in wartime. In peacetime, demand regulates supply, and as any number of economic pundits have noted, demand is actually encouraged because the capitalist system *needs our needs*. The economy depends on "the endless inculcation of envy," said political commentator George Will.

Controlling spending is another alternative for controlling luxury. Sumptuary laws have been used throughout history to keep a rein on consumption. With one type of sumptuary law such as Prohibition, a tax on furs, or the recent limitation on travel outside the country imposed by the French government, no one group is favored or punished. With the other type, certain groups of people are not allowed particular foods, clothing, or household goods. This is usually done to keep the lower class from living like the upper. In ancient Rome, for instance, only members of the royal household could wear ermine; during the reign of France's Charles IX, trimming on clothes correlated with rank; sixteenth-century German peasants were forbidden to wear red; King Edward III decreed the points on commoners' shoes could not protrude more than two inches; and for centuries, purple, a dye that comes from Tyrian shellfish, was deemed a royal color because it was so rare.

Feudal Japan probably had the most detailed sumptuary laws

in history: what people could eat, what they could wear, the minutest details of their houses were all legislated. A peasant's standard of living was indexed to his rice production. A 10-bushel farmer was not allowed large teacups and could only eat soup, never a roast; a 100-bushel farmer fared a bit better but was not allowed that Japanese necessity—floor mats; a 500-bushel farmer had larger teacups, floor mats, and more than soup to eat, but still no parlor or tiled roof.

The sumptuary laws on our books today, such as the ban on crocodile handbags and leopard coats, are aimed, for the most part, at saving endangered species. There are no laws against Neiman Marcus's annual "Can you top this?" Christmas gift catalog, consumed by 1,500,000 people each year plus millions more who vicariously enjoy the ritual announcement of the His and Hers gifts on their TV news. Supposedly the public has a need to know even if they can't afford twenty-four-carat gold wigs; his and her Chinese junks and mummy cases; $90,000 leases on natural safety deposit boxes dug out of a granite mountain in Utah; and $17,500 robots.

The most effective way of controlling consumption may be to control *desire*, something sociologist Emile Durkheim figured out a hundred years ago. People must be convinced that "they do not have the right to have more." Moral pressure, peer pressure, media pressure, etiquette, and various rewards are all used to inhibit or postpone desire—just as they are used sometimes to increase desire. Where would savings banks be if today's cravings could not be put off until tomorrow?

The Moral Squad

The enforcers, in this method of control, are not the government, they are "we the people." Our neighbors' budgets occupy us as much as the federal budget, making consumption grandstanding a major spectator sport. Since each person saves and spends at a different rate, we find it particularly hard to comprehend one another's idiosyncratic spending habits. One person likes to make a few mega-purchases each year. Another spends just as much, but on a succession of bitsy buys—as does the woman who admits having to buy something, no matter how small, for her house *every day.* One man thinks it is sinful to eat in expensive restaurants, yet plunks down $15,000 on a solar greenhouse; one woman thinks a dishwasher is an extravagance, yet drives a splashy sports car. Another woman has a fetish about keeping the refrigerator door closed to save energy, yet, rather than bothering to *repair* a small defect in her floor, will have a new parquet floor installed.

To make consumption ethics even more complicated, people in different economic and social classes have different standards of spending and living. It is especially difficult to make sense out of the spending habits of folks a distance away from us in the economic order. Those who accuse others of using their homes to show off are often of lower social status misreading "normal class differences," said sociologist Herbert Gans. Misunderstanding upper-class spending habits, a juror in the trial of John Hinckley, President Reagan's would-be assassin, concluded that Hinckley had to be insane to fly to distant cities and spend only one day in each place. It was inconceivable to this working-class juror that anyone in his right mind, even the son of a successful oil executive, would waste a costly plane fare on a one-day trip. By this man's standards, everyone in the jet set could be declared non compos mentis.

Each person thinks his or her own spending and conserving habits are the righteous way. To justify their consumption, some people become devoted bargain hunters. Instead of buying less, they buy more, but more cheaply. Bargain hunting is just another form of conspicuous consumption, said anthropologist Myra Bluebond-Langner. "It's a preoccupation with possessions in an age of austerity. Embarrassed by their desire, people make a religion out of their shopping and their objects. There are many ways to pray."

In one of those ubiquitous newspaper opinion pieces castigating consumption, a writer pushing for "smaller is smarter," insisted that "those energy-wasting gadgets we spend so much time acquiring must finally be put in the toy chest where they belong." Was she suggesting that Walter Cronkite, who is known to be a "great fan of electronic games," must give up his computer? That Henry Thomas, the young actor who played E. T.'s friend in the film, must stop spending his $5 weekly allowance on video-cassettes? Do Walter and Henry tell that reporter how to spend her time and energy?

The critics we pay most attention to are in our own social

groups. Peer pressure has always been an extremely powerful mode of control. In Victorian England there was an agreed-upon standard of living that varied with the ups and downs of society's resources. Middle- and upper-class Victorians felt it their duty to live as *elaborately* as they could afford. Ostracism, ridicule, and exclusion from sources of power were all used to make sure the right people kept *up* appearances. Although there were reformers who criticized the rigidity of society, people knew what was expected of them.

There is still pressure to conform—the difference between then and now is that there are a greater variety of life styles to conform to today. We use ridicule, too, but more often to encourage keeping *down*, not up. When some people thought Nancy Reagan went too far, she was crowned queen of materialism on a postcard depicting her in a royal tiara and ermine cape. When someone less well known crosses the unmarked but not unpatrolled border into crass materialism, morally outraged letters to the editor suffice.

Clearly, the Sunday observer has replaced the Sunday sermon. Today, our ex cathedra pronouncements emanate from the news media; they keep us up to the moment on prevailing moral and pecuniary standards—which are constantly being debated and adjusted. But the news media send mixed messages serving up *guilt* on the editorial page where we get our moral lumps on the plight of the homeless, and *desire* on the style page, which informs us where to buy $1,000 clocks that only a Ph.D. could tell time by. Both pages are underwritten, of course, by advertisers who whip up more desire.

But why blame the media? The news media are *us* and they suffer from the same ambivalence we do. It has been observed that Americans oscillate between two opposite poles of values— the American Dream of "individual elitism" and the egalitarian ideal of "liberty, equality, and justice." The *elitist* ethic, embodied in the Reagans, is based on the idea that if people earn money through ability and hard work, they have the right to spend it as they please. The *egalitarian* ethic, embodied in the Carters, values understatement and the simple life. It's up to each of us to choose our modus vivendi—that's what living in a pluralistic society is all about. But it's hard to choose without more information. We have heard all about the down side of possessions. Don't they have any redeeming qualities?

What Are Things For?

As anyone knows who has seen a house turned inside out at a yard sale, furnishing a home entails the acquisition of more objects than there are in a spring housewares catalog. With all the time, money, and space we devote to the acquisition, arrangement, and maintenance of these household possessions, it is curious that we know so little about our relationships to our possessions.

"It is extraordinary to discover that no one knows why people want goods," wrote British anthropologist Mary Douglas in *The World of Goods*. Although no proven or agreed-upon theory of possessiveness in human beings has been arrived at, social scientists are coming up with new insights on our complicated relationships to things. Whether or not it is human nature to be acquisitive, it appears that our household goods have a more meaningful place in our lives than they have been given credit for. What comes across in a wide variety of research is that things matter enormously.

Our possessions give us a sense of security and stability. They make us feel in control. And the more we control an object, the more it is a part of us. If it's *not mine*, it's *not me*. It would probably make sense for everyone on the block to share a lawn mower, but then no one would have control of it. If people are reluctant to share lawn mowers, it should not surprise us that family members are not willing to share TV sets. They want their own sets so they can watch what they please. Apparently, that was why a Chicago woman, furious with her boyfriend for switching from *The Thorn Birds* to basketball, stabbed him to death with a paring knife.

Besides control, we use things to compete. In the late nineteenth century the Kwakiutl Indian chiefs of the Pacific Northwest made war with possessions. Their culture was built on an extravagant festival called the potlatch, a word that means, roughly, to flatten with gifts. It was not the possession of riches that brought prestige, it was the distribution and destruction of goods. At winter ceremonials that took years to prepare for, rival chiefs would strive to outdo one another with displays of conspicuous waste, heaping on their guests thousands of spoons and blankets, hundreds of gold and silver bracelets, their precious dance masks and coppers (large shields that were their most valuable medium of exchange), and almost impoverishing themselves in the process.

Today our means of competition is the accumulation and display of symbols of status. Perhaps in Utopia there will be no status, but in this world, every human being is a status seeker on one level or another—and a status reader. "Every member of society," said French anthropologist Claude Levi-Strauss, "must learn to distinguish his fellow men according to their mutual social status." This discrimination satisfies human needs and has definite survival value. "Status symbols provide the cue that is used in order to discover the status of others, and, from this, the way in which others are to be treated," wrote Erving Goffman in his classic paper, "Symbols of Class Status." Status affects who is invited to share "bed, board, and cult," said Mary Douglas. Whom we invite to dinner affects who marries whom, which then affects who inherits what, which affects whose children get a head start.

Today what counts is what you eat (gourmet is better than greasy spoon), what you fly (private jet is better than common carrier), what sports you play (sailing is better than bowling), where you matriculate, shop, and vacation, whom you associate with, how you eat (manners count), and most important, where you live. Blue Blood Estates or Hard Scrabble zip codes? as one wizard of demographics calls them. He has figured out that "people tend to roost on the same branch as birds of a feather." People also use status symbols to play net worth hide-and-seek. When *Forbes* profiled the 400 richest Americans, its own in-house millionaire Malcolm Forbes refused to disclose his net worth but was delighted to drop clues telling about his status entertainments—his ballooning, his Fabergé egg hunts, his châteaux, and his high life style. It is up to others to translate those obviously costly perks into dollars.

A high price tag isn't the only attribute that endows an object with status. Status can accrue to something because it's scarce—a one-of-a-kind artwork or a limited edition object. The latest hard-to-get item is Steuben's $27,500 bowl etched with tulips that will be produced in an edition of five—one per year for five years. "Only one bowl will bloom this year," is the headline on the ad for it. Status is also found in objects made from naturally scarce materials: Hawaii's rare koa wood, lapis lazuli, or moon rock. And even if an object is neither expensive nor rare, status can rub off on something if it is favored by the right people, which explains why celebrities are used to promote coffee, cars, casinos, and credit cards.

If you've been associated with an object long enough you don't even have to retain ownership. Its glory will shine on you retroactively. Perhaps that is why a member of Swiss nobility is having two copies made of each of the Old Master paintings in his collection. This way, when he turns his castle into a museum, both his children can still have, so to speak, the complete collection, mnemonics of the pictures that have been in the family for centuries. And the most potent status symbol of all is not the object per se, but the *expertise* that is cultivated over time, such as the appreciation of food, wine, design, or art.

If an object reflects a person *accurately*, it's an index of status. But *symbols* of status are not always good indices of status. They are not official proof of rank in the same way a general's stars are. So clusters of symbols are better than isolated ones. Anyone with $525 to spare can buy one yard of the tiger-patterned silk velvet that Lee Radziwill used to cover her dining chair seats. But one status yard does not a princess make. A taxi driver in Los Angeles gets a superior feeling from owning the same status-initialed luggage that many of her Beverly Hills fares own. "I have the same luggage you have," she tells them. "It blows their minds," she brags. But two status valises do not a glitterati make. Misrepresenting your social status isn't a crime, just "a presumption," said Goffman. Like wearing a $69 copy of a $1,000 watch that the mail-order catalog promises will make you "look like a count or countess on a commoner's salary."

"Signs of status are important ingredients of self. But they do not exhaust all the meanings of objects for people," wrote sociologists Mihaly Csikszentmihalyi and Eugene Rochberg-Halton in *The Meaning of Things: Domestic Symbols of the Self*. The study on which the book was based found that people cherished household objects not for their status-giving properties but especially because they were symbols of the self and one's connections to others.

The idea that possessions are symbols of self is not new. Many people have noticed that *having* is intricately tied up with *being*. "It is clear that between what a man calls *me* and what he simply calls *mine*, the line is difficult to draw," wrote William James in 1890. "Every possession is an extension of the self," said Georg Simmel in 1900. "Humans tend to integrate their selves with objects," observed psychologist Ernest Beaglehole some thirty years later. Eskimos used to *lick* new acquisitions to cement the person/object relationship. We stamp our visual taste on our things making the totality resemble us. Indeed, theatrical scenic designers would be out of work if Blanche DuBois's boudoir could be furnished with the same props as Hedda Gabler's.

Csikszentmihalyi and Rochberg-Halton discovered that "things are cherished not because of the material comfort they provide but for the information they convey about the owner and his or her ties to others." People didn't value things for their monetary worth, either. A battered toy, a musical instrument, a homemade quilt, they said, provide more meaning than expensive appliances which the respondents had plenty of. "What's amazing is how few of these things really make a difference when you get to the level of what is important in life," said Csikszentmihalyi. All those expensive furnishings "are required just to keep up with the neighbors or to keep up with what you expect your standard of living should be."

"How else should one relate to the Joneses if not by keeping up with them," asked Mary Douglas provocatively. The principle of reciprocity requires people to consume at the same level as one's friends. If we accept hospitality, we have to offer it in return. And that takes the right equipment and the right setting. But we need things for more than "keeping level" with our friends. We human beings are not only toolmakers but symbol makers as well, and we use our possessions in the same way we use language—the quintessential symbol—to *communicate* with one another. According to Douglas, goods make the universe "more intelligible." They are more than messages to ourselves and others, they are "the hardware and the software . . . of an information system." Possessions speak a language we all understand, and we pay close attention to the inflections, vernacular, and exclamations.

The young husband in the film *Diner* takes his things very

seriously. How could his wife be so stupid as to file the Charlie Parker records with his rock 'n' roll records, he wants to know. What's the difference, she wants to know. What's the difference? How will he find them otherwise? Every record is sacred. Different ones remind him of different times in his life. His things *take* him back. Things can also *hold* you back. Perhaps that's why Bing Crosby's widow auctioned off 14,000 of her husband's possessions—including his bed. "'I think my father's belongings have somehow affected her progress in life,'" said one of Bing's sons. And things can tell you where you stand. Different goods are used to rank occasions and our guests. Costly sets of goods, especially china and porcelain, are "pure rank markers. . . . There will always be luxuries because rank must be marked," said Douglas.

One of the pleasures of goods is "sharing names." We size up people by their expertise in names—sports buffs can converse endlessly about hitters' batting averages, and design buffs want to know whether you speak spongeware, Palladio, Dansk, or Poggenpohl. All names are not equal. We use our special knowledge of them to show solidarity and exclude people.

In fact, the social function of possessions is like the social function of food. Variations in the quality of goods define situations as well as different times of day and seasons. We could survive on a minimum daily allotment of powdered protein mix or grains and berries. But we much prefer going marketing, making choices, learning new recipes. "Next to actually eating food, what devout gastronomes seem to enjoy most is talking about it, planning menus, and remembering meals past," observed food critic Mimi Sheraton. But it's not only experts who thrive on variety. Menu monotony recently drove a Carlsbad, New Mexico, man to shoot the woman he was living with. She served him green beans once too often. "Wouldn't you be mad if you had to eat green beans all the time?" he said. If every meal were the same, and if everyone dressed alike and furnished alike all meanings in the culture would be wiped out.

The furnishings of a home, the style of a house, and its landscape are all part of a system—a system of symbols. And every item in the system has meaning. Some objects have personal meanings, some have social meanings which change over time. People understand this instinctively and they desire things, not from some mindless greed, but because things are necessary to communicate with. They are the vocabulary of a sign language. To be without things is to be left out of the conversation. When we are "listening" to others we may not necessarily agree with what this person or that "says" with his or her decor, or we may misunderstand what is being said; and when we are doing the "talking" we may not be able to express ourselves as eloquently as we would like. But where there are possessions, there is always a discourse.

And what is truly remarkable is that we are able to comprehend and manipulate all the elements in this rich symbol system as well as we do—for surely the language of the home and its decor is one of the most complex languages in the world. But because of that it is also one of the richest and most expressive means of communication.

1

What Is Home?

Ph.D. Phone Home

■

Home Fires Burning

■

Home Sweet Privacy

■

*Would You Mind
Closing the Door, and
Other Privacy Devices*

■

Honk If You Want to Be Alone

■

*People in Glass Houses
Shouldn't Throw Away
Their Curtains*

■

*Make Room for Daddy,
Mommy, Sis and the Kids,
and Aunt Mary*

N INETEEN EIGHTY-TWO will be remembered as the year in which three words—"E. T. phone home"—triggered tears and sobs in a multitude of adults and children. E. T. wanted to phone home to tell his "people" where he was and to come and get him and take him home because he was frightened and lonely in this alien place and longed to return to the safety of familiarity, a place where he belonged.

The leathery extraterrestrial was expressing a primal human emotion—the feeling of being lost, frightened, out of place, vulnerable, homeless. The only antidote for those feelings is "home," four economical letters that combine to form one of our most enduring symbols, signifying safety and familiarity and love. By applying just the right pressure to the G-spot of our hearts, Director Steven Spielberg demonstrated in 118 minutes what a bunch of big thinkers in the social sciences have been grappling with for the last fifteen years. The primacy of "home."

Ph.D. Phone Home

"Look homeward, ologist" is the order of the day. Never in history have so many social scientists been studying so many supposedly mundane things. Instead of analyzing the symbolic schema of tribal houses in Polynesia, the academics are studying the symbolic schema of their neighbors' houses. See the researchers out in force, cruising around the cul-de-sacs of suburbia in their subcompacts, lugging their Nikons and their tape recorders, their university-issue clipboards filled with checklists and open-ended survey questions, gathering data—data on whether Mom and Dad sit side by side at the dining table or opposite; what percentage of people knock on bathroom doors before entering; how long it takes before Levittowners convert their carports to fourth bedrooms; the subtle differences between the things that people store in attics and cellars—all to unravel the meaning of home. In the process of studying habitats, ologists are discovering what real estate agents have suspected all along—that home is much more than shelter and a wood-burning fireplace.

Waxing poetic, these savants have produced a passel of potentially familiar quotations about home that, though pithy, may not be symmetrical enough to replace Home Sweet Home on needlepoint pillows.

"Home is our corner of the world . . . our first universe, a real cosmos in every sense of the word," said Gaston Bachelard, the French philosopher and guru of the new cottage industry of residential introspection. "Home is an ordering principle in space . . . a place that is loved or a place of loving . . . a place where one has some degree of control . . . an option to modify," said architectural phenomenologist Kimberly Dovey.

Home is "the territorial core," "a preferred space, and a fixed point of reference" around which people structure their daily lives, said geographer J. Douglas Porteus. Home "is the presence of children and the activity of family life," plus ownership, with the attendant feelings of control that "make a house a home," said political scientist Robert Rakoff. If ownership is what it takes to make a house a home, however, there are an awful lot of psychologically homeless people in this country. Only 50 percent of Americans own their own homes. What about the half that don't?

A few years ago D. Geoffrey Hayward, an environmental psychologist who was a renter himself, decided to find out whether a person had to own a house for it to feel like a capital-H home. "What is home?" he wondered. "Is it a set of relationships? A group of possessions? A feeling state?" Based on a study of hundreds of New Yorkers, including many high-rise dwellers, Hayward isolated nine dimensions of home, only *one* of which was bricks and mortar.

Home is, first, not an object at all but the presence of other people, said Hayward. A place where "someone cares for me . . . a sense of belonging, love, and togetherness." Home is "a social network . . . friends, neighbors, community, shopkeepers." Home is self-identity . . . "a reflection on my ideas and values." It is also "a personalized place . . . that reflects my taste." It is a "place of privacy and refuge—a place of peace and rest, where I can do what I want, and be safe and secure." It is "a base of activity . . . where one's day starts and ends," as well as continuity, a familiar place of permanence and stability. Home is also, not surprisingly, "a physical structure," a room, an apartment, a house, land. And, last, for many people, Hayward said, home is not where one lives at all, but "one's childhood home or roots." If we can't go home again we often try to re-create it—like the woman in Chicago who was raised in a log cabin and now collects log furniture, explaining, "I guess it's my way of buying back that home."

If Hayward's findings are accurate, you don't need to own a home to feel at home. Ownership may just be the means of ensuring that you can do what you want and have continuity in a place. Certainly a house of one's own is the epicenter of the American Dream. The fantasy of ownership is that when you own your home you will be in control—no one will be able to evict you or raise the rent or tell you how to raise your children or whom you can share your space with. Although freedom and control are never total—there are always zoning laws and the pressure of community standards—owning does offer more control than renting. "It really is a joy to have something of your own. It means you own a piece of the rock," said Amelia Samuda, when she won the right to buy a three-story brownstone in Harlem for $5,000 in a housing lottery. "It means I'm a homeowner, a property owner," rejoiced Priscilla Ashley, another winner. "It means I have tangible assets to give my son."

Sad to say, home is most appreciated when it is at risk or when one is homeless. If you want to understand the significance of home, talk to people who have had their dwellings condemned for a freeway or lost them in a divorce settlement. Look at the statistics on the elderly who have been transferred from nursing homes that were condemned as firetraps to other nursing homes. Leaving "home" accelerates their death rates. Read about people who have been displaced, whose houses have slipped down a canyon, been washed away by floods, or burned down in brush fires. Often they rebuild in the very same place, even though there is a good chance that the same disaster will recur. During the recent war in Beirut when people were driven from place to place looking for shelter and each successive shelter was destroyed, residents flocked back to the remains of their residences like homing pigeons. "We thought, well, if we have to die," said one grocer, "we should die at home."

Home Fires Burning

But nothing brought home to me the meaning of home more keenly than the statements of the American hostages who were released in January 1981 after 444 days in captivity in Iran. Their whole existence during that time was a struggle to create the rudiments of "home" in an alien world while longing to get back home. Their statements are touching testimony to Hayward's study.

"When I dropped my toothbrush into the glass next to Dottie's toothbrush," said Richard Morefield, "I knew I was home. We were together again." Home for him at that moment was loved ones.

"There I was standing in the bedroom of my boyhood," said Michael Metrinko. "Nobody was threatening me. No one was calling for my death. I was home." He was talking about home as a place of refuge.

"This is a real homecoming day, coming back to your home neighborhood," said L. Bruce Laingen from the steps of his Bethesda, Maryland, home. Home as social network.

Back home in Georgetown, Moorhead C. Kennedy, Jr., "ran his fingers over the objects in the living room, den, and kitchen. 'I thought a lot about this house,' Mr. Kennedy said. 'This was a sentimental journey.'" Home as a place of permanence and familiarity.

He recalled the constant moving he was subjected to by his captors, from hiding place to hiding place. "The first twenty-four hours in a new place were the worst, till you made a little home again. . . . The worst part of it was just when you'd made a home for yourself—got your photos pinned up and your few possessions arranged—they'd move you." Home as personalized place.

"Whenever I moved," said Richard Queen, who was released earlier than the others because of poor health, "I took everything I could." Postcards, letters, games, ashtrays, thumbtacks, plastic cup, knife, fork, spoon. The most mundane possessions became fragile defenses against loss of identity. Describing his homecoming in his memoir, Queen said, "I felt so good, so safe surrounded by my family. . . . Home not only meant my family's house, but America, my big wonderful country." Home as roots.

After "having no control . . . the degradation of having to ask to go to the bathroom . . . being watched twenty-four hours a day," being "dependent on the Iranians for everything . . ." said Queen, "I can't describe the feeling I had when I spent the first night in my own apartment—a free person living as I chose to live. No chanting mobs . . . no stained mattress on the floor. Why, I could get up and walk around at 2 A.M. if I wanted to. I could have two cups of tea instead of one; I could go to the bathroom all night if that's what I wanted to do. Freedom . . . made life wonderful."

Home as a place of refuge and privacy.

Home Sweet Privacy

Until recently, privacy was never mentioned as a basic human need. It wasn't included in the oft-quoted hierarchy of human motivations psychologist Abraham Maslow drew up in the 1940s: air, food, sex, safety and security, love and a sense of belonging, self-esteem, and self-actualization. Privacy still wasn't a hot concept two decades later, when anthropologist Robert Ardrey observed in *The Territorial Imperative* that privacy seemed to exist among social animals, but its value had "never been explored." Today, however, a number of psychologists believe that *privacy* is the key to understanding the meaning of home and decoration.

What in the world, you might ask, does *being alone* have to do with deciding between stripes and cabbage roses on the wallpaper? What could a room of one's own have to do with Americans spending tens of billions a year on home furnishings?

The first step to understanding is to stop thinking of privacy as "I want to be alone." Think of privacy as your right to determine what is communicated to others about you and to control access to your self, which is the essence of individuality and freedom. Privacy allows you to be you. "The ability to control and regulate privacy is essential for self-identity," said psychologist Irwin Altman, who is in the vanguard of theory development on privacy and its relation to home. "If you have no boundaries, no secrets, no hiding places, no privacy for bodily functions, you are literally nothing."

We need varying degrees of privacy for sharing secrets, planning ahead, looking back, daydreaming, cogitating, evaluating our lives—being creative. We need privacy for keeping secrets and controlling who knows how much about us, something Elizabeth Taylor's lawyers fought for in the lawsuit to stop filmmakers from dramatizing her life. Privacy lets us drop our smiles, our masks, and our roles temporarily, suspend etiquette, scratch an itch, curse, cry, fall apart, pull ourselves together. Zsa Zsa Gabor claimed—and complained—that to maintain the illusions of one of her husbands, she had to go to bed with her makeup on every night. But most of us can't bear to wear masks without an intermission. At some point it is time for being "at ease."

Privacy for body maintenance, elimination, and sexual functions is deeply rooted in our culture—and in many other cultures. In a study of American families, 96 percent of the respondents said they closed the bathroom door when showering, 99 percent said they closed the bathroom door when using the toilet, and only 5 percent allowed other people in the room while they were using the toilet, bearing out a statement by Alexander Kira, author of *The Bathroom,* that husbands and wives often "draw the line" at elimination functions; even nudists do. Spouses will generally knock on the bathroom door before walking in on each other, sociologist Barry Schwartz wrote in his essay on privacy, "not as a token of deference to nudity," but to allow the other person to decide how he or she wants to be seen. It is said that after her mastectomy, Jacqueline Susann, author of *Valley of the Dolls,* dressed and undressed in a closet because she didn't want her husband to see her scarred body. Even mates who would seem to have nothing to hide have moments when they prefer not to be fully exposed. The basis of intimacy is closeness, yet without "distances and intermissions," said sociologist Georg Simmel, intimacy loses its attractiveness.

Privacy *from* is as important as privacy *for*. Most Western people don't like being subjected to the sights and sounds of other people's intimacies; they don't even want to be witnesses of innocuous everyday events they haven't been invited to share. In a study of "cluster housing" in Australia it was found that many people didn't use outdoor areas that were designed for neighbors to share because they didn't like "being observed" and they were embarrassed to be "intruding upon their neighbor's privacy."

Would You Mind Closing the Door, and Other Privacy Devices

The new thinking is that privacy is not necessarily a one-way "keep out" situation—Thoreau in a cabin on Walden Pond. Rather, it is a moment-to-moment *process* of boundary mediation between "me" and "you" and "us" and "them." As Barry Schwartz put it, we maintain our identities by the "ability to hold back as well as to affiliate."

Therefore we are constantly trying to achieve the comfortable balance of standoffishness and sociability for each activity. For some activities we want privacy "to the max," we don't want to be seen, heard, sensed. For others we want more interaction. At various times we want to be alone by ourselves, alone together with one or more others, alone in a crowd, or psychologically removed—and thousands of points in between. It takes two to tango, four for tennis doubles, and thank you, I'll take my bath by myself. But maybe you want company in yours.

To regulate degrees of privacy we use a whole repertoire of privacy mechanisms, each reinforcing or subbing for another and adding up to a privacy *system*: words, gestures, body language, customs, the bubble of space around us, even other people such as bodyguards, butlers, and appointment secretaries. The glare, the vacant stare, making appointments, "come in," "call back later," can all be used together to mean "stay away" or "let's get together." But one of the most effective privacy control mechanisms is territory and *territoriality*, which involves the ownership, control, defense, and marking of space to let others know "this is mine." Many animals appropriate space and mark their territories with secretions and excretions, chirps and roars. The antelope rubs a bit of musk from its antorbital gland on tree branches in its home range and the area takes on the pungent smell of occupation. But comparing humans to animals is tricky. Animals don't commute to work or take vacations in exotic places, they rarely have second homes, and if they collect anything it's food for the winter ahead—not art or demitasse cups.

Humans operate in multiple territories and have a much wider range of devices for controlling space. An office, a seat on the bus, a pay phone, a turn in line, or a restaurant table are territories over which we have only temporary rights or limited control—they're called secondary or public territories. But home is a primary territory, a space where a person or group has exclusive control, and because of its versatility, home is one of the most effective privacy regulating mechanisms ever invented. All its parts—the house, landscaping, walls, doors, furnishings, possessions—can be used to the owner's advantage. To mark home base, some humans use scents, just as animals do. Berbers rub a little tarry secretion on the four corners of the house to let the evil spirits know whose place it is, but we lean more often on visuals, using everything from nameplates, signs, fences, hedges, smoke curling out of the chimney, well-tended lawns, locks, and interior decoration to give our home territories that "occupied" and "fortified" look.

Territoriality serves privacy needs in two major ways. First, it allows us to be who we are—to raise our families, take care of biological needs, withdraw from community interaction, develop ourselves. And, second, when we modify our homes, personalize them, mark them with symbols of our selves, we are using territoriality to assert our individual identity as well as our allegiance to a neighborhood, an ethnic group, a taste culture, or a class.

We rarely use one territorial privacy mechanism alone. More often we use one or more to reinforce another. The teenager hangs a Keep Out sign to give extra clout to his or her closed bedroom door. A welcome mat suggests that behind the closed front door there is hospitality. A Beware of Dog sign reinforces the muscle of the garden gate. On the way to bed we announce, "I'm really exhausted," to tell those staying up we're serious—please do not disturb.

Different people have different privileges in our spaces, and to be part of a culture is to "know your place." Salespeople cannot get more than a foot in the door; acquaintances get as far as the living room; good friends can sit in the kitchen; intimate friends can sit on the bed, but only special people can get in it. A Philadelphia woman remembers with horror the evening a couple she had recently met and invited for drinks went into her bedroom and stretched out on her bed. That was the end of the friendship.

Many privacy mechanisms are used to warn of the approach of outsiders. Ceremonies of arrival and departure are ritualized in all societies. We like having notice that people are coming. We don't want to be caught out of costume, out of role. Telephones, doorbells, intercoms, doormen, knockers, and the Victorian custom of leaving calling cards in advance of paying a call are all part of elaborate customs for warning of intrusion. The Iroquois Indians used a slanted stick across the door to say "We're out." If the Tarong of the Philippines are not receiving, their ladder is pushed away from the raised porch. Lauren Bacall and Humphrey Bogart would turn the light on over their door to signal special friends that dropping in was okay.

Good manners among Arabs is to leave immediately after dinner. Etiquette teaches Westerners never to arrive before the performers are ready. But we linger on, believing "It's not nice to eat and run." However, "Don't overstay your welcome." If you do, a host might say, "Let's call it a night" and start turning out the lights. That's more civilized than the pygmies—they force their guests to leave in embarrassment by beating them at strip poker.

In those cultures where community members are not required to announce themselves before walking into a residence, there are elaborate mechanisms for *ignoring* the guests. In Java, where people come and go in residences unannounced, privacy is a "general lack of candor in speech and behavior," said anthropologist Clifford Geertz. In rural Ireland where neighbors come and go, dwellers are not required to acknowledge the guests until they are finished with whatever they are doing.

When certain cultures appear to have no customs that resemble privacy as we know it, we often assume, mistakenly, that they have no privacy regulation. But the society without any barriers is rare. Short on space but long on resourcefulness, many people throughout history have learned to find privacy among others. Sancho Panza was never out of Don Quixote's presence, but having servants by one's side at all times was not a problem in those days. Knowing your place, socially, was a substitute for walls. For the Puritans, privacy was a diary. For the Victorians, it could be a window seat. The English, unaccustomed as children to rooms of their own, learned to be quite reserved. When Arabs need to withdraw, they stop talking. Japanese have traditionally given and gotten privacy by sitting in the middle of their spaces, away from the paper walls, and conversing softly. But because of severe crowding, couples have been forced to patronize "love hotels"—a new institution—to have sexual intimacy without being observed. The Mehinacu of Brazil appear to have no spatial privacy whatsoever, but they practice what Alan Westin called "rules of avoidance." Personal questions are not asked, and if they are, the Mehinacu lie a great deal.

If you don't have material devices such as doors, walls, signs, and so on for privacy, you have to be willing to be unsociable, to clam up or calm down or shut up or lie.

Honk If You Want to Be Alone

How strong our barricades are depends on how hard people are trying to get to us. It is something like resistance training in weight lifting. The more pressure from outside, the more resistance we have to apply. "Stardom is a house without shades," observed pop groupie Candy Darling, and no one knows the problems of privacy better than celebrities. The Secret Service could not protect Henry Kissinger from an invasion of the garbage snatchers and Scotland Yard could not protect the Queen of England from the bloke who shinnied up a drainpipe at Buckingham Palace to get an audience with her. A garden variety sunbather can tan in the backyard without having her strap marks splashed on the cover of the *National Enquirer,* but Cher considered installing a retractable sunroof on her Holmby Hills house to circumvent the picture snappers; and Victoria Principal was forced to brick up her windows "against paparazzi."

The rank and file use etiquette and house rules for border control. One person lets it be known she welcomes drop-ins, another acts like she's a fine restaurant and demands reservations. It's good manners to learn what time our friends go to bed. No one is more of a pariah than the person who calls someone after bedtime. Phones off the hook, refusing to answer the doors, lights out, window shades down, Larry Hagman's speechless Sundays, are all good ploys. But if people want to reach you badly enough, they'll send telegrams, slip notes under your door, rap on the window, send skywriters up with messages. The price of resistance is guilt. Your right to privacy is always countered by your friends' and family's and fans' rights to have access to you.

If the level of privacy we crave is different from the level of privacy we get, the result is discomfort—and worse. The inability to regulate social interaction can actually be dangerous to your health. It is now believed that each of us has an optimum physiological level of arousal, depending on introversion and extroversion scores, just as we have our own blood pressure levels. Extroverts have a *low* arousal level, so they become arousal *seekers*. Conversely, introverts have a *high* arousal level and therefore protect against added stimulation. They prefer enclosed spaces, shield noise by putting up double windows, keep doors locked, and discourage sociability. Constantly having to protect against extreme complexity in their surroundings sets off a chain of stress reactions, including lowered blood pressure and, in extreme cases, fainting.

People in Glass Houses Shouldn't Throw Away Their Curtains

Judging by the results of one study, many Americans are not satisfied with the level of privacy they have achieved in their home lives. Getting too much? No, too little. Not surprising. A combination of elements—a national disposition to openness, a 75-year design trend to more and more open-plan housing, and a housing crunch that is turning adequate space into a luxury item—is jeopardizing our ability to control our residential privacy.

Openness does seem to be part of the national character. In 1832, after a visit to America, Mrs. Frances Trollope complained that "No one dreams of fastening a door in Western America . . . I was told that it would be considered an affront to the whole neighborhood." In 1933, George Bernard Shaw remarked, "An American has no sense of privacy. He does not know what it means." Openminded, open-hearted, open-handed, Americans are known for open spaces, the open society, the open-door policy, and "open" golf tourneys. No wonder it was a cinch to sell them open-plan houses. That's where one room segues into another and room boundaries are so indeterminate you can't decide where to stop the floor tile and start the carpet.

The open plan was, fittingly, an American invention. Pioneered by Frank Lloyd Wright in 1908 in his Robie House, the doorless interior plan was adopted by European designers and returned here in 1932 when the Museum of Modern Art staged an exhibit of International Style architecture, launching a fashion for what was already feasible because of central heating. And in 1934 the Crystal House, an all-glass house displayed at Chicago's Century of Progress Exposition, which opened in 1933, introduced the picture window to the masses. The postwar building boom in ranch houses that continued through the 1950s showed home shoppers that sliding glass doors and the open plan could be a good buy.

Meanwhile, architect Philip Johnson gave openness a lot of visibility and more than a touch of class in 1949 when he took the genre to the brink of unlivability and built himself a one-story glass box in Connecticut. It had almost no interior partitions—the only fully enclosed space in the house was the circular bathroom—and little sense of protection from the outside. But why not? He lived alone on many acres. He didn't have to worry about nosy neighbors looking in. Before long, Johnson built three closed-in living modules within walking distance of the glass house. When tired of full disclosure, he could mosey over to the underground art gallery, the fully curtained guest house, or duck into the windowless study he built for himself that had only a skylight. Or head for his pied-à-terre in the city, in which, he admitted recently, he spends most of his time. While Johnson cultivated his image as a supreme ascetic—a man with no dirty dishes or bad habits to hide, a man so secure he didn't need a corner to nestle into—he had a choice of enclosed spaces to dwell in.

It wasn't long before new American houses became as see-through as a Rudi Gernreich blouse. Modest windows lowered their necklines to become picture windows, the breakfast room did a quick change to a breakfast counter, the kitchen got a bare midriff pass-through, and the dining room stripped down to a dining area. Houses became so transparent that you could stand outside the front door and look straight through the foyer and living room into the garden. It was in this climate of openness that the newborn family room flourished. The family room wasn't a place to get away from one another. It was an alternate place to be together at home—a place where you didn't have to worry about getting Brylcream on Mom's prized sofa. This room was the physical embodiment of a new social order. Togetherness. "Togetherness sought to resolve the opposing demands of privacy and society by eliminating privacy," wrote Robert Ardrey with hindsight. He knew it had no future. "It was too boring."

In fact, mothers found togetherness so hard on the eardrums, they started campaigning for a room of their own. In 1956 over one hundred middle-class housewives testified at a housing policy hearing sponsored by the Housing and Home Finance Agency (later renamed HUD) that fewer mothers would go to mental wards or divorce courts if there was one tiny room in the house where they could have "peace and quiet without the television and radio." But who pays attention to housewives or housing commissions?

The 1960s and the sexual revolution brought a different sort of togetherness. The door being stormed was the door to shame. Without shame there would be no need for doors and, as time went by, the door was given the door whenever possible. Even the bedroom door in some "good design" houses was replaced by eye-stopping, but not sound-stopping, room dividers; before long, open sleeping lofts started cropping up. It seemed as if the only solid doors in the contemporary house were in front of the TV screen, which was considered an eyesore.

By the 1970s "full exposure" was a decorating style. It was okay to keep everything from Jockey shorts to work boots on open shelving; women were hanging their jewelry on the bedroom wall for decoration, and when designer sheets begat the unspread-bed-look, even the beds showed us their Underalls.

Then *House & Garden* advised its readers that the new luxury was *space*. Enter the loft, the higher-rise version of the open-plan house. Good-bye rooms, hello space, as in "I love your space." To advertise a loft on a real estate page you have to cite its square footage—because it has no rooms per se. In the beginning it was considered bourgeois to break up a loft into rooms with—ugh— walls and ceilings. Nothing was supposed to interfere with the flow, certainly not such middle-class values as privacy regulation. If there were no children and only one intimate relationship housed there, if you didn't mind light in your eye while you tried to sleep in the bed zone and your loftmate or POSSLQ (person of opposite sex sharing living quarters) read in the living zone, and if you both liked Bruce Springsteen, the who-needs-doors open-plan worked well enough. Lofts made up in square footage what they lacked in barriers, something that friends had to remember when they called and it took ten rings before anyone answered the phone. To get away from one another, all loft dwellers had to do was go to opposite corners.

But when architects brought a touch of loft to the standard postwar apartment by "opening up the space," the wide-open spaces made some people yearn for claustrophobia. One New York hairdresser lost his cleaning woman after he took the door off the second bedroom to "open up the space." When she arrived one morning to find two naked same sex bodies in the guest bed, she quit. She was not about to be what is called in the sociology of privacy "an unwilling spectator."

Almost the only door left to remove besides the front door was the bathroom door. Though a harder sell, there are always a few folks who want to be the first on their block. Bathroom Lib gave a number of style-setters the chance to prove they had no shame. But one artist's mother took a stand, which many would applaud, and refused to visit her daughter's loft until a door was put on the bathroom.

The privacy pendulum appears to be swinging in the other direction now. "It almost seems like a joke," wrote one re- porter, but designers of lofts "are being asked to build separate rooms. . . . Even the door is having a revival." In another article heralding the privacy revival, architect Peter Wilson said, "People today seem to be tired of living in one loftlike area. . . . Most of my clients ask for the privacy of enclosed rooms, but at the same time they want a feeling of more spaciousness."

So architects are giving them semiprivacy—*partial* walls,

which stop short of the ceiling and adjacent walls. A partial wall may obstruct the *view* into the next room—but not light, sound, or cats. In one newly built home that has partial walls there is a peekaboo effect that wasn't anticipated by the builder. When the children and their friends sit in a special spot in the living room and turn the lights off, they can see, reflected in the skylight, Mommy getting dressed or undressed in her walk-in closet, which has a partial wall. This embarrasses Mommy. To retaliate, she employs what Professor Irwin Altman would call an "alternate privacy mechanism"— she gets dressed with the light out.

Make Room for Daddy, Mommy, Sis and the Kids, and Aunt Mary

It's bad enough we have to fight design trends to protect our privacy, we also have to fight city hall and a propaganda effort that is hammering home a new message—the right to a place of your own is a luxury this country can no longer include in the gross national promise. For decades government, savings and loan associations, and home magazines promoted the benefits of home ownership, and we responded by integrating the single-family home into our expectations, our retirement plans, our status hierarchy—and our behavior.

Now, all of a sudden they have recalled the American Dream for adjustments. The cliché editorial today is the one preparing us to share housing. "A nation that can no longer realistically provide private housing for its population must generate alternate 'dream houses'. . . . The concept of multiple dwellings must be projected as a positive housing norm," said one *New York Times* editorialist. A *Time* editorial in the same vein suggested that Americans are spoiled—they want too much space and privacy. With hardboiled egghead condescension for "all those folks in the Eisenhower years grinning out from their patios," writer Lance Morrow reminded us that the "Russian 'sanitary housing norm'" decreed that each citizen was entitled to "100 sq. ft. of space." Since Americans occupy "140 sq. ft. on average," he said, "by most of the world's standards they live like caliphs." In other words, let them double up in bedrooms, wait in line for the bathroom, take turns using kitchens, and resort to time-sharing of the living-dining room.

Americans are already tightening their belts housing-wise. In the 1970s a typical first house had from 2,000 to 2,500 square feet. In 1982 it had shrunk to between 850 and 1,400 square feet. We may have to return to the social workers' nightmare, *taking in boarders,* the practice that legions of turn-of-the-century settlement workers deplored. A peek under the roofs in most communities today reveals more parents moving in with adult children, more adult children moving in with parents, more unrelated roommates, all trying to get along without getting in one another's hair.

Sharing sounds so sensible. There are plenty of cultures in which the norm is not one house for each nuclear family. But living ensemble is a way of life not always compatible with the democratic ideal of individuality and the old wives' injunction that there can only be one boss in the kitchen. For each pioneer willing to live in a commune or to share housing, there seem to be a thousand who would rather have a tiny place all to themselves. A California woman made the news recently when she said she preferred a prison cell to a semiprivate room in a nursing home. Miss Mae Lang, a ninety-three-year-old paroled murderer, asked to be declared a parole violator so she could live out her days in a prison where she had served thirty-nine years. The rationale? "I knew if I went back I'd have a room of my own."

Living with in-laws is an alternative that generates almost as much animosity in Duluth as in Melanesia's Dobu Island where married couples alternate living one year with the wife's family and one year with the husband's. The humiliation and abuse customarily heaped upon the Dobu spouse in alien territory would keep Henny Youngman in mother-in-law jokes till the year 3001.

The chief benefit of this housing alternative seems to be that the hostility generated keeps the adrenaline flowing. Living with in-laws serves the same purpose on TV sit-coms such as "All in the Family," where the spectacle of Archie Bunker locking horns with his resident son-in-law Mike was always good for a laugh. Living *en famille* gives many a TV show its vigor if not its *verité.* How many women do you know like those two slinky daughters-in-law on "Dallas," who would for so long have put up with living in their mother-in-law's homestead? Only on TV would Pam Ewing, a millionaire's wife, suffer, in addition, having to sit down to grits and grousing every morning with a venal brother-in-law like J. R. Ewing without demanding a more stately ranch of her own. To have nothing but a bedroom in the house of in-laws is about as conducive to what we have come to think of as a "good relationship" as taking your parents on your honeymoon.

In modern America, the urge is for "my place." The twenty-two-year-old who has just entered the work force knows very well why he doesn't want to live with his dad and stepmother in their space-tight city apartment, even though they haven't rolled up the welcome mat and he can barely afford to live in the style to which he's accustomed. He wants to be able to get phone calls late at night without his father howling, he wants to be able to entertain, he doesn't want to have to explain why he's spending the night elsewhere or coming in so late—in short, he wants a private life and a place that represents him.

When young people start yearning for and acquiring the things that define them—the special foods, stereo systems, home computers, cookie jar collections, and cabinets to house them—the charm of shared housing begins to wane. Identity needs can be submerged for a while in favor of economic considerations, but eventually there comes the time when they want a home of their own where they are in control.

People need more than minimum space for sanitary functioning, more than breathing space and elbow room. Not only must we satisfy our biological drives—"hunger, thirst, sex," said psychologist Harold Proshansky—but also our "needs for affiliation, achievement, success, and other complex social motives. We need space to acquire things which help to define us."

But how will identity be defined in the latest solution to the housing problem that's been dreamed up by builders—the "mingles" house? It has two master bedrooms, each with its own bath, plus a living room, family room, and kitchen to share. In one 3,286-square-foot mingles house, there is also a hot tub, a pool, and a lanai. This arrangement supposedly allows unrelated people to have the amenities they couldn't afford on their own "without sacrificing individual privacy," as one design journal put it.

There is just one hitch. The mingles house is predicated on the assumption that the only place in a house people need or want privacy is in their bedrooms. Gosh, where have these builders been all their lives? Have they never gone to the kitchen in their underwear, hugged in the hall, or argued on the patio? And have they got any brilliant suggestions about whose taste will reign in the living room? Don't they know that when you can't control what goes on in a space, when you don't feel responsible for the care and decorating of a space, you don't feel at home? A recent study showed that even children who had to share rooms with siblings felt disenfranchised. In the final analysis, no matter how many hot tubs, lanais, and other communal areas it has, your house is your home *only* when you feel you have *jurisdiction* over the space.

2

What Is Decorating?

The Geography of the House

■

Places, Everybody

■

Decor as Symbol of Self

■

Paint Your Wagon

■

Messages to Ourselves

■

Mirror, Mirror

■

Making an Impression

IT WAS A day like any other day—in decorating. In Los Angeles, Jill St. John was scouring the decorating boutiques for an unusual nightstand; Stephanie Mills eased on down the road to the design district looking for a glitzy Art Deco dining table; Grizzly Adams was foraging for a pair of Moderne console tables for his Beverly Hills bungalow; and five people in a row asked one purveyor of Orientalia if she had any exotic folding screens. Across town at a branch of RB Industries, one of the largest furniture chains in the country, a woman bought a champagne-beige "playpen"—modular seating for the sociable—and a young couple bought four rooms of furniture for their new condo.

In Atlanta, retired Atlanta Braves star Hank Aaron popped into Domus, a trendy housewares store, looking for patio furniture, and walked home with six butterfly chairs; and a lady with storage problems exited smiling after ordering an 84-inch-wide wall unit that could do double duty as closet, chest, and bookcase in her space-tight bedroom. In Texas, where decorators are so busy there's hardly time to get their cowboy boots shined, a Fort

Worth designer figured out how to make the living room of a couple "on the move" double as a dining room with two tables on wheels.

Meanwhile, back in New York, Lauren Bacall was making the rounds of fabric houses with her decorator; on the advice of a friend, a Bronx couple ordered—with trepidation—their next biggest purchase after their sofa, pink vertical blinds for their living room; a woman who changes her decor as frequently as Liz Taylor changes husbands called in her decorator to discuss, yet again, the design of her canopy bed. Her teenaged son put in his order for a loft bed, beige walls, and a place for his Apple computer.

Before leaving for the office, a Grand Rapids accountant stood in his basement and surveyed with pride the bookcase he had been building for the last three weeks with his new Shopsmith equipment. And in a small town in Indiana, the owner of a local wallpaper shop was making her appointed rounds. By 8 A.M. she had polished off a doughnut and a second cup of coffee and had made the first sale of the day to a woman who ordered sheer satin draperies with a silk slub for her bedroom. Then a house call to an expectant mother who wanted yellow blinds for the baby's room. The husband, a tree surgeon, asked how he could get an outdoor feeling in the basement family room he was renovating. The wallpaper shop-owner suggested a wall mural of a forest scene. At her next stop, she suggested putting wallpaper in panels in the customers' foyer to save money and explained how they could stencil the living room themselves. Her last stop was at her own shop where she taught twenty women to sew folded stars for quilts and potholders and pillow shams.

The bottom line in the furniture business may be sagging because of the recession, but, based on anecdotal evidence and a spate of industry surveys, the decorating urge is on the increase at every income level. In 1980 *House & Garden* reported that its 677,000 subscribers had spent an average of $1,667 on furniture in the previous twelve months; 7 out of 10 of those readers said they were more interested in decorating than they had been five years before—in fact, it was one of their favorite activities—and 89 percent were planning to do some refurbishing in "the near future." In a 1981 report, *Architectural Digest* stated that 51 percent of its 550,000 subscribers had done some decorating or redecorating in the previous six months and another 48 percent had done some within the previous three years, spending a median $4,800. In a 1982 study, *Better Homes and Gardens* claimed that 70 percent of its 8 million subscribers said they enjoyed decorating their homes "very much"; a quarter of them had spent up to $500 and another quarter up to $1,000 on furnishings in the previous two years.

Americans spend $50 billion a year on furnishings, from asphalt tile to zebra rugs—with bolsters, café curtains, credenzas, dhurries, Flokatis, highboys, lowboys, parquet, rattan, shutters, terrazzo, and wicker in between. We buy umpteem million decorating books and magazines and keep tens of thousands of decorators busy from Miami to Honolulu. Wouldn't it be simpler and cheaper to sit on the floor, use orange crates for tables, and get our esthetic kicks from sunsets and rainbows? Simpler, yes, but not as satisfying.

Most human behavior can be explained. People seldom accept and participate in activities "without meaning and without goals," said sociologist Leonora Davidoff. One way to learn why people take an interest in decorating is to ask them why they do it. "For beauty," "for pleasantness," "for social position," they answer; "to express myself," "to make a statement," "for comfort." Others insist "it's a substitute for a good relationship," "so I can feel good about myself—be proud of my home, express things about myself I wouldn't tell people," "for change—if I change my space maybe I can change myself." "It's busy work for women," said one skeptic. "It's pressure from advertisers." "It's fear," said another, meaning decorating is a performance that will be reviewed and those who are inept will be ostracized.

Are they right? Partly. The activity you and I call decorating social scientists call personalizing. Personalizing is marking your environment to let people know where your boundaries begin and end, and putting your personal stamp on a space and its contents. When you add a room to your house to accommodate an addition to *your* family, knock down a wall to make room for *your* cherished Steinway, mount *your* sentimental doorknocker, hang the pictures *you* unearthed in the flea market, adjust the shelves in the cupboard to *your* height, throw scarves over the lamps à la Scavullo to get the ambience *you* like, buy Miss Piggy mugs or mugs with *quel* other symbol (tennis racquet, Garfield the Cat, or hockey team) *you* identify with, make everything in your home conform to *your* standards of beauty and comfort, you are personalizing—custom tailoring your space to your image, monogramming it with your crest, imprinting it with your *geist*, spirit, personality, and life style.

Personalizing is the human way of adapting to environments. Making them fit us physically and psychologically and socially. It serves two important functions: one, to regulate the social system in a house—direct traffic, keep the peace (and the quiet), and thereby control privacy; and two, to express identity, tell the world—and ourselves—who we are.

Most personalizing involves two processes, which decorators refer to as "the plan" and "the scheme." The *plan* is the geography of the house. It locates people and activities spatially, marks out relationships, and thus has a lot to do with regulating the social systems in a house. The *scheme* is the topography of the house. It has to do with color schemes, ambience, style, patterns, and collections, and is closely related to the second function—expressing identity. Are you a blue person or a green person? Early American or Contemporary?

But life is never so neatly compartmentalized. In real life, the plan and scheme overlap and reinforce each other, helping to control what takes place in our spaces and define identity. Giving little Johnny and little Sally separate but equal rooms seems a clear-cut *plan* decision that defines ownership of a space and limits bickering. But by giving the kids rooms of their own, we are also communicating that we are solvent enough to afford separate bedrooms for our children. When Sally plasters her room with Wonder Woman or Strawberry Shortcake paraphernalia, it may be her way of expressing her identity, but all those personal touches can serve to remind Johnny that this is Sally's room. As long as we realize that both plan and scheme work together and reinforce each other in accomplishing the two functions of personalizing, we can talk about them separately.

The Geography of the House

Before a paint chip is chosen or a picture hung, we must divide up the space. "Settling in a territory is equivalent to founding a world," said Mircea Eliade, an authority on early religion. Thus each time we set up housekeeping in a new place, whether it's a freshman dorm, a one-bedroom condo, a three-bedroom split-level with a 25-year mortgage, or a rental at the seashore, we organize the space according to our *imago mundi*—our image of the world. We create our microcosm of the world according to our values and beliefs. Of course, we do not make "foundation sacrifices" to get spiritual protection. We do not bury slaves alive in the postholes as the Maoris or Tahitians did; sacrifice the mason's wife, as they did in Greece; or build the walls of our houses on the bodies of volunteers, as they did in Japan. We're less superstitious and more humane. Our sacrifice is the interest on the mortgage. The chimney or smoke hole, the sacred center of a preliterate person's cosmos, is no longer considered the ladder to heaven—just a symbol of domestic warmth.

Step number one in decorating is much like the initial decision on the first day of camp. We have to settle who sleeps where and who puts his or her things in which cubby. Animals divide their spaces into areas for eating and drinking, bathing, sleeping, food stores, lavatory, sunbathing, and backscratching. We need all of those, plus places to store skis, stand trophies, hang pantyhose, do taxes, play video games, and engage in America's favorite indoor sport—talking on the phone. The telephone is so important that deciding where you want to do your talking is the first decision in many decorating plans.

Decor defines decorum. The way we divide up space, furnish, and equip it defines the situation and reminds residents and instructs guests how to behave appropriately, which simplifies life and makes it predictable. Woe to the guest who barges into the master bedroom and hangs his parka in the bedroom closet instead of in the hall closet, where we've left room and fancy hangers. What's the matter with this guy? Doesn't he know how to act? "Settings have plans for their inhabitants' behaviors," as psychologist Roger Barker noted.

But how do we make these spatial decisions? Apparently they are largely cultural. All spaces are not equal. Like the divisions of space made by traditional societies, some of our spaces are sacred, others are profane. The geography of the house is based on a whole range of spatial poles such as front/back, clean/dirty, male/female, and yours/mine, that are, if not a blueprint of the way we live, guidelines we follow. How fancy should the living room be? Is it "for show" or "for blow"? A choice between a *gemütlich* family-kitchen and a formal living room is not a decorating decision—it is a value choice between two ways of life.

Almost every society differentiates front (our face to the world) from back (where we can be ourselves). But the more technological a society, the more it cares about fronts. Apparently, high technology leads to high mobility, which leads to high anxiety about making a good impression on all those neighbors who don't know a thing about you except the way you maintain your home. To keep up a front, so to speak, we invest quite literally in the fronts of our houses. They must be decorative and respectable. With paint, hardware, and a bit of molding we can communicate that "this ornate or especially large door with the overhang is the 'front' door where guests are supposed to enter and this plain door is the 'back' door for deliveries, family, and close friends." "Around here," said Joe Duncan of Plano, Texas, recalling the fateful night when a location scout rang his bell and asked if he would rent his ranch out as the South Fork ranch on "Dallas," "you know it's a stranger because folks you know always come in the back."

Many people refer to the living room as the "front room." No matter how infrequently the room is used, the space is not wasted. "It's the face of the house, which speaks composedly and smiles for the rest of the body," said Mary Douglas. And you can tell from the arrangement and care we give this room that you are not supposed to come in here with your dirty jeans and throw your leg over the arm of the chair or put your boots on the coffee table.

When front matters, children are relegated to the back. Children are a threat to decorum—and white walls. They can't be trusted to preserve the sanctity of the sofa, the purity of the wall-to-wall. The Gauls and many other early peoples sent their children away to foster homes to be raised. We just send them to their rooms or out back to play. Front and back divisions are the bane and boon of the furniture industry. An industry newsletter warns manufacturers that the life of a "wrap bedroom" (jargon for modular wood bedroom sets) is twenty years or more because "bedrooms are not 'public' rooms, so the replacement priority is low." Better to sell upholstered pieces that go in front rooms—high priority spaces for consumers.

Another geographical distinction is deciding where to eat and where to do laundry and what fixtures will be in the bathroom.

These choices are dictated by one's definition of clean and dirty, and vary tremendously among cultures. "No cooking in the house" and "no death in the house" are ancient proscriptions. Some societies still remove the dying from their beds and their homes. The kitchen is not supposed to be visible from the living area in a Japanese house. The toilet is often in its own compartment in French homes, separate from the sink and tub. The kitchen in the French house is traditionally an inconvenient distance from the dining room reflecting a distaste for cooking odors during the meal.

People who speak the same language often find one another's clean and dirty distinctions incomprehensible. In a study comparing the English and the Australian division of household space, an Australian architect discovered that the English regard the kitchen as a dirt removal place—they will do laundry there, wash dishes there, even bathe in the kitchen, but they don't like eating in the kitchen. If there is no separate dining room, the English prefer to eat in a living-dining room. Australians, on the other hand, see the kitchen as a place having to do with all aspects of food—preparation, eating, and clean-up. If there is no dining room they will eat in the kitchen. And while they may iron in the kitchen, they will never wash clothes in the kitchen. That is considered dirty.

Americans follow the lead of the English in decorating but seem to be more like the Australians in their codification of clean and dirty. Architects here have noticed that Americans *abhor* doing their laundry in the kitchen but *adore* eating there. As Matilda and Mario Cuomo prepared to move to Albany to become the governor and first lady of New York State, they lamented not being able to take their kitchen along. Not only do they eat there, said Mrs. Cuomo, "it's the hub of our family."

You cannot decorate a room before you know its gender. The Western home may not be as rigidly divided into male and female space as the Moslem home where male guests must not get a glimpse of the women of the house, but we still make some sexual distinctions. Gender jurisdiction lives in our dens, garages, and basements which are still male territories, and in the kitchen, living room, and dining room which are still predominantly female territories—no matter how many women are bringing home the bacon these days and how many men are frying it.

Even a couple's bedroom, which is inhabited jointly in most

homes, has a gender—female. The custom of the connubial bed being the woman's place and her husband being a guest in it is close to "universal" and dates from Biblical times, according to Lord Raglan, a British anthropologist. That the husband is a guest in his wife's bedroom is obvious, judging from all the ruffles and flounces in master bedrooms. Let us not forget that the most powerful man in the world, the president of the United States, sleeps in a peach bedroom with birds flying on the wallpaper, and Hugh Carey, when governor of New York, slept in "a peach and flowered bedroom."

"Yours and mine" is another polar distinction in a house. Consider the master bedroom. Before you can choose night tables or install the phone jacks, you need to know who sleeps on which side of the bed. Before you can design a closet you must know which side of the closet the skirts will hang on. How do couples divide control of space? Flip a coin? Ladies first? First come, first served? Traditional cultures decide these things by the sun and sexism. Most traditional cultures face east, cosmologically. When you face east, the south light is on the right, which is equated with power— and power is always male. The dark left side is profane and female. Only the Chinese see the left as honorable, said University of Minnesota geographer Yi-Fu Tuan. That is because the Chinese ruler traditionally faces south. His left is to the east where the sun rises. Thus for the Chinese, left is light, honorable, and male, and right is less honorable and female.

Modern societies have lost their bearings and prejudices on who is the rightful owner of left and right—everything is negotiable. Other than seating an honored guest on the host's right at a banquet, we orient ourselves to the god of convenience. The left-handed mate sits to the left of the right-handed mate so as not to knock elbows or chopsticks when eating. We choose sides of the bed the same way we select window or aisle seats in an airplane— by preference to be near the radiator, the window, or the bathroom. In *Tootsie*, Dorothy, the woman Dustin Hoffman was impersonating, wanted to sleep on the side of the bed near the bathroom to be near her bag of disguises.

Still, some people long for rules. One young woman subscribes to her parents' notion that a man should sleep on the side nearest the door to protect the woman from intruders.

Places, Everybody

Whatever system you use, knowing which side you're on is as important in a home as it is in politics. Modern young adults who pride themselves on their good sportsmanship are often surprised, when they start living *á deux*, how upset they get over minor territorial infractions. They are embarrassed by their selfishness. Would Romeo begrudge an extra shelf in the bathroom cabinet to Juliet? Mutuality, cooperation, and sharing are noble until their roommate appropriates the dining table for a desk, their favorite mug or chair or all the hangers.

Love doesn't mean never being allowed to say "that's mine." A family is as much a social system as an office staff or a submarine crew, and members need to know their places internally. Who sits at the head of the table and who gets which chair in front of the TV? When the Reagans first moved into the White House, Nancy Reagan said, "It takes a while to settle in, to develop your own living routines, like what chair he sits in and what chair you sit in [in] the family room."

Because marriage presupposes a certain amount of togetherness, it was unusual some years ago when architect Robert Venturi designed a couple's bedroom and divided it as rigidly as East and West Berlin with a line down the middle of the room dividing his side from her side. The king-size bed straddled the line. Everything on her side including half the bedspread and her name in eight-foot-high letters on her closet doors was to be blue; everything on his side including his half of the bedspread and his name on his closet doors was to be gray. After divorce derailed the project, the wife was fond of saying, in retrospect, that the architect must have sensed a house divided. Why else partition the space so unequivocally? If two hearts are beating as one, people don't need to be possessive about space, do they?

In fact, they do. The more territorial people are, the better they seem to get along. In isolation studies done for the U.S. Navy with two people sharing a small room for ten days, the pairs who *did not* make rules early on about who owned what space were unable to stick it out for the full length of the experiment. The pairs who decided on the first day how to divvy up the space and organize their time were able to remain in isolation to the end.

Robert Frost may have been initially skeptical about good fences making good neighbors, but being possessive about space actually helps people live in harmony. Life would be a constant trial if every day we had to renegotiate who slept on which side of the bed, whose towel hung where, and who sat where at the table.

As more and more people move into lofts and alternative housing where space is undesignated, or try to fit themselves into old housing stock that was designed for different life styles, they must struggle to adjust their preconceptions about front and back, clean and dirty, and male and female with existing room arrangements, positions of the plumbing stacks, windows, and the doors. Not until they've diagrammed the spaces for various activities and figured out systems for keeping out of one another's hair and diaries can they begin to think about expressing themselves with "the scheme"—picking colors, choosing furniture—the beauty part that most people think of when they think about decorating.

Decor as Symbol of Self

The other aspect of personalization is the big I—Identity. Making distinctions between ourselves and others. "The self can only be known by the signs it gives off in communication," said Eugene Rochberg-Halton. And the language of ornament and decoration communicates particularly well. Perhaps in the future we will be known by our computer communiqués or exotic brainwaves, but until then our rock gardens, tabletop compositions, refrigerator door collages, and other design language will have to do. The Nubian family in Africa with a steamship painted over the front door to indicate that someone in the house works in shipbuilding, and the Shotte family on Long Island who make a visual pun on their name with a rifle for a nameplate, are both decorating their homes to communicate "this is where our territory begins and this is who we are."

Even the most selfless people need a minimum package of identity equipment. One of Pope John Paul I's first acts as pontiff was to send for his own bed. "He didn't like sleeping in strange beds," explained a friend. It hadn't arrived from Venice when he died suddenly.

Without familiar things we feel disoriented. Our identities

flicker and fade like ailing light bulbs. "Returning each night to my silent, pictureless apartment, I would look in the bathroom mirror and wonder who I was," wrote D. M. Thomas, author of *The White Hotel*, recalling the sense of detachment he felt while living in a furnished apartment during a stint as author-in-residence at a Washington, D.C., university. "I missed familiar things, familiar ground that would have confirmed my identity."

Wallpaper dealers wouldn't need fifty or sixty sample books filled with assorted geometrics, supergraphics, and peach clamshells on foil backgrounds if everyone were content to have the same roses climbing their walls. Chintz wouldn't come in forty flavors from strawberry to licorice, and Robert Kennedy, Jr.'s bride Emily wouldn't have trotted him around from store to store "for ten hours" looking for a china pattern if the home wasn't an elaborate symbol system—as important for the messages it sends to residents and outsiders as for the functions it serves.

In the five-year long University of Chicago study into how modern Americans relate to their things, investigators Mihaly Csikszentmihalyhi and Rochberg-Halton found that we all use possessions to stand for ourselves. "I learned that things can embody self," said Rochberg-Halton. "We create environments that are extensions of ourselves, that serve to tell us who we are, and act as role models for what we can become." But what we cherish and what we use to stand for ourselves, the researchers admitted, seemed to be "scripted by the culture." Even though the roles of men and women are no longer so tightly circumscribed, "it is remarkable how influential sex-stereotyped goals still remain." Men and women "pay attention to different things in the same environment and value the same things for different reasons," said the authors. Men and children cared for action things and tools; women and grandparents cared for objects of contemplation and things that reminded them of family. It was also found that meaning systems are passed down in families from mothers to daughters—not to sons.

Only children and old people cared for a piece of furniture because it was useful. For adults, a specific piece of furniture embodied experiences and memories, or was a symbol of self or family. Photographs which had the power to arouse emotions and preserve memories meant the most to grandparents and the least to children. Stereos were most important to the younger generation, because they provide for the most human and emotional of our needs—release, escape, and venting of emotion. And since music "seems to act as a modulator of emotions," it is particularly important in adolescence "when daily swings of mood are significantly greater than in the middle years and . . . later life." Television sets were cherished more by men than women, more by children than grandparents, more by grandparents than parents. Plants had greater meaning for the lower-middle class, and for women, standing for values, especially nurturance and "ecological consciousness." "Plateware," the term used in the study to cover all eating and drinking utensils, was mentioned mostly by women. Of course, "plates" are the tools of the housewife's trade. In many cultures they are the legal possession of the women of the house.

The home is such an important vehicle for the expression of identity that one anthropologist believes "built environments"—houses and settlements—were originally developed to "*identify a group*—rather than to provide shelter." But in contemporary Western society, the house more often identifies a person or a family instead of a group. To put no personal stamp on a home is almost pathological in our culture. Fear of attracting attention to themselves constrains people in crime-ridden areas from personalizing, lack of commitment restrains others, and insecurity about decorating skill inhibits still others. But for most people, painting some sort of self-portrait, decoratively, is doing what comes naturally.

All communications, of course, are transactions. The identity we express is subject to interpretation by others. Will it be positive or negative? David Berkowitz, the "Son of Sam" murderer, didn't win any points when it was discovered he had drawn a circle around a hole in the wall in his apartment and written "This is where I live." A person who fails to keep up appearances is stigmatized.

Paint Your Wagon

Each material aspect of the home, from its location to its size, siding, and screen-door monogram can be manipulated to express identity. But exteriors can fool you. Neighborhood rules and apartment house regulations keep many folks from giving self-expression their all on the exterior. There are rules about making *interior* changes in apartment houses and rentals, too, but on the whole the interior is where you have the most freedom. Paint the place orange, do a graffiti mural, tent the ceiling—as long as your neighbors don't have to endure the sight of it, express yourself— each according to your means, skills, values, free time, passion for purple, greenness of thumb, ethnic origins, esthetic preferences, social striving, local customs, materials on hand, and appreciative- ness of cheering section.

When John Warner was chairman of the Bicentennial Commis- sion, he wallpapered his house in patriotic red, white, and blue. Don Henley, the Texas-born country and western singer, gave his California home a Texas touch by fencing it in with a down-home cactus garden. A prominent architect wrote his mentors large, stenciling his dining room with a frieze of names such as Beetho- ven, Michelangelo, Frank Lloyd Wright, and others who had been influential in his career. The hallways in Yoko Ono's apartment are lined with John Lennon's "gold and platinum records, his litho- graphs, his little presents to Yoko"; and Yoko, who is an Egyptol- ogist among other things, has furnished her dining room with ancient Egyptian chairs. Iconoclastic fashion designer Betsey John- son spent a great deal of time searching for a decorative identity that was "truly me and not anyone else." God knows she won't see chartreuse living-room walls like hers and cabbage roses on the shower curtain coming and going. But arriving at that scheme re- quired a months-long introspective journey into self, with the ther- apeutic assistance of an interior designer. "I realized I wanted a tropical environment. . . . Stainless steel was just not me," she explained.

The well-to-do may do it more extravagantly, with more skill and the sophistication to justify their selections, but personalizing isn't their exclusive domain. "Every housewife of every taste cul- ture who can afford to buy furniture seeks to make her rooms into a work of beauty expressing her standards," said Herbert Gans. In the mid-1970s, fascinated that identical spaces could look so differ- ent, New York photojournalist Barbara Pfeffer photographed al- most all the living rooms in the middle-class apartment house in which she lived. None of the rooms was a candidate for a decorat- ing magazine, yet the residents managed to make personal state- ments using the scheme, possessions, and division of the space to express aspects of themselves—their nationality, sex, values, life style, even income. In every instance the decorating was as loaded with personal significance as a pillow with feathers.

"I feel my place is very feminine," said the lawyer with the piano in the pale blue living room. "We used everything old because I think old things are warmer," said another young woman whose TV was in the bedroom since she considered watching TV with company "crude." "We have Turkish rugs because my husband is Turkish," said the woman who described her decorating style as "poor man's modern." Almost everything in the art-filled living room of the husband and wife psychotherapists had "sentimental value." A divorced mother made her living room a children's playroom. A composer and his wife whose parties always ended up as songfests hung musical instruments on their walls. And a couple who valued "being different" expressed their identity by what was missing—they were proud to have the only apartment in New York *without* plants.

Using the services of a professional decorator can express identity, too, although some homemakers feel that's cheating, like using a pony for an exam or a professional hairdresser for the Miss America contest. "I couldn't imagine hiring an interior decorator," said Berkeley city planner Clare Cooper Marcus, who wrote the classic paper on the house as a symbol of the self. "To me that would be a cop-out. I want to look at my house and think about my taste and my needs and make the decisions and do it."

"I like to make my own mistakes," said Edward Albee, who has been working on his Montauk house and grounds for eighteen years without the aid of a landscape architect or interior designer. "I'd rather have my home less than perfect and less integrated and something I've made for myself."

If someone else decorates your home, is it less personal? We live in houses designed by architects, why not interiors designed by decorators? Using a decorator is another way of expressing your identity. The decorator is like a designated hitter doing identity work in your name—and one hopes in your image—helping you to create a proper setting for the person you think you are, and acting as a role model for whom you could become. But most of all, a decorator allies the client with people of means, education, taste, and discernment who know that a home can be more than a cozy nest adorned with calendar art—it can be a work of art. The woman who expressed the hope in an *Architectural Digest* interview that one day her apartment, designed by Ward Bennett, "will be considered a twentieth-century classic of modern design," was probably speaking for many design clients. Using a designer makes the client a patron of the arts, which is an entrance card to the upper reaches of society. Thus, if the design isn't totally home-made, it doesn't matter. When you use a decorator, your identity comes from your design appreciation and patronage.

Messages to Ourselves

Our homes are as much messages to ourselves about our-selves as communications to outsiders. Settings remind us who we are. "My settings support me, help me play my roles," as Harold Proshansky, dean of New York's City College Graduate School, put it.

Multiple acts of personalization that aren't any more world-shaking than figuring out where to hang a picture, deciding how many plants to put on the windowsill, selecting which vegetables to grow in the garden, or choosing the sheet pattern add up to a sense of competence and control. When we decorate we take a no man's land of nondescript space and make it "habitable and per-sonally significant." To be surrounded by things we have chosen ourselves gives us a sense of security. Certain possessions remind us that there are people who love us, bring back happy occasions, affirm what we believe in—religion or art or success or family. And in the process of choosing, arranging, buffing, puffing, and caring for our things—working to pay for them—we become bonded to them the way parents bond with a child. Writer Dora Landey ex-plained the passionate bond she felt with the tea caddies, humi-dors, and Staffordshire plates she and her husband, actor Tony Lo Bianco, collect. She can remember when she bought each piece, what she paid for it, even the weather and whom she was with at the time. "It's better than a photograph album," she said.

Oddly enough, a guest can be confronted by a dozen items in the host's bookcase and never know which of those items has the most significance for him or her. To the outsider, the vase or the book or the plate is just that, but to the resident, the cherished item fairly glows with significance. The object can stand for the donor, for the occasion when it was acquired, for personal development, or for memories. But there seems to be a special force to objects that are symbols of beginnings, especially the beginnings of a marriage. "Formative periods," said sociologist Barry Schwartz, "are marked by the magic, attraction, and prestige of origins." It takes time, events, perhaps even loss, to heighten the meaning of some objects till they take on mythic status for a family—their own tooth of the Buddha.

Such was the case with one Cuban woman. Mercedes Menendez de Lopez always loved fine things. Her most cherished possession was her graceful set of Baccarat crystal—goblets, wine glasses, champagnes. You didn't have to be Napoleon or the king of Siam or the czar of Russia to own "the crystal of kings." You could be schoolteachers like Mrs. Lopez and her husband Alfonso. Their set wasn't quite complete, however, because in postwar Havana in 1945, the year they were married, it was not easy to acquire full dozens of their delicately cut pattern. But arranged and reflected behind glass doors in the mirror-lined mahogany breakfront, it was never apparent to outsiders that three glasses were missing.

But what are beautiful possessions without political freedom? In the 1950s the Lopezes, both school principals, became well-known anti-Castroites. Following Batista's fall in January 1959, Mr. Lopez, by then the head of Havana's board of education, decided to emigrate to the United States to wait for the day when Castro would surely be overthrown. On August 1, 1960, the Lopezes with their two children, little Mercedes, ten, and Alfonso, Jr., fourteen, fled Cuba, taking with them only those things that could be crammed into eighteen hastily purchased suitcases: clothing, linens, a hand-embroidered matrimonial bedspread, antique jewelry, a Baby Jesus statue, a camera, little Mercedes's dolls, Alfonso, Jr.'s baseball mitt, school records, yearbooks, a tiny radio, a knife, and a pressure cooker. The cherished glassware was packed in several crates along with some other possessions and hidden in various relatives' homes for safekeeping until the Lopezes' return.

It was a forty-five-minute flight to Miami and back to square one, economically and socially. Hoping for better school and job opportunities, the Lopez family headed for a Cuban enclave in New Jersey and a series of substandard apartments. The fact that they were living out of suitcases, sitting on boxes; that Mrs. Lopez was doing sewing in a factory and that Mr. Lopez was working as a furniture salesman didn't make this proud family feel ashamed. It was, after all, a time-out situation. Mr. Lopez was certain they would be able to return to Cuba soon.

But after three years in exile, they began to realize that they might be staying in the United States permanently. Not until then did Mrs. Lopez finally face up to the loss of the things she left in Cuba. "Only the person who has experienced it can know what it feels like," she said recently. It was too late in her life to recoup her losses. Making sure her children could acquire the possessions and the way of life she left behind became her mission.

By the mid-1970s, little Mercedes, with a master's degree, was in a position to reach her mother's goal. A researcher in a major ad agency and engaged to Tony Morgan, an advertising research director, she was as determined as her mother was that she must recover the material things, and the respect that comes with them, that the family had lost. Mrs. Lopez didn't hesitate to give the newlyweds her pension money to furnish their apartment.

And then it arrived, a glossy gray box tied in white satin ribbon, holding the gift Tony and Mercedes were fated to receive—six Baccarat goblets. The family ritual would be perpetuated. It didn't matter that Mrs. Lopez's pattern had been ornately cut and that Mercedes's was perfectly plain. What was important, said Mercedes, "is the whole idea of having them in the family." Although Mercedes shopped for two years to find the right cabinet to display the glasses, she rarely uses them, and Tony complains that they don't have a whole lot of utility.

Of course, though, the glasses do have a very real utility. They serve a symbolic function representing a hard-earned status passage. Mrs. Lopez understands it and so does Mercedes. "To go from having nothing to get back to Baccarat crystal," she said, "you have to have come a long way."

Mirror, Mirror

But symbolism can also prejudice us against possessions. As cartoonists understand so well, most people are extremely sensitive about being caught in settings that are out of character. In one *New Yorker* cartoon, a couple refuse to buy a house because of the address: "Mr. Tetlow feels he couldn't live with 114 Pussy Willow Lane on his personal stationery." In another cartoon, a young man breaks up with a woman, telling her in all seriousness, "I honestly don't think it could work out. You're Nantucket and I'm Martha's Vineyard."

Decorating folklore is rich with "not me" anecdotes. The wallpaper was brand-new and costly in a New York condominium conversion because the apartments had been used as a decorating showcase. But when the apartments were sold, each and every new owner steamed off the paper and started from scratch. Why? "Not me." The bachelor thought he had found a painless way to get his townhouse fixed up when a decorating magazine offered to do a "before and after" story. After the "after" he sold all the objects of the make-over to a friend. Nobody had asked the bachelor if he wanted a pink and green living room. He didn't. "Not me." Mario Cuomo's first act as governor was to remove the full-length mirrors inside the master bathroom shower at the Governor's mansion. "I told the construction worker if my mother sees them she'll break them with a hammer," said Cuomo. Not him.

To have their way with a room, consumers will endure long waits for the "right piece." If there was a choice between two pieces of furniture "both in the style you want, one is available immediately but not in the color and/or pattern you want, the other piece is exactly what you want . . . but will take six to eight weeks," which would they buy? asked *Better Homes and Gardens* of its consumer panel. More than 96 percent said they would wait for the piece in the color or pattern of their choice. Only 3 percent would take the less preferred piece immediately. In fact, a large segment of the furniture industry is built on the premise that people will wait.

Few things in life are as satisfying as seeing yourself reflected in your things, as the cartoon in the Bell Phone Center ad demonstrates: "Finally, Charlene," says the bug-eyed gent to the bug-eyed woman about the bug-eyed phone on display in the telephone store, "a phone we can identify with." Finding the right piece is like love at first sight or discovering your long-lost twin. "I knew instantly it was what I wanted . . . the perfect look . . . a strong design," said Burt Lancaster, describing how he felt on spotting the dining table of his dreams at an artisan's workshop. He saw himself reflected in it. Strong, handsome, top quality, rich materials—black-enameled wood with brass inlays—and a perfect fit for his life style. It seats six or eight people—"My ideal number for a dinner party," said Lancaster.

But don't expect him to be wedded to it forever. Identity is always in a state of flux. "A person's identity is not necessarily coherent or stable over time," said the late Berkeley psychologist Donald Appleyard. "We can be successively the person we would like to be, the person we wish we were not, and the person we think we know we are." Our decors ebb and flow accordingly. Those who *can't* afford change move furniture; those who *can* afford change redecorate. A close reading of decorating magazines can give you a clue to the wobbly identities of the most identifiable. On her bed, Tiffany designer Angela Cummings had a blue-and-white afghan made by a friend, "to satisfy a passion I once had for all the shades of blue." Regine, the nightclub impresario, has changed her apartment from crowded *fin de siècle* to white and light Art Moderne.

Those who can most afford to change don't redecorate, they just add on residences and express a different aspect of self in each one. French couturier Karl Lagerfeld is the master of multiresidence, multi-identity decorating. At last count, he had four different homes in four different styles—a bright surrealistic apartment in Monte Carlo, an eighteenth-century-style palace in Paris, a high-tech apartment in which he likes to work, also in Paris, and a black and white Weiner Werkstätte flat in Rome. "I feel quite different in each place and I like that," he said.

Making an Impression

It's nice to feel "at home" at home, but personalizing is also a message to other people about ourselves. Why else would 1,200 readers of *Metropolitan Home* (from every state but Wyoming) last year enter their decors in a home beauty contest which involved propping their rooms in a perfect imitation of design magazines, snapping photos, and submitting them within six weeks to be judged? All so that the winners could have their home on the cover of a magazine for every person buying a lottery ticket at a newsstand to see.

The need to have people "see me, see who I am" is strong

and spiked with competitiveness. Studies show that bicycle racers go faster when there is a strong competitor nearby, fishermen wind tackle faster when other people are watching, and homemakers personalize more when they are expecting company. In studies of the elderly, those who had hardly any visitors took much less interest in fixing up their homes than those who expected visitors. Psychologists call this the "social influence" or "social increment." Furniture people call it the "having company syndrome," and they're thankful for the boost it gives their business in late summer when people start thinking ahead to holiday entertaining. As any hostess knows, the hardest part of a dinner party is getting the house in shape for the party.

People want to present themselves from their best angle because they suspect that others make judgments using every clue they can see, hear, or sense to sum up the situation. And their suspicions are correct. Numerous studies have shown that individuals equate certain qualities in rooms with their occupants. A study of how psychotherapists chose therapists for themselves found that inferences about people were drawn from the decoration of their offices. One therapist was rejected because "He had plastic plants in his waiting room"; another because "Her personality, like her office, was furnished like a motel."

And so homemakers try hard to manage the impression they will give others, pretending that it took no effort. They would be mortified if their peers knew about the bouts of self-doubt, the experiments and mistakes, spats with spouses, financial sacrifice, and pure panic that went into setting the domestic stage for audience performances. "To furnish a house so it will express simple, quiet dignity," wrote Erving Goffman, "the householder may have to race to auction sales, haggle with antiques dealers, and doggedly canvass all the local shops for the proper wallpaper and curtain materials."

A few secure people have no shame about the way they manipulate the impressions they give. The legendary public relations counselor Benjamin Sonnenberg was quite frank about his efforts to manage his identity through his home—a lavishly furnished 37-room townhouse with ballroom, movie screening room, and paintings by van Gogh, Vuillard, Degas, Ingres, and Sargent. He admitted he wanted his house to counteract the fly-by-night image of public relations. "I want my house and office to convey the impression of stability and to give myself a dimension, background, and tradition that go back to the Nile."

The more decisions, the more anxiety about the choices. "I can blame Grandma for the rocker she left me," said one woman, "but if I make a bad wallpaper selection, it's my mistake—there for God and everyone to see." Building a house from scratch is the ultimate identity crisis. It is your choice from the color of the brick to the height of the fireplace hearth. That is why dream-house clients are such a nervous and irritable bunch. "They feel as if the whole world is going to judge them by the house," said one architect who has designed his share of custom residences. "Every decision is a painful one."

Decorating anxiety fluctuates with the importance of the guest. The kiddie party rates an E.T. disposable paper tablecloth and high-ranking guests get the embroidered linen cloth that has to be washed by hand. Housekeeping is especially reactive to rank. Nobody makes the bed just because the plumber is expected, but let someone discover that royalty is coming to see how the masses live and watch the dust fly. To prepare for a queen or future king, a new carpet and more would not be out of the question. Prince Charles recently remarked that one of the drawbacks of the royal lot is to suffer repeatedly the smell of fresh paint.

Even those who deny caring about the opinions of others may have one possession that embarrasses them. "I don't care about fancy furniture and doing 'the right thing' with space," said one New York businessman. "If something is less than perfect, I wouldn't redo it. I care about comfort—that's all." But every time company was expected, he nagged his wife about replacing the old slipcovers.

It takes money and total dedication to make every object and room from front parlor to back porch live up to your standards year-round. That's why many people designate a certain time of year as "our time to shine" and decorate seasonally. Many people "do Christmas." See all the Santas flying over suburban houses and the crèches on the front lawn, the pine boughs, cranberry chains, and lights strung inside the house. Wreaths and candy canes can conceal a multitude of decorating indecision. Other people "do summer." If the living room is empty, it doesn't matter, as long as the patio is furnished.

Another option is to designate one special piece or set of

equipment to speak for you and make an impression on special occasions—a vintage car that is pushed out of the garage and parked in front when guests are coming, a set of "good" china, a handmade lace tablecloth with feathers, the chairs which are hidden under plastic slipcovers until guests are expected. A jukebox. In the French 1950s film farce *Mon Oncle*, the family had a fountain in front of the house in the shape of a fish. Whenever the doorbell rang the husband and wife would trip over each other to turn on the fish—their major status symbol.

One object, however, is rarely enough to define identity. We need a whole esthetic complex, a total identity package to truly represent us to ourselves and others. And sacrifices will be made to assemble the package, especially among people moving up the social ladder. "I always wanted to show people, hey, I've really got nice things," said Rosebud, a young Virginia woman who owns a greeting card shop. Her husband is an accountant. In order to have nice things, she squirrels away whatever she can from her household money to buy furniture. "It takes a lot of work to get nice things. I don't have cheap, off-the-rack stuff," she said. "That sounds kind of braggedy but I don't mean it that way. I have a real leather chair and a solid wood table and a nice sofa. These things weren't important to my parents but they've always been important to me. . . . Our house is not in a ritzy-ditzy area. Everyone's kind of down-to-earth here. But I think my house shows taste."

Rosebud uses her home to send messages in two directions —to her family and to outsiders. "I want to show my parents that they didn't fail, that my life is good, that I'm successful. And I want to be special. And I want people to think, 'She's a nice person, she really tries hard.' I do strive for that. That's important."

But communicating an intended identity with your environment depends, as architectural theoretician Amos Rapoport has pointed out, on the "cues being noticed and the meaning understood." For this reason people usually put their finest identity equipment in places where they are sure to be seen—out front or up front inside the house, in the entrance hall, over the mantel, on the coffee table, over the sofa, in the breakfront. The eighteenth-century noble kept his prize bronzes and curiosities in his *cabinet*, a private study off his bedchamber where he received only the power elite. Our front rooms are one big *cabinet*. You're not likely to find any prized coromandel screens in corridors.

To make sure identity equipment is not ignored, further attention is called to special items with elaborate frames, pedestals, spotlights, and, as a last resort, not-so-casual references such as "the museum wants to borrow our Picasso"—or spittoon collection or whatever—"for an exhibition." Once noticed, the meanings of objects have to be understood. Are those $762 per pair Scalamandré tassels on the tiebacks or five-and-ten-cent store window shade pulls? Is that an original Matisse or a poster shop reproduction? Esthetics are nice, but most objects speak a language that transcends mere visual delight—they have meanings that can only be understood within one's group or culture. Barbara Walters would not have a clue that the fish-bird decorations on a chief's house in the Trobriand Islands denote high rank, and the chief would not have a clue that Miss Walters's spacious living room designed by Angelo Donghia denotes high rank—and high income.

So that the identity he is projecting in his Minimalist apartment will be noticed and all the objects properly appreciated, one New York designer—let's call him Mr. X—hands out to guests a mimeographed raison d'être comparing his personality to his decor, an austere ambience of black lacquer walls, black quilted divans, black slate tiles, and Art Deco bronzes. The printed statement explains that Mr. X, who dresses in black to match his decor, "is quite as trim in appearance as his rooms are . . . [He is] convinced that the way a person chooses his environment is a clear indication of who he is." The release describes Mr. X's attention to detail, the way the grouting in the floor tiles lines up perfectly with the channel quilting on the sofas. "Some people call me a perfectionist," Mr. X is quoted as saying.

One feels rather caddish for mentioning this, but if Mr. X is a perfectionist, why is his printed material riddled with misspellings? Unintended messages can always contradict the intended ones used by observers to locate people "in social space." Discrepancies can be embarrassing since most of us try to give the impression that we are deep down what we purport to be. "No impostors here. My taste is not rented for the occasion but integral with myself."

If all the world's a stage, some things are certain: the *Playbill* will have misprints, the Scotch will be weak tea, we will all fluff our lines from time to time—and people will see through our little deceptions. The most we can hope for is that as we become more comfortable with ourselves, our decor will fit like a skin, not a glove.

3

The Creative Imperative

T

HEY CONVENED ON a Saturday morning in March with stars in their eyes, diamond solitaires on their left hands, and place settings on their minds—a gaggle of brides-to-be along with a smattering of mothers-of-the-brides-to-be and best friends, and one husband-already—250 in all, the most that Tiffany's could squeeze in on folding chairs between the sterling silver gravy boats and the engraved notepaper.

They came for The Word on the three most "important esthetic decisions every bride must make"—her china, her crystal, and her flatware. The Word was spoken by the *Bride's* magazine tabletop editor with the blessing of Tiffany's bridal registrar. There were no drumrolls and no fanfare to underscore The Word, just the resoundingly clear *ping* of Tiffany's swag-patterned lead crystal and the authority of the Tiffany pulpit.

The Word was: "When you choose your place settings, you must consider what will give you personality and creativity. You've got to make that personality come through. You want your home to be *yours,* your own personal style and taste." The bridal expert wasn't suggesting that these young women, who had a higher median age and education and more and better jobs than any group of brides in history, should make sofas out of bathtubs in the madcap manner of Holly Golightly in *Breakfast at Tiffany's*. But if a bathtub divan was their choice, who was to stop them when even this establishment which used to see the world according to Hoyle is teaching brides to *express themselves*.

The bridal registrar would prefer that they express themselves at formal dinner parties which "we believe in." And to that end the brides were briefed on why tulip-shaped champagne glasses were better than wide-mouthed ones (fewer bubbles escape), why salad servers should be vermeil (vinegar won't tarnish it), and the fact that cocktails were coming back (better stock up on martini glasses). But nothing they learned at breakfast at Tiffany's that morning was more important to the new generation of brides than the cultural credo, *"You've got to make that personality come through."*

The Way It Is: Express Yourself

Apparently, there's as much need to explain why your house has to be *you* as there is to explain why we eat with utensils instead of with our bare hands. Your personality has to come through because . . . because lately everyone says it must. And how do you make it come through? By differentiating yourself decoratively. This is not the creative option, this is the Creative Imperative.

"There is a great deal of pressure to express yourself," allows Stanley Barrows, the well-known design educator who has guided many of the country's top interior decorators through the crosscurrents of style and taste. "We live in an age of personality. Everyone is supposed to be different. People think they're special, that they have something terribly thrilling to offer the world and they're going to show this in their homes. They try a little of this and a little of that and it all comes out a big hash."

But what does Barrows expect? The pressure is on the consumer in every quarter to "express yourself." In August 1980 *Better Homes and Gardens* gave its readers a sermon on "Me"-decorating: "Personality Decorating—How to Make Your Home Say You: The rooms we live in can reflect our values, tastes, and interests." That same month *House & Garden* advised its flock on "What You Can Do to Develop Personal Style. The style you give your home is what makes the difference between being in your home and the one next door. . . . Style is like personality. The point is to develop yours so it is memorable." That was the doctrine, then came the parables, including an article on Picasso, whose life was as "original as his works of art"; an interview with author Jill Robinson, who told how she tried to live with "less" but finally succumbed to "more"—revealing her true accumulative nature. "A house is who you are, not who you think you ought to be," said Mrs. Robinson, lip-synching the latest doxy; and finally, a feature on born-again individualists who built a house in Chicago that looks like a circus wagon. "We're proud of our house," said the owners, "because it's really our *own*. There's not another one like it in the world." Hallelujah.

Okay, readers, said *House & Garden*, repeat after us: "Style is not a roomful of furniture from one source, a house done all-in-a-period, as a museum, a rigidly matching scheme demanding conformity." You're entitled to your look, your needs, your things, you deserve it. Go for it. Reach inside yourself; find that personal style that is lying dormant—"pull it out, fine-tune it. Be brave! Develop your own point of view." The creative imperative!

If you need role models, the media will give you role models, See in the *New York Times* how cartoonist Charles Addams turned a van into "an idiosyncratic heap," a rolling haunted house. See in *Architectural Digest* how Sylvester Stallone personalized his Los Angeles place with a portrait of himself in the bedroom by Warhol, boxing sculptures in the living room, and his initials inlaid in ebony in the dining table. See in *People* how Robert Redford put his point of view all over his New York apartment with western paraphernalia and Indian objets d'art and Utah sagebrush. What could be more creative and personal than Lola Redford driving a station wagon full of certified sagebrush all the way from the Redfords' Rocky Mountain hideaway through Colorado, Missouri, Illinois, Indiana, Ohio, Pennsylvania, and New Jersey to their Manhattan apartment house? That's making the personality come through. That's making it say "us." Thirty years ago everyone laughed when Liberace sat down at his piano-shaped swimming pool. Today he'd get a design award for it.

The Way It Was:
Express Yourself, but Not Too Much

If personal style and self-expression are the law of the landscape, why do we need all this prompting, how-to instruction, and examples, examples, examples? Why can't we just get out the Magic Markers and the slipcover fabric and start expressing ourselves?

For one thing, most people don't have that much experience in the decorating medium. We shop for clothes on a continuing basis but we take on only a handful of decorating projects in a lifetime. Furnishings are also big ticket items, so we are inclined to play it safe. Once we make our bed selections, we lie in them a long time. Artists start out copying the Mona Lisa before they find their own unique style. Who can blame homemakers for copying Versailles or Winterthur or their neighbors?

But the most pervasive reason for holding back on ego decorating is that individuality is a risky business. Most of us have received precious little affirmation of our personal taste from the very people who are exhorting us to express ourselves. Personality cheerleaders can be remarkably uncharitable after they've sold us their bill of goods. Look at the fashion world: *Women's Wear Daily* touts the latest outlandish fashion; readers buy the latest fashion; then *WWD* labels those readers in the latest fashion "fashion victims." Gotcha.

For more than eighty years we've been getting double messages. Express yourself by not expressing yourself. Express yourself—classically, carefully, suitably, tastefully, functionally, or excessively, depending on the decade. At the turn of the century, good taste took precedence over personal taste. No one advised brides to express themselves. That was for parvenus. Many socially ambitious Americans followed the lead of the British who believed there was as little place for originality or personal expression in the proper house "as in the dress of the man who inhabits it." *The Decoration of Houses,* the influential haute how-to book by novelist Edith Wharton and architect Ogden Codman published in 1902, emphasized the importance of following the rules of classical design. Readers were warned that individuality was not "the cheap originality" of "putting things to uses for which they were not intended." The only individuality tolerated was "the desire to be comfortable in your own way." There were rules regarding almost every aspect of the decor from the height of doors to the proper metal for andirons and the color of walls.

Elsie de Wolfe, the mother superior of modern-day decorating, preached correctness and suitability in her 1913 book, *The House in Good Taste*. "Homemakers are determined to have their houses . . . correct according to the best standards." So she taught standards. She believed self-expression would take care of itself. "You will express yourself in your house, whether you want to or not." Gotcha.

Hygiene, good housekeeping, and functionalism were top decorating priorities in the 1920s until fear of the "alienating" machine gave personal style a shot in the armchair. A decorating guru in *Creative-Art* magazine assured readers that the new trend to harmonize rooms with sectional furniture and coordinated accessories would not make for "drab uniformity" but should actually emphasize "individuality." It wasn't the pieces you used but the *way* you combined them that would be individual. Thus, a harmonized, depersonalized-looking room by architect Joseph Urban was proclaimed in *House & Garden* to be the very model of personalization. "To be happily livable," the magazine explained, "a room should express the thoughts of the designer who controls the scheme and makes the room artistic and should contain furniture and articles cherished by the owner." The cherished articles in this case were one vase, two candlesticks, and some books. Individuality was invited to the party but it was hardly the guest of honor.

Emily Post's *The Personality of a House*, first printed in 1930 and reissued a number of times in the 1940s, appeared to endorse self-expression while it actually eroded the readers' self-confidence. A home "should unmistakably suggest *you*," she told her readers. But "you" had better not be a pretender. "If you choose to live in a palace, not only must all your appointments be of suitable dignity and quality, but so also must *you*." In the best "how-to" tradition, Emily intimidated with fear tactics—and bad taste was public enemy number one. "Two chairs or carpets or rolls of wallpaper are offered to two women," said Emily. "The one who has taste chooses this item and the one who is ignorant chooses the other. . . . Quite often the good item is of less cost than the bad." How the reader could acquire the taste to discriminate and express her personality without being the fool who paid top price, Emily found more difficult to explain.

By the 1960s, the decorating terrain was thick with celebrations of self, but not the sort Her Etiquetteness had in mind when she said "personality." The chartreuse underbelly of personality was exposed. Everywhere you turned people were revolting against the authority of good taste. Into the language came "conversation pits," "fun furniture," "wet-look," "water beds," and "total environments," and into the living room came neon, Mylar, billboard sheets, stretch walls, and Brillo-box end tables. All this regurgitation of taste spoke to the "soul rather than . . . the dictates of fashion and social position," wrote Norma Skurka in *Underground Interiors.*

Say goodnight, Gracie, to narrow definitions of good taste and good design. Suddenly, pluralism reigned. The antisocial self-expression of the late sixties and early seventies was like a giant tidal wave that rolled over the past and washed away conformity and self-denial, leaving in its wake what came to be called "focus-on-self." Why put off till tomorrow what you can buy today? While Tom Wolfe didn't *invent* the new narcissism, he spotted it first and focused a 15,000-watt arc light on it in his 1976 article, "The 'Me' Decade." A subsequent spate of consumer research backed him up. Authority was out, said the market researchers, the people who had America hooked up to a battery of life-style sensors from its Maine head to its Texas toe. The researchers' "focus group" interviews with real people revealed that the prevailing mood was "nobody is going to tell us what length to wear our skirts and what style of chair is in." Although they wouldn't mind a few suggestions from their favorite life-style magazines.

Happy to help, the magazines and advertisers pitched the nonconformist focus-on-self theme right back to the folks the focus groups were typical of and the idea reverberated in every medium. Conformity is dead. Express yourself. Meanwhile, one newspaper started a You Section; Burger King sang, "Have it your way"; Frank Sinatra crooned, "I did it my way"; and a wall covering industry association began to test a commercial—based on research into what motivates people to redecorate—showing self-satisfied consumers, one after another, in flocked and flowered rooms exclaiming (with no screen credit to Wolfe), "It's me"; "It's me"; "It's me"; "It's *moi*."

After enough media bombardment, even those who are on the fence, expressively, begin to think it is written in their DNA that their home should be self-expressive. Long live the creative imperative.

"I believe absolutely in a house being a creative expression. I would find it very depressing if my house looked like any other house in the area," says Paula, a forty-year-old woman who lives with her husband, a successful lawyer, and their three children on Philadelphia's prestigious Main Line in a Tudor house decorated in a mix of antiques and trendy modern pieces. "I think my house is very personal, very much an extension of myself. . . . I think of myself as a creative person. My house certainly doesn't look like my mother's house. I wouldn't have anything silver-green—my mother's whole house is silver-green." Paula buys things that have meaning for her. Designs she considers innovative. "My house is very much me. It's a symbol of me artistically and visually, and if it looks confused in places, I'm confused in places." What does she admire most in decoration? "Quality and the guts to be innovative."

But just two miles away from Paula lives Binky, forty, whose decorating philosophy predates Edith's, Elsie's, and Emily's. Binky, who is listed in the *Social Register,* is a real estate broker, mother of two, married to an ad man. The creative imperative has barely touched her. "Nobody on the Main Line [meaning her crowd] wants to be creative in their homes," she says. "They'll work for Planned Parenthood but they're scared of doing anything different in their decorating. They won't buy modern houses, they won't even talk to an architect about building a house. I don't *dare* to be too different. I am getting a Berber rug for my hall and I know everyone is going to ask what's that." When Binky did make an attempt to differentiate herself from her crowd, which leans to Oriental rugs, eighteenth-century English antiques, horse prints, and rooms suitable for hunt breakfasts, she was rebuked by her teenage son who had already absorbed the values of their social world. "I did a sitting room over recently and I bought a chrome table," said Binky with amusement. "My son says it looks like a dentist's waiting room."

Binky is typical of the holdouts—whole groups of people who could afford to express themselves but insist, instead, on looking like their neighbors. Why don't they get with it? Don't they read the papers? Haven't they heard about the new accent on self? Why don't they break out of their furniture uniforms, get rid of their old school tiebacks? Why? Because some people have other priorities.

The Way of the World:
"Me" People versus "Us" People

It is now very fashionable to think of the home as a symbol of self, said James Duncan, a geographer at the University of British Columbia. He has been studying homes all over the world, *especially* homes of the wealthy, because only they can afford to make their homes conform to their values. Duncan and his wife and colleague, Nancy Duncan, created a furor in Bedford, a posh exurb of New York, by studying landscape taste. They found that the people with the cutesy painted mailboxes, who decorated the outsides of their houses with signs of Americana—eagles and wagon wheels—were the least likely to be members of the local historical society, which cost only $5 to join. From this the Duncans concluded that the wagon-wheel people weren't interested in history at all, but in the status symbolism of history.

According to Duncan, the home and its decoration is not always a symbol of one's personality, it can also be a symbol of group membership, or a combination of personality and membership in varying proportions. While the "Me's" are multiplying in the Western world, there are still pockets of folks among them who could be called "Us" people, for whom the house is more representative of group values—ethnic, religious, social world—than personal ones.

Duncan believes that most societies can be categorized as individualist or collectivist. *Collectivists* are stable groups of kith and kin; they don't move "up" and "out" when they get a windfall; they stay put in the old neighborhood; they do business with one another, socialize with one another, and marry one another; they share the same values and often the surplus wealth by entertaining one another, preferring to give a big bash for the group rather than indulging themselves. Among collectivists, men have higher status than women; men socialize outside the home at pubs and clubs while women stay home and raise the children; and the house is less a status symbol than a "container of women."

Individualists have "open social groups" and high mobility. Ambition is approved and success applauded; outsiders can break into the social milieu—one doesn't have to be a relative to get a job; values shift according to fashion; and individuals are encouraged to pursue their own interests, even if it takes them away from the group. Men and women are not rigidly segregated—the men spend time in the home and take an interest in its decoration; family life is more private with fewer relatives living in, while the house itself is more public because outsiders are invited. Individualists use the house as a status object—affirming identity. "The more individual a society, the greater dependence on object display," said Duncan.

"Me" Decor versus "Us" Decor

In 1979 Gerry Pratt, one of James Duncan's students, published "The House as Expression of Social Worlds," a study of two groups of wealthy women in Vancouver and the differences in how they expressed themselves in their homes. Her premise was that self-expression in the home was not in the genes but rather a "socially relative phenomenon" having to do with group affiliation. Pratt looked at fifty-four women and their homes in two separate elite social worlds in Vancouver. Half were the *old elite* of Shaughnessy and half the *new elite* of West Vancouver. Both groups decorated their houses. Both groups used the services of decorators, but there the similarities ended. One group believed that it was important to express themselves in their homes; the other group used their decoration to show their *membership* in a social group. Shaughnessy and West Vancouver were ideal contrasting behavioral sinks because while the women living in each area could afford the same standard of living, they were not comparable socially.

Exclusive, dignified Shaughnessy, a stately residential enclave south of Vancouver, which was developed by the Canadian Pacific Railroad in the first decades of this century, is home to the Old Guard—the established business elite whose social life centers on private club memberships. Shaughnessy's English Tudor revival houses and tree-lined boulevards, said Pratt, give the area "a

sense of a stable environment where generations had grown up."
She found Old Guard Shaughnessy women "quite provincial." Most
of them had been raised together in the area and their friendships
had developed over a lifetime. They had exceedingly large social
networks because they all did philanthropic work and belonged to
the same clubs. Since they were born at the top of the social ladder, they were not socially mobile.

If Shaughnessy is a "lady" in a cashmere sweater and circle
pin, West Vancouver (known as British Columbia's Riviera) is a
cosmopolite in designer jeans. Originally a summer colony, West
Vancouver is a twenty-one-mile-long waterfront stretch where
people live in glass houses "that cling like barnacles to the massive
rocks or stand on slender stilts, jutting at dizzying angles over the
cliffs." The architecture, whether Frank Lloyd Wright organic or
steel-and-glass International Style, is blatantly twentieth century.
West Vancouver's residents run the gamut socially from successful
physicians to business tycoons, with a football star and nightclub
proprietor in between.

People in this area have neither "geographic nor cultural continuity." More than a third of the sample had surpassed their parents socially and financially, and more than half of the sample and
their spouses had grown up in other countries and emigrated to
Vancouver. Thus the West Vancouver women had smaller networks of friends and acquaintances. They didn't see themselves as
part of a group. "The private self," said Pratt, "has become the
source of gratification."

The social differences in these two communities made for
vast *taste* differences. The definition of good taste in Shaughnessy
was very subdued, classic, and timeless. The term "individual expression," said Pratt, was never mentioned. Nine out of ten
Shaughnessy women said that their home was *not* a creative statement. They expressed themselves in their jobs or committee
work. The majority of them felt they got their taste from their
parents. Most of their furnishings were inherited and the rest
bought over a period of time. The few women who subscribed to
interior design magazines said they "certainly wouldn't copy anything out of one." People who changed their belongings on a regular basis were considered "rootless, shallow, sinful."

Seventy-two percent of the Shaughnessy women felt their
homes were *similar* in decoration to their friends' homes. "We live

in the same way," said one Shaughnessy woman; "we all went to the same schools, generally our houses are the same. You could take my Chesterfield [sofa] and drop it into a friend's living room and it would fit." Meaningful possessions were invariably "family heirlooms." In this group, said Pratt, "conforming to the group canons of good taste was enough."

West Vancouver might as well have been a thousand miles away. There, home was considered "an expression of individual creativity," said Pratt. Most West Vancouver women felt their taste was completely different from and not influenced by their parents. Their taste was influenced "by peers and magazines." West Vancouver women were susceptible to fashion. They confessed to "marked shifts" in style preferences over the years. Possessions were cherished, not because they were inherited but because they signified something *personal* or a shared memory with a spouse. Bad taste in this milieu was considered a room with "no personality" or "no thought put into it." Good taste was "what I like." Almost 80 percent of the West Vancouver women said that their homes *differed* decoratively from their friends' homes.

Given these group profiles, you'd expect Shaughnessy women who value creativity so little to decorate their houses themselves and West Vancouver women who value it so much to use decorators. But it was just the opposite. Shaughnessy women used decorators more often and for bigger jobs than the West Vancouver women. The decorators consulted in Shaughnessy were usually members of their clients' social world, and women didn't object to having the same decorator as their friends. Decorators were used as "legs"—to fetch fabric samples and expedite the job—not for their artistry. The highest praise for a decorator was to be known as someone who left the house looking as though a designer hadn't been there. In this group with its "traditional values, group orientation, community obligation, and deprecation of the house as an expressive medium," said Pratt, the designer is a craftsman more than an artist, but especially "the guardian of group taste." *Our look. Our taste. Our traditions.*

It was just the opposite in West Vancouver, where designers were used not for legs, but for their *ideas*—"to make your house special." And apparently it wouldn't be very special if you used the same designer all your friends used. West Vancouver women wanted their houses to be different. A good proportion of them believed a woman should decorate her home herself so it would look more personal and less faddish. A few West Vancouver women who had used decorators pretended they did it themselves, something that probably sounds familiar to many decorators around the country. *My look. My taste. My way.*

Pratt's study demonstrates that not everyone with money wants her or his house to be "me, me, me, *moi*." To people in group-oriented societies or in certain collectivistic worlds within individualistic societies, such as the old elite of Shaughnessy or Philadelphia's Main Line, the house symbolizes "group values." On the other hand, in all those areas around the globe in which individualism is becoming more and more the dominant theology, whether it's West Vancouver or on the Main Line where Paula lives, the house reflects the owner's personality, status, accomplishments, and self-concept, said Duncan. The "Us" people versus the "Me" people. But the "Me's" are gaining.

When the Caste System Meets the Cult of Personality

It's not just North Americans who make elaborate displays with their homes. The last place you'd expect to see a decline of group orientation would be in India, where social station is assigned at birth. Yet in India the Duncans found there are now groups of affluent people using their homes to express their personality and status. And it's not only well-to-do people who use their homes to express individuality. There is evidence that even the Zapotec Indians of Mexico—a classic group-oriented society— are turning away from the collective life toward focus-on-self. How do you say "me" in Hindi and Zapotec dialect?

In a study comparing the houses of the old elite and the new elite in Hyderabad, India, James and Nancy Duncan found the same dichotomy that Gerry Pratt found in Vancouver. The wealthy, educated *old elite* in Hyderabad lived in the old walled city and were unconcerned with the appearances of their houses whose design style was best described as "faded grandeur." Walls were dingy, the only decorations were family portraits draped with dusty dried garlands of flowers; furniture was sparse and shabby. But appearances didn't matter. Strangers were rarely entertained. Most guests were relatives. "The host," said the Duncans, "does not need to use the interior of his house as a cue to his status because his status is established." Money was spent on the group for weddings and gifts.

In the new part of Hyderabad and its suburbs resided the *new elite*—well-educated, high-salaried people with managerial jobs who came from many castes and many areas of the country. They lived in "elaborately decorated and well-maintained" houses which they used as membership cards in the new society. Rooms were coordinated and furnished in Western style with copies of European furniture, built-in bars, tape recorders, electric barbecues, and that ubiquitous local status symbol—a refrigerator in the formal dining room.

The groups were hostile to each other. The new elite thought the old elite's large family parties a waste of money. The old elite thought the new elite's houses were ostentatious.

In Mexico, "Me"-ism is making inroads at a lower socioeconomic level. The Zapotecs of southern Mexico, influenced by upwardly mobile mestizos (people of mixed Spanish and Indian blood), are turning away from the old collectivistic system. Instead of chipping into the group sombrero with relatives and staging a fiesta for the benefit of "the community, the ancestors, and the saints," the Zapotecs are thinking about improving their humble houses, which often have dirt floors and no plumbing. When researchers asked the Indian women how they would spend a "windfall profit," they sounded like new elite Hyderabad Indians and "Me" generation North Americans. "Most replied they would fix up their house," said Duncan. A house of costly adobe with a tile roof and a cement floor is now a status symbol—a sign of being civilized. The creative imperative, Zapotec style.

The principle operating in all these examples is the same. When you live in a social world where everyone knows you from the day you are born, you are likely to spend money on parties or other consumption rituals that the whole group can share. Your house is kept up to the standards of the group and those standards vary cross-culturally: among the Zapotecs the house is primitive; in India it's shabby; in Vancouver the standard is a tasteful but not ostentatious house. Only when you are a stranger in a society, said

Duncan, does "the house, the address, and its façade as well as its interior, affirm one's status in the eyes of strangers."

A similar premise on the function of clothing was advanced some years ago. "Most human interaction is structured in terms of the judgments people make of one another," wrote sociologist Thomas Ford Hoult in one of the first controlled studies linking clothing with status. Hoult dressed up a number of college professors first in their gardening clothes and then in their going-to-a-meeting outfits and took their pictures to show to rating teams. According to Hoult, clothes "made the man" only when the man was being judged by *strangers*. Time after time, raters unacquainted with the men they were rating gave high or low attractiveness ratings depending on the clothes the test subjects were wearing. But clothes had nothing to do with the rating when the subject was being judged by people who knew him. The person who was known got the same rating whether he dressed up or down. Naturally, if you're always interacting with people who know you, you don't have to dress up your clothes—or your home.

Why "Us" People Cater to "Me" People: Business as Usual

Which brings us back to Tiffany's and the creative imperative. It's comforting to know that Tiffany's is preaching the values of the new individualists while its own chairman is a charter member of a collectivistic world that is as inbred as the old elite of Hyderabad. Harry Platt, one of the last uncontaminated collectivists still available for study, is chairman of the board of Tiffany & Co. Great-grandson of designer Louis Comfort Tiffany, Platt was born with a vermeil spoon in his mouth and raised on the 600-acre family estate on Long Island where, "both sheets on every bed were changed every day." But friends were rarely changed. Platt still skis and sails and foxtrots with many of the men and women he grew up with.

Although Platt's living quarters are a far cry from the shabby houses of the old elite of Hyderabad or the dirt floor houses of the fiesta-giving Zapotec Indians, his way of life is comparable to theirs. Obviously Platt could afford to live in any style he wanted to. But he lives modestly for his position in a one-bedroom apartment near his office which was decorated by Billy Baldwin, a designer who always said he tried to make his work look as if a designer had not been there.

Like the old elite of Hyderabad, Platt *never* entertains strangers in his home. In fact, according to published reports, he rarely entertains anyone at home and does almost all his entertaining at restaurants and clubs, and once every two years he gives a major bash—a fiesta—at a hotel for, in his words, "a group of people that belong to the setting." His crowd. The people he grew up with. As James Duncan would say, Harry Platt spends his money for "the benefit of the collectivity" and doesn't worry about *impressing* anyone with his home, although it is probably furnished up to the standards of his social set.

Meanwhile, back at the store, Tiffany's is catering to the needs of both the new individualists and the traditional group-oriented people who still want to look like one another and not stand out. The latter group is no problem. But the individualists will find that Tiffany's has standards. Fads and bad taste are not welcome at breakfast at Tiffany's or any other time. Tiffany's will not sell colored crystal—no red or blue or green goblets: Tiffany's will not sell gold- or silver-rimmed glasses; no silver-edged china; no colored wedding invitations or ones with "kooky" wording; and on its table settings there will be no napkins folded to look like origami butterflies, or "amusing" saltshakers.

But Tiffany's isn't stuffy. It doesn't object to brides mixing butter plates of one pattern with dinner plates of another; it has nothing against informal earthenware—not every bride needs Limoges. And Tiffany's has a sense of humor. It didn't get exercised when socialite Mrs. John Drexel 3d, invited to do an in-store table setting, did a breakfast for champions complete with Wheaties box; nor did Tiffany's complain when social whirler Betsy Bloomingdale staged a TV dinner with a Sony parked right on the table; or when Andy Warhol cheekily made a Campbell's Cream of Tomato Soup can the centerpiece de résistance on his table setting. That was making the personality come through!

But, while the creative imperative is indisputably good for business, dear me, sometimes the Old Guard saleswomen yearn for the good old days when there were standards and everyone wasn't getting carried away with creativity so they could show the world the real "me, me, me, *moi.*" Perhaps one day the pendulum will swing back again to collectivism. In the meantime, another 250 brides are due in April for breakfast at Tiffany's and The Word— "You've got to make that personality come through."

4

Who Am I?
The Living Room
and
Class Connection

MOST LIFE STYLES have their disease—smoker's cough, tennis elbow, the Type A person's heart ailment. The black lung disease of focus-on-self is the *identity crisis*—a favorite theme in books and articles in every area of contemporary life, including decorating. The quintessential decorating book for the age of "Me" was the 1980s *What Do You Say to a Naked Room?* That title said it all: the *angst* of homemakers confronting the blank canvas of a room feeling naked and ashamed, unable to present themselves till properly clothed. But what to wear when there are supposedly "no rules" and the rule of thumb is *express yourself?* A fate worse than death is having ho-hum rooms with no sense of style. Boring, boxlike rooms, untransformed, signify boring people. The whole world is your mail order catalog. All you have to do is *choose*. ChooOOOoooOOOse. The word ricochets off the sides of the tunnel of indecision. But you can't choose till you solve the big puzzle—Who am I? Instead of the existential "To be or not to be," the contemporary question is "What to be?"

Am I a princess in a palace, an ultrasophisticate in a penthouse, a peasant in a farmhouse; am I satin or homespun; porcelain or pottery; marble or marbleized? The price we pay for liberation from convention is that we must constantly invent ourselves, be Pygmalion and Galatea simultaneously—artist and creation in one.

In a typical example of identity-crisis journalism, one writer confessed recently to "furniture flings" with Japanese, Victorian, and English country chintzes. She despaired of her "inability to light on a 'look,' plan, or scheme and stay with it," but resolved to overcome her "decorating indecisiveness this year." It was taken for granted that readers of the New York *Daily News* would understand and identify with her need to be reflected in a decorating style.

Oh, to be like Ali MacGraw, sitting pretty and self-assured on her puffy white sofa amid Indian rugs, plants, books, and pottery in a full-page ad for *Architectural Digest.* Obviously, she didn't have any trouble making conversation with a naked room. Her philosophy is headlined across the ad: "I want a place where a ten-year-old boy can eat an ice cream cone without my getting uppity about his making a mess on the sofa." The fact that most good housekeepers reading the ad would never let an ice cream cone near that white sofa makes it all the more intimidating.

Hello, Central, Get Me an Affluent, Extroverted Hedonist

Know thyself, advised the Seven Sages, and God knows we try, using everything from horoscopes to biorhythm charts, handwriting analysis, phrenology, color tests, numerology, est, and psychoanalysis. We are not alone in this quest for self-awareness. The livelihoods of numerous occupational groups depend on their knowing us well enough to predict our actions. Psychologists need to separate the masochists from the sadists, the neurotics from the schizophrenics, and they use a battery of tests with exotic names such as TAT, MMPI, CPI, and Rorschach to do this. Market researchers have to sort out the "outgoing optimists" from the "apathetic indifferents" so that advertisers can target their messages to the receptive consumers. Using interviews and questionnaires, consumer analysts have raised psychographics—the charting and codifying of people's attitudes—to an art form. Plato divided men into gold, silver, and brass. He'd probably be aghast at the array of taxonomies that have been devised to pigeonhole us now. Low, middle, and highbrow; consciousness I, II, III; Puritans, moderates, hedonists; experimental, transitional, traditional; formalistic, sociocentric, personalistic; worriers, sociables, independents, sensory types.

Personality is a complex thing. Who you are is more than your four humors, sense of humor, body type, head bumps, brow height, birth order, and possession in varying quantities of 350-odd character traits. If you think your passion for blue-and-white china, your affection for old quilts, or your affinity for shiny new furniture is an expression of your inner psyche and *nothing else,* you are mistaken. The personality of your house is related to factors *beyond* your biological uniqueness—variables such as your age, your sex, and most especially your social status. Social class is a major determinant of what your house looks like. In decorating matters, no man is an island. We are all part of some taste archipelago. According to Henry Murray, the eminent Harvard psychologist, personality is determined by internal needs and external pressures. And so is decorating taste. Despite the myth of "free will," sociologist Kai Erikson said, "the world is full of invisible forces that press in on people and shape them in certain ways." We live "in an invisible network of rules, traditions, and customs." While we are all unique individuals operating on the basis of our own "idiosyncrasies . . . there are common rhythms in the midst of all that uniqueness."

The common rhythms and external pressures in furnishing the home are invariably social milieu. That is why one of the major determinants of what your house looks like is your position in the social pecking order. To talk of social class differences smacks of snobbism. Americans hate to admit there are class differences. But social class "is a cultural reality," according to sociologists James Bossard and Eleanor Boll. It is recognition of the fact that "people live and work and play and think at different levels. The differences between classes are not merely financial or ostentatious." They are differences in life style. Today, the components of style of life include occupation, consumption habits, speech, dress, values, pastimes, family life, and more. Income, number of children in the family, and size of home can affect discipline and family organization, all of which affect personality.

The term "life style" irritates newspaper copy editors, who feel it is overused. It is used so much because it means different things to different groups (each of which spells it differently). To furniture people, "lifestyle" is a trendy category of goods—the inexpensive, carry-out, and assemble-it-yourself items that appeal to the first apartment crowd. To psychologists, "life-style" is a personal coping style; Freud's associate, Alfred Adler, used "life-style" to describe the mechanisms that children, as they develop, rely on to deal with their sense of inadequacy and attain a sense of superiority. And to sociologists, "life style" is what Max Weber called "style of life" and defined as standard of living, the way a family allocates its resources.

Focus-on-self hasn't lessened the hold that class differences have in our culture. Just because you see Jack Klugman in an ad hugging his Canon personal copying machine and proclaiming, "Finally, a copier for the most important person in my life. Me," doesn't mean he has no external pressure—no group to conform to. Why does he need all those copies? One assumes he needs them to edify the people he is bound up with socially and economically.

If Klugman and his fellow "Me's" are subject to the press of outside forces, the non-"Me's" are pressed even more. And their numbers are significant. According to Daniel Yankelovich, 20 percent of Americans still live by the old rules, saving money for a rainy day and sacrificing for the family's future. Another 63 percent mix and match some old-fashioned self-denial with some new-fashioned self-indulgence; and only 17 percent devote themselves to themselves wholeheartedly.

Even these fully committed "Me's" answer to some fashion authority. Human beings have a need to be the same just as they have a need to be unique. Because of this, even so-called style-setters and fashion individualists are not practicing bizarre, out-of-this-world uniqueness—living in pink cabooses in the middle of a street of Colonial homes. Some degree of social obedience usually accompanies individual differentiation. Even the dandy who wears white suits when everyone else wears dark suits, wears suits. He doesn't wear togas.

Toe-the-line conformity may be a declining neighborhood, but affiliation is still six prime blocks on the Boardwalk, a key buying incentive. Most often the group we want to affiliate with is our own or the one above—socially. Fashion in material things is "a product of class distinction," said Georg Simmel in 1904, and eighty years later, despite occasional slumming into lower-class fashions such as jeans and my old Kentucky homespuns, it still holds true.

A person's willingness to conform depends on many variables, but the very nature of decorating predisposes to conformity. Psychological studies have shown that the more difficult the task, the more people lean on others for guidance—something that we see all the time in decorating. In situations where there are no absolute right or wrong answers (decorating is one of those), people have been found to be more willing to go along with others; and, most important, people are more willing to conform to "a group that has had a past history of success than to one that has consistently failed." Upper classes certainly have a history of success, which is one reason their homes are so popular as decorating role models.

Small wonder *Metropolitan Home*'s most popular feature is the one that instructs its upwardly mobile readers on how to imitate an expensive style at a fraction of the cost—the $37,000 English country drawing room in pink flowered chintz that you can reproduce for only $4,000, using Diane Von Furstenburg's new chintz from Sears. "What your home could have in common with the Met, the Tate, and the Louvre" is the hook used in a mail-order ad for limited edition prints. The need to affiliate with a successful group also explains why *Beverly Hills World,* the short-lived materialist's guide to Los Angeles, inaugurated a shopping column called "Word of Mouth: Personal Recommendations by Those Who Know . . ." The column established linkage between recommended goods and prestigious people who owned them. The soft-sell was unabashedly affiliative. Worried about getting into modern art? Don't be. The November 1982 issue informed readers that two successful entertainment figures, record mogul David Geffen and director Paul Mazursky, owned the red, Abstract Expressionist poster by Sam Francis and readers could own it, too, for a mere $100 (signed) or $25 (unsigned). As they say on "The Price Is Right," "Come on down." Come on down to modern art; get in the art swim with the big boys. In the December 1982 issue, *Bev-*

erly Hills World readers learned how to affiliate, pillowcase-wise, with Sophia Loren, Pope John Paul II, Elton John, Johnny Carson, and assorted princesses—all of whom sleep on Pratesi 300-thread-count linens, "the costliest sheets in the world"; the sheets on which "much of the European aristocracy has been conceived."

In every era, various styles become associated with membership in groups. Status groups tend to monopolize styles and genres. The more status a group has, the more likely members are to make certain styles and special objects their own. They hold onto their symbols with the same fervor that traditional clans and tribes held onto their given names and passed them on in the family. During the Depression of the 1930s, Old Guard New England families who had fallen on hard times would consign their family heirlooms to dealers in distant cities to keep their status objects from being sold, heaven forbid, to the local nouveaux riches.

Today, the meritocracy is pressing in hard on the old rich—buying their homes, aping their style, patronizing their lampshade makers whose formerly hush-hush addresses are now the "service" in such social-climbing guides as *Town & Country* (the self-described "magazine of privileged information"). How does the Old Guard protect its symbols? Sumptuary laws are patently undemocratic. One of the few prerogatives left to them is the head start. In New York each winter, the social upper crust and the most prestigious antiques dealers collude in the name of charity to give the "right" people first crack at the rare objects that the dealers have been holding back for the annual Winter Antiques Show, the toniest social and antiques event of the year. Committee members and their cliques have first call on the $125 preview tickets, and there are never enough to satisfy the demand. Despite the chance to make more money for its charity, the committee doesn't see fit to issue more tickets. The goal is not unqualified profit, but profit with honor—and that requires making sure the finest objects are offered first to those *Women's Wear Daily* calls the "Quality people."

Decorating is like art, which one sociologist described as an expression of the "desire for beauty . . . through sanctioned form." Yes, we all have our personal tastes and the need for harmonious surroundings, but it is difficult to resist the pressure to find beauty in forms that are *approved*. Inevitably, people in the same class express themselves in similar forms. Shared *style of life* and *style of living room* may have replaced the pleasures of shared religious experience.

The pursuit of beauty in some circles resembles religious zeal—styles are sects, and conversions to a certain period or idiom can make connoisseurs feel they have found "the way." Each specialist feels his or her stylistic faith is the *divine* one, an idea that is encouraged by merchants who defend their particular "denominations" with religious fervor. "People who like eighteenth-century [English] antiques are highly discriminating—true connoisseurs of beauty," proclaimed Philip Colleck, a New York dealer in the genre, in a magazine interview. "The people who buy French eighteenth-century furniture are the happy few," insists Leon Dalva, a fine French furniture dealer. "The person who collects Victoriana has to be more sophisticated, more tasteful, have more imagination, because it is out of fashion," asserts Hervé Aaron of Didier Aaron, the prestigious firm selling an eclectic mix of antiques. "Anyone who says Victorian is bad taste, I will punch his face."

Accounting for Taste

Realizing that taste marked the boundaries between social groups, in the 1970s Herbert Gans divided Americans into five "taste cultures" which he said were highly reflective of education, which in turn is often related to income. Gans suggested that people in the various "cultures" would share similar tastes in literature, art, music, and home decoration, but perhaps because he was less attuned to differences in decor than to other cultural indicators, he was a bit vague on how different interiors would look in each taste culture. In his hierarchy, high-culture people set standards, are interested in form, and appreciate innovation and experimentation; upper-middle-culture people value simplicity in design and borrow the most popular aspects of high-culture taste; lower-middle-culture people lean to romantic and representational art; and low-culture people like their visuals colorful, ornate as in rococo, or overblown as in Hollywood modern. Gans's fifth taste culture included quasi-folk culture, ethnic culture, and youth culture, all of which give higher priority to feeling than reason. People straddle cultures upwardly for status-seeking, and they straddle downward for relaxation.

Class and taste connections are not just an American phenomenon. In France, sociologist Pierre Bourdieu published *La Distinction*, a monumental study correlating taste in furniture, music, art, cinema, cuisine, TV, vacations, and haircuts with social class: an equation of income, education, and father's occupation. Questionnaires (administered in 1963) probed respondents' preferences for Edith Piaf versus Petula Clark; westerns versus musical comedies; da Vinci versus Picasso, Dali, and Van Gogh; the Modern Museum versus the Louvre; permanent waves versus chignons, and so on. In addition, Bourdieu asked people whether their furniture was modern, antique, or rustic; which three adjectives best described rooms they would like to live in: tidy, comfortable, composed, understated, warm, functional, intimate, *soigné*, fanciful, easy to maintain, classic, harmonious; and how they acquired their furnishings—at the flea market, from department stores, or were they inherited.

Bourdieu found what Gans found, that people in different social groups affiliated with people at the same level and differentiated themselves from those at different levels in measurable ways. Standards were set by the dominant middle classes—the intellectuals and the wealthy bourgeoisie. The scorned petit bourgeoisie or lower middle class attempted to learn what was proper. All of the above looked down on the taste of the working class, who returned their disdain.

In interior decoration as in other consumption matters, said Bourdieu, people were using distinctions to express their superiority to the groups below. Intellectuals leaned to a composed look, country antiques, restored farmhouses, and an ascetic understatement that matched their Left Bank taste in art (Kandinsky) and music (Boulez). If the intellectuals saw the world pessimistically as *la vie en noir*, the bourgeois industrialists saw life optimistically as *la vie en rose*. They had a Right Bank mentality—preferring luxury and comfort in decor, Impressionism in art. The petit bourgeoisie sought correctness in decor and preferred the "Blue Danube Waltz," while the working classes valued function in furniture and sentiment in their art. By endorsing the taste of one group and not others, said Bourdieu, the taste establishment maintains a virtual caste system.

But taste, like Pac-Man, is always in motion. Whistler's Mother was considered *highbrow* in the late nineteenth century, *middlebrow* in the 1920s, and *lowbrow* in the 1940s and 1950s, according to the classic map of the painting's downward mobility in *The Tastemakers* by Russell Lynes. The *only constant* in taste is the process of using taste to affiliate with the aspired-to group and to distinguish oneself from everyone else.

And where do these incremental distinctions in taste become most self-evident? At home. While class barriers are breaking down in many areas of culture, "the culture that is closest to family and home seems to express class position more than culture which is publicly consumed," said Herbert Gans recently. For this reason, he said, home furnishings correlate strongly with class. And the living room correlates the strongest. In the living room, personal taste is the most hospitable to class ideals. More than any other room, the living room is the center ring of symbolic interaction where the id is overruled by the superego—where "I" meets "them" more than halfway, where we show how well we have internalized the esthetics and values of our class.

The Living Room: More Than a Touch of Class

East is East and West is West but just about everyone in the world needs a place to receive honored guests and demonstrate credit-worthiness. In the hierarchical world of the home, the living room is *sacred* as opposed to *profane, front* as opposed to *back,* the *stage* as opposed to *backstage*, where, as Erving Goffman observed, "Performances for guests are most often given." "The living room stands for how it should be, not how it is," wrote architect Harold Alexander. "For many American families, the living room is as close to being a sacred place as any area in the home, although it rarely contains altars, religious objects, or shrines," said Irwin Altman, who has been studying the average American home in Salt Lake City. Rather, the living room is sacred in the psychological sense, serving as "a symbol of the family's status and values." It is a family's corporate identity symbol, reinforcing—and sometimes upgrading—the symbolism of the neighborhood and the exterior of the house, over which people have less control.

As W. H. Auden observed in "The Common Life," a poem from *About the House*:

> A living room . . . confronts
>   each visitor with a style,
> a secular faith: he compares its dogmas
>   with his, and decides whether
> he would like to see more of us.

The living room is a testament to a family's taste and sophistication, family centeredness or accomplishments. It can even show one's disdain for those values. Are the residents pretentious or family-oriented; ecologically inclined; politically active; cultured or crass? The living room will tell. A woman whose only claim to sociological savvy is that she's an astute observer of the bicoastal decorating scene, laid her cards on the coffee table: "It's the room where you show how successful you are." She hesitated to use the term "status symbol," but made the point by saying, "It's where people put their art." She understands full well that art and furniture are clues that people use in "taste exchanging," the mutual sniffing out people go through to decide if they are socially and intellectually sympatico.

No wonder the living room is the space where the resident curator tries to be the most discriminating, the housekeeper the most meticulous, the exchequer the most liberal. "Sloppy Joe" yellow pine furniture is okay for the family room but for the living room we need something better. Performances here will be reviewed. Judgments will be made. Reputations established. Who wouldn't set aside some space and money for this purpose? Those who wouldn't shouldn't underestimate the extremes to which others will go to demonstrate their status and values.

Decorating folklore brims with tales of velvet ropes across the doorways of middle-class living rooms; sofas protected between social calls with clear plastic slipcovers; families spending evenings in living-room avoidance, and silent agreement among middle-class consumers that certain objects are inappropriate in the living room—TV sets, telephones, recliners, trophies. Some people even feel books don't belong there. All to protect the immaculate conception of the living room, an ironic name for a room no one lives in.

In view of the evidence that people go easy on this room, using it as infrequently as possible, an inordinately large share of household resources are lavished on it. Year after year, home furniture industry studies show, more money is spent on furnishing the living room than on any other room in the house. Many more living rooms are carpeted than master bedrooms and dining areas. Sixty-nine percent of *Better Homes and Gardens'* consumer panelists say they would spend the most money on the living room if they were buying home furnishings. Only 14 percent would spend the most on the family room. Living rooms are also the bread and butter of the residential interior design business. In 1980 *House & Garden* subscribers were planning to redecorate the living room more than any other room in the house; and in 1981 *Architectural Digest* subscribers had done more recent redecorating in the living room than in any other room. It would seem they had good reason to as *Digest* asserts its average subscriber entertains sixty-five people per month.

If the furniture industry were really savvy, it would push *entertaining.* That's the real hot button for furniture sales. Nothing triggers living room redecorating more than anticipatory shame— the thought of this room being exposed to the glances of guests, respected guests. The floor tile can be coming up in the kitchen, the ceiling can be peeling in the bedroom, but the living room has to measure up. The drapers, upholsterers, carpet installers, and wallpaper hangers can tell you what reduces clients to alternate fits of rage and supplication—the specter of the living room being unfinished in time for The Party. Would the client demand that the upholsterer move heaven and earth to complete the furniture for any other room? Even the eminent professor who told me "I don't know anyone who decorates, we furnish," makes living room obeisance to guests. "We clean up for a party and remove the things of daily life," he said.

If *invited* guests inspire insecurity, the thought of a visit from *unexpected* guests can be even stronger incentive for living-room completion. Why was the Long Island woman shopping for fabric for her living room? Hadn't she just redecorated a few years ago?

asked a friend. "My mother is very old. She could die any day now. My living room has to look good when people pay condolence calls," explained the shopper.

There is even anticipatory *posthumous* shame. When Barry, a New Jersey dress manufacturer, learned he was terminally ill, he looked around the living room and thought about his funeral. He pictured his friends and colleagues calling on his wife and the impression his home would make, and he did not like what he saw. Even though they realized he probably wouldn't be around to see the job completed, Barry and his wife, Sylvia, asked a designer, a good friend, to redo the living room—fast. When Barry died there were still a few details unfinished. The morning of the funeral Sylvia asked the decorator to do what he could to make the room look finished, saying, "I want it to be perfect for Barry."

The living room is so important that when people do not have what they consider "a *proper* living room," they won't entertain. Take Beverly, an intense, dark-haired young woman. When she first moved to New York from Texas, she furnished her own room respectably with a convertible chaise longue, willow table, and chairs. Then she started collecting clothes. Soon they covered every inch of the tiny apartment. Now the apartment is essentially a large walk-in closet with a bed in the center, a room "dedicated to getting dressed," says Beverly. She looks on her clothes as children and she can't send them away the way her mother, a rubber lady in a circus, sent her away when she was twelve. Yet, her apartment embarrasses her. "You're not supposed to live like this," she said. "You're supposed to live with all your clothes put away. You're supposed to have a living room. I care what people think. Of course I care. Which is why I don't let anyone see my apartment."

Living Room at Risk

Meanwhile, the space crunch is on. A housewife on a recent Phil Donahue show complained she needs a three-bedroom house with a living room and a family room, but she can't find one she can afford. She'll have to scale down her aspirations. What will she give up? As real estate prices soar and living space shrinks accordingly, space-starved residents eye the living room the way shipwrecked sailors eye one another after ten days without food. Should they defy the cultural prohibition on cannibalizing the living room? Some people say they should.

Despite all indications that the living room serves an important symbolic function, there are living-room critics—efficiency experts who probably Xerox on both sides of the paper and use their soap till it's as thin as tissue—who relieve their personal anxieties by insisting that the world should operate sensibly. The idea of dedicating an expensive piece of real estate to Keeping Up Appearances is as extraterrestrial to them as having two sets of china, one for "everyday" and one for "good." They vote thumbs down on the living room and justify it as triage. They're not killing the sacred living room, they're saving the profane family room. "There appears to be a continuing need for a place where . . . people do not 'go to all the trouble of keeping up with those pretentious Joneses,'" said one living-room detractor. I'd like to introduce him to Charlan Graff, a psychologist at the University of Indiana. Graff believes it's important for a home to have *two* living spaces, one for family, one for guests. The informal room promotes identification with the family, she says; the more formal room teaches children "who we are and how to act." If *she* were on the triage committee, she would suggest that the children double up in bedrooms rather than sacrifice an extra living area.

While the debate goes on, builders have invented the high-ceilinged Great Room—a living-dining-family room combination that diverts the buyer's attention from the fact that there is no place else to sit down in the house except on the beds. If builders slim down the basic American home much more, social life could return to the front stoop from whence it came. "Street life is not a choice but a necessity, born of lack of space in the dwelling," said Herbert Gans. But considering that only 3 percent of the housing stock is replaced or added to each year, the living room is not obsolete yet. Just endangered.

Interior designers have done their part for the austerity effort by perfecting the double-duty living room. It looks respectable but is designed to withstand Nikes on the sofa, soda cans on the coffee table, assertiveness training meetings, and the spilled popcorn of Superbowl Sunday. But it requires constant vigilance and self-consciousness. And for heavy living-room users, having to entertain in the same room in which they watch TV every night has all the sex appeal of a subcompact car—which Americans are forsaking whenever possible for larger cars. If all home buyers can afford is one living area, they'll make do, but as soon as there's enough money, they will trade up to a house that has one living area to mess around in, and another for "good."

The Living-Room State of Mind: Nature or Nurture?

One psychologist believes honesty is the best living room policy. She thinks it's a shame that we are embarrassed to let outsiders see our "homeliness." She decries the fact that "we feel obliged to sweep away the smell of dinner and the items that mean the most to us when company comes." It's so artificial. Why can't we be natural?

When "natural" is respected in everything from fibers to childbirth, it may seem rearguard to mention that there is no "natural" way to behave and never has been. "There is no zero point in . . . human development," wrote sociologist Norbert Elias in *The History of Manners.* "In both 'primitive' and 'civilized' peoples, there are socially induced prohibitions and restrictions, [and] anxieties." Living-room anxiety and the resulting artifice is related to the same civilizing process that gave us etiquette and table manners. They all evolved from the feelings of shame and embarrassment at undisguised bodily functions that developed in the Middle Ages and accelerated in the sixteenth and seventeenth centuries. In those years, for instance, forks were adopted, not because they were more hygienic, but because it became revolting to be seen eating in public with bare hands. "The whole process of civilization," said Elias, is the progressive movement to "the hiding 'behind the scenes' of what has become distasteful." But there was one other reason for the adoption of table implements: they were status symbols par excellence, distinguishing the nobility from the vulgar rabble.

The respectable living room is a social implement with similar honorific properties. It is, at once, a symbol of our civilization, a container of our emblems of honor, and the site of the social rituals by which we communicate and reinforce our group memberships and status claims.

The interest in home decoration that is rising like bread dough is supposedly a response to trying times. "In times when life is threatening," said *House & Garden*'s editor-in-chief recently, "home materially and spiritually becomes a kind of haven, a controllable space where you can build your own world." That may be part of the fermentation in home improvement, but the yeast in this trend has got to be the status factor. With increased social mobility and education, taste is becoming the last bastion of differentiation. And if there is one thing that will keep the living room safe from the wrecker's ball, it is that this room has yet to be replaced as a prime coefficient in the old math—status arithmetic. Cavil and joke though we may about social accounting, it is an activity with respectable sociological credentials.

The Living-Room Status Test

In the late 1920s, sociologists woke up to what Henry James and socially sensitive homemakers had known intuitively, that the American living room could be used as a measure of "social status," a relatively new social index then. In earlier times, distinctions had been purely economic and limited to two poles: nobles and serfs, rich and poor, capitalists and workers. With the rise of the middle class in the nineteenth century and the ensuing multiplication and diversification of styles of life, sociologists were concerned with differentiating *economic* class (determined by income and property ownership) from *social* class or social status, which Max Weber defined as "social honor"—the amount of respect the community gave a family. But how could you measure social honor? F. Stuart Chapin, chairman of the University of Minnesota's sociology department, found a way.

"Almost everyone is jealous of his social status and will put up a struggle to maintain it," noted Chapin. He felt social status was a complicated equation of income, occupation, education, culture, standard of living, and position in the community. He believed that, with few exceptions, income level was related to occupation and education. And he believed that people treated others differently depending on the nebulous entity called social status.

Looking for a way to quantify social status, Chapin began in 1926 to assign points to middle-class families on four scales—income; material possessions (furnishings and household equipment); cultural possessions (books and musical instruments); and community involvement (clubs and committee memberships)—and to add them up. The bottom line of the four columns was unexpected. It showed you didn't need *four* scales. Material possessions was enough. It wasn't necessary to know how much money a family had or what country clubs and political committees family members belonged to. All you needed to know was whether certain objects were present in their living rooms.

THE LIVING-ROOM STATUS SCALE, 1933

Hardwood floors; +10; softwood: + 6
Large rug: +8
Windows with drapes: +2 per window
Fireplace with three or more untensils: +8
Artificial light: +8; kerosene lamp: −2
Piano bench: +4
Library table: +8

Armchairs: +8 each
Desk: +8
Bookcases with books: +8 each
Sewing machine: −2
Sofa pillows: +2 each
Alarm clock: −2
Radio +8

Three items could be in rooms other than the living room:

Filled bookcases: +8 each
Newspapers and magazines: +8 each subscription
Telephone: +8

Points were also gained or lost for
4 categories of taste and condition:

Items spotted or stained: −4
Dusty room: −2
Disorder: −2
Order: +2
Furniture repaired: −2

Furniture in good repair: +2
Bizarre clashing schemes: −4
Drab and monotonous rooms: −2
Harmony: +2

This was heady stuff. What accounted for "The Living-Room Scale" being so accurate? It must be because most people select their living-room furnishings to reflect well on the family and consequently "to determine its position in the community," said Chapin. The scale went through several modifications. There were 48 items on the 1931 scale. The test was so simple it could be administered in five minutes by a fieldworker just looking around the living room. Various points were assigned for tables, chair, desk, sofa, lamps, clocks, pottery, books, magazines, radio, telephone, as well as for taste, cleanliness, and good repair.

By 1933 Chapin had honed down the list to 17 items.

The possession and condition of these objects proved to accurately separate the destitute (0–24 points) from the blue collar (25–99), from the average middle class (100–124), from the upper middle class (125–149)—a hard pill to swallow, perhaps, for those who think that material possessions do not count. In 1933 they counted the most when they added up to an upper-middle-class 149 points.

The problem with the Living-Room Status Scale was that social scientists soon realized changing fashions could make it obsolete. To remain accurate it "would have had to be constantly revised," said sociologists Richard Coleman and Lee Rainwater recently. They are the authors of the impressive status study, *Social Standing in America,* published in 1978. Today most people have the same basic package of goods. Checking off the presence of certain items wouldn't be enough anymore. You'd need to measure the subtle semiotics, the messages each item gives off. Is the bookcase from the unpainted furniture store or fine cabinetry? Is the club chair covered in Naugahyde or genuine leather? Now that even budget sofas come with a bunch of back cushions, you'd have to give different scores for Dacron filling and pricey down. In fact, those who could accurately decipher the subtle differences would deserve status points themselves.

"It is well known that objects tell a great deal about the social status of the owner," if one can decipher the code, said French sociologist Jean Baudrillard. But rarely are rooms all of a piece. Some things denote "factual status," while others tell of "level of aspirations," or "fidelity to original class." People play with the code of meanings, he said, "break its rules . . . speak it in their class dialect," making it hard for anyone outside the same status group to interpret it.

Good Neighbors Make Good Status-ticians

For those reasons the next generation of status accountants developed a new technique for doing status arithmetic in homes that could be described as, "Don't send a fieldworker—just ask a neighbor." In the 1930s, social anthropologist W. Lloyd Warner was working on *Yankee City*, the seminal study of status in Newburyport, Massachusetts, which became the touchstone for all subsequent status research. Warner defined status groups as "networks of equal rank." It made sense to him, therefore, to use peer groups to do the social accounting. Better than outsiders, people in the community could evaluate those around them—their memberships, friends, homes, living rooms—and could convey those evaluations to researchers. Based on interviews within the community, Warner isolated six status levels in "Yankee City": upper-upper, lower-upper, upper-middle, lower-middle, and upper-lower, and lower-lower class. And in each group, the home had a different symbolic function.

For the two upper classes, said Warner, the house is "the very heart of the technical and symbolic apparatus necessary for maintenance of self-regard." Their symbols express "the significance of their way of life" to outsiders but also remind the dwellers "of the superiority of their world." Warner found that the upper-upper class (the old rich who could trace their ancestry back to the golden period around 1815) spent the smallest percentage of their income on home equipment, while the lower-upper class (the new rich) spent the largest percentage of their income. This supported his thesis that the lower-upper class went in for "conspicuous display" while the upper-upper class people were more "sober-minded." They could afford to be—their inherited furnishings and paintings and their low rate of house-moving helped keep down material expenditures.

Influenced by Chapin and Warner, Harvard's James Davis in the 1950s asked Cambridge housewives to arrange photos of living rooms according to social status, something he found they did quite accurately. Apparently you'd have to blindfold people to keep them from doing living-room status arithmetic. Why did Davis choose the living room? Because almost every family has a living room, he said, and since it is accessible to outsiders, "it is furnished from a social as well as an individual point of view." He concluded that making status judgments from living rooms was "an institutionalized phenomenon," that people had very clear perceptions of a status hierarchy, and that the judgments they made were about other individual's economic worth although their judgments became less accurate the more removed they were socially from those they were judging. Obviously, people couldn't be such accurate status-ticians if there weren't unwritten but agreed-upon standards of living-room equipage that are conformed to at each level.

In 1970 sociologists Edward Laumann and James House took living-room status testing a step further by correlating taste for specific styles of living-room decor with social milieu. After studying the backgrounds and attitudes of the upper class in the Detroit area, they found that those who chose traditional furniture and those who chose modern furniture were on different sides of the social divide. The "traditionals" tended to be established, white, Anglo-Saxon Protestants. They set the standards for the middle class who followed in the WASPs' traditional-style steps. The "moderns" were new rich, upwardly mobile non–Anglo-Saxons, often Catholic, who were "making it" for the first time and did not socialize with the traditionals. Since the social contacts of the new rich did not give them the prestige they craved, they turned to conspicuous consumption, with taste as well as money. "The nouveaux riches," said Laumann and House, "spurn the style of the traditional upper class in favor of newer fashions . . . to establish their tastefulness" while "showing their disdain of the 'snobby' traditionals."

This refuted something taken for granted since the turn of the century when Veblen in his send-up of leisure class "conspicuous consumption" asserted that the old elite set the standards while those beneath them emulate them. The old elite do set the standards for the middle class, said Laumann and House, but not for the very new, very rich. Style preferences may come and go, but what is constant is the challenging group's need to differentiate itself from the already ensconced group.

In the 1970s another team of researchers focused on life style as an indication of status. Housing is a major life-style expense that is closely indexed to income; economists have hammered home for years that up to 25 percent of income was the proper amount to spend on rent, and most people complied by buying the most housing they could afford. Furniture is also indexed to income, it has been found. "There is a strong acceleration of furniture spending as income increases," said one furniture industry analyst. Because of this, the house has come to be an index as well as a symbol of income level.

Once you have the yardstick, you can't help using it. People judge other people by their standard of living, stated Coleman and Rainwater. In search of a status picture of America, they asked Kansas Cityans and Bostonians in all walks of life to place themselves on the status ladder vis-à-vis their neighbors. The result was yet another status ladder, this one with seven ranks in three classes—*Upper Americans*: old rich, new rich, and moderately successful professionals and managers; *Middle Americans*: comfortable and just getting along; and *Lower Americans*: working poor and welfare poor. The task of pegging people was made easier, said the authors, because "Americans generally, regardless of class level, are almost continually judging each other as socially superior, inferior, or equal." Coleman and Rainwater found that income is the most important component of general social standing while education is the most important cause.

Since people are not privy to one another's bank statements, what basis do they use to make these judgments? A major test of income is a person's home. "It is questionable whether a family is regarded as a full participant in the good life, no matter what its income, if it does not own a suitable house," said Coleman and Rainwater. A suitable house, in this study, meant one with the proper number of rooms for each level of the social ladder. The respondents agreed, to be a comfortable Middle American you would have to own, not rent, "a single-family house with six regular rooms (living room, dining room, kitchen, and three bedrooms) plus one and a half baths." To lead a good upper-class life, a house with a living room, dining room, and a family room plus three bedrooms is needed; to lead a *very* good upper-class life, an eight-room house with a family recreation center is necessary; and to be at the top of the upper class, a "super-luxurious" home, plus a second home, is a must. Certainly, other things count in status assessment (cars, vacations, jobs, club memberships), but the more rooms one has, the more they count.

Nine Styles of Life and Styles of Living Room According to SRI

You might think it would be impossible to play the living-room status game today when we are so fragmented, demographically and decoratively. The growth of single-person households, the increased divorce rate which often divides a family's income in two, the decline in family size, the new culturally approved informality, added to the amazing plurality of decorating styles, all conspire to confuse living-room status mathematicians.

With art directors dropping out of high-salaried jobs to become struggling painters, scions of the Rockefeller family going back to nature, and a big-bucks movie star like Jane Fonda keeping a low profile, today's living room would seem to be the last place to find accurate clues to status. But the living-room status test lives—requiring ever more complex categories to pigeonhole people and a sharper eye for status inconsistencies.

Enter VALS, short for "Value and Lifestyle Program," a market research project of SRI, the sometimes controversial Northern California think tank formerly known as the Stanford Research Institute. SRI maintains itself with fees in excess of $150 million per year from government, commerce, and industry. A long list of Fortune 500 companies each pays SRI $27,000 per year to get VALS' help in targeting more accurately to consumers their beers, rental cars, magazines, whiskey, and grandfather clocks. No consumer topology seems more exhaustive. VALS has sorted the 226 million Americans into 3 divisions and 9 categories. The term social status rarely appears in the reams of printed matter SRI generates on VALS. Yet the VALS hierarchy appears to be a jazzed-up version of the all-American status ladder—with a heavy marketing orientation.

An eclectic mix of ideas from previous studies in psychology and sociology, VALS stresses that people of similar economic level can have very different values, and it is the values that influence the life style. As any sanguine social status-tician would expect, the living room is one of the major places where people show their VALS.

The VALS status ladder (3 divisions, 9 levels) has a distinctly Northern California silhouette. It is shaped like an artichoke, the regional vegetable. According to VALS' associate director, Gloria Esdale, people move up from one VALS stage to the next through a combination of psychological maturity and increased financial ability. And they regress because of insufficient funds to maintain a particular life style. SRI has prepared a number of reports projecting how people in different VALS levels can be expected to relate to certain categories of products and services. One of these studies is called "The Home." It confirms that the American living room hasn't lost its status symbolism yet.

THE VALS ARTICHOKE

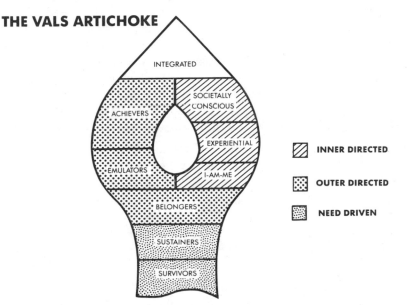

INTEGRATED

SOCIETALLY CONSCIOUS

ACHIEVERS

EXPERIENTIAL

EMULATORS

I-AM-ME

BELONGERS

SUSTAINERS

SURVIVORS

▨ **INNER DIRECTED**

▨ **OUTER DIRECTED**

▨ **NEED DRIVEN**

Here are some highlights of the VALS topology from the bottom up. All quotes are from "The Home." In the stem of the VALS artichoke is the Need Driven group which includes *Survivors* and *Sustainers*. Survivors account for about 6 million households—1 percent of the total home furnishings market. Among the *Survivors* are the people *Ms.* magazine recently called the "Nouveau Poor"—elderly widows and divorced women with many children. *Survivors* had incomes of under $4,200 in 1978, the year of VALS' statistical base; they spent their money on essentials and "bare-bones furnishings." *Sustainers*, 8 million households, younger and largely ethnic, accounted for 5 percent or $20 million worth of home-related expenditures. These people live with a lot of secondhand furniture—hand-me-downs. Sometimes they splurge on Princess phones.

There are two avenues of upward mobility in the SRI status artichoke, the Inner Directed and the Outer Directed (terms that SRI uses without apology to Harvard's David Reisman, who coined almost identical terms and used them differently). To the left is the

Outer Directed route, the traditional American way, which you climb from *Belongers* to *Emulators* to *Achievers*.

Belongers are conventional, traditional, formal, sentimental, old-fashioned, and family-oriented. Not particularly affluent, they are society's stabilizers, tending, like Archie Bunker, to prefer old values and traditional ways. The Belonger's home, like Archie's or the widower police sergeant's on "Gimme a Break," is a refuge and a haven, a symbol of belonging to the community and a particular way of life. Belongers "don't like big parties for casual acquaintances, partly because of a fear of not being acceptable." When Belongers do entertain it may be outdoors. The living room is "the most important room" in a Belonger's house, which is not likely to have a den or family room. The TV set is the focal point of the Belonger's living room, which is accessorized with family photos, trophies, mementoes, handicrafts, plate collections, and symbols of patriotism. Often unsure of their judgment, Belongers tend to buy brand names or matched sets of furniture. They are not interested in making a personal statement with their decorating, preferring comfortable, no-hassle furnishings.

Another 6 million American households are *Emulators*, including many blue-collar workers, blacks, and career women. They account for 11 percent of household furniture expenditures, nationally. "The Jeffersons" of TV fame, whose theme song is "Moving on up to the Big Time," would seem to be Emulators. "Emulators are conspicuous consumers, materialistic, status conscious, on the leading edge of voguish fashions, show-offs; they prefer overstatement and are very upwardly mobile," all in the quest to imitate and outdo the Achievers, the group above them in the VALS scale. Emulators favor expensive-looking housing with the trappings of wealth—pools, saunas, glamorous lobbies; in furniture they're "drawn to examples of ultra-modern" found in the magazines and images of Hollywood. "Not able to afford the original they cut corners . . . not really seeing the difference." Emulators begin decorating in the most public spaces. Thus the living room is the focus of their attention. They like to entertain and are good customers for souped-up video and stereo equipment. Style takes precedence over comfort or function. Clues to Emulators, at least in 1978, were shag rugs, fur throws, crushed velvet, mirrored walls, expensive sound systems in the living room.

Achievers (13 million households accounting for 36 percent of all furnishings purchases) are the high rollers: physicians, lawyers, stockbrokers, and corporate executives, some of them millionaires. Achievers are successful—and eager to give evidence of that success. They are also "individualistic, materialistic, pacesetting, competitive, interested in efficiency and comfort," and buy top-of-the-line luxury items. Their focus is on entertaining and self-exposure. Achievers supposedly live in fine old houses or architect-designed new ones; they can afford to indulge their preferences for exclusive neighborhoods, multiacreage, privacy, security, tennis courts, pools, and greenhouses. In their living rooms, Achievers are on a first-name basis with Oriental rugs, pure silk, wool carpeting, art objects, collectibles, rare books, and timepieces. They entertain frequently and can dedicate one living room to guests because they usually have a den, family room, or bed-sitting room where they watch TV. Having multiple living rooms seems to be one of the marks of an Achiever. Jacqueline Onassis's hideaway in Martha's Vineyard is said to have *three* living rooms— a living room and a family room in the main house, and another living room in the guest house.

But not everyone wants to move up the traditional way. The alternate upward mobility route is the route of the Inner Directed, "a leading-edge group." Its ladder is on the right side of the VALS artichoke and also has 3 levels: *I-Am-Me, Experiential,* and *Societally Conscious.* Often children of Achievers and Emulators, Inner-Directed people are the fastest-growing consumer category. Numbering 12 million highly educated households in 1978, VALS predicts they'll be a not-to-be-sneezed-at 22 million by 1988, and an important market for soaking tubs, hot tubs, whirlpools, and skylights.

The least affluent are the *I-Am-Me's,* mostly students. What they lack in income they make up for in style. They are young, zippy, exhibitionistic, narcissistic, dramatic, impulsive, and fiercely individualistic. I-Am-Me's are supposedly better customers for bedrolls than for standard bedding. However, when they settle down and go to work, they move up economically to *Experientials* (leaning toward parapsychology, yoga, and knock-down furniture) or the more affluent *Societally Conscious,* in the company of, I presume, such people as Jane Fonda, Gloria Steinem, Governor Jerry Brown, and Ralph Nader. Whichever rung they're on, Inner Directeds can be found leading lives of "voluntary simplicity" in the

country, self-expression near college campuses, or creative renovation in lofts in changing industrial neighborhoods, using "honest," durable materials.

The living rooms of both the Experientials and the Societally
Conscious are in strong contrast to those conspicuous consumption living rooms of Achievers. The Inner Directed's living room
may be an expanded kitchen with a solar greenhouse or other multipurpose room decorated with natural wood, exposed brick, floor
cushions, beanbags, hammocks, tree-trunk tables, hand-woven
fabrics, hanging plants, hand-thrown pottery, wood stoves, and
$2,000 stereo component systems assembled after "much com-
paring of brands and prices." The accompanying photographs in
VALS' "The Home" indicate a certain shagginess, from the fringe
on the hand-loomed shawls to the hanging ferns and macramé plant
holders.

The constrasting portraits drawn by VALS, on the one hand,
of the sleek, one-purpose Outer Directed living room, and, on the
other, the shaggy, multipurpose Inner Directed one, seem to be
caricatures. But surprisingly, the VALS depictions were confirmed
in a recent study of California homes by two anthropologists who
found that the absence or presence of a clearly defined living room
is the easiest way to separate a counterculture family from a conventional family. In a conventional home (what VALS would call
Outer Directed), the California study said, rooms have predictible
functions. A living room is a living room. In a counterculture living
room (what VALS would call Inner Directed), functions overlap.

Crowning SRI's artichoke are the *Integrateds*—2 percent of
the population. When someone who works at SRI wants to get on
your good side they tell you you seem to be an Integrated. Integrateds are a cross between the top-scoring Achievers and the
top-scoring Societally Conscious. Integrateds "have it all together," said SRI's Gloria Esdale. "They're psychologically mature
and comfortable with themselves—like Einstein and Arnold
Mitchell," the VALS director.

What happens when an Achiever is married to an Emulator? Good question. That's a "mixed household" in VALS lingo.
"Ideally, all household adults would belong to the same type and
therefore agree on most elements of the home environment." But
often that's not the case. When the husband is an Achiever and
wants to decorate for success and the wife is a Belonger who

wants to decorate like her mom—"homey, conservative, and family-oriented"—there can be trouble. The solution, according to VALS? The wife, to please her husband, "lets a decorator do the living room and dining room and does the other rooms in her [own] taste." There's the living room emphasis again!

What happens when the household moves up from Belonger to Emulator, or from Emulator to Achiever, or moves sideways from Achiever to Societally Conscious? Do they bring along the furnishings that express the previous values and life style? VALS has the answers to this one, too. The new home will contain a "mix of products," or else there will be "sufficient desire" to alter the home "to reflect the change of attitude."

Yes, Virginia, they will redecorate. It's not only that "rank must be marked." It is also that new values must be made visible. And pent-up needs and desires that could not be afforded before will be satisfied. In order to belong to a group, you need the trappings of the group, the right stuff. To count, those things have to be visible.

For most people, the living room is the handiest shorthand symbol of their status. But identity is made up of more than social status and is expressed in more areas of the home than in the living room. If you are asking yourself, Who am I?, you have to consider your sex role, your stage in the life cycle, and your personality as well.

5

Sex Role and Decorating Role

T

HE DOORBELL WAS ringing. It was kaffeeklatsch time in a modest Long Island suburb, the hour when once upon a time the proverbial little woman was at home, making beds and softening fabric. But times have changed. On the morning in question, Jerome Tognoli, a psychology professor at C. W. Post College, was waiting for the oil burner repair people. His wife, an instructor at another college, had left earlier to teach a class. Tognoli and his wife had bought the house the previous year with the understanding that he would do the major share of maintenance and supervise the renovations until she finished her doctoral dissertation. And he really didn't mind. Until moments like this.

As he went to answer the door, Tognoli recalled, he could hear one of the repairmen saying, "Here she comes now." "They just assumed it would be a woman at home. I was in my running clothes, and, I must admit, I felt self-conscious, as if I were answering the door in my bathrobe. We had just vacuumed, so I asked the men to go around to the back door, but I felt fussy doing it. Then, while they were working I started washing the breakfast dishes and I wondered, 'What must they be thinking of me?'"

Tognoli is no stranger to sex role issues. He teaches a course called Images of Home in Psychology and Literature. "In my course," he said, "we talk about attitudes. One student told me that her father refused to go marketing because 'that's for fags.'" The problem men have doing things around the house, he explained, "is fear of being judged feminine—which is intermingled with fear of being homosexual."

"The home is the core aspect of human experience, yet men seem to feel uncomfortable when relating to it," he noted in a study of men's attitudes toward their homes. Men have traditionally gone outside the house for their social activities. "Men typically do not invite men friends into the home to socialize unless done in the safety of women's supervision," and when they do invite men, "it is under a highly formalized context," a gin game or a TV tribal ritual: watching the Superbowl, the Kentucky Derby, the World Series, the Academy Awards, or the Election Night returns.

Little wonder that the last thing many young bachelors are concerned about when they furnish is how many people they can seat at the dining table. "I'm never going to entertain," a typical, twenty-eight-year-old bachelor assured his decorator. A stool in the kitchen for breakfast was his idea of dining-room furniture. Not until he became engaged and his fiancée insisted, did he relent and order a table and chairs. In Barry Goldwater's Washington, D.C., condominium (in which the doorbell chimes the Air Force song), the dining room is devoted to a ham radio station, and the pantry is a gun-making shop. His wife resides full-time in Arizona and Goldwater commutes between the two residences.

For evidence that men living alone have different socializing patterns than women do, consider the gender segregation experiment conducted by John Ofrias and Tognoli. Two families that were good friends (whom I'll call the Allens and the Butlers) split up temporarily and recomposed themselves according to gender. The women in one house. The men in another. For seven weeks, Mrs. Allen, thirty, Mrs. Butler, thirty-two, and her fourteen-year-old daughter, lived together in the Allens' suburban house, while the males, Mr. Allen, thirty, Mr. Butler, thirty-five, and his ten-year-old son, all lived in the Butlers' house. Copious notes were taken, charts filled in, diaries kept, and friends and relatives interviewed.

During the experiment, the two women had visitors on many occasions. However, Mr. Allen and Mr. Butler didn't have a single male guest—not that they didn't invite any. But men who had been good friends refused to visit, and even seemed to avoid them. Why? The cause was made clear in questionnaires filled out by some forty friends, relatives, and neighbors as part of the study. One of the Allens' neighbors, a man who had previously spent a lot of time with Mr. Allen and Mr. Butler but wanted nothing to do with them during the course of the study, wrote sarcastically: "Is it an experiment to find out their compatibility toward each other?"

"The home is perceived as female and as the seat of intimacy," said Ofrias and Tognoli, "and for other men to socialize in it might suggest too close an association with femininity and intimacy—qualities the male sex role dictates should be avoided at all costs." In fact, what worried Mrs. Butler's mother most about the experiment was that it might lead to homosexuality.

Home: Whose Place Is It?

Obviously, there are very real differences in attitude about home between men and women, but when it comes to gender and decorating, this is the Age of Denial. Even usually observant people take the Fifth if asked whether they notice any differences in the homes of men and women living alone.

If men and women are created equal in decorating skills, how come no one cried foul at *Starting Over?* There was certainly a ring of truth to that scenario when Jill Clayburgh moved into Burt Reynolds's gloomy place with her quilts and her plants and her *tchotchkes.* Do we really need to take a household inventory of 3,000 single persons' living quarters to recognize the fact that men have been flexing a different set of muscles in the homemaking department? Even when men receive assistance from professionals in getting their places together, they seem to have different priorities from women. James Bond, with his souped-up electronics, is a more important decorating role model for males than James Beard, with his state-of-the-art kitchen, even though Beard is gaining. Just because Paul Newman is marketing his own salad dressing doesn't mean that men's lives and role definitions have changed nearly as radically as women's have in the last decade.

Men can't be blamed for their nesting disabilities. Years of playing with dollhouses, toy kitchens, helping mother, taking "home ec," and pursuing needlecraft hobbies have given women an edge. The only thing men are expected to know about the house, judging from ads run by bookstores before Father's Day, is the inside of a home repair manual. Men are expected to be fluent in "handyman" from Adhesives to Z-bars. They have to know that studs are 16 inches on center. The message that is still reinforced repeatedly in our culture is that a woman's place is—you know where—cooking, cleaning, caring for the sick, marketing, selecting the curtain fabric. As President Reagan said in a TV interview with Dan Rather, "Nancy tells me what color the drapes should be and I tell her what we're doing about foreign policy."

In the world according to TV, a prime medium for teaching children the real facts of life, women get out of the house much less frequently than men do. In a recent study researchers analyzed the thirteen TV shows most popular with children, aged two to eleven, including "Mork and Mindy," "Laverne and Shirley," "Loveboat," "Bugs Bunny," "Chips," "Eight Is Enough," "Sesame Street," and "Charlie's Angels," to see whether men or women were shown most often *"outside, inside, or inside, at home."* And sure enough, the person-in-setting count showed that girls and women were constantly depicted in interior settings, while boys and men were more often shown in exterior settings, with certain exceptions. When men showed up inside more than usual, as occurred on "Laverne and Shirley," they were being served dinner by women. And on "Mork and Mindy," Mork had an excuse for spending so much time in the house—he came from another planet. Even Charlie's audacious angels could not get out of the living room. On that show, the three female detectives got their orders from a disembodied Charlie who was heard but never seen. The males on the show were shown outside more than inside, while the three angels were seen *inside* almost twice as often as outside. If that doesn't convince you, the office from which the women worked was a living room, which contained a single desk. Bosley, Charlie's male assistant, was the only one who ever used the desk.

This study confirms what many feminists suspect, that ideas about what spaces are male and what spaces are female are passed down through custom, a system of control that has a much higher pass-along rate than genetics, which is subject to the laws of mutation.

Women Inside, Men Outside

The woman inside and the man outside are common roles in many traditional cultures where sex roles are strictly defined. The Berbers, who are Moslems, have a series of maxims on the place of men and women that would probably inspire Phyllis Schlafly to praise Allah. The Berbers believe "Man is the lamp of the outside and woman the lamp of the inside." For a Berber man, "the house is less of a place one goes into than a place one goes out of." Eating, sleeping, and procreating take place in the intimacy of the house, a woman's domain, as opposed to the man's activities, which go on outside. A Berber man who has respect for himself is supposed to leave his house at daybreak. "The man who stays too long in the house during the day is either suspect or ridiculous."

"'Woman's place is in the home' is a relatively new prescription," insisted Nona Glazer-Malbin in her classic feminist essay "Housework." Knocking the myth of "inevitable domesticity," she explained that women started becoming housebound with the rise of agriculture in the Middle Ages. Although many women worked alongside their husbands in the fields, and a few, like Joan of Arc, even went to war, women generally stayed inside, while men went outside.

A man without a woman to take care of his house lived like a beast, said one fifteenth-century preacher. He compared the bachelor's bed to a ditch: It "was never shaken up and smoothed . . . the sheet was never changed until it fell apart from age . . . on the floor lie the rinds of melons . . . the platters he washes as little as he can." Far be it from the medieval man to take these duties upon himself. Masculine and feminine roles were prescribed. "Details of housekeeping he should commit entirely into her hands," advised one manual of the period. With the exception of wealthy widows who had special status, women were not yet the consumers. It was the wife's job to keep track of what was needed in the household, but it was up to the husband to do the purchasing. He was also the one who commissioned a house from an architect, and he was undoubtedly in charge of furnishing it.

Men were still doing the purchasing in the eighteenth century—a period when English and American gentlemen were vitally interested in the decoration of their houses, and in competition with one another to be the first to have the latest styles. Like his contemporaries, George Washington had a passion for china and even occupied himself with selecting ornaments for his table settings when he was president. In 1758 he wrote his china purchasing agent, saying, "Pray let it be neat and fashionable or send none." That same year when it was the style for curtains and upholstery *to match,* Ben Franklin sent his wife fifty-six yards of printed cotton in one color for curtains and in another color for "chair bottoms," because, he wrote her, "these were my fancy." Men in those days were the tastemakers, and historians say they have no real evidence that upper-class eighteenth-century American women had much say in the decoration of their houses.

It was not until the early nineteenth century that women became chained to the house. At this time, home and workplace, which had been synonymous, became separated as industrialization began to change the structure of society. Men went to work outside of the home, and women were left to care for the family and the house. In 1845, when historic records show that a Vermont couple went to New York together to buy furniture—considered an important clue—the role realignment became evident. To women's domestic duties had been added the responsibility for home furnishing. The house was now seen as a symbol of "the man who earned it," while the interior of the house—the mood, the taste, the activities that took place there—stood for the woman who ran the house. Man's house, woman's home. In 1869, a physician wrote that it was "man's business to earn money and [woman's] to spend it."

But running the house and spending money did not come naturally. The multitude of advice books churned out to teach women of the emerging middle class the ins and outs of homemaking and decorum, including not picking teeth at the table, as well as the duties of wifehood, show us that there was nothing innate about woman's role. She was treated as if she were ignorant and incompetent. With the rise of eclecticism, there was much for women to learn and the educators treated them as if they were all inept. On top of that, there was a new stereotype which first appeared in the 1840s—the frivolous woman who wanted to impress with her house. From then on, the housewife was continually accused of being extravagant and demanding, and putting on airs.

Such accusations got passed along from book to book like a

torch in an unending relay race while a whole generation of women whose grandmothers had been self-sufficient—spinning, weaving, making soap and quilts—now had to be reeducated into the task of being good consumers. As household technology gradually liberated women from their overwhelming housekeeping and maintenance responsibilities, they were left with few outlets for their energies, and authority figures were looking for tasks to tie women down. "Our whole social fabric would be better for it. Too many women are dangerously idle," said the *Ladies' Home Journal* in 1911. One task that could keep them busy besides motherhood and germ warfare, was homemaking-as-art-form. The recipes and the patterns for a cozier home marched forth, month after month, and still do. Women's magazines taught kitchen organization, the so-called psychology of color, découpage, china painting, needlework, do-it-yourself, and space planning.

How Girls and Boys Learn the Facts of Life

If there was any doubt about the fitness of women for the interior realm, psychiatrists came up with the proof that it was their natural habitat. Based on results of free-play experiments with children, Erik Erikson, the noted psychiatrist, said in 1963 that women were innately inner-oriented and men innately outer-oriented. Girls, he observed, routinely built interior scenes filled with people and animals and furniture, while boys put their people and animals outside and built elaborate structures with cannons and turrets.

As it is with concepts that fit a society's prejudices, Erikson's theory took on a life of its own. He wasn't credited when the idea surfaced, as if written in stone, in the *Washington Star* in 1979. "Spatial relationships are anathema to most women," wrote architect John R. Miller. "The fields of architecture and engineering are open to women, but these areas are dominated by men." No mention of the fact that some of the major architecture schools, founded in the last quarter of the nineteenth century, would not even admit women until around 1910. Miller was puzzled "at the success with form that some marvelous women interior designers have."

"Has the female a characteristic way of structuring the world that is different from the male?" asked Yi-Fu Tuan. He wasn't the only one who wanted an answer. It was a question vital to the women's movement. Is woman's place *inside* and man's *outside* engraved in their respective DNA, or are these leanings culturally induced? That is the question.

Woman's attachment to the home and man's separateness from it are bred into us, said Harvard's Carol Gilligan in her book on women's development. Girls are taught to be girls, and boys are taught to be boys from the day of birth, and by age three, gender identity is firmly in place. Girls see themselves as like their mothers who are usually the nurturers, and their identity comes from attachment, while boys see themselves as different from their mothers, and in order to develop an identity they must separate from their mothers. These identity routes become ways of relating to the world. Thus a woman's identity is built on attachment, sensitivity, relationships, nurturing, and caring, and a man's identity is founded on separateness from others, which allows him to compete for personal success.

A recent study of children and their experience of place by environmental psychologist Roger Hart seemed to support Gilligan's theory that the sexual division of space is culturally ingrained. By tagging along with kids to their favorite stomping grounds, hideouts, and watering holes, and from interviews, diaries, and maps made by children, Hart pieced together how children learn to relate to the physical environment. He found, as Erikson did, that when girls built houses they concentrated on the interiors, and when boys built houses they were primarily interested in the shell of the structure and not the interior—furnishing it with only a bed, a chair, and shelves for comic books. But there were reasons for this. Stereotyped activities were bred into the children from the earliest age with rules about how far they could roam. In fact, boys were allowed to roam nearly twice as far from home as girls; boys went on errands, mowed lawns, and delivered papers—activities that gave them a head start in spatial ability. Parents set the limits of where and how far a child could go to play, and boys were allowed to break the rules more than the girls.

Girls are given a double handicap, said Hart. Not only are adventure and exploration restricted, but girls are also anchored inside by custom. They are encouraged to be homebodies, expected to do more chores around the house, and to babysit. The resulting lack of outside experience diminishes their skill in spatial abilities. Inside the house, boys and girls are treated stereotypically, too, according to other studies. Parents decorate children's rooms differently and give them different toys, depending on their sex. A content analysis of the rooms of children under six years old showed that parents gave daughters more dolls, doll houses, and furnishings with lace, fringe, ruffles, and floral motifs; they gave boys more vehicles, machines, military toys, sports equipment, and furnishings with animal motifs.

By the time children go to college, there is a decorating and attitudinal chasm between the sexes. In a study of dorm decor it was found that women spent more time in their rooms than men and were more concerned than men about personalizing their rooms and making "a homelike environment," which may explain the "orgy of Dior Rose sheets and pillow shams and dust ruffles," recalled by one Wellesley graduate. These attitudes carry over into marriage, with women spending more time in the home and more time on home maintenance, and being more likely to think of the home as part of their identity, even when they have jobs and outside interests. But while women consider the home their burden, they also get more satisfaction from it than men do.

Men, for the most part, aren't nearly as wrapped up in the interior of the home as women are, nor do they spend as much time at home as women do. They don't depend on the harmony of the living room for their identity. They get their identity from the neighborhood they live in, the value of the house itself, and, of course, from their work.

In a study of a suburban community, Princeton's Suzanne Keller found that 39 percent of the women, but only 13 percent of the men, spent sixteen or more hours a day in the home. Other studies of suburban life showed that men were consistently less emotionally involved in their homes than women, even though they were more satisfied with the move to the suburbs than their wives were. Apparently, men prefer living in the suburbs because it guarantees the status quo of traditional sex roles. It may be an "unconscious desire . . . to assure that their home will be taken care of by a woman with few other options."

In Sweden and Britain there have been similar findings. British husbands, it's been shown, take pride in their neighborhood, the view, recreational facilities, schools—and their heating systems. For the wives, satisfaction with the home comes from having enough space for the children's activities, a roomy kitchen, attractive furnishings, and friendly neighbors. Husbands and wives were responding not biologically, said David Canter, a leading British environmental psychologist, but from their "role perspectives."

But that's all changing, you might argue. Today men are being given permission to be caring, sharing, domestic, and paternal. In a recent commercial for canned soup, we saw a husband at the stove fixing the chowder as the wife arrived home from the office; in an *Esquire* fashion spread we saw a liberated daddy holding his baby during a poker game with his cigar-chomping pals, and in another photo, a young man mastering the art of French cooking.

Meanwhile, the women's magazines have fashioned a new male role model—the househusband. He stays home with the children, takes charge of the house, and keeps a diary of the experience for a woman's magazine while his wife, in scenario number one, is the family's major breadwinner and gives her all to her job, or, in scenario number two, goes back to school. TV's Ted Koppel is probably America's most famous househusband. He stayed home for nine months once while his wife went to law school. The househusband makes good copy, but it's not likely that the Marlboro man will be seen wearing an apron in the near future. A word-processing repairman who got no publicity for staying home for a year to care for his nephew while his wife finished her course in electronic maintenance, said he could have kept at it for two years at the most. "Then, I'd have to get out of the house."

Not that men aren't doing some household chores. They are helping out more with the children. And they are cooking more. One man in three cooks one meal a week; 13 percent cook three or four times a week, says *Bride's* magazine. But study after study shows that men are masters at avoiding housework. In two-paycheck families, men are *not* sharing the housework. Nor is the next generation overly enthusiastic about revising the balance of power at home. In a Harris study of the American family, a majority of teenagers with both parents working believed "that one parent should stay home with preschool children. . . . There is some feeling that it doesn't matter which parent stays home, but virtually no one says it should be the father." As Berkeley geographer Bonnie Loyd said, the sexual division of space "is one of those cultural definitions enshrined in myth, taught to children, repeated by friends, and confirmed by experience."

Marrying the House

When Elizabeth Taylor was young, she wanted to "grow up and get married and have a house with a white picket fence and six children and one maid and lots of dogs, cats, horses, and cows." Marilyn Monroe, at the height of her celebrity, enjoyed thinking about giving dinner parties; she wanted a comfortable chair built for a man and a chandelier with real candles. No matter where she's headed or where she's coming from, almost every woman feels the magnetic pull of being mistress of a house—a house where she can bring people together around a table, nurture relationships, express herself. Now, in a commercial, Revlon's Charlie agrees it is time to settle down; in an ad for her favorite magazine, the Cosmo girl dropped the bombshell that she was buying a house; and in a *Rolling Stone* interview Bette Midler mused about what a terrific wife she would be. She knows what the job entails. "It means being an artist on your own planet. You get to have your own home, your own stage where you get to use your visual and color senses."

Women may be working, making their own money, marrying later, and divorcing more, but they are still interested in marrying the house. Why should this surprise us? Like swimming against the tide, it takes a massive effort to resist the pull of sex roles that were internalized in childhood. Culture accomplishes in humans what nature facilitates in animals.

In lovebirds, for example, hormones trigger nest-building. After mating, the female lovebird begins building her nest with grass. As egg-laying time nears, she starts losing feathers from the underside of her breast, exposing a bare piece of skin. This brood patch, as it is called, gets an increased blood supply which the bird will need to warm her eggs. As the patch becomes more sensitive to grass, the bird feels impelled to collect *feathers* to line and soften the nest.

Hormonal action may prepare a young woman for marriage, but decades of custom and dozens of wedding gifts help her feather her nest. Until recently brides were marched through the prenuptial preparations in a behavioral lockstep passed along from one generation to the next. The details of the rituals surrounding the knot-tying may have varied over the years and from group to group, but the intent was the same. To get the daughters firmly ensconced in their own homes. The bond between a young woman and her household possessions forged over months of shopping and selection, discussion—and perhaps dissension—and, finally, compromise with her fiancé, served the perpetuation of the species. A woman's involvement with her housewares was an umbilical cord to her home.

The young woman who had shopped for her silver pattern with the diligence of an airline purchasing agent deciding between a DC-10 and an L-1011, choosing from among hundreds of patterns before settling on *hers,* made her selection public in some store's bridal registry, unwrapped the place settings as they arrived one by one, taking the flawless pieces from their soft Pacific cloth bunting, was not merely furnishing a house. She was working her way through the most important status passage of her life. She was marrying her house. The gifts were the estrogens of the home-making experience, stimulating the idea that my place, my things, my home, and I are one.

While the furnishings were a couple's joint possessions, it was *her* initials that went on the silver and linens. In the bridal registry the selections were filed under the bride's maiden name—Jane Smith—and after the wedding, under *Jane* Jones, not Mrs. John Jones. And she was the one who got that exquisite feeling of pride when she set her table. If she became an important enough hostess, it was she who would be asked by a magazine to pose beside her exquisite table setting. Men were invariably posed beside their cars. It was just as important to nurture these home feelings in a woman as it was to encourage maternal feelings. She would think twice when she had a disagreement with her new husband before chucking it all. Celebrations of marriage with the accompanying gift-giving demonstrated the culture's approval of the idea of family, and reinforced sex role stereotypes.

In the late 1960s and 1970s it all seemed to change. If young people were marrying, they were doing it untraditionally. Down with white satin bridal pumps—barefoot in the park was the wedding style. Down with possessions, down with registering. Who needed porcelain dinner plates in the Peace Corps or the commune? Marriage rates declined. Birth rates declined. So many people were living together the Census Bureau had to find a new designation for people of the opposite sex sharing living quarters. For the parents of these unwed couples, the big topic of conversation was "Should we or shouldn't we dignify the relationship by allowing them to share a bedroom when they come home for a visit?" You can be sure that the older generation wasn't about to reward out-of-wedlock lovemaking and homemaking with the material prizes that were supposed to accompany matrimony. When a young woman moved out of her parents' house to set up housekeeping with a man, or on her own, Mom and Dad might have sent over a set of pots and pans, but capital-G gifts were not forthcoming. China patterns were not selected and registered for. The young woman needed plates to eat on, but there was no sense that the choice of those plates was meaningful. They were just plates. Not the sacred implements of matrimony, the tools of the new trade.

But now, there is a new dimension to the tabletop market. Store officials and manufacturers are smiling from ear to ear. Brides are registering again. "Even brides who live in communes are registering," said one wedding consultant. But that's not all. A trend has been spotted by a tabletop consultant for the Lenox China company. Singles who have no intention of marrying in the foreseeable future are registering. The only explanation is, they want it all. First they wanted *sex* out of wedlock. Then they wanted *children* out of wedlock. And now, they want *gifts* out of wedlock. China, flatware, crystal, placemats, candlesticks. "It's the beautiful accessories on your table that create the subtle variations, the lasting impressions that your guests will long remember," advised the April/May 1983 *Bride's* magazine. Just because they're not marrying doesn't mean they don't want to express themselves with their table settings. They still want to marry the house.

Her Place: Investing in Togetherness

Single women are becoming just as home-oriented as the married ones or the formerly married ones. Being single is a more varied experience than the demographic designation implies. A woman can be suddenly single, stubbornly single, temporarily single, or single-and-settled. A person's state of mind affects her state of union with her home. "When you're twenty, you wait for the phone to ring to have a social life," said a twenty-eight-year-old TV producer. "You think, the way I live doesn't matter—any minute now I'll get married and build my dreamhouse. By the time you're twenty-four, you realize that if you want to control whom you see, you need to be able to entertain. To entertain you need a cute place. Between twenty-five and thirty-five if you're still single, this way of life suddenly seems more permanent—you begin to earn more money, maybe you sign a five-year lease or buy a condo and say to yourself, 'I'm not waiting for some guy to give me a nice place—I'll give it to myself.'" At this point the single woman becomes more like the formerly married woman who has been conditioned to have an expressive home.

Pam, thirty-six, has been living alone for eleven years since her divorce. After college, the Peace Movement, three years of marriage, six years of social work, a series of jobs in the cosmetics industry, she considers herself lucky to afford a one-bedroom apartment in Manhattan. Many of her single friends are still folding the bed back into the sofa every morning in studio apartments.

Ever since she moved out of her marriage and moved in alone, she has made an effort to create an attractive home, however minimal, using hand-me-downs such as a nice antique chest from her mother, a comfortable chair, a rug, pictures, books, mementoes. Pam still has the modular bedroom set she had as a teenager: sectional white cabinets topped with bookcases, and the cattycorner desk that works perfectly as a dressing table. To these bedroom furnishings she added an old table, skirted with a sheet, and her prized extravagance—a blanket cover and pillow shams from Pratesi. When Pam saw the movie *Rollover,* she was so busy adding up the value of the bedding—"$4,000 worth of Pratesi"— she missed the notorious love scene. Her admitted goal of having a bed swathed in, and a linen closet filled with, Pratesi is really a desire to be able to afford quality at this stage of her life. "It's so hard for women to earn a living that they can't afford the values they've been brought up with," she complained.

Sometimes it's easier to say you are immobilized because of money than to admit you are waiting for a change of life. Finally Pam faced up to it. She would give herself a nice home. She wanted a living room that looked—she can't put it into words—

"done; of a piece. I wanted an environment where I could feel proud and comfortable and elegant and stylish."

And so she committed all of her savings, several thousand dollars, and hired a young designer. "A single man would have invested in an oil well, but I put the money into having my floors scraped and my walls lacquered," she said quite seriously. Her storage wall—built by a cabinetmaker, not a carpenter—is a BMW in a world of Chevettes. Her custom-built, 100 percent down sofa—L-shaped and covered in the palest blue cotton despite her mother's warning that it would be hard to keep clean—is capital-Q quality. It pleased Pam that nowhere in her twelve-by-sixteen-foot living room was there any Workbench, Pottery Barn, Crate and Barrel, Pier One, or Azuma knock-down tables, no chairs stuffed with beans or rattan picture frames or plastic umbrella stands that she sees in every divorced man's apartment. Her only snipped corner was the stereo. Pam's brother helped her select the components. It killed her to pay $650, although she realized that most fifteen-year-old boys paid more for a stereo than she did.

By the time she finishes, Pam will have spent three times more than she originally budgeted. But she doesn't regret it. The apartment has the "togetherness" that she values. Not that Pam has given up on the other kind of togetherness. "I want a husband and a family and a nice worn rug to go under my coffee table."

Wife-Decorator

Once a woman marries, the decorating wish list lengthens. The more income a family has, the more attention is paid to the appearance of the house. "Caring for the house-as-status-symbol" takes time. Not only is there cleaning and maintenance to be done, rearranging and provisioning, but also *decorating*. According to Bonnie Loyd, one of the few people writing on women's issues who acknowledges that decorating is different from housework, "Decorating . . . is a major task for American homemakers, whether they decorate consciously with the help of a professional designer or casually by simply ensuring that the family has adequate furniture." As housework becomes more automated, the decorating escalates. "A 'nice' home reflects a good homemaker, a good wife, a good mother, and so a good woman."

Even if a woman is not a traditional homemaker, and, like 50 percent of American women, has a job or a career, she is still interested in her home. The second paycheck is vital to the middle-class family. One category of things it buys is home improvements. Better living. While men are getting more involved in the buying decisions, testing the chairs, okaying the colors, the wife is still the purchase instigator on living-room and bedroom furniture, major appliances, small appliances, carpet, mattresses, and vinyl tile.

Take Chris Evert Lloyd. She "picked out the colors, drapes, carpeting, and wallpaper" for her and husband John Lloyd's villa on the Amelia Island Plantation. Did John have any decorating input? No, said John. "I leave it to my little lady to choose, and she does very well." Husbands are more often purchase approvers or purchase vetoers. To make all these furnishing decisions a woman has to educate herself in consumption, style, and taste. It takes as much skill to select and harmonize the contents of a home as it does to buy a million widgets for a gasket factory.

At a certain income level, a family needs a wife-decorator. Actually, even though she may be working, she is trying to live up to the lofty standards set by the lady of leisure, one of the heroines of Western history. Her job description was spelled out by Cornelius Vanderbilt Whitney in his 1979 diary, *Live a Year with a Millionaire*, which he published for his friends. Outlining his wife Mary's role in their marriage, he said: "First . . . she always dresses beautifully for whatever scenario we are in. . . . Second, she decorates and furnishes all of our homes in ways that please me and her. . . . Third, she invites the guests, seats the tables. . . . Fourth, she is a truly great cook," and keeps her husband in good physical and mental health. His own role, said Mr. Whitney, was to keep working, enjoy his life, and encourage his wife in her projects.

The wife-decorator usually has her husband's support. He needs the proper setting as much as she does. Sometimes, however, the wife takes the decorating so seriously it becomes a full-time preoccupation. On any weekday you can see the wife-decorators with their shopping bags full of fabric samples cruising the design centers in major American cities. Karla, a thirty-eight-year-old wife and mother, works part-time for a number of arts institutions in Chicago, serves on charitable boards, and takes postgraduate courses in business. Yet, reviewing her life, she realized she had invested a major share of her productive capacity fixing up a continuous succession of homes for her family—two girls, one boy, and husband Michael, an electrical parts manufacturer.

Her most recent design problem was the indoor pool. What started as a simple exercise pool had become a major project. It was dug once. Then Karla decided it was in the wrong place. The hole was filled in and redug again a few feet farther west. For what it cost in the end, she complained, "We could have had the finest architect in America do it." But since it was just for Michael, not for show, she had designed it herself.

This is the fourth house she has renovated since she and Michael were married. The first was a little rented house in the De Paul area where she did "a big number. . . . We used to pick up furniture on Wells Street," she said, "go to auctions. Little by little we furnished the house and it was fabulous. I thought it was the best of all my friends' houses." Next came a small house in Old Town, which they proceeded to change from the ground up. Their moves could be considered budding acts of art patronage because, for structural changes, Karla and Michael always hired promising young architects. Michael loved working with them. The decor was Karla's job. "I thought I was equipped to handle anything." Michael, who loved to wheel and deal in real estate, came home one day with yet a larger townhouse in Lincoln Park. And the process started all over again. And now the house in Highland Park, which almost caused a divorce. "It was a horrible house," said Karla. "When I saw it I was in deep depression. Faced with the mess of reconstruction, inadequate help, and the demands of children, I felt hysterical. All this responsibility. I never could share it with anyone. Michael just disappears after he's made the purchase. I looked at this one as a chore." But still she accepts the job. It is part of her role in her social class to be a woman of style. And necessary to her self-esteem.

While she complains that her "entire life is maintenance of possessions," her home study course in the good life has taught her there is more to aspire to. She would especially like a new house to tackle. Something in "the big league." Meanwhile, there is a long list of future decorating projects in her present house. "It sounds like I need a full-time staff person for all this maintenance. But I'm the staff. I guess anyone could do it, but I like to think I can do it better than anyone else—and anyway, everyone likes to be needed."

When He Decides

Despite the woman's clear franchise to be chairperson and chief executive officer of the home decorating projects, there are some men living with women who take total charge of the furniture buying and make the taste decisions—and the woman is lucky to get veto power. What causes a man to go against the old role model of deferring to her, or the new ideal of joint decision making? When a man takes over the decorating, unless he's an Arab sheik or a South American tycoon who both operate by medieval standards in these matters, there is usually a good reason.

I'll leave the men who are competing with Mom for Dad's attention to their psychiatrists. But there are men who take charge of the furnishing because they were severely deprived as children. Perhaps they had to share a bed with their brother, and work from the time they were eight. They trust no one else to fulfill their needs. "All my life I wanted a pool table," said one New York man who took over the decorating decisions. "All my life I wanted a canopy bed," said the well-known Mr. T., who gave himself one recently when he decorated his Los Angeles apartment. Yet another type of man needs total control, for any number of reasons. Decorators describe him as the one married male client in twenty who won't defer to his wife. He gets involved, takes full charge, deals with the decorator on a day-to-day basis, attends all the meetings, and approves every fabric swatch and color chip.

There is also the man who doesn't trust his wife to manipulate the iconography of the home, especially if he has married beneath himself, socially. When Reginald Vanderbilt married Gloria Morgan in the 1920s, she "discovered she had moved into a way of life that had existed for a quarter of a century." She was informed by her husband that the butler would run the household because "he understands me," and "I would like conditions to remain unchanged."

Probably no married man is more interested in his home than the design professional. Among male designers and their spouses, the issue of who is in charge of furnishing the home is the high casualty crossroads of sex role and work role. Male architects married to nonarchitect spouses call the decoration of the home "the combat zone." The architect's wife would be happy to have her husband build a house. But young architects are rarely in a position financially to build a dreamhouse. So they'll settle for doing the living room. "You're just learning to be an architect," said one forty-year-old architect who has done battle in this field and survived to talk about it. "You have all this education. You need to manipulate and control. Having a place of your own to try your wings is a godsend." But the wife isn't always thrilled to give up her prerogative. "If he's honest," he said, "there isn't a male architect alive who won't admit to having problems in his marriage over this."

Probably the most celebrated architect who decorated as he pleased without consulting his spouse was British architect Edwin Lutyens, who designed many great English country houses at the turn of the century. A recent memoir by his daughter reveals that although Lutyens "made a show" of checking with his wife, "he had very strong views and tastes" on decorating. Before their marriage he promised her a cheerful house with white walls and sofas covered in "jolly" fabrics. Instead, he gave her what he pleased— glossy black walls in the parlor—just as he once gave a client who asked for an oak staircase a black marble one. To his wife's dismay, Lutyens valued space over comfort, and bought houses he could not afford to heat so he could have large rooms.

Occasionally an architect's wife will be delighted to be relieved of the decorating responsibility. In years past, she would have had to do the job she found odious, and her husband would have had to hold back. But today each does what she or he prefers. David, an architect, and Tina, a law student, fit into this category. Tina claims she has no interest in the decoration of her home, and that most of her classmates aren't involved in their houses, either. "I can't imagine anyone who has a demanding job getting involved with the house," said Tina. In fact, if a friend were going to marry an architect, Tina would advise her: "Let him do everything to the house he wants to."

David has just finished renovating their house and most of the furnishings are built in. Very little furniture had to be bought. Only dining chairs. "David picked them out. I said, 'Sure.' It's an identity symbol for David, not for me," Tina insisted. She admitted, however, taking hundreds and hundreds of pictures during the renovation. More than necessary or normal. "I think I was trying to say it was my project, too. It was an attempt to relate to it in some way." One way Tina would have liked to relate to the house was to hang one of her family's quilts over the bed. But David used one of *his* family's quilts because of the colors. "But my quilts are better quality. It really pisses me off," said Tina.

Of all the reasons for men being involved with the decoration of the home, one particular reason seems to be on the rise. That is, simply, taking an interest. With sex roles blurring, men are now free to become involved in activities that were formerly considered feminine. Market researcher Judith Langer distinguishes the Old-Fashioned Man who expects to be pampered by women from the New Expressive Man who is more open about his feelings and beginning to share responsibilities with women. The New Expressive Man tends to be under thirty-five and doesn't live in the South. But he can also be an older man in a second or third marriage. It's not so much the age of the man as the age of the relationship, said Langer. "Men in long-term relationships resist change," even when the wife's role has changed from housewife to working woman. Men who started a relationship "in the feminist era" are more likely to participate in home furnishing decisions. As the wife of one New Man said, "My husband would be furious if I bought a window shade without him."

Henry, a thirty-year-old Farm Bureau official in Omaha, is representative of the New Expressive Man. He is totally involved with his collection of nineteenth-century furniture and accessories. Most people are surprised to hear Henry is an antiques collector— a bit artistic for a civil servant. But Henry and his wife, Anne, an executive with a family-owned newspaper, have been collecting since they were first married and Anne's grandmother suggested that for a wedding gift they pick some old furniture out of her storeroom—things that no one else in the family seemed to want. They selected a grand old four-poster bed, an elaborate dresser, and an original Belter sofa, the kind with two humps on the back. Henry refinished them all himself, something he had never done before, and found he had a real feel for it. Impressed with the results, Anne's grandmother told them they could have anything else they wanted. Like many newlyweds, Henry and Anne made their furniture decisions together; but when Anne got busy with their first child, he began shopping alone. "If I thought a piece was good enough I would bring it home to replace something we had. I know Anne's taste as well as mine; I can buy for our house and it's always been acceptable." When relatives and friends began asking for help in choosing an oak table or the kind of bed Abraham Lincoln slept in, Henry's hobby became a weekend business. Meanwhile, he was taking charge, more and more, of the furnishing of their home. If wallpaper, a rug, or hardware was needed, he chose it. Anne had veto power. "It's easier for her and usually it looks good once it's done," said Henry.

How does Anne feel about her husband taking over the job that many women still view as theirs? "It's like having a live-in decorator. I really don't have the time to go out and search for things, and he just absolutely *needs* to do this. He cares the most," said Anne. "I have never wanted anything common," said Henry. "I don't want people to come in and say, 'Gee, you got everything at J.C. Penney's.'"

His Place: Aural Eroticism and Fear of Flowers

But what about the men who live alone? Not since the Second World War have so many men lived unaccompanied by women. Between 1970 and 1978, the number of women living alone increased 41 percent, while the number of men living alone jumped almost 80 percent, pushing this category to 10 percent of American households. Who are these men? Some are never-married men, whose numbers have doubled; others are divorced men whose ranks increased 118 percent.

And one of their biggest problems when they move in alone is how to fix up their living spaces. Large numbers of single women are widows who have more furniture then they have space for. But most single men are furniture poor. They are starting out or starting over. Because so many of these single male households are in the twenty-five to forty-four age group, *Home Furnishings Daily* has dubbed them the "New Target." From his statistical profile, the New Target is often a management executive, a salesman, or a professional making over $20,000 a year. Twenty-four percent of these men make over $35,000. He spends an average of $762 a year on clothes and is now venturing into the home furnishings marketplace in sizable numbers.

But no matter how interested a man is in his home, the process of furnishing is often bewildering. As a rule, men don't read magazines that give furnishing ideas. They are short on time and have little experience or patience with shopping. Retailers are full of contemporary folklore about the single man who buys the complete contents of his home in one two-hour shopping trip—not necessarily because he knows what he wants but because he hates indecisiveness. Conran's president, Pauline Dora, recalled the bachelor who filled five shopping carts with everything from china to furniture, and the owner of Studio 54 who outfitted his apartment himself in a single shopping spree. And it is single men who purchase Bloomingdale's model rooms, *in toto*.

If a man doesn't want to make his own decisions, he is extremely adept at getting help. Men are masters at delegating, especially those who are older or more affluent, and they often assign their home furnishings purchases to significant others, insignificant others, secretaries, sisters, ex-wives, even Mother. The woman who makes furnishing purchases for a man may get the mistaken idea that she is mistress of the house. Jean Harris, convicted in the shooting of the Scarsdale diet doctor, testified that she had a chair reupholstered for Dr. Tarnower, bought curtains, watercolors, a bird print, bathmats, and plastic pillows for the outdoor chairs, a plastic bench, a pillow for the doctor's bed, monogrammed towels, various plates, glassware, and an iron. Her defense attorney tried to prove that these domestic chores were evidence that the doctor's house was really Mrs. Harris's New York residence.

In some ways, having a lesser emotional investment in the decor than a woman has can be an advantage to a man. He has no hesitation about using a decorator, if he can afford one. But the price he may pay is that his home is less authentically male. A decorator is in some respects like a wife. He or she will domesticate the less "civilized" instincts of the man. If the man wants his trophies or his paperback collection in the living room, his decorator will shunt them into the den. When he says he absolutely does not want any plants, the decorator will send one as a gift. But, because a man comes to a designer with few illusions that he could do the job better than the professional, and little competitiveness, he can be very appreciative of good advice. After six years in his completed apartment, one bachelor was still so satisfied and so grateful to his designers that he sent them each a $100 bonus.

If design professionals are to be believed, his very first concern when he moves in alone is how to hang up his ties. Supposedly, after settling the tie problem, his major purchases, in descending importance, are a bed, a comfortable chair, a lamp, a TV set, a sound system, and a popcorn machine. It is assumed that the stereotypical bachelor homemaker never goes beyond buying these basics. But many men feel hurt by this image—they reject the cliché. While there are few things you can say about the differences between men and women that are not open to debate, it is generally agreed that men view their homes more as functional objects. They furnish their homes in their own image, which they define as more rational, less emotional, and today many men are willing to stand up and be associated with a distinctly male style of decor.

Bloomingdale's senior vice-president Carl Levine says the single male furniture customer falls into three categories. The first is the stereotypical bachelor who really does exist, and in large numbers, said Levine. "He wants a glorified college dorm. All the furniture clichés. A brown sofa, reproduction Oriental rug, double pedestal desk, Breuer dining chairs, chrome and glass coffee table, chrome etagère for stereo and diplomas—the stuff that he's seen over and over and so assumes it must be right."

The single man in the second category may have been exposed to more sophisticated decor, perhaps coming from a family that had beautiful furnishings, or may just want to impress in a sex relationship. This man is after more individuality and higher style design in his apartment and seeks help from a variety of sources. He is willing to mix old pine and contemporary and is aware enough of trends to say, "I hear the radial look [with marshmallow edges] in upholstery is in."

A third type of male consumer, whose numbers are fewer, said Levine, is sophisticated, extremely adventurous, reads design magazines, and is likely to do his place himself quite capably or use a designer. In Levine's opinion, contrary to popular mythology, a man's sexual orientation does not account for his interest in style. Men in creative fields, straight or gay, have more sophisticated tastes than men in other fields. And "the gay customer who works in a hospital or in law may not do his home any differently from the traditional bachelor."

One group of artifacts is standard equipment in the male den: the high-techtonics. Susan Shins, a New York decorator who specializes in helping men start over, said it is not unusual for her clients to spend one-quarter of the decorating budget on the sound and video system. One client spent $11,000 on audiovisuals and $30,000 on everything else. Heaven for the typical male home-maker resembles a recent Sony ad. A cartoon by Charles Saxon shows a young executive type in suit and tie, reclining in his leather Eames chair, feet on ottoman, surrounded by his electronic menagerie—the large-screen projection TV, Betamax, tape deck, dictating machine, clock radio, amps and preamps, woofers and tweeters ugly enough to make an art history major cry.

All these possessions are to the male what the accouterments of the dinner party have traditionally been to the female. The same pride and sense of identity a woman has been conditioned to get from a china pattern which stands for her taste and her social class, the audiophile gets from his multi-amp sound vehicle. The quality of a man's equipment is a symbol of his success, and his connoisseurship. "The only difference between men and boys," said one gadget-loving bachelor, "is the price of their toys."

The male fascination with equipment probably comes from an interest in knowing how things work, which women, one study discovered, find boring. Because men generally have no fear of equipment or technology, they have also become the best market for the $250 pasta machines, the costly electric gelati makers, microwave ovens, and professional knives.

The bachelor slob may be becoming as obsolete as the nine-teenth-century fop, but one thing has not changed in ages in the interior world of men and women. Single men do not want their homes to look feminine any more than they want an aftershave lotion that is "soft and gentle." They like a little sting in their after-shave and some toughness in their furnishings. Not that their rooms have to look like a men's club, a barracks, or a pub. An office or a spaceship will do.

The decor of Bruce Keiser's four-level Philadelphia loft features streamlined detailing reminiscent of 1930s trains and lobbies. Bruce is representative of the new male attitude to the home. He is so interested in his home and its decor and so unwilling to compromise that he does not want to live with his woman friend, Diane Gingles, an owner of clothing boutiques. Instead they live in side-by-side industrial buildings that are connected via the roof. "We used to live together, but it's always compromise, sharing taste and sharing objects," said Bruce. "I'd rather live in my own space and visit." Bruce and Diane's living quarters are almost caricatures of the differences between the homes of men and women today. "Diane's space is much more feminine," said Bruce. "She has more objects around, more flowers, more coffee table books, more vases and statuettes, a real kitchen, and a bathtub. Her house is designed for having company—she has a big sofa and a cocktail table in front of a fireplace, and she can seat eight at her dining table, so we're more likely to entertain there."

His place is designed for one person. There's only a shower and no door on the bathroom, a small living room, not geared for entertaining, and his kitchen is designed only to accommodate his built-in professional wok—he is an accomplished Chinese cook. Bruce admits he is very conscious about the gender connotations of his decor. "My place is not feminine looking and I don't want it to be. It's more pared down than a woman's place. I'm against compulsive accessorizing." Nonetheless, he said, "a lot of people jump to the conclusion that I'm gay. They believe that any man who has style must be."

Emily Post understood the primal fear of emasculation and its connection to decoration. "That any normal man should be repelled by the least suggestion of effeminacy is only natural," wrote Miss Post in her 1930 decorating book *The Personality of a House*. In the chapter devoted to rooms and houses for a man, she went to great lengths to spell out the gender of various decorating elements as if they were French nouns. Modernistic furnishings were well suited to men, she said. Empty spaces, the absence of ruffles and curtains, and beautifully polished surfaces of wood and metal were masculine. "No woman loves the finished surface of leather, or wood, or metal the way a man does." Floor-to-ceiling books were suggested for decoration. Chintzes and cretonnes were "entirely suitable," but "not chintz of the pink-roses-and-blue-bow-knot variety—scarcely!" As for style, in the 1930 edition she suggested that Elizabethan, Spanish, or Georgian were masculine, but French was too feminine. By the 1948 edition, Early American and Modern were also certified as manly. "Every open-beamed doorless bare-walled room is obviously masculine." As were high ceilings. But, low ceilings, she warned, had "feminine tendencies."

Today, male anxiety about appearing effeminate often manifests itself in avoidance behavior limiting men's choices for everything from paint to sheets, towels, and cocktail napkins. One thing the New Target man does not want—something that sold well to women—is surface decoration. The toasters, coffeepots, and microwave-proof bowls had to be stripped of their decorations. No more stampings and decals of butterflies, palm trees, snowflakes, and the hottest hot-stamp of all—the hex-axial variant rosette.

"It was all brown, very boring male furniture. It wouldn't even make an interesting den," complained David Stockman's bride of her husband's bachelor-pad furnishings. Well, what else is new? Male living rooms are being dressed in the same neutrals their inhabitants wear: navy, black, gray, brown, beige, and luggage tan. And their beds are being made up with sheets in patterns that have connotations of Euclidean logic and rationality—neat geometrics, plaids, stripes, checks, herringbones. Martex recently introduced fashion designer Perry Ellis's sheet designs featuring patterns of houndstooth checks and stripes. Why no flowers and lace? Ellis said he looked at all the sheets on the market and saw that "everything was flowers and lace, that there was no room for a man in a bedroom." And he didn't think that was right. You can be sure that if Prince Charles were living alone, his sitting room would not have contained a pretty pink sofa with pink and white flowered and ruffled throw cushions on which he was recently photographed with his wife and son for the *Ladies' Home Journal.*

Fear of appearing effeminate is also a factor in the housekeeping style of single men. If they are too meticulous, it is seen as not masculine. "People say things to them such as 'You'll make someone a great wife,' and they hate it," said Judith Langer. So they feign nonchalance. "I'm not very houseproud," insisted one bachelor whose tastefully renovated apartment, published in the *New York Times,* belied the disclaimer. The major difference between men and women when it comes to homemaking is not that a woman designs her home for interaction with other people, while a man arranges his home for his own entertainment, even using the kitchen to clean his motorcycle or the dining room for basketball practice, both of which men have been known to do. No, the major difference between men and women is that men don't feel ashamed or guilty about cleaning a motorcycle in the kitchen or housekeeping lapses. "When a guy's apartment is a mess," said a single, twenty-eight-year-old New York playwright, "he'll say, 'Come on up, the place is a mess.' When a girl's place is a mess, she won't let you come up." "Women have more of a sense of conscience about things in the house than men do," observed a male student at Harvard Law School.

The New Frontier

It has been observed that there is beginning to emerge a new type of person: "the androgynous personality" with "sex-role flexibility." This new modal type, said Florine Livson, the late Berkeley psychologist, is "equally at home with masculine instrumentality and feminine expressiveness, regardless of gender." And the benefits of role-blurring are measurable. They go beyond freeing men from the sole burden of making a living, and giving women a chance to become doctors and lawyers and firemen. Apparently, people who have sex-role flexibility are at an advantage in later life. Studies show that men and women with more androgynous personalities adjust better to aging. Women who have been conditioned to be helpless in their adult years are particularly at risk when they are older and widowed. And men who have been conditioned to be assertive and nothing else do not adjust well to retirement.

Therefore, it doesn't matter whether he warms up Lean Cuisine or dishes up nouvelle cuisine, whether the sheets he selects are striped or flowered, whether he paints his walls gray or aqua or shell pink. What matters is that men are beginning to be less home-phobic. While women are learning to become more comfortable outside of the home, men are becoming more comfortable inside the home. And that is one large step for woman- and mankind.

6

Home Cycles: What Time of Life Is This Place?

IT WAS AN April-November marriage—a nymphette and a mogul. The mogul, Meshulam Riklis, sixty, Rapid-American wheeler-dealer and Las Vegas hotel owner, was giving a journalist a tour of his Beverly Hills mansion, complete with hot tub and pink exercise room, in which he was playing house with his pubescent bride, aspiring actress Pia Zadora. Whether Riklis wanted to disclaim credit for "the look" or just wanted to explain why he seemed a bit out of place in the energetic surroundings, he told the reporter something that deserves to be memorialized on a needlepoint pillow: "It's decorated young."

It's decorated young! What a wonderful expression. It brings to mind Donald Reilly's *New Yorker* cartoon. A middle-aged couple dressed in their country club best arrive at a suburban party. As they wait for the front door to open, the husband cases the party through the window and exclaims to his mate: "Uh, oh, cushions on the floor."

Cushions on the floor separate the young set from the midlife-crisis crowd, whose real crisis is getting up from a fourteen-inch-high sofa seat; cushions on the floor separate the work-out-aholics from the have-you-got-a-straight-back-chair senior citizens; the traditionalists from the nonconformists; and the haves from the have-not-so-muches. Cushions on the floor are definitely "decorating young." But like high chairs, they are eventually outgrown. It's a sure sign of life-cycle transit when someone who has decorated young trades in floor cushions for chairs, claiming consideration for her guests. "I knew I didn't want pillows on the floor anymore when the commissioner of football came to visit. It was pathetic to see him sitting cross-legged on the floor," said a thirty-five-year-old veteran of the lotus position.

Age is the underrated issue in the psychology of home and its design. Almost every aspect of behavior "can be shown to relate to [chronological] age," said David Canter. But we often overlook the fact that age accounts in large measure for a person's different needs, choices, and responses to surroundings.

The Ides of Decorating: Sic Transit Mahogany

It has been observed that "life cycle is the universal escalator on which everyone rides," and there is no doubt that consumer researchers, furniture people, builders, and social scientists are all fellow travelers. Marketing people divide up the life cycle by the requirements of *body* and *role*. Are we potential buyers of baby powder or denture powder? Are we students, workers, or retirees; freshman wives, freshman mothers, senior mothers, mothers emeritus, or consultant grandmothers?

The home furnishings industry is especially interested in our size and motor function, the better to take care of our ergonomic needs from cradle to coffin. There are bassinets for newborns, cribs and playpens for infants, strollers for toddlers, youth beds and bunk beds for preadolescents, bean bags for restless teens, rocking recliners for the sedentary midlifers, adjustable beds for seniors.

But taste also separates the cohorts of one age from those of another. In fact, changes in taste act as a kind of carbon dating system in decorating. Bloomingdale's Carl Levine divides old taste from young according to the following checklist, which is subject to change without notice: mahogany is old, light woods are young; Duncan Phyfe is old, rattan is young; sofas are old, modulars are young; club chairs are old, armless slipper chairs are young; matching lamps and matching end tables are old, pharmacy lamps and trunks for end tables are young; chandeliers are old, track lighting is young; breakfronts are old, wall systems are young; boudoir lamps are old, drafting lamps are young; deep-cut glass like Waterford is old, flat-cut glass like Baccarat is young; silver plate is old, stainless steel is young; cups and saucers are old, mugs are young; Oriental rug reproductions are old, dhurry rugs are young. And the youngest of all are *cushions on the floor.*

Every home has its age spots. Not even so-called timeless design can save a room from revealing the ages of people dwelling there. Having nothing on any tabletop usually denotes a toddler is in residence. Only the Manus of New Guinea have been able to train their children *not to touch anything.* And barnacles of family photos clinging to every tabletop, and bookcases filled with 1940s Book-of-the-Month Club selections are clues to advancing seniority.

Rooms inevitably change and age over time, yet this is rarely acknowledged in the fixed plate view of the home shown in interior photographs. Homes evolve as lives evolve. Training wheels come and go. Nests fill, nests empty, and sometimes fill again. Jobs change, spouses are changed, income changes, values change. Just when the newlyweds get every one of their new purchases in place, they may find a baby is on the way. The master bedroom has to be converted to a nursery and the living room to a bedroom. If it's not a family addition, it's an unexpected guest. Spouses, lovers, relatives, and friends come through the revolving door. Someone becomes bedridden; an aged parent moves in; grown children return home for a few months. These are not one-in-a-million happenings, they are the very fabric of life. And the home has to respond to these life revisions as rapidly as an army supply depot reacts to action at the front. Quick, bring in the crib; open the hide-a-bed; put up some shelves; add a room; convert the garage; finish the basement.

In addition, we have to adjust our homes to technological changes. Where do you put the microwave when every inch of the kitchen is spoken for? Even *Future Shock* author Alvin Toffler didn't predict he might one day take on another computer when he originally laid out his office. "The place wasn't designed to hide the wires of two of them."

If the house can't expand or contract properly, we move, if we can afford to. The social mobility of American society is mirrored in its residential mobility with almost 18 percent of the population moving each year. We rarely die in the houses we were born in. Not surprisingly, the three basic reasons for moving are all related to life cycle. A change in family configuration—marriage, divorce, a new baby, children leaving home, a death—is the first motivation. Soon after their marriage, William Agee and Mary Cunningham bought a house in Oyster Harbors on Cape Cod; on the heels of her scandal-making divorce, Roxanne Pulitzer had to vacate her $1.5 million Palm Beach manse and move into an apartment; when little Ricky started bumping into the props, television's Lucy and Ricky Ricardo forsook their apartment and moved to a house in Connecticut; and following the death of Natalie Wood, Robert Wagner moved the kids and their growing menagerie of dogs, cats, goats, chickens, and three Arabian horses into a larger and more private house with stables.

The second reason for moving is a job transfer. Patty Hearst's husband, Bernard Shaw, is leaving the San Francisco police department for a security post with the Hearst Corporation's New York office, and finding a home in New York is their first priority. Athletes, politicians, and corporate executives are the most visible job-related movers. Their house hunting ordeals and good or bad adjustments are staples of newspaper feature pages. When George Foster left the Cincinnati Reds to join the New York Mets, his wife Sheila wrote a first-person piece about the trials of moving. When basketball player Scott Hastings was drafted by the New York Knicks, his bride Judi "was not at all happy at the prospect of living in New York. . . . She'll grow to like it or she'll go home," said Hastings. And when the Reagan appointees swarmed into Washington, we learned Mike Deaver had to leave his grand piano behind; the Caspar Weinbergers left their California rose garden just as it reached perfection; and Alexander Haig couldn't find a house he felt was grand enough. Which brings us to the third motivation for moving: to downgrade or upgrade housing.

When homeowners have a reduction in income, one of the first things they do is get rid of the house they can't afford, cut down overhead. Because of business reverses, Billy Carter had to trade down. People generally upgrade to bring "their residences into line with their prestige needs," said sociologist Peter Rossi, and they search the longest and look at more houses when they are upgrading than when they are moving for any other reason. This is because the house must fit a person's social aspirations as well as space needs. And those aspirations usually center on a particular neighborhood as well as a special home. In Texas, said *Ultra* magazine, people look for three things in a residence: "location, location, location." Understanding the need for the right address, New York developers whose apartment buildings have entrances on a side street off Park Avenue give them Park Avenue addresses, which apparently can bring 20 percent higher rents. And in Los Angeles, 2,500 homes just north of Beverly Hills use a tony Beverly Hills address, which is said to add 10 to 15 percent to their value.

Life-Style Lodgings

The home building industry has been the Rip Van Winkle of stage-of-life marketing. Only recently did it wake up to the need for different housing for different seasons of life. In the 1950s and '60s there were basically two options in housing: the single-family detached house, for sale, and the attached house or apartment, for rent. Although American families were shrinking, houses weren't. The Irvine Company of Newport Beach, California, among the most successful developers of planned communities in the country, was one of the first builders to realize you couldn't sell that many four-bedroom houses to families with 2.8 members, and it started building houses to fit the new consumer needs.

"The Browns are really excited about moving into their first home. They have been married for about a year, living in an apartment and saving every penny. . . ." "The Jacobs have just been transferred from the Midwest. Tom works for a national electronics company as a designer, Sue is employed as a legal secratary. They entertain friends often. . . ." "The Masons are moving up from a townhouse. . . . They love the yard space for the children." These are profiles of potential home buyers, created from market research by Irvine.

Whether you're twenty-one or sixty, want to spend $70,000 or $2 million plus, have a boat and no children or triplets and a dog, Irvine has a house for you—or a lot on which you can build a dreamhouse. The Irvine people know you better than you know yourself. They know that if you're young, you want your fireplace in the living room; and if you're older and more successful, you don't want soot on your living room wallpaper and prefer your fireplace in the den. And they know you want an extra room for hobbies, but that you'll end up using it as a guest room or children's room.

Irvine builds for thirteen market segments, providing housing for every conceivable life style except communal living. It has condos for *Young Singles* like Laverne and Shirley; accommodations for *Adult Singles* who give noisy parties and want their friends to be able to come and go discreetly; houses for working *Young Marrieds #1* with one kid, and *Young Marrieds #2*, who have two careers and a sports car. It also has houses for the *Never Nested,* the grown-up two-career couple at their earnings peak; places for the *Compact Family Move-Down,* which became compact when it left its large family home; and special layouts for the *Compact Divorced Family,* which needs a generous family room and a master bedroom suite separate from the kids; Irvine understands that the divorced parent craves privacy for new relationships. In addition, there are houses for the *Family Move-Up,* which moves up to get more bedrooms; and for the *Established Family,* which needs room for teenagers and three cars and a house to match the peak in the family's "economic and social life-style curve." *Luxury Families* that "have arrived" get a formal house—detached, of course. Irvine also recognizes differences among peripatetic *Empty Nesters,* gadabout *Active Retireds,* and *Retired* stay-at-homes. There is even a double master bedroom house for couples to share.

But sentiment and house attachment are not a strong component of the Irvine experience. If you need another bedroom, you don't necessarily add on to your house. Instead, you're supposed to trade up to another house, just as you would trade in your car for a larger one. Your roots are supposed to be on the ranch, not in a particular house there.

Irvine is just one of the multitude of builders catering to special interests in housing today. It has been estimated that there are 600 communities around the country especially geared to older adults. Of the 74 million Americans over forty-eight, 2.5 million live in adult communities which are likely to be equipped with card rooms, clubhouses, and shuffleboard courts. Meanwhile, condominium communities for singles, divorced people, and two-career couples in their thirties with no children are also mushrooming. These fitness-oriented market targets are lured with such amenities as jogging trails, swimming pools, exercise clubs, tennis courts, paddle tennis courts, hot tubs, and pool tables.

Every Time Has a Place

Just as we have different houses for different times of life, homes mean different things to us psychologically at different life stages. While there have been a number of investigations during the past decade into the stages of the adult life cycle, none of them has correlated stages of life to housing. But surely having the right residence for each stage is a necessity. After all, how can you become your own man or woman if you are still living with your parents?

How many stages of life are there? Solon, the early Greek poet, believed there were ten; Confucius thought there were six; Shakespeare, seven; philosopher Ortega y Gasset, five; psychiatrist Erik Erikson, eight, three of which are adult stages. In Erikson's view, the young adult's task is intimacy, "to lose and find oneself in another"; the adult's task is generativity, "to make be" and "to take care of"; while the mature adult's task is "to face not being."

Although times of arrival and departure in a stage vary for each person, today's life-cycle theorists generally agree that one's early twenties is a time of breaking away; the late twenties is devoted to the search for intimacy; the thirties is a time of materialism and striving to consolidate a career; the forties is a time of *sturm und drang,* the last chance for a major change—a redefinition of identity—and involves a switch from self-centeredness to nurturing and mentoring (if this has not occurred earlier). In one's fifties, most life-cycle experts agree, there is a mellowing, a settling down, an interest in immortality, a sense of physical vulnerability, a fear of mortality, and the special problem for women— anticipation of widowhood. So far, the fifties is the end of the line for the life-cycle theorists. For your passage beyond this point, you must transfer to gerontologists who will tell you that the next stage, which occurs at different times for different people, is a return to the dependency of childhood.

No matter what stage you're in, the right home can help you through your developmental tasks, but the home that's good for one stage can impede your progress in another. "If the commune prevents loneliness before thirty, it perpetuates it afterwards," said psychiatrist George Vaillant in *Adaptation to Life,* a long-range study of healthy men. "A person's residence is in part a place to sleep, to eat, and maybe a place to raise a family," said Daniel J. Levinson, author of *The Seasons of a Man's Life,* a major study of the male life cycle, "but beyond that, it is often a center for one's life. The place you go to be replenished, part of one's leisure life." He can see that the four or five moves he and his wife have made coincided with important changes in their lives. One apartment "had a transitional quality . . . we couldn't get rooted in it. It wasn't an adequate base for the rest of the life." A rented home was "a firmer richer center," and contributed to a sense of "going home." And buying a house for the first time coincided with expecting a child and feeling more settled. "Each home reflected important things in our lives, but the meanings changed over the life cycle."

The primary requirement of the young adult's home is to have a place for intimacy. But by age thirty or thereabouts, it's time to settle down, choose a new life style or affirm a former one. This is the age for "making it" socially, as well as for gains in income, power, fame, creativity, and quality of life. If there are children, there are the worries about play space—indoors and out—and nearness to schools, but social life for the parents matters, too. A home for this stage of life needs to support sociability, which in turn raises identity issues. As one lawyer approaching forty said, "It's time that I had a home that expresses my acomplishments." But that usually takes money, more money than is available. One's pocketbook is usually out of synch with one's image of self.

Dissatisfaction with the amount of money earned reaches its peak between thirty-five and forty. Nonetheless, the emphasis in this period is on outward appearances rather than inner satisfactions, and many people go into debt to make the right appearance. The thrift shop chic of one's first pad seems jejune now. There is a sense that it is appropriate to live in a certain way—one can't beg off anymore. Even Andy Warhol's Factory headquarters have aged stereotypically, evolving from the silver mylar youthquake look of his thirties (complete with transvestites) through a series of taste cycles in his forties to the current downright-upright look of his fifties (complete with rare Irish Regency and Art Deco furnishings and pre-Raphaelite paintings)—the culmination of managing director Fred Hughes's plan to "establish the Factory socially as well as artistically."

When it comes to your residence, the *transitions* between the stages of your life are as crucial as the stages themselves. It is during life-cycle transit that you may become sensitive to the fact that your home doesn't support the new direction in which you're heading—and often dissatisfaction with the home can signal a change in your life you hadn't fully recognized or verbalized. In most cultures, transitions are heavily invested with ritual and meaning and one stage must be formally ended in order to begin another. "To mature we all have to 'die' from a previous state," wrote anthropologist Victor Turner, "and to be reborn finally as persons in control of our lives at a more challenging level." In our culture, ending one stage involves evaluating the past, deciding which activities, relationships, interests, residences, and possessions to keep and which to discard. We may send some things to the attic, other things that don't stand for us anymore we send to the thrift shop, some objects are demoted to rooms of lesser status, and still others promoted to positions of more respect. But people can't discard things until they are ready. "Throwing away any possession, however useless," said French social psychologist Perla Korosec-Serfaty, "means tearing it off the fabric of one's experience, giving it up." This can't be done before one is psychologically prepared. Each person has to determine his or her own time for getting and for letting go.

Breaking Away

The hardest time in any family, said Jay Haley, the noted family therapist, is when someone is coming into a family or leaving it. "Leaving home is a crucial time in one's life, when one has to move away from the family and create an independent home base." Frequently, departure is not a precise moment, but a drawn-out *process*. It often begins with children spending more and more time away from home while their summer clothes, skis, knapsacks, spelunking gear are still in residence. It's not a real decampment, just a leave of absence, which isn't the kind of leave parents have in mind. As far as they're concerned, it's checkout time. They have other plans for the room. "I was dredging out my son's room, hoping to discover a guest room in its depths," said one Pennsylvania woman in a letter to the editor of a newspaper.

Anxious to get on with their own transitions, parents often make a child feel abandoned. When an eighteen-year-old leaves home for college, she is just rehearsing for the big break. She still thinks of her parental home as "home." But her parents don't wait for the kid's mattress to get cold before they move in with their desks and home computers. There's a sofa bed there for the daughter, of course, but it's no longer *her* room. From then on, she's a guest. No teddy bears on the bed, no glass animal collection on the shelves, no school pennants on the walls. And she doesn't like it.

New York decorator Noel Jeffrey tries to discourage his clients from dedicating rooms to grown children. He tells parents that "once away the children won't want to come home." But he notices that "mothers simply don't want to hear this." Actually, in this situation, Mother knows best. Until the children are out and established in a place of their own, said Jay Haley, "they really need the feeling of having a home, and having their own room does that even if they are not there. At the point you visit your parents' home and don't have a room there, you really have left home," he said. "Our daughter is in college and we keep her room exactly as if she were there. Not that there aren't other things we could do with the space."

Leaving the safety of your parents' home and establishing your own home base is the first step in entering the adult world and thinking of yourself as an adult. Loading up a rented van with your clothes, your TV, your stereo, a new mattress, and some dishes and moving them into your own space is the beginning of breaking away. But it takes more than one's name on a mailbox to feel truly "at home." At-homeness doesn't happen overnight.

Feeling at home in a place creeps up on you in three stages, said psychologists Jerome Tognoli and Jaime Horwitz. The first phase is transitional—you may be living in a dormitory or group house, or a "real" house or apartment (or series of them) that you aren't attached to, or aren't ready to become attached to, that is perceived as "not home." In the second phase, you may be living in the same place and there is an incipient awareness of home—it's beginning to feel a little more like home. But eventually there is a moment when you realize you require a place that truly feels like home. It could be precipitated by a desire for more space or more privacy and control, or it may just be a need for a place you can feel more attached to. Feeling really at home comes with recognizing your needs and learning to satisfy them. Some people can't feel at home, said Tognoli and Horwitz, until they give up the fantasy that some other place, perhaps the parental house, is their real home. In that case, they may never feel at home any place else until their parents die.

Another pair of researchers have characterized the first home as "a perch, not a nest." In their study of thirty-nine newly married couples in the Cambridge, Massachusetts, area, Florence Ladd and Kathryn Allott found that, "Frequently the husband-to-be occupied the apartment and somewhat later the wife-to-be moved in with him." At the "lowest point in their economic growth," most couples were happy to be able to locate a decent apartment within their budget. It was furnished with secondhand furniture, hand-me-downs, and a few new pieces, including a bed, the couple's major purchase. The husband "felt possessive about his desk and stereo." The wife felt possessive about "her plants, the sewing machine she had had since she was seventeen, and an overstuffed chair that she had bought for eight dollars." The rest of the things they considered "theirs." Newlyweds gave relatively little thought to the way their day-to-day living would mesh with the layout of their apartment. When the apartment included a study, it was more often "his" study, and the wife felt deprived of a place for her homework and hobbies. It took experience for young people to be aware of their needs. No matter how many rooms they had, newlyweds spent much of their time in the same room because being together mattered to them. The focus of the first home is definitely *inward,* said Ladd and Allott.

Please, Mother, She'd Rather Do It Herself

A clean break from one life stage is vital to the success of the next, but the process of weaning yourself from your parents can often persist into middle age. Certainly cutting the mother-daughter cord is difficult. Because house and mother are closely linked, decorating can be one of the most trying experiences of a woman's life, said New York psychiatrist Milton Sapirstein in his controversial 1955 essay, "More Stately Mansions: The Paradox of Decorating a Home." Despite the passage of nearly three decades this point is still valid. When a daughter sets up her home, it is "the final declaration of independence from her mother," asserted Sapirstein, who happened to be married to a decorator. "It says, 'I have equal status.' " And if there have been unresolved differences between the two, disagreements over decoration are often used to act out old enmities.

"The need to imitate one's mother is a strong, deep force that few daughters can permanently ignore," wrote psychiatrist Roger Gould in *Transformations*, another major study of life cycle. By giving parents a "small but often irritating degree of power over us," he said, we get an "illusion of safety." By their own admissions, daughters often allow, even encourage, their mothers' intrusion in the home furnishing process, and once involved, mothers are not above playing power games. Some mothers see imitation as fealty. If you love me, you'll love my favorite style. For her first home away from home, Averil Meyer, granddaughter of the late New York Mets owner, Joan Payson Whitney, asked her decorator for a bedroom just like her mother's, a garden of flowered chintzes. Apparently such homage is not unusual among the upper classes. A *House Beautiful* survey found that upper-middle-class daughters were more likely to copy Mom's decor than lower-middle-class daughters, who were "more likely to rebel and want something different." But rebellion is not unknown in the upper middle class.

The seeds of mother-daughter decorating conflicts are often sown in childhood, maturing slowly into later conflicts. Nancy, a Houston mother, admits to having made the mistake of "putting up what *I* wanted in our six-year-old daughter's room. She persisted in pulling the paper off the wall, not once, not twice, but three times. I tried everything. The calm heart-to-heart talk, the screaming and wringing her neck. Finally we made a deal. In two years we would redo it." Ironically, Nancy admitted, she was doing exactly what her mother had done to her when she was a child. "My mother made my room the way *she* wanted it. Nothing could be moved. It was all white. Much of the house was all white. Everything was *'Look, don't touch.'*"

Whose room is it anyway? Usually an adolescent's first step toward independence is taking possession of his or her room. It's partly an issue of control, partly young people's attempts to find and define their own identity. But some mothers can't abide their children's taste if it isn't identical to their own. "I arrange my room in the summer the way I like it and when I come back home from college over the Thanksgiving holiday, the room is totally different," complained Dorothy, a nineteen-year-old from San Francisco. "I'll put all the stuff I don't like in the basement, and after I go back to school, my mom will go down and get it and put it all back. I have a favorite pillow that I like on my bed—she'll put it on my window seat. I use Scotch tape to put posters up. She doesn't like posters that aren't framed. At Christmas my mother said my room was a mess, so I proceeded to clean it bare—not one thing on the dresser—and she came in and put a little vase of fake flowers there. I took it off. Of course, my mom has really good taste. I know I should listen to her, but I really prefer a cleaner look to all those arrangements." Dorothy worries that she'll carry this hassle into the next stage of her life. "I've told her many times, when I get married she won't get into my house."

Furnishing disputes often do carry over into marriage. In-laws are responsible for a large share of early marital problems, many of which are played out as furniture disagreements. A new husband can be jealous of the closeness between his wife and her mother from which he is excluded when so much time is spent shopping for furniture. If newlyweds are too closely connected to parents, they can't connect properly to each other, and both spouses can resent the demands imposed by gifts of furniture. Not until she was in the throes of a divorce after five years of marriage did Anthea, an Oklahoman, learn how much her husband had resented his mother-in-law's interference with the decorating. Her mother is, in Anthea's words, "an absolute lamp freak, so I have fabulous looking lamps—and a lot of them. That's probably why I'm getting a divorce. My husband said recently, 'There's not a goddamn piece of furniture in this house that your mother and dad didn't give us or bring in here personally.'"

Some mothers or mothers-in-law fear being overshadowed by a daughter's or daughter-in-law's home that is more beautiful than their own. Mavis, a Detroit woman, has been married for more than thirty years and her mother-in-law has always been jealous of her furnishings. "If we acquired something she liked," said Mavis, "she would decide it was too good for us and we would trade. I always let her have it. I knew it would come back. We bought a set of Chippendale dining chairs that were almost identical to hers. But she felt ours were finer and that upset her. So I suggested we switch. Then she would come for dinner and watch in horror as the children dropped food on her brocade. The chairs that I had given her were covered in a sturdy needlepoint and nothing could hurt them. They were perfect for the children. So, after maybe two months, we traded back." No matter how willingly she acquiesced to her mother-in-law's whims, she could never get her approval—something both daughters-in-law and daughters crave.

There are mothers who try to keep control by withholding approval. Carrie, a Pittsburgh mother, was very much the family matriarch, proud of her taste and her traditionally furnished home. Her daughter Sonia rebelled by furnishing in a totally different style. When Sonia and her husband built a ranch house, Carrie could never do anything but criticize. "It wasn't until after she died," said Sonia, "that I learned she was a lot prouder of me than I realized."

Please, Mother, You Do It

"Some girls run away at fourteen, I rebelled at thirty-five," said New York journalist Blair Sabol. "My break with my mother was over the decorating scheme. For the past seven years, I have had a total lack of responsibility for my surroundings. I was put in a high chair and my mother took charge of the choice of chairs and I let her. But two weeks ago I sent the furniture back to Mom. I realized recently I have never used any living room my mother decorated for me. My place reeked of my mother's friend, the decorator. After seven years I wanted it all trash-compacted.

"My mother is the kind of person they call eclectic—she uses Oriental rugs with Pop Art things mixed with Navajo stuff. I think eclectic means you can't make up your mind. When in doubt, buy both. Our house in Philadelphia was very nice but it was suffocating. When I was young I wanted a canopy bed. Mother hated canopies so she gave me a *half*-canopy which was like a dumpling on the wall. It was horrible. All style decisions were made *for* me. As a result, I never cared how I lived. In fact, as I got older I noticed I liked hotels better than I liked my home.

"I moved to New York when I was twenty-eight. My first place, a two-bedroom apartment, was also a pied-à-terre for my mother. She decorated it, mostly with furniture she already had. She appliquéd the doors between the living room and dining area with tin chocolate molds. My bedroom was a bust. I hated it. She said, 'You need a dark room.' So she did it in a burgundy high-gloss paint. The bedspread was covered with little mirrors. It was like living in an Indian store. It was so dark I could never get dressed in there—I always ended up with one red sock and one black sock.

"I decided to redo the bedroom myself. I wanted to do it *light* in gray and peach. But I fell flat on my ass. I discovered gray is a terrible color to paint walls and sisal on the floor is terrible on the feet. Mother did the 'I told you so' number. I always had this problem wanting acceptance from my mother. So back I went into my shell, thinking I must have terrible taste. I can't do my own surroundings.

"Then I got a job in Los Angeles. There I discovered a whole new world. A friend took me to this rental place and we did the house in two minutes. We picked out the chrome and glass table and the chrome and glass étagère, the white shag rug, the bentwood chairs—the only trouble was every house you went to had the same furniture. Next I moved to a beach house in Malibu. Mother came to visit and said, 'Well, what are *we* going to do with this?' and I realized she had come out to decorate. When I got involved with a guy, that stopped her. She couldn't stay with me, and from three thousand miles away she had no control.

"When I moved back to New York two years ago, I took a major step, I found the apartment myself. I wanted it to be airy and light like Los Angeles. Mother made it dark again, rust and brown. She did the living room from 'stock'—she keeps some things in a locker at a moving company in Philadelphia, she keeps others in my brother's attic, plus she also has furniture in what I call the Storage Pavilion, a storage room she built in the back of our house. It was eclectic—thick baroque Jesuit chests, Oriental rugs, a massive French Provincial coffee table, fabrics from Provence, a Brighton Pavilion chair, an Art Deco lamp, tortoiseshell-finished bamboo blinds and some Moroccan mirrors thrown in. Mother's friend the decorator would send over a table and say, 'You know, Blair, it's absolutely stunning,' and I'd say, 'It doesn't exactly *go*,' and she'd say, 'Go? It doesn't have to go, it's an antique. Of course you like it, Blair. There's no discussion.'

"I always thought my mother had marvelous taste. It never occurred to me she had terrible taste *for me* until, one day, I was running around the reservoir with a friend, talking about *decorating*. I said I couldn't care less about it. She said, *'Obviously.* Your apartment is awful.' I knew it was cluttered but I never knew it was awful. She said, 'If I were you I'd get the crap out of there.' And I said, 'I'll call my mother.' And she said, 'No. That's the point.' But how could I do an apartment without Mother?

"Recently I stayed at an ashram in Tucson. It literally had only a mattress on a board and a good reading lamp. No chair. No place to hang your clothes. Just hooks. That was it. The style I wanted. Zen Trappist monk. My mother said I could never live like that. So finally I made a decision, and I didn't discuss it with Mother. I just called up her movers. I said in forty-eight hours I want you up here. When they arrived I gave them everything in the living room except a few pictures that were dear to me and my mauve sofa which I had picked out myself. I knew I had done the right thing when the moving man said as he was leaving, 'Boy, you really had a lot of stuff. I bet you're glad to get rid of all this.' Then I called my mother and told her the furniture was on its way back and I was doing my apartment on my own. She said 'That's very good. You're almost forty, it's about time.'"

Midlife Real Estate Crisis

Life cycles are like singing rounds in camp. While kids are merrily, merrily, merrily, merrily leaving home psychologically, parents are row, row, rowing the boat into middle adulthood. By age fifty, nurturing is on the decline and people must deal with the loss of youth. Whatever has been neglected in life must be attended to. Around that time of his life, playwright Neil Simon fulfilled the fantasy of having an apartment in New York's ritzy Ritz Tower. He had been there when he was much younger to visit

Goodman Ace, one of the great radio writers, and told himself, "If I ever could afford it, that was where I'd want to live."

After their children were grown, Kate Lloyd, editor of *Working Woman* magazine, and her husband John, a fund-raiser, traded in the townhouse they had lived in for thirty-two years for a loft in Greenwich Village. They are using their old furniture, but if a piece doesn't look right when the loft is finished, said Mrs. Lloyd, she'll change it. With tuition bills behind them, she doesn't have to make do anymore. "This is my final resting place, and if I hate the way the furniture looks, I'm going to get something new."

This is also the season of life when people reevaluate their lives and commitments. Spouses aren't always in agreement about how they want to live. There are marriages in which one spouse may feel trapped by a home that is too expensive or too hard to maintain or in the wrong city, while the other partner has finally attained what he or she wanted. Who will give in? Talking about Los Angeles, where he has lived since 1960, actor Peter Falk said recently, "I never have felt and never will feel connected out there." However, when he suggested moving back to New York, his wife said, "I'd go in a minute, but I can't get the house on the plane."

In *The Fall of a Doll's House,* author Jane Davison, in her own words, threw "snowballs at the single-family house, the word *housewife* . . . and home ownership as a creed." Tracing the history of the single-family suburban house and the myths surrounding it through the homes of her grandmother, her mother, and herself, she concluded that being the keeper of the dreamhouse was not worth the sacrifices. Despite her family history of attachment to houses, she warned others about getting too involved in their homes, admonishing them to save their emotional energy for important relationships rather than squandering it on symbols of themselves. "When the home-as-object threatens to dominate its occupants," she argued, "they should remodel or move out at once."

The midlife years are also a period of changes in the body, especially for women, who must deal with the loss of attractiveness and capacity to bear children, as well as a decline of power within the family. "It is an extremely common phenomenon of middle-class and upper-class life," said Levinson, "that a woman remains in a bad marriage to keep her husband's income and social standing, which she may do a great deal to sustain." If a woman has children, they are leaving home, perhaps taking with them the mother's raison d'être. Some middle-class women defend against the decline in physical beauty and the decline in nurturing by sublimating their bodies to their homes. The house and garden are cultivated with the same energy that sexual attractiveness once was. If the body can't measure up, at least the home can. It becomes a narcissistic object that exists to be noticed and admired. A recent survey by the American Society of Interior Designers found that empty nesters were significant users of interior design services. "I like people coming to see my house and telling me it's beautiful and they enjoyed being here," said one woman who gave her home a facelift when she was forty-five, although she admitted it was in perfect shape. "I just said to my husband, would you mind if I got rid of everything and started over?"

Senior Sensibility

Three generations—a grandmother, her daughter, and her two grandsons in their twenties—were driving to a family wedding. The seventy-five-year-old matriarch was rambling on enthusiastically about her project of the last few months. She had taken a lifetime of family photos and finally mounted them in albums. When her grandsons teased her about her growing obsession with family legend, she turned to her daughter and asked quite seriously, "How come the younger generation has no sentiment?"

They have no sentiment because they are still looking forward to their lives, not back over them, while for the older generation the view is definitely through the rearview mirror. A major preoccupation of the elderly is what has been termed the "life review," the obsession with going over the past, in pictures, in memory, in conversation—helping them deal with their mortality.

In aging, we regress to a new kind of dependency as a result of a decline in power that comes with physical, economic, and social limitations. The elderly inhabit a different sensory world from younger people. "My mother's house is beginning to look like the lair of *The Madwoman of Chaillot*," said one thirty-five-year-old woman whose mother used to pride herself on her fastidious home. "Lately, she has everything she ever owned crowded into one little room." The homey clutter we associate with grand-mother's house is not necessarily an esthetic preference but a physiological one. Small rooms filled up with many things, said German psychologist Ernst D. Lantermann, compensate for the failing senses and give older people a feeling of control. Impaired vision, changes in depth perception, color perception, hearing, and sense of smell all account for the different sensibilities of older people. These perceptual changes affect the way older people ar-range their surroundings.

How can you keep an eye on your things if they're too far away for you to see them? For people with reduced vision, glare on surfaces has to be controlled, the glitter of a chandelier is annoy-ing, the shine on the floor is hazardous because it appears to be water or ice. Busy patterns on seating can hide objects resting on them. Their vision doesn't adjust easily to the dark. And there is trouble distinguishing among blues, blue-greens, and violets. Older people do much better with reds, oranges, and yellows. The most important thing in decor for people with poor eyesight is to have a contrast of shades among different surfaces, especially be-tween walls and stairs. Painting her brown kitchen chairs white so they contrasted with the dark red floor made all the difference to a woman with retinitis pigmentosa. She also found that a dark bathmat, dark soap, and striped towels made it easier to differenti-ate these items from the white tiles and fixtures. Even light col-ored mugs were necessary for her to see coffee in them.

With auditory impairment, hearing doorbells, the TV, conver-sation, rain on the roof, approaching footsteps, the teakettle whis-tling can all be a problem. Chairs that were better for conversation at right angles now need to be face to face for lipreading; the TV has to be closer to the recliner; telephones may need amplifiers; doorbells may need flashing lights. Rooms need more sound-absorbent fabrics to keep down echoes.

Even the resistance to change that characterizes the elderly is physiologically based, the result of their slower response to stimuli. Redundancy is security; change takes too long to process mentally. Better to leave the telephone books in the *hard to reach* but at least accustomed place under the table skirt rather than move them to an accessible but *hard to remember* place on an end table. "I like to live in a place that I know blindfolded, where I can find my cigars without looking," said actor George Burns, when he was eighty-six. "Mary Benny says it's time for me to move, but I tell her I can't move, because I finally know where my handkerchiefs are."

Because of decreased agility, dull is the safest finish for a floor that can be hazardous for old people when it is waxed. And while a pleasant view is more important than ever to the person whose life is rooted in the house, wet leaves on the ground are a frequent cause of falls and broken hips. Their homes have to be challenging enough to keep the elderly active while not so challenging and hard to negotiate that they withdraw into inactivity.

But the most important and most overlooked aspect of housing for the elderly is its symbolism. Just because certain furnishings get little use doesn't mean they have no function. The home is often the sole remaining source of self-esteem for an elderly person. For this reason senior citizens depend on the decoration of their homes to stand for themselves, for their life history, and for special events in their lives. But decreased income can force them into housing that is too small to accommodate the most precious of their possessions. According to MIT's Sandra Howell, a specialist in environments for the elderly, the pieces of furniture most symbolic of self to widows—the double bed, the husband's high dresser, and the formal dining room set—can't be fitted into the space-constrained apartments of public housing. While these items may not seem all that necessary or functional to an outsider, they have an important function for the older woman. To give up these possessions is to lower self-confidence and self-esteem. Familiar possessions and places remind us who we are. Without them, we risk psychic disintegration.

Older people also need familiarity with their communities. Some people who move late in life never overcome the feeling of outsiderness. Belonging to an area gives a person more status than being a newcomer, which is especially disadvantaging to people who are already devalued because of their age. If the move is *involuntary* and if the new home is not an improvement over the old one, moving can be traumatic. "Transplantation shock" can result in higher mortality rates, especially in the first three months after the move.

But relocating needn't always be a negative experience. Under the right circumstances it can have positive effects. Moving to another community voluntarily and getting involved in new activities can compensate for the role losses that come with age. It appears that the one trait that is vital to making a good adjustment to relocation at a later age is the *willingness to take risks*. Studies show that people who have successfully moved to a new community viewed the move as a gift to themselves. They planned ahead to be able to "establish a new life style *apart and separate* from younger people," among people who were "young-old," energetic in spite of being elderly. Admittedly, their aim was to create a life where there was no bad weather, no bad news, and no bad apples.

The most satisfied and well-adjusted relocators can be divided into four types: Explorers, Helpers, Comfort Seekers, and Fun Seekers. Explorers put a low priority on comfort and possessions; they are adventurers who see retirement as a chance for a new start. Helpers find a new identity in "doing for others" as does the retired man in Queens who has adopted a public park—mowing the lawn, among other chores. Comfort Seekers devote themselves to their decorating projects, spending a great deal of time in their new apartments which are usually an improvement over their previous homes, while Fun Seekers enjoy the sociability of retirement. When one Fun Seeker bought an apartment in Florida fully furnished, her friends were surprised. They couldn't understand why an interior decorator wouldn't want to fix it up herself, put her stamp on it. But she had her reasons. "At this stage in my life, I don't want to waste time fixing it up. I want to have fun. I don't want to be running around fighting with contractors." An internal alarm was buzzing. "It's time. Time to enjoy."

She would have been shocked twenty years earlier if a crystal ball gazer had told her she would one day be so casual about her environment that she could relinquish control of it. But attitudes and behaviors that seem to be personality traits often turn out to be related to one's stage of life and change as we age. This is not always welcome information. We like to believe we're unique, that we make decisions for ourselves, that we don't follow the pack, or act in stereotypical ways. But age as well as sex and class can influence our choices in our homes. Personality enters into it, too, in other ways.

7

*Making It You:
Preference and
Personality*

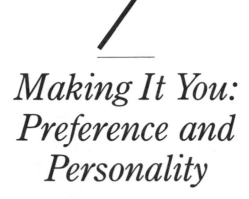

*The Slipcover Justification:
Proof Positive that Decorating
Is Good for You*

■

*If I Like It,
It Must Be Good for Me*

■

Modus Decorandi

■

Picking and Choosing

■

*Picking and Choosing:
Color Connections*

■

*Picking and Choosing:
Style Connections*

■

The Arrangement Makers

■

The Good Housekeepers

■

The Rescue Squad

■

The Master Builders

■

The Garden Brigade

A RECENT EVENT in Cambridge, Massachusetts, qualifies as one of the Great Moments in Decorating. Psychologist Norbett Mintz had just been appointed to the staff of the Harvard Medical School. An office came with the territory. It was unrelievedly gray—gray walls, a cold northern exposure, and a closeup view of the rear of a gray building.

The office would have to be painted, he told the powers that be. That was impossible, he was informed, the room had just been painted. Then he would paint it himself, he said. That was completely out of the question, he was told. Union rules. Union rules? "Either this office gets painted," replied Mintz adamantly, "or I'll bring down the union." Within the week the office was painted the tannish yellow of his choice.

Another professor might have made do. Academics are supposed to have loftier thoughts on their minds than the color of the walls. Decorative disarray and stylistic nonchalance are such staples of academia that when a scientist has an untidy laboratory, one study found, he is perceived as being important. Why, then, was Mintz so insistent upon sprucing up his office?

Very simple. If there is one person who has firsthand proof of the benefits of pleasant surroundings, it is Norbett Mintz. In 1955, when he was a research fellow at Brandeis University, Mintz and his mentor, Abraham Maslow, the late renowned psychologist, were discussing the fact that people seem to behave differently in different settings; yet no psychologist had ever explored the effects of room esthetics on behavior. There had been studies of the effects of color (Mintz had done some of those himself), and the effects of music, but never the effects of "beauty." They decided to look into it.

The Slipcover Justification: Proof Positive that Decorating Is Good for You

The first experiment Maslow and Mintz undertook was called "The Effects of Esthetic Surroundings: I." It was designed to measure the short-term effects of three rooms—one "beautiful," one "average," and one "ugly." Would people, in looking at pictures and making judgments about them, evaluate them differently depending on the esthetic quality of the room in which the task was performed?

Three rooms were prepared as the experimental sites. The "beautiful" room was Maslow's own comfortable beige-walled office furnished with mahogany desk and bookcase, club chair, Navajo rug, draperies, paintings on the walls, and sculpture by Mrs. Maslow. The "average" room was an ordinary no-frills, no personality, university-issue office with battleship-gray walls, metal bookcase and filing cabinets, two standard desk and chair combinations, window shades, and a daybed covered with a neat green spread. Tidy but institutional.

Creating an "ugly" room was more difficult. "What is ugliness?" asked Mintz, reminiscing recently about the landmark experiment. "We finally settled on disarray and messiness as being unpalatable." A basement room was tricked up to look like a janitor's disheveled storeroom. There were two straight-backed chairs, a bare mattress and spring, dirty, torn window shades, tin cans for ashtrays, broom closet paraphernalia, and assorted refuse.

To make sure that the rooms would, indeed, be perceived by

others as beautiful, average, and ugly, a control group of students was asked to comment on them. The beautiful room was rated "very pleasant," "very nice." The average room evoked such responses as, "Well, how should it look, it's an office." And the ugly room elicited such remarks as "hideous," "horrible," "disgusting," "repulsive," and "ugly."

In that case, how did the students in the control group feel about working in these rooms? Did they think they would feel any different spending time in one or another of these rooms? Good question. Certainly, no one wanted to spend any time in the ugly room. But neither did any of the students foresee a benefit from spending time in the beautiful room as opposed to the average room. Being in the beautiful or the average room would be "equal," the students predicted. Were they right? Did esthetics make no difference?

The decorators, furniture and wallpaper dealers, and paint manufacturers of America are going to like this. In fact, beauty seemed to make an appreciable difference. Stationed in each of the three different rooms, an "examiner" asked students, one at a time, to look at ten negative-print photos of people's faces and to rate them for energy or fatigue, well-being or displeasure. Students judging photos in the average room found more energy and well-being in the photos than the students who were rating them in the ugly room. And students in the beautiful room found even more energy and well-being in the faces than those judging the same photos in the average room. According to Maslow and Mintz, the only thing that could account for the different ratings was the esthetic differences in the three settings.

In a follow-up experiment, Mintz examined the long-term effects on the examiners of working day after day in the beautiful room compared with working in the ugly room. Again there was a notable room effect. Examiners stationed in the beautiful room over the course of three weeks felt powerful, comfortable, energetic, enthusiastic, and weren't at all anxious to stop their tasks, while those working in the ugly room suffered a whole range of unpleasant reactions, from headaches to fatigue, irritability, hostility, and room-avoidance. When the examiners were asked what they thought might have accounted for their moods, only a few of them saw a possible connection between the room and their state of mind. The rooms definitely affected people, but only a small percentage of the subjects involved were aware of it. For most, the effects of the environment were subliminal. If Maslow and Mintz were right, the more pleasant the room, the better people feel in it, the more energy they have there, and the more positively they regard the tasks they perform there.

For anyone who needs a slipcover justification or a redecorating rationale, these studies should do nicely. Were furniture industry folks as well read in psychology as they are in flammability standards and housing starts, Maslow and Mintz would have been made Men of the Year by now.

Of course, the idea that beauty is functional is hard for Americans to accept. Studies have shown that skepticism about the benefits of beauty and the usefulness of esthetic experience runs deep in our society, contributing to the attitude that beautiful surroundings are *nice,* but not *a necessity.* This undervaluation of a pleasant environment may stem from ignorance about the nature of esthetic experience.

If I Like It, It Must Be Good for Me

It is probably no coincidence that the expression "good taste" is the semantic term of esthetic choice as well as of biological survival, said Norbett Mintz. Infants develop a taste early on for foods that are good for them. Bad-tasting food can kill. And bad taste in surroundings—that is, any taste that is not our taste—makes many of us feel physically threatened. The esthetically sensitive repeatedly use food metaphors to describe environments that displease them. "Ugly rooms are like a bad meal," said one designer. "Some rooms have so much color I could gag," said another. "I hate those candy sweet colors, those pale yellow rooms with peach windows and mint on the furniture—it's like being force-fed pralines and cream. They make my gums ache."

These are apt metaphors. Esthetic experience is as much physical as it is psychic. It is the search for pleasure and the avoidance of pain, and involves attraction, arousal, stimulation, and satisfaction—and their opposites. To endure surroundings that are not your taste gives you more than visual indigestion, it can cause measurable stress. "Psychic satisfaction is related to physiological well-being," said James Marston Fitch, the noted architecture critic and Columbia University professor. While we perceive our surroundings with our eyes and our senses, we react to the slightest changes in combinations and intensity of color; to odor and order; monotony, complexity, and disarray; noise and music; the familiar and the unknown—*physiologically*, with gut reactions that reverberate throughout the immuno-, cardio-, and adrenal systems, affecting brain arousal, steroids, and hormonal balance. We can't really like a place unless it feels good physically.

Human habitats are almost uterine, said Fitch, and the body reacts violently to extremes of sensory experience. It is known that sensory *overload* can destroy rationality, and sensory *deprivation* can reduce people to gibbering incoherence. So we should not be surprised that there are physiological responses to less radical situations. In fact, pleasant sensory stimuli can make the heart beat faster and provide a physical sense of well-being and satisfaction. Most people, not to mention chimpanzees used in esthetic experiments, will go out of their way to get those pleasure rewards from visual and other sensory stimuli.

But *mental* satisfaction can also be had from esthetic experience. There is strong evidence that the appreciation of beauty has evolved from the basic human need to make sense of our environment—to understand what is good and bad for us in our surroundings. Both humans and animals have to distinguish the noxious from the harmless. In order to predict events and plan behavior, experience has to be organized, every stimulus has to be noticed, evaluated, classified, and appropriate action taken. It is not only the obviously dangerous conditions such as fire or lack of oxygen that must be evaluated and acted on, but also the weather, the terrain, and the presence of other humans or animals. Decisions have to be made: Is this good for me or bad for me? Will I feel good in this place or bad in it? What can I do about it? Esthetic judgment is developed by noticing relationships of materials and objects to one another over time and reacting to them. It involves recognizing balance, harmony, complexity, and rhythm—the likeness tempered with difference in objects, sounds, sights, and smells—and then relating these to previous experiences, deciding whether to eat an object, fight it, flee it, or ignore it.

The capacity for making distinctions on which life and death decisions are based has developed over time into esthetic awareness, said animal biologist Nicholas Humphrey. Just as there is pleasure in sex *without* procreation, there is pleasure in sorting things out for no other reason than the enjoyment of looking at pictures, selecting a color scheme, searching for a special shell, naming that tune. Indeed, being sensitive to one's surroundings is a sort of calisthenics for the mind, which is entertaining, challenging, satisfying, and good for you.

But how do we know what sort of physical situations are good for us? One way is to turn to studies. Certain environmental investigations have shown that we leave more packages on the bus when the barometer drops; under noisy conditions and in hot weather we are less helpful; a request for a salary increase in a noisy room nets a smaller raise than if the request is made in a quiet room; and we tend to disclose less to our therapists in cold, bare rooms than in cozy spaces.

When scientists want to measure the effects of certain environmental stimuli—the color of the walls or the level of light—they hook their subjects up to sensors in the laboratory and chart how the heart and brain react to a red room or a dark room. But most of us can't spend our days tethered to machines to ascertain when the moderate and pleasurable arousal of novelty in a setting becomes the heartburn of too much complexity. We can't have technicians in attendance measuring how much overstimulation prompts the heart to compensate by slowing down heartbeat. And, luckily, we don't have to.

Each of us has a built-in mechanism for keeping the body from self-destructing. It's called *preference*. "An organism must prefer those environments in which it is likely to thrive," said psychologists Stephen and Rachel Kaplan. Preferences may not replace stress tests but they "are important indicators of environments in which people can be constructive and effective."

But there's a hitch. Even when we know what we like, we can be convinced otherwise. Beauty, unlike the color, form, weight, or odor of an object, is not an innate attribute. Designating something as beautiful is a subjective judgment, said Fitch, an award conferred by the mind. And the human mind has other priorities than pure pleasure. Every day we forgo gratification for social rewards. We give up sweets to be thin, meat for Lent, sex for religious or moral reasons. Similarly, we may reject houses, objects, and perfectly good solutions to our homemaking problems because we don't like their connotations. Judgments of beauty or ugliness are never based purely on formal esthetics or gut level preference. They can always be prejudiced by the meanings that become connected to a style, pattern, or object.

A person who values honesty in materials is embarrassed that her wood floor has an easy-care polyurethane finish. "It's not what I believe in." Another person won't have any patterns with birds in her home because she feels it's bad luck; people of one religion rule out patterns with crosses, those of a different religion reject designs that have a hint of a six-pointed star. And comes the revolution, of course, there is always a change in taste. What was coveted the day before is suddenly despised. After the French Revolution, Frenchmen did a taste about-face wanting nothing to do with the cabinetmakers popular with the court.

If religion or politics or symbolism doesn't prejudice us against a style, fashion will. Yesterday's avant-garde favorites, such as supergraphics, log furniture, and arc lamps, are now as passé as bell-bottom trousers. Fashion is a perpetual game of Us against Them, a balance between conforming to one group while setting ourselves apart from another. As soon as the group from which we are differentiating ourselves adopts the fashion of our group, we must switch course, adopt a new style.

Modus Decorandi

If esthetic preferences can be so easily ruled and overruled by outside forces, what role does personality play in our place-making? Psychologists believe that personality differences can reliably predict one individual's fascination with possessions and another's disdain for them, as well as different orientations to privacy, the penchant for antiquarianism or tinkering, the taste for the suburbs or the backwoods. Although theory is still in the formative stages, the hot topic in personality and environment research is *dispositions*—and it is related to preferences.

Human personality is composed of a complex variety of interconnecting needs, motives, values, attitudes, temperaments, actions, and traits that operate as a whole system. Psychologists believe that our preferences are clues to personality traits, but there is no agreement on whether traits remain constant over time and across situations. Therefore, many psychologists prefer to talk about dispositions. An infatuation with purple or Queen Anne style furniture is a passing preference that may come and go with one's moods and whims. But a disposition is a behavioral trend, an individual's unique and recurring method of activity and problem solving, a style of operation, a modus operandi. Each of us tends to personalize space in characteristic ways, becoming a specialist in color coordination, tabletop arrangements, lawn maintenance, or other creative endeavors.

To dope out your own dispositions, you don't have to take elaborate psychological tests. According to Canadian psychologist Brian Little, all you have to know is this one rule of thumb: *"You are what you prefer to do."* If you have a particular way of relating to your home, if you repeat it, and if you find it satisfying, it's probably a disposition. Thus, recurrent choices, activities, or ways of attacking a project that a person finds salient add up to a summary statement of one's personality.

But don't be misled. What appears to be a disposition for one thing can be a disposition for another. Taking on a major house-building project doesn't automatically mean one has a disposition to build. "I built my house myself," said Kansas State University architect and psychologist Paul Windley. "I did it for economic reasons. I would never have attempted it except for the fact that my father-in-law is a contractor. To think of building a house for fun is not in my repertoire." Rather than a disposition to build, he said, "Perhaps it was a disposition to save money."

And when Francis Gabe, an Oregon housewife, built herself a Rube Goldberg-type wash-and-wear, self-cleaning house with sprinklers in the ceiling to dispense detergent spray, her motivation was not so much an interest in good housekeeping as a loathing for it. Cleaning was her excuse, but when someone works eight years on building a house, you can be sure she has a disposition to build.

Abilities can influence dispositions. "The more competent you are in a domain," said Little, "the more you like to do it, the more you do it, the better you get at it, the more interested you are in it, and the more it stands for you." Certainly abilities have a lot to do with one's choice of homemaking activities. Depending on how frequently you engage in them, and how skilled you are at them, these activities can be merely leanings or full-blown dispositions— in which case you would incorporate them into your self-definition.

As the kids would say, " 'A' my name is Alice, my favorite color is avocado, I come from Alabama, and I adore antiquing."

The five modes that are most often used to make our homes our own are selecting and acquiring; arranging and organizing; housekeeping; conserving and restoring; and handiwork and gardening. (Collecting is an aspect of selecting and acquiring, but because it is such a unique endeavor, it needs to be treated separately.) If you become known by your compulsions or your pastimes, it's a sure bet they are dispositions. Barbra Streisand is an antiques selector and acquirer nonpareil. Lady Diana is emerging as a compulsive organizer. "If her shoes are cleaned, she wants them put back precisely in line in the cupboard. She is obsessed that everything around her be perfect," said a palace informant. Joan Crawford was known for her compulsive cleanliness, which was put to the test daily in her fabled white carpeted living room. New York consumer reporter Betty Furness is a dedicated needle-pointer of rugs and pillows and her home was designed as a background for her handiwork. Jimmy Carter is a woodworker; astronaut Colonel Jack Lousma likes to build things around the house, as does actor Hal Holbrook. And Joyce Ride, mother of astronaut Sally Ride, is casual about housework but a diligent gardener.

Specialists in one or another of these areas tend to approach problems from their own perspective. Given a shortage of storage space, the shopper would think first of buying an armoire; the arranger would turn some shoe boxes into space organizers; the good housekeeper would clean out the cupboards to make room; the conservator would convert an old wardrobe trunk into an extra closet; and the builder would construct some extra shelves.

Picking and Choosing

How seriously one regards selecting and acquiring material possessions for the home depends on how one relates to objects. In the course of our daily lives, we have all noticed that certain acquaintances care more for things than for people, or more for people than for things. Elsie de Wolfe's biographer observed that Elsie found houses and furniture "a happier adventure" than the people she met or the parties she attended, and that she was "far more comfortable expressing her passion for buildings and objects than for people." Apparently one's disposition to things—whether one can take them or leave them—is a basic aspect of personality, which is just beginning to get the attention of social scientists.

A recent study by two psychiatrists found that infants can be classified as either *thing-* or *people-oriented*. Thing-oriented tots learn the names of things first. When they play house they are interested in the equipment, and to calm them, parents have to offer an object—a stuffed animal, a doll, a ball. People-oriented children learn the names of people first and play roles when they play house. To calm a people-oriented child, parents have to offer themselves.

Brian Little believes that two categories aren't enough. He has isolated four types of "specialists," as he calls them: Thing-specialists, Person-specialists, Self-specialists, and Generalists. Thing-specialists not only care about things, said Little, but are also intrigued by them. They are fascinated by the physical properties of objects, their form and their function, often disregarding their social impact. So what if the chair isn't comfortable? It looks good. Person-specialists are sentimental, they associate things and places with people and tend to personify them. Their homes may not be visually coordinated, said Little, "but every place in the house is sacred." They want their chairs to be comfortable for family and friends, and to heck with the looks. Self-specialists see everything from a personal point of view—the chair has to suit themselves alone. Generalists balance an interest in people and things. They care about comfort *and* esthetics. "You'd want your designer to be a generalist," said Little. Every selection one makes for the home will be influenced by these attitudes to things.

Picking and Choosing: Color Connections

The rich may commission their homes and have a say in the design, but the majority of people *"select* rather than create," as the late psychologist Donald Appleyard put it. Even when we're not open to buy, we are choosing. When one passes a store window or looks at a mail-order catalog, one is constantly assessing whether an item of furniture or apparel is "For me or not for me. What could I use it for?" Shopping and comparing is one of the ways we flex our visual senses. How much we like something has to do with its familiarity or its novelty. The familiar can range from comfortable to boring; the novel from exciting to outré.

But to avoid stimulus overload and total chaos, we all have to make choices of goods and activities. While it's not likely that a preference for this color or that could be termed a disposition, an interest in color and color aptitude is a disposition. Color memory, the ability to match and discriminate among colors, is inborn, but the eye can be sharpened with training.

Color is the front line in esthetic choice. That may be because infants can distinguish color before they can distinguish form. Experiments have shown that baby chicks will open wide for a red stick, mistaking it for the mother's bill. Unless you are color blind or indifferent to visual discord, color coordination is the easiest way of ordering the environment. Besides, having a favorite color reduces anxiety on the way to the checkout counter. In a world where everything from candles to soap, scrub buckets, can openers, paper plates, tissues, and directors' chairs are available in a rainbow of hues, having a preference is defensive—it helps avoid time-wasting indecision.

Once a decorating color identity is found, color coordination can be quite obsessive. Beige was the favorite of Elsie de Wolfe, who on seeing the Acropolis for the first time supposedly exclaimed, "It's my color." Red is Diana Vreeland's signature. Yellow is Dinah Shore's. And who doesn't know that lavender is shared by Miss Piggy and Liz Taylor? Writer Phyllis Theroux defined color favoritism as a kind of loyalty: "I always pick blue gingham, if available. Blue gingham constellates a galaxy of memories (beach, ocean, the first placemats in my first house) that confirm me."

We tend to feel self-conscious about our color choices because we have been told our color schemes will betray us. Color experts would have us believe that color preferences are related to character or personality and have the same meanings for and effects on all people. They advise us that the colors we choose have deep intrapsychic significance, that behavior can be controlled by the color of the walls and people can be analyzed by their choices. Color preferences are "as telling as body language, as revealing as psychology, as inescapable as astrology . . ." is the claim on the book jacket of *Color Your World* by color authority Faber Birren. He called red the color of extroversion and manic depression, yellow the color of high-mindedness and mental deficiency, a prefer-ence for green a trait of people who are probably overweight, middle class, and never engage in extramarital activity.

In *Psycho-Decorating,* Margaret Harmon (with a master's de-gree in psychology) proposed a system for doping people out from the colors of their living room decor. A room done in one color, Harmon said, means the woman who decorated it has "a highly developed conscience. . . . Bright red is associated with willing-ness to give in to other's wishes . . . brown reflects a capable attitude." Neutral colors on the sofa reflect an "independent man-ner," but on the windows "self-doubt"; black "reflects a rational attitude . . . an interest in accomplishing things" and is related to "a desire to stand out from the crowd." And green is popular with so many different types of people, said Harmon, it has no psychologi-cal significance.

Yet another color psychic cares not what a color tells about you, but how it can influence your behavior. Alexander Schauss, a former counseling psychologist in the prison system, has gotten an extraordinary amount of media mileage from his claim that a raving mad prisoner could be calmed down for twenty minutes by placing him in a cell painted bubble-gum pink, although Mr. Schauss admit-ted there have been no controlled experiments to prove this claim, which many scientists have found questionable. But proof doesn't stop Schauss from making this and other color presumptions. He advised against using pink in a bedroom. "Pink affects muscle strength and the penis is a muscle. Pink puts a male in a weakened condition. . . . Sex, after all, is an aggressive act," he said. He also claimed to have found a color that will help manic depressives, as well as a shade of green that increases strength but he'd rather not disclose its exact hue for fear "some sadistic individual might use it to drive a person wild."

How seriously should we take all these color psychics? Can color really control us or reveal us in predictable ways? Beware of sweeping claims about the power of color. No aspect of psychology is as susceptible to review. "More nonsense has been written about color effects than about any similar phenomena," cautioned Corwin Bennett, professor of industrial engineering at Kansas State University and author of *Spaces for People.* Many of the innu-merable studies on color are contradictory, which may be due, he said, to poor research but more probably to the fact that "many reactions to color are *very small effects.*" Color undoubtedly affects people, but its effects vary from person to person, said Norbett Mintz. "Some people wish for colors that *contrast* with their personality, others want a *similarity* to their personality."

To be told that color analysis is specious is like being told there is no Santa Claus. We hate having color-voyancy debunked. We want color to have magic properties. We long for it to be significant, to have effects we can count on. "I believe in color vibrations," said actor Ken Page of Broadway's *Cats,* who decorated his bedroom with purple walls and ceilings because "purple for me, being a Capricorn, is supposed to be a very good energy color."

What is underrated in most color preference work is the power of symbolism, context, custom, as well as fashion, all of which have influence on our reactions to color. This is a perfect example of "I know what I like but I can be convinced otherwise." Color has at least as much power over us through its symbolism as through its wavelengths. All colors are not equal. Certain hues and shades are considered appropriate or inappropriate for certain situations. If you doubt it, just listen to people howl when someone commits a color crime. In Litchfield, Connecticut, the residents were up in arms when the Methodist Church was painted gold, blue, and brown, and in New York City there was a stir when the Art Commission tried to paint the city's bridges in designer colors.

Color was one of man's first symbols. In traditional cultures colors had power and their meanings were known and shared. Today, colors are still surrounded by a web of symbolism. Yellow, a popular theme color for weddings in this country, is not considered suitable for wedding decorations in France, where it is the symbolic color of the cuckold. White is the color of mourning in many cultures. But in the early twentieth century, white walls and kitchens signaled "sanitary awareness." White rugs and upholstery, on the other hand, were a sign that one was wealthy enough not to have to worry about getting the furniture soiled. The all-white room, often credited to decorator Syrie Maugham in the 1920s, was actually inspired by the wife of a wealthy British coal merchant who decorated her house all in white—the antithesis of coal, and a symbolic color choice if ever there was one. While red is probably the most popular color in the world, there's a big difference, as one psychologist said, between a red bus and a red breast. With color, if you like it, it's probably good for you. But what you like has a lot to do with other factors than color appeal.

Picking and Choosing: Style Connections

After people choose their color, they usually choose their style. The real estate agents want to know what kind of house is desired—a house with a flat roof, a peaked roof, or a butterfly roof; the furniture salesperson needs to know whether to show the shoppers through the Colonial Corner or the Urban Gallery; the wedding guests want to know if the newlyweds are modern or traditional. Are they like the readers of *Colonial Homes* magazine who "don't live in the past, they just visit"? Which era do they visit? The gift giver must decide between an ice bucket with clawfeet (traditional), ball feet (contemporary), or no feet (modern).

A strong and repeated style preference for country or traditional or modern, carried out with a passion, can be considered a disposition and is probably based more on the meaning of a style than on some pure esthetic response to it. Perhaps you thought that style decisions were totally independent, free of outside pressure, a matter of formal esthetics between you and the pattern perception center in your brain. Sorry to disappoint you. Like color choices, decisions about form are influenced by outside forces. The *associations* a style has for you can influence your perception of it. What you pay attention to, what you prefer in forms, ornament, and proportions depends on your past experiences and the cultural meanings that attach to a particular type of design. It is almost impossible for most of us to separate our affection for furniture of a certain period from its meanings.

If you don't inherit prejudices for or against certain styles from your family, you pick them up along the way. Those who can't read the sign language of furniture can always turn to a semiotician who will interpret for them. In the nineteenth century architect Andrew Jackson Downing decreed that rustic arbors on a house gave it an "impression of refinement and taste." And Charles Locke Eastlake, pushing the quaint Queen Anne style, said the use of wooden pegs in a piece of furniture "had 'sincerity,' a nail did not." Later John D. Rockefeller called the Williamsburg, Virginia, restoration an example of high purpose and "unselfish devotion of our forefathers to the common good." Styles represent moral judgments—and affiliating with a style bears a certain resemblance to converting to a particular religion. If styles weren't meaningful, why, in 1967, would NASA have furnished its Houston lunar reception area in imitation Colonial?

Colonial has been riding high ever since 1885 when the Daughters of the American Revolution and other reform groups, in a xenophobic reaction to European style, led a campaign to Americanize. Nothing is more popular today than some form of traditional styling, whether it is native American or Old World. Symbols of tradition link people to ancestors or family values, said Berkeley psychologists Maryann Jacobi and Daniel Stokols, providing "a sense of continuity and identity within relatively unfamiliar surroundings"; they also show one's commitment to carrying on a tradition, and emotional links to some other time and place.

Often in decorating, however, the past people attempt to link up with is not their own family's but a more illustrious one. Old furnishings give a sense of family genealogy—the illusion of legitimacy. "Kinship is so entwined with social class," said sociologist Anselm Strauss, "that a deficiency of kinship memories means also deficiency of class memories." And to compensate for this, rooms must look as if the furnishings have been in the family for generations. This may explain why in order to snare the plum residential jobs, young designers who used to turn up their noses at traditional are all boning up on Eighteenth century. Rooms "must not look new," said established New York decorators Robert Denning and Vincent Fourcade. "They must give the impression that they evolved over generations, never touched by a decorator." "Newness is something I generally find disagreeable," said New York decorator Mark Hampton.

Actually, the whole concept of antique is modern, Yi-Fu Tuan reminds us. Reverence for the old has to do with a culture's concept of time. The Chinese don't revere old furnishings, they revere old *ideas*. In Japan, the design of the Shinto temples, which are rebuilt every twenty years, is considered more important than the original structure. In the Renaissance there was no compunction about using stones scavenged from the Colosseum to build other

structures. Not until the eighteenth century when it was prestigious to collect odd relics was there real interest in the past.

But perhaps the most subtle reason for the popularity of
things that are old or look old is fear of the future. "When people . . . feel they are in control of their destiny, they have little
cause for nostalgia," said Tuan. What better example than the
home of astronaut Sally Ride, which, according to published reports, is decorated with souvenirs of the space age. She faces her
future squarely with space-shuttle dishes, NASA posters, and a
large framed photo taken on the moon. However, when people
think change is occurring too fast "nostalgia for the idyllic past
waxes strong," Tuan said.

Americans may be fascinated with the future, but they don't
want to live in it. After spending an evening with Princess Leia and
Luke Skywalker in *Return of the Jedi,* they go to sleep in their
Early American, Eighteenth-century, or Mediterranean beds. The
home computer is the fastest growing consumer product category,
but contemporary-style furniture has only a 27 percent market
share. Even people who like new furniture aren't necessarily interested in *new styling.* In a recent *Better Homes and Gardens* survey
the majority of readers preferred new furniture to "secondhand,"
but only 15 percent of those people wanted the latest style.

A taste for the new is often a reaction to the past, which is
what worries the establishment. When Napoleon became em-
peror, he sent the contents of Versailles packing, stating he
wanted to "make new, not buy old." People who live with old
things seem to take it as a personal assault when they read about
extreme new styles. They see any home that is a radical departure
from their own as a rejection of their values, and therefore their
way of life. With limited money, the young rebels can shake up the
establishment by merely declaring torn draperies beautiful. Two
New Wave designers in New York who use glitter and pearlized
paint and car upholstery proclaim that their work is "a process of
breaking unwritten design laws." That's what worries the people
who like things that are old.

Another aspect of the new is its moral attitude toward excess.
The old look in decor is full and complex, the new look is spare,
simple, and "minimal." Minimal is a style of restraint, an appetite
suppressant for possessions, a room on a diet, in reaction to a

lifetime binge on materialism. "My main project this fall is getting rid of things," said an anonymous writer in *The New Yorker*'s Talk of the Town column. "Suddenly I'm bored with possessions. . . . I realize I don't want to die and leave behind a pile of little boxes from Azuma." But once you shed the *tchotchkes,* you have to go on a maintenance diet—vow to live a life of unparalleled neatness, dedicate yourself to the upkeep of space rather than objects, resist buying the unnecessary, and if you can't, store your things in someone else's house.

For a room to qualify as minimal it's not enough to dispose of everything. The emptiness must be designed. What this style lacks in clutter it makes up for in detail. When most people want their furnishings movable, the minimal look depends on elements that are unrelentingly immovable—built-in steps, platforms, ledges, and niches. Plain backgrounds are as costly as embellished ones because it's more difficult to get a perfectly smooth plaster doorjamb than it is to hide the joints under moldings.

When designer Hazel Haire chose to simplify her life, she and her husband put themselves in the hands of a designer. One might think that it wouldn't take long to prepare a minimal space for occupancy, but as it turns out, minimal requires more work than maximal. "It all seems so simple, it looks as if we didn't do anything, but it took an army to get us to this stage," said Mrs. Haire. What was supposed to be an eight-week job took a year. With the walls austerely blank, there was no place to put the books they absolutely couldn't part with. So the Haires began looking for a second home in the country to house the overflow.

Here again is a case of knowing what they liked—books—but being convinced otherwise. Minimalism is actually "conspicuous austerity." Its exquisite emptiness is not a sign of poverty but the height of luxury. Like the Japanese tea ceremony, it is the epitome of consumption, not the rejection of it.

The Arrangement Makers

Planning, making order out of chaos, seeing relationships and connections among disparate things, are all part of the arranging disposition. The arrangements we make can be large- or small-scale, and people who are drawn to this activity fall into two distinct types—the macroarrangers who concentrate on moving furniture and the microarrangers who see mantels and tabletops as their canvas.

Macroarrangers think big. These are not the people who arrange their chairs, sofas, and tables once and forever. Fuzz balls do not grow under their breakfronts. They move their inventories continually, anxiously, always looking for better juxtapositions. The stereotypical chronic furniture mover is a neurotic housewife, presumably expressing her unhappiness by changing the position of her sofa rather than changing her life. Furniture moving can be a signal that aspects of one's life are out of order, but it can also be a constructive attempt to improve on the existing order. We can't truly possess our furnishings until we control them and we make them our own by deciding how they'll be deployed.

Sometimes the macromover is a space planner trying to familiarize herself or himself with the terrain. "Man's feeling about being properly oriented in space runs deep," said anthropologist Edward Hall. It is linked to "survival and sanity." To be disoriented in space is to be "psychotic." We need to be familiar with our spaces not only to live in them comfortably but also to be able to escape fast in an emergency. When the smoke alarm goes off, it's good to know where the foot stools are.

Other furniture movers are social directors trying to improve communication. How far chairs are from one another and whether they face or adjoin can influence how chummy people get. When your conversational partner is seated twelve feet across the room, it's like having an intimate discussion on a speakerphone—you hesitate to ask for unpublished details of the palace coup. The chronic furniture mover may also be an explorer, open to change. In a study of an Ithaca housing development it was found that 50 percent of the people who rearranged their furniture did it for variety. Nineteen-year-old Amy is known in her Boston college dorm for her furniture-moving disposition. By the middle of her sophomore year she had rearranged her furniture no less than four times. Why? "I do it when I'm bored," she explained. It's also a way of getting approval. She and her roommate "had a lot of compliments" last year when they improvised bunk beds.

Pamela, a California woman, moves furniture for stimulation. "I really love change," she said. Some of her furniture moving episodes coincide with changes of season. In the summer she likes to put the secondhand dining table covered with the spiderweb scarf near the window and the view; in the winter she sets it in front of the fireplace. "When I move furniture there's so much energy, it starts my mind thinking about how I can make other changes in my life. After I move things I end up making changes in myself, my hairstyle, my work, my job."

Making small-scale arrangements is, in decorating jargon, "accessorizing," which is not far from what hot-rodders do to their cars. Formerly the bailiwick of the elite who collected the type of curios that you'd find in the storeroom of a natural history museum, accessorizing caught on with the bric-a-brac-mad Victorians, and interest in the art has never flagged. Shelter magazines show exquisite closeups of tabletops and mantels laden with bouquets, teensy picture frames with photos of the Queen Mother, marble eggs, china ladybugs, Battersea boxes, and bronze dogs, and homeowners feel obliged to accessorize. Every tabletop a still life.

Ideally the memorabilia on your shelves and mantels and coffee tables should be accumulated over time and have meaning for you. But when you read in your favorite Home Section that accessories "can make or break rooms," and that "tabletops should have a composition just as a painting does," you almost feel obliged to go out and fill your shopping cart with the right objects. No self-respecting amateur arranger will settle for less than the Billy Baldwin minimum—a discreet and artful arrangement of exotica on each and every tabletop; here a few turtles, there a cachepot, Oriental boxes, a lacquer tray, a small oil painting propped up on a stand, a pair of candlesticks, a decoy. Accessory anxiety is not exclusive to the upper and upper middle class. Taking advantage of the middle-American woman's accessory-inferiority complex is Mary Crowley, a Texas matron who poses for her publicity photos holding a mink-covered Bible. She heads a $400 million Home Interiors & Gifts business that is modeled on the Mary Kay cosmetics sell-it-at-home sessions. To ensure "that no home in America is ever dull or unattractive," Crowley pushes brass leaf wall plaques and flying gull wall ornaments, mirrors, candlesticks, and "permanent foliage," meaning fake ferns.

But once you have the stuff, you still have to arrange it. Loretta, a young Texas matron, used to depend on her mother to make her still lifes. "I'm good at tearing down walls and picking colors, but I can't arrange things," explained Loretta. "Mother was wonderful about putting knickknacks around and displaying things in the bookcase." Since her mother's death, a friend of the family has taken over visiting Loretta every six months and reorganizing her accessories. In between visits, "if one of the kids moves something," said Loretta, "it stays there until 'Aunt' Rae comes back."

Styles of arrangement are grammatical, suggested psychologists Jurgen Ruesch and Weldon Kees. Some people arrange by "subject," they said: all the ladybugs or horse pictures together. Others arrange by "predicate" such as high things or green things together. Books are a perfect example. Scholars often file their books by subject, putting a diminutive book on butterflies next to a large one on the same topic. The more visually oriented person tends to file by predicate. Architects, for instance, are prone to arrange books by size—all books under nine inches in height grouped together; and decorators are not above grouping books by jacket color, irrespective of subject. Making extreme predicate arrangements, perhaps putting lemons and yellow pencils in the same place, is supposed to be a sign of schizophrenia.

Each of us has a preferred way of deploying his or her regiments of relics. Piling, filing, hanging, grouping, shelving, and aligning. A gentleman in San Francisco liked to arrange his towels side by side with the diagonal stripes heading in alternate directions so they formed a chevron pattern. Some people must have balance. "I think of symmetry as comfortable, asymmetry as not," said Colline Dufresne, the former Warhol groupie known as Ultra Violet, who organizes by subject, keeping pots with pots and candles with candles. And the Duchess of Windsor once said, "I get ulcers if anything is crooked."

When objects are placed directly on a surface it is called "naked contact." But some people must have an intervening membrane between object and tabletop, plaster rosettes between ceiling and chandelier, a doily under every teacup, coasters under crockery, and antimacassars between occupants' arms and chair arms. They cover everything from toasters and Cuisinarts to toilet tanks and put plastic covers on lampshades.

There is also the "vertical orientation" and "horizontal orientation." Verticalists tend to decorate upward, building arrangements of pictures up to the ceiling; they fill the wall space over the mantel. Horizontalists concentrate their arrangements on the ledge itself, stringing their things out like toys on parade. The most recent manifestation of horizontal orientation requires standing pictures on the largest accessible horizontal surface in any room—the floor—and leaning them against the wall, which could cause *Homo erectus* to regress back to walking on all fours.

The Good Housekeepers

Many women, and even some men, define themselves by their housekeeping or cleanliness fetishes—polishing, scrubbing, or tidying up diligently. In the housekeeping department they need to be "10's" all the time. Why can't they tolerate the sight of dirt?

"Dirt is matter out of place," said Mary Douglas in her classic, *Purity and Danger.* "Dirt offends against order." Getting rid of it is a constructive and creative endeavor to organize our surroundings. Thus, spills on the dining table, crumbs on the floor, dust on the windowsill are all matter out of place. Knowing what belongs where gives us a sense of security.

A New York dancer is so fastidious, he opened a house cleaning service to capitalize on his disposition. Theatrical agent Swifty Lazar is supposedly so obsessive about cleanliness, he refused to meet with client Dorothy Parker in her own house. "She wasn't very tidy." In the elegant barefoot world of Palm Beach, an obsessive Mrs. Clean has had all her furniture upholstered in white canvas. When her sockless husband falls asleep on the white chaise, she dashes to the kitchen for her bucket of suds and not so gently washes his feet and slips a towel under them. In that case, the husband seems to be matter out of place.

Cleanliness is also "conspicuous morality"—a prerequisite of respectability. It is assumed the resident has some control over it. Of all the qualities that are valued in a residence or neighborhood, cleanliness and upkeep may be the most important, especially among people who are short on status in their dwelling and possessions. The less affluent woman has nothing but her housekeeping to speak for her. Cleaning is the way she personalizes and asserts her own and her family's identity. "So they think at least I'm a decent housekeeper," said one resident of an Ithaca housing project. In Baltimore, the famed white marble steps worn down by ritual daily scrubbings are in a working-class neighborhood, not a posh one. But the well-to-do can be equally obsessed with their housekeeping. Estée Lauder "is pleased that her hardwood floors are shining, that there's no dust on the antique side table. 'I love everything shiny and clean . . . it shows you care,'" she told one interviewer.

Cleaning can also serve a cathartic function. It takes a crisis to make some of us compulsive housekeepers. During the hostage situation with Iran, Mary Lopez, mother of one of the hostages, controlled her depression by concentrating on picking up tiny bits of lint and dust. And when her husband was dying, writer Joan Gould kept her house from going to pieces to keep herself "from going to pieces."

Different dirt offends different people. Some people are obsessed with laundry, never allowing one family member's clothes to be washed with another's. Others focus on floors, kitchen counters, the inside of the refrigerator, mirrors, windowsills, toilets, or the ring around the bathtub. Some people are more fastidious in one room than another, especially parents of teenagers, who are finding it easier to condone *matter* out of place in their children's rooms than to deal continually with *anger* out of place.

But when cleaning is obsessive, it could be motivated by the repressed memory of past humiliations. Being a model housekeeper is an attempt to be perfect, because only then can one be loved. Beth admits she cleans for fear of contempt. She and her husband Chris, a missile engineer, and their two children, Donnie, seven, and Dana, six, are the family that casting directors must have in mind when they say, "Get me Middle America." Their home is in a neat subdivision in America's heartland. Beth, who works part time in a carpet store, is never idle. She knits and makes Christmas wreaths and flower arrangements—work that takes a lot of patience. But her major way of relating to her home is via housekeeping. Neatness was drilled into her and sometimes punished into her by parents who "kept things nice and wanted me to."

She remembers all too vividly her childhood when, if she forgot to make her bed, her father would strip the sheets off. When she was in a hurry to go out on a date and left clothes on her bed, her father took all the clothes out of her drawers and dumped them on the floor. She had been warned. Today, Beth is cleaner and more orderly than her parents. "I want everything perfect," she admitted. Her obsession drives her to empty ashtrays while people are still using them, clear the table while the family is still eating, and wash dishes before she puts them in the dishwasher. The rituals of Beth's war on disorder—brushing her teeth five and six times a day, having the beds made before nine, the table set for dinner and dinner started in the morning, making sure the kids put away one toy before taking out another—are exhausting her now that she works, but she can't change her habits.

She is raising her kids the way she was raised. Recently, she said, she had had it with Dana. She dumped everything in one of Dana's messy drawers on the floor and told her to fold it; if it wasn't folded right she would dump it again. "Dana's just like me already," said Beth proudly. "She told me when she gets married, she wants everything to be just perfect."

The Rescue Squad

It's easy to recognize the rescuers. They subscribe to the *Old House Journal,* support their local preservation efforts, and always seem to be stripping paint off something. The urge to preserve, rescue, and reconstruct is basic in humans. Repairing toasters, renovating houses, and restoring whole towns are all related to the need to conserve. Today, with housing prices out of sight, you can *double* your pleasure by saving money while salvaging a house. This twofold satisfaction has turned the urge to rescue houses into a boom activity, with close to a million people across the country involved in rehabing, restoring, and renovating—and their ranks are increasing every day.

"After thirty years of married life," said Harold Proshansky, "I realize that my wife and I are constantly engaged in a hidden practice. Every environment we pick to live in always has a lot wrong with it. We have to fix it up and change it. So I have rebuilt houses, ripped out partitions, extended bedrooms." "I love seeing something really depressing made into something beautiful," said British designer Jenny Hall after turning a decrepit 140-year-old house into an *Architectural Digest* subject. "Whenever I've finished putting one house right," she said, "I long to rescue another."

To rescue a house one must have a missionary's faith that the old place is worth redeeming. Restoration is part of a three-step process of "birth, death, and redemption," said geographer J. B.

Jackson. First there has to be a golden age, remote enough in time for us not to have any memory of it, which may account for the current rise in the popularity of Victorian—a style that is finally sufficiently distant to inspire nostalgia. Then there has to be a period of decline and neglect. When the house has decayed sufficiently to take on a sacred quality it is ready to be rediscovered and gentrified.

Some rescue operations garner more respect than others. It is not enough to rehabilitate a house. You have to "rehab right" (as the book of the same name advises). That means fixing up the house without sacrificing the sacred original architectural assets. Although lower-middle-class homeowners have been responsible for most improvements in urban housing since the late 1940s, middle- and upper-middle-class people outnumber them in rehabing right. As one back-to-the-city expert explained it, blue-collar people have had their fill of deteriorating housing; their dream is *new* housing, where the plumbing works. They don't care to restore the past—they want to improve on it. Their mission is better housing. Not concerned with authenticity, they "rehab wrong," at least by the standards of the gentrifiers. Rehabing *wrong* means gift wrapping the house in a fake stone façade, adding elements and colors that weren't present in the original; doing *artificial restoration*—modernizing—which may *save* the house but also *transforms* it into a new house. It may take a few decades before these houses are considered sacred vernacular architecture and worth saving.

The Master Builders

"The fellow that owns his own home is always just coming out of the hardware store," said folk humorist Frank McKinney Hubbard over fifty years ago, and it still holds true. According to the Do-It-Yourself (DIY) Institute, more than four out of five Do-It-Yourselfers are homeowners, and in 1982 for the first time more money was spent on Do-It-Yourself supplies than on new housing; $28 billion to be exact. Do-It-Yourself home improvements (home repairs and additions, painting, papering, floor laying, bathroom remodeling, lawn and garden projects) have become such big business that more than three out of four American households did a major project in 1981. Add to that all the stitching of pillows and curtains being done at home and you realize we're not *passive* consumers.

Many of the DIYers today are working women who could afford outside help but can't stay home and wait for repair people. It's easier to do it themselves. But while a growing number of women are taking on heavy-duty chores, there are still many more men than women wielding skill saws and climbing ladders. Do-It-Yourself is the only home improvement activity in which men outnumber women. Men do 62 percent of home repairs and improvements; and in spite of all the ladies' garden clubs and flower-arranging courses, men do almost two-thirds of the lawn and garden work. Perhaps this accounts for the fact that when men talk about their homes, they invariably talk about the work they have put into them, not what they look like. Because research and observation have shown that women still make most of the style decisions and men still do most of the installations, Lowe's, a major Do-It-Yourself chain, lays out its stores with carpet, wallpaper, lighting fixtures, vanities, and mirrors on "the women's side," and bulk lumber, electronics, and plywood "on the men's side." Hardware, a unisex category, is along the back wall.

With hammer and nail, needle and thread, rake and trowel, the armies of home improvers put blood, sweat, and tie beams into their houses—and what they get out of it is a lot more than a new bathroom, an enlarged kitchen, or an afghan. They get pride and a sense of control, a feeling of "I made this happen." Building a deck may not be as momentous as having a baby or building a bridge, but there is still a tremendous sense of accomplishment. Do-It-Yourself projects are not just money savers but stress reducers, providing, said one market researcher, "some tangible accomplishment in a world increasingly moving away from specific, completed tasks." "I think the initial impetus of Do-It-Yourself projects is saving money," said planner Clare Cooper Marcus, "but the conscious—or unconscious—payoff is a much deeper connection to one's dwelling. You look at something and say, 'I made that' and you feel proud of it."

Jason is a New York lawyer with two sets of tools: a small set in a toolbox in his city apartment and the heavy duty stuff lining the basement walls of his country house. Jason has a list of projects that will take him a year of weekends in the country. Insulate the basement, build patio furniture, repair the deck, finish the attic—in addition to his landscaping chores. He could afford to hire professionals to do some of the work but he'd rather do it himself. You might call it a family ritual. While his country neighbors cook out on store-bought barbecues, Jason cooks the fish he catches on a brick barbecue pit he built himself. It was his first project after he and his wife Helene took possession of their country house. While Helene moved in on the kitchen cabinets with scissors and shelf paper, Jason paced out the spot for the barbecue, just as his dad had done thirty-five years before.

"I always built things with my father," said Jason. "It was something that brought us together and it was fun. When I got married the first time, we had a small apartment. I built bookcases. One of the reasons I wanted to buy a house was that I was tired of sawing wood in the bathtub. So we bought a house in the suburbs with a basement where I could have a workshop. I did a tremendous amount of work in that house. I did it to save money, but I liked doing it. I worked like hell and I got a big kick out of it."

The Garden Brigade

In a section of Honolulu where the landscaping is decidedly Occidental, one house stands out for the formal Japanese garden in its front yard. In New Jersey, a landscape architect has planted acres of sunflowers in the fields beside his house. In a modest community in Rockland County, New York, owners of a bungalow have monogrammed their rock garden with a big S inlaid in pebbles. In Stonington, Maine, a woman has created an elaborate lily pond behind her house.

If we can believe a recent survey of our leisure activities, Americans spend more time gardening than making love. Perhaps that's because gardening has something for everyone. It provides a wealth of beautiful and exotic natural materials with which to experiment and express oneself. And judging from the enormous number of members in garden clubs and begonia societies, it's an extremely sociable endeavor, although at the same time it's a fine way to get solitude—even if portable telephones threaten to intrude on the tranquillity that gardens have traditionally offered.

You can buy into this activity for $1.99, which will get you a young geranium, or you can plow a million into rearranging a few acres artfully as one gentleman landscaper is now doing in Bedford, New York. Both an outdoor and an indoor sport, gardening is a science, and an art form with a bountiful harvest of history and folklore.

It is usually assumed that people garden because they like the activity of it, but there are those for whom the payoff is the end result. Beyond the joy of exchanging bulbs and know-how, getting righteous backaches and status thorn wounds, going on garden tours and finding seed catalogs in your mailbox, there is pragmatism. For those who like their activities to be productive, without too long a wait there is an abundance of parsley, sage, rosemary, and zucchini to share with neighbors; for those who seek delight and centerpieces, there are 5,700 varieties of flowers; and for the competitive, there are beefsteak tomato contests and specimen tree collecting.

"I love seeing things grow, effortlessly," said one of New York's more affluent rooftop gardeners who specializes in corn and tomatoes. "I don't have any money, but I love beautiful things," explained a cable TV repairwoman whose specialty is begonias. Creating a view, replacing the tarmac or the wilderness with a planned landscape in the backyard is what motivates many other people to pick up trowel and hoe.

According to one team of researchers, the attraction of plants is almost primordial, a genetic imprint dating from prehistory when vegetation was essential to human survival. Most people find green things as endlessly fascinating as fire and water and caves, although it is only since the seventeenth century when the pleasure garden, the flower garden with no other utility but beauty, superseded the garden of vegetables, spices, and 400-odd medicinal herbs.

"I think of my garden as a *place, not an activity,*" said Rachel Kaplan who, with her husband Stephen, a psychology professor at the University of Michigan, has been studying the psychology of interest in nature. "I like to look out the window at our garden as I write," she said. She and her husband garden not for the exercise or activity but for what they call "the content," the end result, the garden itself. "We look on it as a park, a source of fascination."

Nature fascination accounts in large measure for the appeal of gardening, and fascination tends to increase as people move from growing vegetables, the first choice of the novice gardener, to flowers, the genre of the more experienced gardener. To garden successfuly requires a certain amount of technical information, but as you become more proficient, you can learn from the experience. "Keeping a garden makes you aware of how delicate, bountiful, and easily ruined the surface of this little planet is," wrote playwright Arthur Miller. "Parsley won't grow in one part [of the soil] but loves another."

There is some indication that the fertilizer people choose may be an important clue to their attitudes about gardening. "The question is the same each year—what method should we use?" said Miller. People who use *chemical* fertilizers seem to have more control over their success but less pleasure, while people who use at least some *organic* fertilizers have less certainty but more pleasure—a greater sense of closeness to nature. Having everything under control is not necessarily the peak experience in gardening. The thrill for many people is the tension between what you know and what you realize you have yet to learn. Demonstrating this, Arthur Miller said, "You simply have to face the moment when you must admit that the lettuce was planted too deep or was not watered enough."

There is no disputing that many people have a disposition and ability to garden, truly enjoying the experience and repeating it often. But it is questionable whether the cultivation of grass has the same motivations. The interest that neighbors take in one another's front lawns and the embarrassment caused by weeds is fabled. The derision heaped on the lawn at the turn of the century by Thorstein Veblen, who called it a glorified cow pasture, did nothing to diminish its popularity. Crabgrass was always good for a laugh when Jack Paar was the host of the "Tonight Show." According to Chemcare, a major lawn care company, there are 25 to 30 million homes with lawns in America and their owner-caretakers, mostly Mow-It-Yourselfers, spend about $1.3 billion per year on lawn care.

Why do they bother? Because a front yard is a "national institution," like having a Bible in the house, said J. B. Jackson. The care you give it "is an index of the taste and enterprise of the family who owns it." And its appearance seems to be a neighborhood affair. People will put off other needs, and make sacrifices for their lawns that would seem out of proportion to their importance.

In his study of the social meanings of suburban housing, Carl Werthman found that homeowners spent money they could barely afford and months of weekends bringing up their lawns; failure to do so was taken by their neighbors as a sign that they didn't care what others thought of them. "Since other people are needed to confer status, and status is the basis of self-respect," lawns take on special significance. If you don't maintain your lawn, you lose not only status but you also risk losing equity. The hidden motivation in lawn care is an attempt to *maintain property values*. One shaggy lawn, said Werthman, can "contaminate the status" of every home and family nearby and send resale values plummeting. Thus, the avid interest in the lawn may not be a disposition to garden as much as a disposition to be a respected citizen—and to protect one's nest egg. But that's part of personality and preference, too.

8

Psyching Out Collecting

Collecting on the Couch

■

The Educated Eye

■

Open and Closed Cases

■

Security Is a Warm Collection

■

Quest versus Bequest

■

Collecting as Fun and Games

■

Collection as Decor

■

Amassing Social Currency

■

The Profit Motive

J OAN BAEDER SPENDS her
days on urban safari in the jungle of executive headhunting and her
nights and weekends at home in a lush suburb of Los Angeles amid
hearts-and-flowers wallpaper and lacy pillow shams. Her walls
and shelves runneth over with collections of things that have a
feminine sensibility—quaint children's books, paper dolls, Victorian toys and games, floral paintings, nineteenth-century stitching
samplers, crocheted and lace hearts, naïve paintings, and her
latest interest, images of women. She has more quilts than she has
moods, more old silk flowers than days in the year, more recent
acquisitions than closets for them. And still she keeps acquiring.
"Why?" asked her housemate of three years. "But, honey," Joan
explained patiently, "you don't understand. I'm a collector. When
you're a collector, buying is a continuous thing. You don't stop just
because the wall is done."

In a Victorian mansion in Northern California, the walls are
never done. Every two years Dolph Gotelli, a design professor at
the University of California at Davis, mounts a Christmas display
that surpasses any department-store extravanganza and opens his

house to tours. Gotelli is probably the foremost collector of Santa Claus iconography in the world. His aim is to keep the image of Santa alive. Meanwhile, he keeps his own adrenaline coursing in a constant quest for yet another St. Nick and the accompanying high he feels in the presence of another Find. The goal is to avoid that terrible sinking feeling that comes when something he wants gets away. "It's like alcoholism," he said, describing the need to spot and acquire.

In San Francisco, they call Lillian Williams "Lillian Quatorze," after Louis XIV, during whose reign Versailles was completed. An avid collector of eighteenth-century furniture, clothing, and ephemera, Lillian has turned her compulsive need to collect and be surrounded with beautiful old things into a total way of life. The proprietor of four shops in San Francisco, one that sells antiques, and three that are decorated with them, Lillian has put her obsession to work for her, full time. "I couldn't be a dentist and do this on weekends," she said. Lillian wants desperately to be an eighteenth-century woman, with operatic accompaniment. Each of the rooms in her thirty-room Sausalito mansion is named after a favorite opera—the Rigoletto ballroom, Manon Lescaut bedroom, Barber of Seville veranda, La Traviata greenhouse and, for her good friend Luciano, the Pavarotti gallery, all of which she has decorated in the spirit (if not the letter) of the opera, using appropriate background music on tape and mannequins in costume.

It has been estimated that one out of every three Americans collects something. Of all the ways we acquire possessions, collecting is the most *active,* and it's as much a disposition as cleaning or building or gardening. It involves gathering, discriminating, making decisions—"I want this not that"—and a strong sense of ownership. Collectors are constantly appraising their things—pruning here, grafting there, reorganizing, trading up, or deaccessioning. The root of collecting is selectivity. A collector is not the same as an accumulator, who saves everything indiscriminately, or a furnisher who acquires chairs, books, cookware for everyday use. Usefulness, in the traditional sense, is rarely the goal of a collector. The collection is a special entity with its own natural order and raison d'être.

"Three of anything is a collection," quipped *Vanity Fair* editor Leo Lerman. To qualify as a collection, the items collected must have some similarity and interrelationship. By being part of the collection, each piece is transformed from its original function of toy, icon, bowl, picture, whatever, into an object with new meaning—a member of an assemblage that is greater than the sum of its parts.

Motivations for collecting have been variously described as curiosity, compulsion, competitiveness, delight in discovery, nostalgia, ancestor worship, miserliness, a reaction to a complex world, anal erotism, and instinct. "I'm a compulsive saver; it must stem from an insecure childhood," wrote one woman in response to an article on compulsive collecting. "Most of us collect for profit," said a *New York Times* reporter. "Money is out, things are in," said another journalist. "There are just three reasons for collecting—and always have been," observed critic Russell Lynes: "love, greed, and ambition."

Collecting on the Couch

Does anyone in the social sciences have a clue to the nature of collecting? Lita Furby, a psychologist, has done a major survey of the literature on "possession," and a number of studies of people and things. One of the problems in studying collecting, said Furby, is that you can't do it in a laboratory with standard methods. It is hard to establish simple cause-and-effect relationships when collecting is so tangled up with an individual's personal and social history. How much weight should a researcher give to the fact that Joan Baeder was praised often by her ex-husband, an artist, for her "eye for beauty"? Is it significant that Dolph Gotelli learned very young that there was no Santa Claus? And how relevant is it that Lillian Williams talks about her collecting—"the tracking, stalking, and haunting," of the past—with the same words she uses to describe going hunting with her father when she was a child?

Most of the theorizing about collecting done in the late nineteenth and early twentieth centuries leaned heavily on an "instinct for acquisition." Charles Darwin observed in his autobiography that his own interest in naming plants and collecting coins, shells, seals, franks, and minerals was well developed by age eight, and he concluded his leaning was "innate"—inborn, not bred.

The instinct to collect was thought to be related to the animal instinct for hoarding food. But most animals don't hoard year-round. They hoard food in winter when it is scarce in order to survive. How could the mania for stamp collecting, which swept the world after the introduction of prepaid postage in England in 1840, be related to chipmunks stuffing seeds in their cheek pouches, squirrels burying nuts in the forest, and bears, wolves, and foxes stashing away food, or a leopard hanging a carcass in a tree for a month of snacking? Surely the survival instinct had nothing to do with the ad placed in *The Times* of London in 1841: a woman wanted enough canceled stamps to paper her dressing room. How many letters could she mail with a roomful of canceled stamps? There was as much mileage to be gotten from those stamps as there is nourishment in millionaire Malcolm Forbes's collection of Fabergé eggs.

One turn-of-the century psychologist linked collecting to the *impulse to construct* that is found in many birds and rodents. Bowerbirds may be the most prodigious and tasteful collector-builders in the animal world. Each species is identified by its particular color preference—for red, white, black, or pink—in construction materials. But can you really compare a bowerbird to the early birds who catch the worm-eaten antiques at flea markets? The bowerbird's collecting activity is genetically built in. It's a very purposeful mating game assuring the perpetuation of the species.

In 1900, Caroline Burk, an educational psychologist, was certain she had proved an instinct for collecting, based on a study of more than 1,200 California children. She found that all but 10 percent of them collected *something*, from cigar bands to rocks, leaves, marbles, and buttons. Burk counted 300 different types of collections. One boy alone had fifty-five collections. Surely it must be instinctive, she reasoned. Her theory was cited and recited whenever collecting was discussed. Not until 1927 was the instinct for collecting debunked by a newer study which found a sizable decrease in children's collecting activity from Burk's day. During the intervening years, a number of pursuits, including the movies, had come along to vie for young people's attention. If instinct was the root of collecting, wouldn't there be as much collecting among children in the 1920s as there was in 1900? Perhaps collecting wasn't instinctive at all, but a socially stimulated activity.

Meanwhile, Freud linked the impulse to gather, collect, and

hoard to the child's fascination with its bodily wastes. In the Freudian view, a child moves from the pleasure it gets from its excretions and the power it gets from holding them back, through a stage of repression and disgust in the name of cleanliness, to playing with mud—sanitized excreta—and then with sand and putty. When pebbles, marbles, buttons, and fruit pits are substituted and arranged in an orderly manner, he reasoned, a collector is born. If the collector graduates to the next phase—hoarding bright, shiny coins—the evolution to miser is complete. Thus, according to Freudian scholar Ernest Jones, "all collectors are anal erotics, and the objects collected are nearly always typical copro-symbols"— symbols of feces.

Very interesting, said Ernest Beaglehole, author of the 1932 classic, *Property: A Study in Social Psychology.* He found Freud's theory of anal erotism ingenious—but unproven. And he didn't buy the instinct theory either. He didn't think instinct explained collecting any more than instinct explained the mania for crossword puzzles that preoccupied Americans during the winter of 1923–1924. No, Beaglehole had another theory. *Grasping,* he said, is the germ of acquisitive behavior. The impulse to grasp objects is in the service of nutrition. The infant's first focus is the mother's breast or the bottle. Growing curiosity and interest lead the child to pay attention to almost anything in its environment which has no repulsive features. From there it is imitation and suggestion that lead a child into the "habit complex" called collecting. Grasping is instinctive, but collecting is a culturally determined activity. It is stimulated, reasoned Beaglehole, "by rivalry, by the desire for that admiration and approval lavished upon the child with better and more complete collections than his fellows—by the desire to achieve, to exploit, to gain superiority and power which is only the reverse side of social approval." Through collections, said Beaglehole, "we taste the joys of superiority, power, and self-esteem."

But what about love? Over and over again we read articles attributing collecting to love—the chemical attraction between collectors and the objects of their desire. "Blind love seems to be the tie that binds collectors together," said one writer. "It's like, well, having a love affair," said another.

The Educated Eye

Saying that love is what draws collectors to their collectibles "is no better than saying people eat food because it tastes good," said Nicholas Humphrey. Humphrey believes he has found a biological basis for collecting that is very similar to bird watching or what the English call "locospotting"—the habit of collecting observations. Birds, plants, license plates, airplanes, and pub signs all have their dedicated spotters who risk life, limb, and pocketbook to collect *observations,* just as collectors go out on a limb for objects.

Despite the emphasis on accumulation and ownership in collecting, said Humphrey, the real thrill of collecting is in the *spotting* and *classifying.* He believes that instead of being an innate tendency to acquire objects, collecting is an adaptive tendency to classify the environment. "Biologists generally assume that most behavior patterns they observe in animals are functional," he wrote. "The traits necessary to be a good collector were once traits necessary for survival." Whether they use the sense of smell or sight, or a combination, "Animals that devised precise methods of classification and enjoyed classifying became good candidates for survival because when they recognized objects they could anticipate events and plan behavior." To classify, they had to be able to distinguish essential characteristics. Many humans have highly developed senses of observation, too. "Collectors of objects as well as collectors of observations are in it not for the material satisfaction but for the mental thrill it gives them. . . . They search for, and value, differences," said Humphrey.

Owning satisfies the ego, but classifying is its own reward, like solving a puzzle or doing a difficult mental exercise. You can spot the spotters—they always talk about noticing minute differences that helped them select their prizes. Invariably, the eye is mentioned. "I have a tardy eye," said one collector, describing how it took a little while for her to get used to 1980s art. "My eye, uncontrollable, is constantly reconnoitering the terrain for any bit of blue and white, Celadon, monochrome," said journalist Bernard Kalb, a Chinese porcelain enthusiast, writing about his "endless affair with my own femme fatale, Lady Porcelain."

The eye is crucial in collecting because, like infants who delight in discovering stimuli that are different, but only slightly, from what they know, collectors get their biggest kicks from seeing new variations on familiar themes. A Santa slightly different from the thousands of Santas he already owns is what Dolph Gotelli looks for on his search and acquire missions to thrift shops, antiques stores, and flea markets all over the world. In a remote London doll museum he spotted his most prized piece, a "nodder," a hundred-year-old wind-up Santa that nods its head. While scanning the crowded shop he made eye contact with the rarity that had eluded him for years—there it was on a high shelf. How did he notice it? By using the same highly developed discriminatory powers that an elephant uses to spot its favorite berries on the mukaita tree, that the koala uses to spot eucalyptus leaves, and that vegetarian animals use to select out their preferred grasses, shoots, barks, leaves, seeds, fungi, and lichens. He compared the properties of the Santa at hand with Santas he had known.

Spotting has always been important to human survival. In landscapes that might appear empty or monotonous to outsiders, pastoralists and aborigines are extremely sensitive to minute differences in vegetation, animal tracks, and signs of human presence. For them, said Amos Rapoport, "the 'empty' landscape becomes very rich." These same powers of observation can be called into service by a collector to distinguish delft from Staffordshire, Hepplewhite from Sheraton, a Ghiordes prayer rug from a Ladik, and better than that, to outwit the professionals.

Spotting something first, or spotting what others have overlooked, is one of the peak experiences of collecting. A good eye helps in this, but so does the ability to put two and two together. There is more than luck involved in being in the right place at the right time. Most collectors do not stumble on their prizes by chance. Being able to predict the best fields for grazing, the direction the birds are flying, is part of the collectors' sensing apparatus—it requires study, training, intuition, the ability to make connections, and a keen intelligence, which may well be the most important trait of a collector. In fact, a study of young collectors showed that the more intelligent the children, the more collections they had.

Armand Hammer, one of the world's foremost art collectors, used his educated eye to outwit the Metropolitan Museum in the

1950s when it deaccessioned what was thought to be a fake Sir
Thomas Lawrence painting—a huge nineteenth-century portrait
of two children. The painting seemed too unbalanced to be the
work of a master. But Hammer had a hunch that the work was
authentic and did some research on its provenance. It seemed un-
likely to him that John D. Rockefeller, its former owner, and a man
with capable art advisers, would have bought a fake. So Hammer
"stole" the picture for a mere $2,700 at auction. After some resto-
ration work, it was discovered that the painting was unbalanced
because a third child had been painted out after the child's death.
When the repainted section was restored, "one of the great Lawrences of all time" was revealed.

Open and Closed Cases

A major difference among collectors is whether they collect
for completion or for repetition. For some collectors getting a
complete set of something is a major motivation. Once the set is
rounded out, it is auctioned off or donated it to a museum. Francis
Garvan, one of the great Americana collectors, asked his agent to
make a list of every major piece of American furniture, silver, pew-
ter, brass, iron, and china so he could go after them one by one.
He eventually gave the collection, which took twenty years to acquire, to Yale. Ryohei Ishikawa recently won a big prize in philately
for putting together what is, in the words of one collector, "the
most phenomenal collection of stamps in U.S. history." Then he
promptly sold his collection. The search was over. It was time to
embark on a new pursuit.

Success after a long quest can be a terrible letdown. For
three years, thousands of people who read Kit Williams's *Mas-
querade* followed clues and dug holes all over the British Isles in
search of the jeweled rabbit buried by the author. "I felt right dejected," said the man who finally found it. "It was all over. There
was nothing to live for." Finding the final object is a kind of death
for the collector, said Jean Baudrillard. It's the end of passion. "Let
us congratulate the person who does not find the last piece," he
said.

The beauty of many collections is their open-endedness. The
series is never complete—like a harem, said Baudrillard. And the

collector is "the master of the secret seraglio," at home in "the bosom of his objects." There is always another prize to be found, giving each successive conquest an addictive quality. "I'm a compulsive buyer," explained New York designer Robert Metzger, who collects objects covered in scaly shagreen—untanned sharkskin in washed-out greens, blues, and grays—which was popular in the 1920s. "When I see a piece I like I feel a tremendous sense of excitement," said Metzger. "I have to have it. Buying it makes my day. I bring it home and put it on my night table. The next day, I look at it a lot. Then I put it in my curio cabinet. It takes another day before I lose interest in it." And the hunt starts all over again.

There are always more hunters than desirable prey and so the competition can be quite vicious. But often the ruthless traders who delight in outwitting one another, who, as Bernard Kalb described, "have lied and cheated to throw a competitor off the scent" of a vase, have nurturing instincts, too, believing it's their mission to save and preserve objects and ways of life. The goal is not to possess, but to rescue. It was partly the urge to preserve that motivated private collectors such as Henry Ford, John D. Rockefeller, Francis Garvan, Henry Francis du Pont, and others to lead the way in preserving Americana and interesting museums in historic preservation.

"I'm a rescue service," said Lillian Williams. "It is gratifying to find things in disrepair and then breathe life into them. I am a custodian. I have an obligation to restore things and put them in good hands." Whether or not she gets pleasure from rescuing because she still feels remorse for breaking one of her mother's antique dolls when she was five, she doesn't feel like the *owner* of her things, just the conservator. "I have chairs that are demented and twisted and broken and legless and armless and they've all been restored because my husband and I are fanatical about restoring things. And restoring them correctly. . . . I am always desperate to find homes for my things; they're orphans, abandoned, lost. And our house is the orphanage." Should a museum send out an SOS for eighteenth-century armoires, *lits à la Polonaise*, harpsichords, candelabra, bonnets, dolls, and authentic silk stockings of the period, said Lillian, she would gladly donate her booty and start all over.

Security Is a Warm Collection

The repetitive aspect of collecting is, like all compulsions, a way of feeling in control. "Everyone tries to develop programs to control life. Some are built in. Some are habit," said Swedish psychologist Rikard Küller. "Collecting is imposing your will. 'I must choose, I must control, I must collect. I must have that object.' By buying it, it is in your possession. Like compulsive eating. The basic mechanism," no matter what you collect, he said, "is an attempt to control anxiety."

If the ability to control an object is, as Lita Furby believes, the "central defining dimension of possession," controlling a whole set of things should be even more satisfying. "You feel insecure, you don't have control, so you amass a whole bunch of something and feel secure," she said. The control you have over your collection is different from the control you have over ordinary household things. It's more total. Designating a possession as part of a collection changes it from an object that anyone in the family can use to an object of value in the collector's *exclusive* jurisdiction.

By calling your six flower prints a collection, you build a protective wall around them. Would your sister-in-law expect you to give her a print to hang in her guest room if it were part of The Collection? Children may have to share their toys, and pass their clothes down to younger siblings, but what unfeeling parent would require a child to share a glass animal from The Collection? A pebble in a collection is no longer an ordinary pebble but the *special pink pebble,* and in the transformation process the object is beatified. The collector decides who may touch The Collection and how it will be displayed. The collector decides when, if ever, coffee will be served in the cups and saucers from The Collection. Objects that would be inconsequential separately become powerful in a group. And their power reflects back on the collector who basks in the glory of The Collection. When it is on loan, it is on loan from "the collection of . . ."

Quest versus Bequest

But where there is power, there are power struggles. Many collections, especially those based on kitsch objects that aren't costly, are susceptible to outside intervention. Julia, for instance, collects artifacts decorated with American flag imagery. Julia's friends know that she collects Stars and Stripes. When they visit antiques stores and see a mug or cigar band with Old Glory screened on it, they think, "Julia would like that." If it isn't too expensive, they'll buy it and give it to her on her birthday, which is, not coincidentally, the Fourth of July. And occasionally it does please her. But Julia, like most collectors, can manage very nicely, thank you, without the intervention of a deus ex machina swooping in with some undiscriminating addition to her collection. Not that she's against sentiment. It's nice to be remembered, but *serious* collectors usually prefer to make their own selections. Butting in on another person's collection is like looking over the shoulder of a crossword puzzle aficionado and suggesting the answer to 23-across without being asked for help.

The reason some collectors resent these intrusions is that they enjoy the fishing as much as the catching; the foreplay as much as the consummation. Searching, spotting, inspecting, comparing, bidding, and bagging the kill are all part of the joy of collecting. Receiving the object of your dreams as a bequest, without the quest, short-circuits the pleasure.

The circumstances of discovery can also affect the pleasure. Certain collectors prefer buried treasures to easily found ones. Sally, a Boston collector of Americana, is admittedly "dying for a pair of Ammi Phillips portraits, really good ones." Phillips was an itinerant painter in the early nineteenth century. Would it make any difference to Sally whether she found the paintings on her doorstep—as a gift from a benefactor—or discovered them herself? "Oh, there's no comparison," she said. "If you found them on your doorstep the whole discovery syndrome wouldn't be there. Having them handed to you takes the fun out. But if I found two of them in an antiques shop, I think I'd go out of my mind. I'd like to find them covered with dust in a little back road shop with an old man, chewing tobacco, minding the store. The fact that I had discovered them off the beaten track rather than on Madison Avenue would be thrilling." Even collectors who have advisers don't like anything acquired for them without their approval. Winterthur's Henry Francis du Pont had a valued adviser but was still known as "a personal purchaser" who scrutinized every prospective acquisition.

Because personal involvement is so important to collectors, they can rarely bond to inherited collections or collections acquired passively, as gifts, with the same intensity as collections acquired actively, by choice. Bill Blass found a saltshaker in the shape of an owl while stationed in England during the Second World War and kept it for a good-luck charm. Over the years friends who didn't know what to give the man who seemed to have everything gave him some 500 owls as gifts. "It got to the point where it was sickening," said Blass. "It got out of hand. The only thing to do was to give them all away and keep the original." Other "involuntary collectors" are equally unenthusiastic about their passively acquired collections. A woman who couldn't stem the tide of gift frogs admitted being ambivalent about them; a man who amassed sixty penguins as gifts said, "It's a good time to call it quits." The gift owl or frog or penguin bonds the recipient to the donor with ties of gratitude, but not necessarily to the owl or frog or penguin.

Collecting as Fun and Games

What keeps people involved in their collections is the reinforcement and camaraderie they get from being a member of the collectors club. The sociability factor in collecting is greatly underrated. The fields of endeavor that hook people and keep them hooked are those that have the most concomitant activities. And collecting—with its auctions, fairs, markets, conventions, exhibitions, guidebooks, lectures, and home-study courses—can hold its own with politics or sports as an all-consuming organizing system for one's life. Whether you pursue art or antiques, are a flea market follower or a collector of political memorabilia, there is a social circuit exclusive to your collection. And, frankly, being the conservator of a unique music box collection or the largest collection of souvenir state capital plates can be as effective in striking up a conversation as two Russian wolfhounds on a leash. The right collection, like the right dog, is an entree to people you would not ordinarily meet.

American antiques buffs can ladle punch from a Paul Revere bowl at Winterthur's annual Twelfth Night Gala. Art pottery collectors get together once a year at the Holiday Inn in Zanesville, Ohio, for the American Art Pottery Association convention. Dolph

Gotelli and other Santa collectors hold regular "Santa Summits." Lillian Williams and her husband Teddy are invited to special candlelight dinners in Paris with antiques dealers who all dress in period clothes. Sally, the folk art collector, attends the major folk art shows in Houston, New York, Philadelphia, and York, Pennsylvania. She and her husband spend summer weekends at country auctions. They even send their children to camp in Maine so they can antique on the way up to attend Visiting Day, always stopping in to see their special "picker," a dealer who supplies other dealers.

Robert Bechtel, a psychology professor at the University of Arizona, not only collects Arizona postmarks but also studies their history, gives lectures, attends meetings, leads expeditions to find lost towns—all on the trail of postmarks. The activities related to the collection are so engrossing that to stop collecting would be like relocating or retiring—one would be cut off from a whole constellation of events and friendships. "Our world is filled with exciting, stimulating, intellectual people," said one art collector. "If I stopped collecting, I'd grow old quickly."

Although dropping dead at an art auction, as one collector is said to have done, is not required to prove your dedication, art collecting can be a total way of life requiring you to put your taste on the line. If a controversial field like modern art is your enthusiasm, your selections can alienate your friends and relatives, even your friend at the bank. But there are rewards.

Modern art, if played to the hilt, can keep a collector's Museum of Modern Art calendar filled seven days a week. Time spent tracking down and making the purchase is just a fraction of the time spent living *la vie en art*. The language must be studied and vocabulary built. Collecting art is never again having to worry about making conversation at a party. "What do ordinary people talk about?" wondered one art collector who talks art on visits to artists' studios, at vernissages, preopening dinners, postopening soirees—and on the analyst's couch. Speaking the language badly is the tipoff to people in the field about your lack of expertise. If beginners refer to difficult art as "avant-garde" or "tough"—decidedly retro language—and ask "Where are the loft parties?" they might as well turn in their Rauschenberg lithos and go back to buying LeRoy Neiman posters. They will not make it in the hard-knock world of modern art collecting. This is a milieu built on scholarship. But don't let that worry you; getting your course credit is more fun than Christmas in Fort Lauderdale. Basic training in collecting requires steeping yourself in specialty magazines and participating in the ritual Tuesday evening openings and Saturday afternoon gallery walk-a-thons. Experts encourage beginning collectors to study before buying. They want you to send your eye to college, so to speak. "Spend your initial funds . . . on books and travel," said one media adviser. Then, a small starter purchase of a drawing, getting on gallery mailing lists, and becoming "a friend" of a few museums will plug you right in to art collecting's social network.

Recognizing that collectors are not born but can be made, the art community does its best to develop collectors by enticing them with prepackaged art-and-camaraderie experiences. In 1981, fifty people were invited by New York's New Museum (an exhibition space catering to art so new the paint has hardly dried) to put some fun in their lives by joining Art Quest: A Contemporary Collectors Forum. The $1,000 membership fee entitled members to ten meetings a year, six at the homes of other collectors; at least four special days of visits to artists' studios with curators present to discuss the artists' work; meetings with artists, critics, museum people; a tip sheet on hot exhibits; discounts on art, membership, and admission fees; a chance to buy limited edition prints available only to members; and a hot line to an art expert for advice. After all this grounding, it's your eye, scholarship, shrewdness, devotion, charisma, and attendance record that will carry you along.

Even if you missed the Jackson Pollack opening at the Beaubourg in Paris, the Craft, Art, and Religion Seminar at the Vatican, the recent Documenta show in Kassel, West Germany, the Zeitgeist in Berlin, and the unfurling of Christo's outer island project in Miami, you can still get in on the upcoming salute to U.S. art in Lucerne, the Venice Biennale, or take a trip down the Nile with a Harvard guide.

"Collecting is a richer context for travel," said dealer Holly Solomon. "It gives you an international family." Wherever you go there are important collectors and dealers to visit—people who will not only show you their etchings but also offer advice on the best doctors and the best tortellini. One of the satisfactions of the art trail is hobnobbing with artists. If you become friendly enough, you might receive a painting for your birthday. This might be the only gift of art a collector would welcome, and a fairly rare one.

Collection as Decor

While the social aspect of collecting has its satisfactions, the end product of all this looking and learning is taking possession of the prizes. If nothing else, you can decorate with the things you collect. The "decorating factor," as art historian Joseph Alsop called it, is very much an issue in collecting. Should you or shouldn't you use a collection as an element of decor? The collectors who have been derided the most on the art circuit are the ones who choose paintings as if they were wallpaper—to match a color scheme.

Actually, there is a long tradition of using collections as decor, at least in the West. In the East, during the high period of Chinese art, a collector wouldn't think of using his prized works of calligraphy to decorate his interiors. Collections were for the owner's delight or to show other collectors—treasures to be put away and protected. In the West, however, the tradition has been, if you've got it, flaunt it. Collections have been used as decor since the very beginning of art collecting in the fourth and fifth centuries B.C. In Greece and Rome, collectors were not above choosing sculpture according to the size of the niches in their houses. Today collectors buy according to the height and length of their walls and the dimensions of the elevators in their apartment houses.

The obsession with housing the collection dates back to the seventeenth century, when having a collection signified that one had leisure, arcane knowledge, and money—the marks of a true gentleman. But virtuosos and dilettanti, as collectors were called, needed places to display and store their curiosities—the sharks' teeth, stuffed serpents, amulets, carved cherry pits, books, inkwells, mathematical instruments, medals, and portraits. As the enthusiasm for collecting caught on, new types of rooms and furnishings—libraries, tribunes, galleries, cabinets, and vitrines— were invented to house them. Creating an appropriate setting for the collection has always been of paramount interest to the collector. In the decorating scheme, The Collection is the favorite child, the guest of honor, the teacher's pet.

One Victoriana collector in the Midwest admits hunting for months for a condominium with a ceiling high enough for his twelve-foot-tall Victorian cylinder desk. He finally settled for a place with a high-ceilinged stair landing to accommodate the piece. In California, a couple added a gallery to their house for their burgeoning collections. In Houston, collectors built platforms on two opposite ends of their large living room as display areas for their collection of French eighteenth-century marquetry chests. In Bel-Air, California, the Bob Newharts had cabinets designed to order for their Steuben glass collection, which started with a gift from Ethel Kennedy. And all over the country, collectors are shopping for proper cabinets for The Collection—or having them made. Sometimes it seems as if the people profiting the most from the collecting boom are the cabinetmakers. In New Orleans, the Manheim Galleries has created a ten-foot-long Chinese Chippendale-style breakfront that can be custom tailored to house as many as thirty-six Boehm birds. It retails for a mere $17,000.

The biggest enchilada, storage-wise, is the modern painting or sculpture, which can be as demanding a family member as any intransigent relative. In the 1960s when many New York art dealers opened up a new territory in SoHo's wide-open industrial spaces, paintings started expanding in all directions like rolled out pizza dough. To be a modern art collector required space. One had to renovate or move. Ben Heller was in the forefront of renovation-for-art's sake when he knocked out a wall in his apartment to make room for Jackson Pollock's *Blue Poles*. "It's ironic," said one decorator, "you can buy a million dollar apartment on Park Avenue, and still end up with only two fourteen-foot-long walls and one twenty-five-foot one."

Even though houses are shrinking, the dimensions of paintings continue to expand—especially the third dimension. Modern paintings are now pregnant with depth. When New York collectors Eugene and Barbara Schwartz bought Julian Schnable's "aggressive" painting with antler horns that protrude two and a half feet from the canvas, they were hard pressed to find a spot to hang it where someone walking by wouldn't be decapitated. The only spot in their apartment with enough clearance was opposite the collectors' bed. "I have to be careful when I go to the closet," Barbara Schwartz laughed. And a large percentage of interior design work seems to be a response to the challenge of creating "a background for art," a favorite phrase in house tour brochures. Sometimes it seems that collectors are more interested in housing The Collection than the family. People will move to find the right space for The Collection; they will enlarge the house by three feet if necessary for The Collection; they will sacrifice a closet to make space for an item in The Collection as one prominent Chicago collector did ("That is the epitome of loving art," remarked one Philadelphia woman on a private tour of Chicago collectors' homes); and they will spend thousands to relocate light switches and thermostats, and install special lighting for The Collection.

California architect Barry Berkus has received notoriety of late as a builder of housing for mingles. But for himself and his family, he has built a palatial modern house in Santa Barbara to share with his art collection. Expansive windows, changing floor levels, vaulted ceilings, swooping skylights, and interior balconies suitable for a Pope's appearances all give the house museum scale. "I designed the proportions of the house for the proportions of the paintings," said Berkus.

Once collectors give their art a suitable architectural hangar, they tend, as the Berkuses do, to open the house up on tours. It's like living in a museum. It puts you in the same league with such personal museum founders as Malcolm Forbes, Norton Simon, Rodin collector B. G. Cantor, Duncan Phillips of the Phillips Collection, and Roy and Dale Evans, who have made their silver saddles, gun collection, and stuffed horse, Trigger, available to the public. "A museum of one's own," said *Town & Country,* "for the impassioned collector, this is the crowning coup, the ultimate status, the surest collaboration with immortality."

Amassing Social Currency

You can't talk about collecting without mentioning status. Collections have been status vehicles for centuries. Of all the objects in the home, works of art—posters, prints, paintings—are the most class related. The University of Chicago study on *The Meaning of Things* found that upper-middle-class people were almost three times as likely as lower-middle-class people to cherish a work of art—whether expensive or inexpensive. Perhaps, said the researchers, this is because art has filtered down from churches and palaces to bourgeois homes as "symbols of affluence and sensitivity." Even Sotheby's isn't above hyping its sales with a reminder that collecting and status go together like love and marriage. In Victorian times, étagères, clock garnitures, bronzes, and silver tea services all "attested to the buying power of the owner," said a Sotheby's newsletter. The status game is still played with collections, although each collector may insist he or she is in it for noble motives while everyone else is collecting for status. It is obvious that status accrues to collections just as status accrues to people, through money. The most expensive collections and collectibles have the most status. And the value of an object depends on its rarity, condition, and beauty, the demand for it, and the status of the people who own it.

It does not detract from the meaning of collecting, said psychologist Walter Durost, "to admit that it may also serve other uses"—whether collecting helps one feel more powerful or whether it provides recognition one wouldn't otherwise be able to achieve. "Most collectors, especially those with new money, are in it for self-aggrandizement," said one jaded New York decorator who has had a hand in improving his clients' collections. Young doctors and lawyers change their collections as their situation improves, he said. "They start with Rhine wineglasses, move on to Doughty birds, and finally graduate to blanc de Chine—white Chinese porcelain."

In certain social sets, people who don't collect feel intimidated by those who do. "I feel pressured to collect," said a New York woman. "All my friends collect. It's one of the practical things to do these days. It's a good investment and it looks good when you entertain—you can talk about your collection." If your collection is large enough, you can invite the museum curator of porcelain or prints or Far Eastern art to dinner to discuss your collection and, one hopes, pronounce it worthy. Even the Philadelphia osteopath who *stole* his whole collection of small-scale art couldn't resist inviting a curator from the Philadelphia Museum of Art for cocktails. He risked being found out for the thrill of impressing someone not easily impressed.

One index of the social capital in a collection is the amount of inconvenience a collector will endure for the sake of it. In tribal Africa the status that accrues from a collection outweighs the discomfort of living with an overgrown inventory. In the African town of Sabo, the married women are ardent collectors of the brightly colored, enameled metal bowls made in Czechoslovakia. All businesswomen, they sink most of their profits from catering into amassing bowl collections, said anthropologist Abner Cohen. "These bowls have become the most important status symbol and women are ranked in status in proportion to the number of bowls they possess," he said. Some women have amassed hundreds of them which they wash and rearrange carefully in tall columns when they are expecting honored guests. "Space is scarce in Sabo," said Cohen, "and husbands are greatly annoyed by the mountains of bowls." The typical complaint, he said, is that "because of the bowls, a man cannot nowadays find space in his wife's room for even his morning prayers." But the women keep collecting because of the power they get from their bowl collections. The more bowls a woman accumulates, the more marriageable girls she will be able to attract to work in her business in return for a dowry of bowls when they marry.

The Profit Motive

Just as collectors deny collecting for status, they also deny collecting for money, although money is never far from their minds. Collecting, like gambling, can break a person. Painter James McNeill Whistler went bankrupt buying Chinese porcelains. But collecting can also be a comfortable nest egg. At a very pragmatic level, collecting is a way of feeling in control of the future, economically. Wouldn't you sleep better knowing your Chinese scrolls had been steadily rising in value since you started acquiring them; that the Grueby vase you paid $15 for at the church auction could be sold for $6,000? Collections are money in the bank—or the breakfront.

This fact has not escaped one couple who are active in Philadelphia museum circles. They were the talk of the New York art circuit recently when, apparently eager to indoctrinate their children, age thirteen to twenty-four, into the pleasures of picking art and profiting from it, they took them to New York for a long weekend of intensive art immersion. After gallery visits, treks to artists' studios, dinners with art aficionados, and the advice of consultants, each child was given an equally generous sum of money to spend as he or she pleased. In five years, so the story goes, the children will be rewarded according to how much their works have appreciated.

But collectors are forever declaring that they don't collect for money. "By and large, today's collectors do not choose their acquisitions for their potential increase in value through the years," said one journalist. "If they do appreciate, their owners say, it is a bonus." If collectors don't think about value, why are they constantly pricing their things; and what accounts for the phenomenal success of the price guides that tell people the market value of various collectibles? Do people study these guides only to learn how to recognize a steal when one is offered to them?

Sally, the folk art collector, doesn't deny the profit potential of her hobby. "I love the products of our collecting. I like adding new things. I only buy what appeals visually. It's exciting looking, making judgments. There's also the element of chance—like at the roulette table, one day you'll hit a winner." A winner? "We constantly check the values," she explained. "We read every auction book to see whether what we have is going up or going down. We never sell. But you know you could if you had to. Having made a good choice is thrilling. When something becomes valuable, you feel you made the right judgment. You spotted something that no one appreciated and then it went up in value." Never for a second did director Billy Wilder think of collecting as a hedge against inflation. "I don't *want* to sell it—do you sell your dog?" asked Wilder. If he didn't think about value, why did he reduce his collection of pre-Columbian art to his ten *finest* pieces? Why not his ten *favorite* pieces?

But not every buy is a good buy, a ticket to the collectors' pantheon. Early purchases made more from enthusiasm than from expertise can be embarrassments when one learns the fine points of a field. Condition, quality, rarity, and authenticity are constantly being assessed. The moment it is discovered that the beloved object is flawed, inferior, or a copy, it ceases to be valued in the same way it was originally. What was deemed exquisite yesterday is suddenly homely. Unless appropriate measures are taken, the devalued item threatens to devalue the owner as well.

Collectors must distance themselves from lesser pieces by disposing of them or disavowing them, announcing they are being retained in the collection for sentimental reasons. Reminiscing about the first piece of porcelain he ever bought, Bernard Kalb spoke of the disenchantment that came with his increased scholarship. "Occasionally I look at that vase and wonder how it could have aroused such lust. Now, I regard it affectionately as my ugly duckling."

As they demote their bad choices they promote their good ones, moving them to better positions in the house. There is more involved here than the satisfaction of having had $20/20$ art vision. The value of a painting or object is of paramount interest to collectors not because they plan to sell it immediately, but precisely because they plan to keep it. An item's value is an index to its quality just as a "Q" rating measures how recognizable a TV star is, or a Dun & Bradstreet measures how solid a business is. The higher the value of the object, the more honorable the collector.

Raina, a California art collector, is not unaware that her painting collection has been steadily rising in value. On Raina's coffee table is a thick and glossy book on New Realist painting. In the book are four paintings in Raina and Norman's collection. "We bought these works of art when the artists were unknown. Now ten of our paintings are pictured in different art books. It's fun because somebody who knows is saying that these artists made it. It affirms the fact that you had an insight, that you had a sense of taste in art or a sense of vision. You are a creator in your own right. I mean the artist is a creator, but the collector is a creator, too."

As Jean Baudrillard said in his essay on the art auction, the value of a painting reflects on the collector who becomes "the equal of the canvas itself" and a peer in the community of the privileged. Art creates not profit but legitimacy, "and it is with this that the art lover identifies."

Fear of Furnishing

N O ONE BUT the telephone man and landlady has ever set foot in the apartment of one otherwise gregarious New Yorker. Not even his best friend has seen it in the six years he has lived there. He suffers from an exotic syndrome that has no research funding and no celebrity benefit committee—fear of furnishing. People with this problem find it more satisfying to picture a penthouse than to risk botching it or having it fall short of their own expectations. The more severe their need to succeed, the less likely they are to start. "It's a matter of not lowering your standards," said Carson, a thirty-two-year-old hairdresser. "My father taught me never to buy things I couldn't afford and my mother taught me to be a perfectionist about my possessions. I know what I want to live with, and if I can't afford it, I won't settle for less."

A Westchester woman suffers from one of the most severe and prolonged cases of fear of furnishing. Hundreds of jonquils are beginning to bloom in the borders around Natalie and Harvey's five-bedroom custom contemporary. But inside the house, the living room is almost empty. Natalie and Harvey have been seeing a marriage counselor for some time. The problem is not sex or money or in-laws—the problem is furniture. For seven years Natalie has been unable to make any but the most makeshift decorating decisions in the living room and dining room. It would be easier to understand if Harvey, an amiable and successful insurance man, was difficult to please or tight with money. Or if Natalie wasn't a decorator. "My mother says it's a disgrace. I can order a whole house from bar cart to soup to nuts for a client, but for myself, I can't even choose a rug. I sent four rugs home on consignment and took them all back. I'm thirty-five, but up to now I have never taken the responsibility for furnishing my own home."

Natalie was still in college when she married the first time. "His parents had just died and he had a house full of furniture so I didn't have to make any decorating decisions," she said. "The only thing I bought was a bedspread and rug and I don't remember having any trouble doing that." In two years she was divorced and living with her mother again.

When she was twenty-four, she married Harvey, eight years older and "fully furnished." "I didn't have to buy a knife," said Natalie. "I just took my seven dresses, three pairs of jeans, and my makeup and moved into his bachelor apartment. I never had to go through that 'Who am I, am I English or French or Deco or Modern, and what is my favorite color?' bit. Even when our first child was born, I inherited a set of baby furniture from a relative." Harvey wanted Natalie to redo their apartment. Another young woman, more anxious to put her stamp on her home, might have jumped at the opportunity. But Natalie said, "Why bother? It's not permanent." Then Harvey suggested they buy a house. "That's when the trouble started," said Natalie.

"I spent three years looking at houses and couldn't find one I liked." In desperation Harvey took over the search. "One day," said Natalie, "he just walked out and bought this house without even consulting me. I cried for a year. I finally made a few haphazard decisions, like selecting some cheap carpet that I wouldn't mind replacing when I decided what I really wanted. When company dropped in we had to pull out folding chairs. I refused to entertain because I didn't like my home and it wasn't furnished.

"I guess my problem is that I want the house to be so wonderful. My nightmare is that when I actually do the house, it will be atrocious. Eventually, I realized I needed some help. I knew there must be a reason I couldn't make any decisions. So, we're in therapy. But I still haven't made much progress.

"Last year, my friend Elaine said she was going to do my house for me. The first thing she did was send me an antique English dining table and chairs. I said, terrific. But I postdated the check so I could change my mind. And I did. I sent them back. Elaine even ordered the jonquil bulbs for our garden and planted them. She said, 'You're going to thank me in March.' And she was right. They're beautiful," said Natalie. "But I can't help thinking, it would have been nice if I had done it myself.

"The house still needs much more. It's not comfortable. It's not warm. Harvey wants to know when we'll be able to invite people over. We're wined and dined in all our friends' homes and he wants to reciprocate. He doesn't care what style I do it in. He just wants it furnished."

To keep from making any decorating decisions, Natalie has developed a new habit of shopping in places that sell things she can't possibly afford. "I make sure I'm not even in my price range." Every once in a while it appears that Natalie is on the verge of a breakthrough. She'll say, "I know I should give up this idea that I have to be so perfect. Maybe I should swallow my pride and hire a decorator. Just to get it done. But, who would I pick? That means I've got to make another decision."

Decorating Interruptus

This is odd. While so many people are talking about decorating, the personally conducted tour of the house has gone the way of the five-cent cup of coffee. Wherever you go, you hear: "I'd love to invite you to dinner but the house isn't finished." When you do manage to get a foot in the door, you're invariably told, "Don't look. It's not done yet." So you avert your eyes. What's the big deal if the living room has no rug, the sofa has seen better days, and the dining room is furnished with a card table and folding chairs? They function, don't they?

That depends on how you define function. Since meaning is an aspect of function, certain connotations can make an object dysfunctional. And the meanings of tattered furniture and folding furniture are all wrong. When people present themselves before

others, said Erving Goffman, their performances "will tend to incorporate and exemplify the officially accredited values of the society." Anyone who has attended enough theatrical performances
knows that the bare stage look is usually a workshop production.
Did you ever see a sign in a model room that said, "Crystal chandelier coming when we can afford it"? Examples of finished-down-
to-the-last-ashtray spaces shown in model rooms and home magazines are supposed to give people decorating ideas. But the idea
that comes through strongest is "It's necessary to be finished."

For some people, finished is when there is no longer a pile of
sawdust in the middle of the room; for others, finished is when the
major furniture bills are paid and they can start taking vacations
again; and for still others, finished is when they work *in* the room
instead of *on* it. But for almost everyone, *finished* is a euphemism
for *right*—the way it ought to be. To be "finished" is to be ready to
be judged by those people whose approval matters—the boss, a
client, or new friends. As one woman who was in the midst of an
endless renovation said, "I can have people to dinner, but I can't
have a *serious* dinner party." This is not frivolous materialism. Her
embarrassment comes from an understanding of the rules of the
social game in our society.

Maintaining a proper front is a role requirement here. In England, a prince need not apply for princedom; no matter how he
conducts himself, he is still a prince. But in an open society, you
have to show an interest in your status and "give a clue that the
status is being maintained," said sociologist Martin Weglinsky. A
home furnished in keeping with one's "position" is such a clue. And
if you don't measure up, you are embarrassed, exposed, as if you
and your rooms were undressed. Entertaining in an empty room is
not measuring up to role requirements in the middle or upper middle class.

"If I like people, I don't care if they are living with orange
crates," said one fully furnished designer, democratically. But if
the people living with those crates believe they should be living
with teak casegoods, the forgiveness of others feels like condescension. For many reasons, it is rare these days for homes to be
ready for inspection and, therefore, embarrassment seems to be
rampant.

Getting on with one's furnishing has a lot to do with faith,
hope, and parity—with one's assessment of job security, future

earning power, and life expectancy. A widow in her seventies saw no hope for improvement in earnings and couldn't imagine living long enough to get her money's worth out of chairs she needed badly, so she refused to buy any. Not until she celebrated her eightieth birthday in good health did she have sufficent faith in her future to make the investment. Feelings of mortality can strike the young as well. A Los Angeles film producer couldn't bring herself to invest in decorating her home until she passed her thirty-eighth birthday. Her mother had died at that age and she had a super-stitious fear that she, too, would die at thirty-eight. Only after that birthday could she make a commitment to fixing up her home.

Some people don't start *or* finish personalizing because they lack commitment to a relationship, a neighborhood, a job, or a dwelling. Often they don't even realize that they are in a commit-ment crisis. Two psychologists hypothesized recently that com-mitment and decorating were linked. But, how to prove it? Not in a laboratory. They chose a college dorm instead. Where else can you find forty blank decorating slates?

During the second week of the fall semester and again nine weeks later, the researchers detailed how forty-one pairs of fresh-man roommates in a men's dorm at the University of Utah "per-sonalized" their rooms—classifying, counting, and photographing the walls over each student's bed. Nothing escaped the research-ers' scrutiny. Snapshots of a student's girl friend and family, peace posters, religious pictures, political cartoons, pictures of sunsets and art reproductions, *Playboy* centerfolds, Dylan posters, sports posters, calendars, clocks, radios, stereos, campus maps, film so-ciety schedules, skis, and astrology charts all were noted.

With every square inch of wall decor accounted for, the re-searchers waited to see which students dropped out—the high-percentage decorators or the low. It was expected that those who decorated more would drop out less. And that's exactly what hap-pened. The "stayers" had covered twice as much wall space in their rooms as the "leavers," who, when they did decorate, used more photos of family, perhaps reflecting loneliness. It proved that decorations can be symbolic of a state of mind in the same way that territorial marking is symbolic of "ownership and intended use." Personalizing is also a sign of intentions. It can mean, "I like it here, I think I'll stay."

If you *don't* think you'll stay, why waste the energy or the money making yourself at home? This can be as true in an office or a house as in a dormitory. A few years ago, Alan Hirschfield, who had just been promoted to chairman of 20th Century-Fox after an eighteen-month power struggle, explained why the only things in the office that reflected his taste were one photograph and a tin of candy: "Since my future at the company seemed so precarious," he said, "I didn't want to waste the company's money." Sometimes the refusal to decorate can be a defiant gesture—a sign that you don't want to be where you are. One woman who moved from a large house to a small one as her family contracted, hated the idea of the move and expressed her depression by refusing to fix up the new house.

Just as a pain in the arm can signal heart problems, an inability to make simple decorating decisions can often signal relationship problems. Should they or shouldn't they renovate the kitchen? wondered one couple. It seemed as if their interest in the kitchen fluctuated with the ups and downs of their relationship. When they fought, they tabled the kitchen design; when they made up, they started planning again. The existing kitchen was a symbol of their poorly operating marriage, just as the plans for kitchen improvement stood for their hope that things would improve. Neither the marriage nor the kitchen did.

Another couple were at an impasse over the sofa. The wife whose "job" it was to make decorating decisions was unable to reach an apparently simple decision about redoing the sofa. Should she slipcover it or reupholster it? What color should she choose? Her indecision dragged on for months. Her husband was pressing her to take action. He was ashamed of the way the house looked— he felt he couldn't invite people over until the sofa was redone. At the heart of the wife's indecisiveness was the issue of whether she and her husband were going to stay together. They had given themselves six months to decide. What was the point of recovering the sofa, the wife reasoned, if the marriage was over? The husband saw it differently. If he couldn't invite people over, there would just be more disagreements—which would doom the trial period. Finally, a therapist mediated the dispute and worked out a compromise. Anything either partner could not decide about, he or she would cease to have jurisdiction over. The results were quite amazing. The husband, who had previously seemed indifferent in matters of taste, took over the sofa project. The sofa was recovered, guests were invited, and at last report, the partners were still together.

Conflicts of Interiors

Sometimes the commitment is there, but there are genuine disagreements about taste that can keep people from reaching the finish line. If home is a symbol of self, whose self is the home a symbol of when there is more than one self living in it—roommates, commune mates, spouses, lovers, siblings, parents, and children?

College roommates often divide their rooms down the middle—two identities in one space, as separate and distinct as two species of fish in the same tank. On the left, the roommate with the Joni Mitchell poster, yellow flowered spread, pillow shams, and wicker wastebasket. On the right, the roommate with the Sex Pistols poster, an unmade bed, a collection of shot glasses, and a broken mirror on the table. And, oh, the disdain, if one roommate doesn't like the other's symbols of self. Crocheted driver heads on the golf clubs convinced one young man that he and his roommate could never be "brothers."

Carmen, a student at the University of Hawaii, is perturbed that her roommate calls all the things she has on display "junk": the cookie tins in which she stores her embroidery, the Bacardi bottles that remind her of parties past, the Confucius book her grandfather gave her, the worn quilt her grandmother made, the rock she found on Kona and painted to look like a wave, and the tennis ball canister she slammed a volley into and dented the first time she played tennis. Carmen scorns her roommate's things, too. Her pet peeve is that her roommate uses her collection of disco glasses to drink from. In Carmen's family, symbolic objects are kept on display—revered. Traditional *poi* pounders are not turned into ashtrays.

But even when your roommate is Ms. or Mr. Congeniality, there can be taste disagreements. Pairs of people who share apartments or houses, but not lives, feel no pressure to adopt each other's values. They choose each other, after a fashion, but theirs is a "marriage" of economic convenience and defensive life-style matching. Each one is happy to find someone personable and solvent who has no bad habits. Do they have to see eye to eye on the decor as well? Not till one housemate's Andrew Wyeth posters face the other's Russian Expressionists do they begin to understand the importance of esthetic compatibility. The roommates would like to give the living room a sense of grown-up coordination. But who has the final say? Each one wants the place done in his or her image. In New York, the young composer thinks a home should be warm and colorful and would settle for framed posters; his apartment mate, the young lyricist, wants substantial Art—the real thing—and he likes his rooms white and stark; the composer calls that "sterile." With close harmony out of the question, they have settled for counterpoint.

If *two* people can't agree on what to hang over the bean bags, *eight or ten* people certainly can't. Commune members finesse the communal identity issue altogether. They don't waste their energy trying to get a consensus on choosing a clan tartan for the living room. The group turf in a shared house tends to be as impersonal as a room in a Best Western motel. It is in the individual bedrooms that personal taste asserts itself.

Indeed, marriage is the only residential situation where cohabitors are expected to make a taste merger and present a united front. Nothing can slow a decorating job down more than the need for consensus. Whose taste should prevail? Whose identity be expressed? His, hers, theirs, hers with his veto, his with her veto, hers in the living room, his in the den? Decorating brings up issues and disagreements that couples never had to deal with before. One person wants the house homey, the other wants it "drop dead." One values things for sentiment. The other despises anything but "good design." One is a saver, the other a disposer. And because of these conflicts of interest, the decorating game is punctuated with innumerable timeouts. How does the decorator reconcile the husband's elephant tusk collection, trophies, and stuffed animal heads with the wife's desire for light, plants, and music? The decorator suggested doing the living room in deep terra cotta. The wife said sarcastically, "My husband will love that, it's the color of dried blood." Back to the drawing board.

Decorating, for some couples, is a negotiated settlement, as any theatrical designer knows. When Paul Sylbert was designing the sets for *Kramer vs. Kramer,* a film about a couple in a child custody battle, he wanted to establish how the characters lived and "who decorated the apartment." At first it was decided that "the talented but suppressed wife, played by Meryl Streep, was the one responsible for the apartment's decor." But then it was concluded that the husband, played by Dustin Hoffman "was too dominating to allow the wife to be in charge." So in the film their apartment "looks as if it were done by her and then changed by him." The modern étagère is filled with the husband's antique firetrucks and "'nifty, goofy art director stuff.' The wife's taste is reflected in finer touches, such as an antique French dessert table, Oriental rugs, and an American Windsor chair."

How well couples work together on self-expression has to do with their residential histories and ritual patterns. According to a study of first homes in first marriages, similar backgrounds make it easier to agree on how to use space and furnish it. Some of the most difficult identity mergers occur in second marriages. Love may be better the second time around, but getting agreement on the identity equipment is as tricky as reaching a prenuptial financial agreement. The pliable clay of youthful taste has long since hardened to ceramic. In Philadelphia, two people with different tastes and backgrounds, and a reluctance to compromise yet again, are having a hard time folding their lives and possessions into each other's without curdling the mix. She wants to collect art. His mother collected art so he prefers to collect vintage cars. She wants a light white interior, he wants it dark. He hates the painting she bought. So she keeps it in the closet.

After years of disagreeing with each other about the decor, nothing hurts more than observing your ex-spouse embrace all your taste preferences, which she or he refused to embrace when you were married. In a typical scenario, the husband who refused to participate in his wife's art collecting interests while they were married becomes a collector and opens a gallery after the divorce; or the spouse who hated her husband's taste for Victorian suddenly rediscovers Belter.

"My ex-husband is an architect with strong ideas about the interior and very good taste," said one city planner. "His taste at the time of our marriage was Victorian funk. I found that awful. My taste at the time was sort of Scandinavian Modern. We kept trying to decorate rooms together and not liking each other's taste." By the third apartment, she recalled, they reached détente. "There were two living rooms, so we each took one and decorated it in our own style and, amazingly, each of us began to spend more and more time in the other person's living room. We began to appreciate each other's taste without having the conflict. Eventually we did get divorced and I would say my taste right now is an amalgam of the two tastes." Which was a sore point. "I bought a secondhand Victorian-style carpet and he was really upset that when we were married I couldn't like that sort of thing."

Getting and Spending

Obviously, money can also be an obstacle to furnishing. It's not necessarily lack of money but, rather, attitudes toward it. Money is the number one cause of arguments in American families, and money is certainly a major cause of disagreement between couples in the throes of furnishing, and between them and the professionals working for them. The props of self-expression come in all price ranges. How much is identity worth, status worth, and comfort worth? Tales abound in the trade of clients who can afford to but can't spend, or clients who delight in spending excessively, oblivious of price.

There are three main stages in every purchase transaction and, generally, your attitude to money hinges on which stage in the process turns you on. According to Georg Simmel, in *The Philosophy of Money*, the first stage is the *possession of the money*. The second stage is the *expenditure of the money*. And the third stage is the *possession of the object*. Different people seem to be stuck in different stages of the sequence. Misers, said Simmel, "find bliss" in the first stage. They enjoy the possession of the potential to buy but never get beyond the almost esthetic pleasure of the promise of happiness that money gives them. Spendthrifts enjoy the second stage, the spending, but are indifferent to an object once they possess it. Spendthrifts are not indifferent to money, contrary to popular myth. In their own way they are very attached to money. They buy the pleasure of the moment at the cost of losing the value of the money. The spendthrift may be overfurnished, and the miser underfurnished. The rest of us enjoy the third stage. The enjoyment of the objects that money buys.

Since there is a bit of miser and spendthrift in everyone, some people's money dispositions are combinations of stages. The compulsive bargain hunter is a hybrid—a combination stage-one miser and stage-two spendthrift—who must save *and* also must spend. The bargains are frequently neither needed nor wanted. There is no pleasure of possession. Often spending habits have no correlation to affluence. As Overspenders Anonymous, a self-help organization, can tell you, those who can least afford extravagance may go the farthest out on a limb, while someone like the Queen of England turns off lights and "watches every nickel like a hawk."

Sarah, a New Yorker, was conflicted between her desire for a tasteful environment and her dread that she would one day need ready access to her funds. It's a time-honored tradition in many cultures that one must be prepared to flee with one's wealth, which is often in necklaces and bracelets of gold coins. Gold and diamonds are among the few objects that can be converted into cash easily. People who want to keep liquid don't put their money into furniture. Sarah knows from tragic experience the benefits of readiness. Daughter of a wealthy Polish manufacturer, she was smuggled out of the Warsaw ghetto under a pile of uniforms in a truck when she was eighteen. She was the only one in her large family who survived, saved by diamonds sewn inside her clothes and hidden in her shoes.

Now she is haunted by the fear that she will have to flee again. One part of her wants the trappings of the good life, a home that expresses her taste and cultural interests. The other part says: "Be prepared." With her children grown and her suburban house traded in for a small rental apartment, she has created a decorating program tailored to her need for security. The accessories of her decor are, in effect, her coin bangles. The major share of her decorating budget, which came from her house sale, she invested in some choice decorative nest eggs.

Sarah's plan is to buy a few things, sell higher, and keep trading up. So far she has parlayed her investment into one fine prayer rug, a Benin bronze, and a small Impressionist drawing. Her one requirement for any purchase is that it must have resale value. "When I buy, I am always thinking, 'Will someone want this?' In my head I am always running." By buying very carefully, she is able to enjoy stage three of the money transaction while being a stage-one miser—fantasizing about the safety that her objects could buy. If her apartment is furnished sparsely, it is because she has other priorities.

Keeping Their Distance with Excuses

Even with furniture fearlessness, commitment, absence of conflict, and no cash flow problems, there can be other interruptions. On numerous occasions in life, due to circumstances beyond their control, people's homes don't measure up to their standards, their status, and their role requirements: after a leak in the roof, a flood, a fire, during renovations; while they're waiting to see whether their building is going cooperative or they'll be transferred by the company; or maybe the problem is a lack of time or plain indecision.

How do they keep their guests from drawing the wrong conclusions about them during those times when their decor is on hold? A great deal of information can be gleaned in the simplest face-to-face situations. Some appraisals a person would like to have in his or her dossier, some not. Ordinarily, the clues presented in social encounters confirm and reinforce a participant's image. But discrepancies may also be conveyed, information that is "ego-alien." This is embarrassing, and confusing to outsiders as well. So what can people do if they don't like the potential implications? They must act to "control the implications," in Goffman's words. Distance themselves from the situation. Posting "Dig We Must" signs or announcing "Don't look, I'm not ready yet," may be a bit extreme, but that's the idea.

These situations require ignoring the old maxim, "Never complain, never explain." Explaining, apologizing, and joking are the three best ways to deny that this place represents you. Through the apology, "the individual begs not to be judged in the way that appears likely, implying that his own standards are offended by his act and that therefore some part of him, at least, cannot be characterized by the unseemly action"—the unseemly lack of furniture, or the wrong furniture.

Those who are too proud to apologize tend not to have guests. "I don't like my house," said actress Angie Dickinson. "I've never had a party because I don't want to apologize to my guests when they arrive." But the decision to forgo entertaining should not be made hastily. Social networks must be maintained—and nothing cements relationships better than offering hospitality. Since frontier days, Americans have prided themselves on being accessible to the right people. The famed Southern hospitality was based on "incessant visiting." Every night, hostesses would set six extra places at the dining table—just in case. This entertaining ritual forged a bond among the people in the ruling class, bringing them together not only socially but also politically. Better to entertain and apologize than not to entertain at all.

Unimpeachable decorating excuses are illness, death, acts of God, and natural disasters. "My wife has been ill; we haven't done any refurbishing in a long time" is a perfect excuse. Other solid gold excuses depend on the decorating initiator being otherwise engaged—working, going back to school to get a degree in law or medicine, running for office, or writing a book. Even Sissela Bok, author of *Lying*, felt the need to explain why she and her husband, Harvard president Derek Bok, don't have a weekend house, something that many people in their circle do have. It's too time-consuming, she said. A popular excuse is "This place isn't me yet" or "I really felt I couldn't deal with it when you said you were coming," which is also flattery, implying great respect for the guest's taste.

But explanations are supposed to be reinforced with signs of good intentions. Having recently moved guarantees a two-year moratorium as long as one announces intentions to furnish. Young people are given an extension on living up to their role requirements if they announce that they're buying on the five-year plan. Leaving blueprints lying about conspicuously, pinning swatches to the sofa, and taping wallpaper samples to the wall are all used to demonstrate intentions to lay claim to one's status via the house beautiful. Saying the furniture ordered in Europe has been tied up in a dock strike also shows intentionality and is quite believable since there is always a dock strike in one country or another. After six months, the ship may have to be sunk. The change of venue is another acceptable explanation. A resourceful young woman explained that she was not finished because, "We *were* going to do it modern but *now* we're antiquing." "I'd like to have you to dinner but the house isn't finished" is one of the most popular role-distancing apologies. It expresses intentions to invite and intentions to decorate according to community standards while buying some time.

Designers are expert at demonstrating good intentions. Not long ago, John Saladino was complaining that his wife insisted on using their living room—which he did not consider finished—for charity events. "I hate it, all these people coming here to judge me," said Saladino. "Everyone thinks our place is going to be serene modern. But it's not, it's just undone traditional." To make sure it was understood that the place was "not me" yet, he explained: "My sense of order is not truly expressed here." And to demonstrate his intention to furnish appropriately, he conducted an imaginary walk-through of his plans: "The French doors will be replaced by a single piece of pivoting glass, there will be a continuous travertine marble step running the length of the room, a catwalk running around the room at bookcase height and a staircase to reach it, the room will be beautifully lit instead of haphazardly, the floors will be bleached . . ." and so on.

The Ralph Laurens also bought some decorating time with statements of good intentions. After they had the basics of their home designed by Angelo Donghia, Ricky Lauren distanced herself from the lack of art on the walls by saying, "This place is like a blank canvas—it lends itself to a lot of creativity. We'll do fur throws in the winter, pastel cushions in summer, and art eventually. But it shouldn't happen all at once. Now is when the fun begins."

There is one excuse that backfires. Hinting that time-consuming disagreements with one's spouse are responsible for the empty living room implies unresolvable differences, which causes friends to keep their distance for fear of being caught in the crossfire. Those who use a more subtle approach explain the new problem-solving techniques they are using to reach agreement. They describe how they are taking turns with their spouses getting their way, and, alas, how they have sacrificed appearances for the sake of improved relations. Depending on the creativity of their excuses and intentions, the decorating moratorium or timeout can be extended indefinitely.

Keeping Their Distance with Jokes

Another ploy used to wiggle out of living up to role expectations is to adopt what Goffman called the "unserious style," otherwise known as the joke, whereby "the individual can project the claim that nothing happening at the moment to him or through him should be taken as a direct reflection of him, but rather of the person-in-situation that he is mimicking." The self-deprecating joke is a handy way of saying this is not the way my house would look if I could afford it. Jokes are the favorite role-distancing method of people who have the *greatest* distance between their ideal environment and their means of achieving it.

As a group, museum curators are usually endowed with extremely high standards. The curator of decorative arts at the Cooper-Hewitt Museum, David McFadden, joked himself a considerable distance away from his nearly empty apartment by calling his decor "Upper East Side Poverty." J. Stewart Johnson, a curator of design at the Museum of Modern Art, poked fun at his incomplete apartment. "It's half finished, the other half is in my mind . . . the plan is so vivid that sometimes it seems superficial to carry it out." The message was clear—it's not me and it may never be.

The joke is especially useful in dealing with a special area of "not me," the buffer zone, the no-person's-land in a multiple-family dwelling that is owned jointly—such as apartment house lobbies and halls—which are really out of the tenants' control, but not out of sight or out of mind. Many apartment dwellers don't want to be associated with their lobbies. This is true not only of people who live in low-cost housing projects but also of the well-off people in more expensive buildings. At a cocktail party for her out-of-town designer at which most of the guests were unknown to her, a New York hostess joked repeatedly that the threadbare lobby of her building left something to be desired. She wanted to make sure the guests did not equate her with that shabby place. "It's not me," she was saying.

The Last Resort—Avoidance

Some people don't want you to see their houses because they are *too* finished, or too accurate a portrait of the owners who want to conceal their life styles. Governor Edmund G. (Jerry) Brown, Jr., made a mistake in letting people know that he slept on a mattress on the floor. He never overcame his image as someone a bit odd. And President Carter's adviser Jerry Rafshoon did his best not to be photographed in a mammoth chair carved like a two-headed eagle. "The image is all wrong," he said. "A trusted adviser of the president, photographed in such a chair? All wrong." By letting the public know that he recognized it was the wrong image for a presidential adviser, he distanced himself from the chair.

Other people are embarrassed by their affluence. They worry that their comfortable life styles will cause jealousy among coworkers or inhibit advancement or contradict some image they have projected. A writer complained that she was not allowed to see best-selling author Fran Liebowitz's Greenwich Village apartment: "Presumably because Fran thinks it bad form to publicize the fruits of her success." When a person's home is too accurate a portrait, not even jokes will do. Avoidance is the only solution. And to keep people away, avoiders can always fall back on that all-purpose excuse, "I'd like to have you to dinner but the house isn't finished."

Some people have nothing to hide—they practice avoidance to avoid wear and tear on the finished decor. Recently, the man of the house, thinking about his daughter's upcoming nuptials at the country club and worrying about his newly decorated living room, told his wife, "I hope the wedding ends so late we can't invite anyone back to the house."

And some people use their unfinished decor to escape involvement. Not furnishing was a surefire way for Denise to avoid a social life. For two years her apartment looked more like a campsite than a home. Those who knew her as the most impeccably groomed interior designer in San Francisco would never have guessed that when she returned to her apartment in the evening, she would eat standing up in the kitchen and pass through the empty living room to a bedroom done in odds and ends. What living room furniture she owned was loaned to a client to fill an empty family room. Once the furniture was gone, Denise didn't miss it. She hoped the emptiness would be the impetus she needed to give herself the kind of home she gave her clients. But the months passed and the motel existence became as hardened as egg yolk on a plate. "I had no desire to create anything beautiful for myself. I think I felt I really wouldn't use it. My life was involved with business. How many hours are left to spend in a beautiful home? I didn't have the energy to entertain and I had no husband or children to make a home for."

Not until Denise came up with the idea of using her apartment for a "before and after" magazine article could she furnish. But finally having a place that looked "done, done, done" didn't change the way she lived. After the pictures were taken, she could not bring herself to put her clothes in the bureau drawers, use the dining room table, or invite any guests. "I still eat in the kitchen," she said. "I've created a stage set, but I'm not living in it."

Interim Decor

Those sociable people whose houses really are not finished, and whose excuses cannot be used yet another year, fall back on an alternate solution—interim decorating, a holding operation allowing one to keep up appearances while postponing the real presentation of self. Interim or temporary decorating can be likened to the theatrical preview where critics can attend performances but are not allowed to review them.

Meredith Brokaw and husband Tom Brokaw, the NBC news anchor, practiced interim decorating when they moved to New York in the late 1970s. It was their fourth home in ten years. "We never stayed in California or Washington long enough to get the house done," said Mrs. Brokaw, at the time. When she arrived in New York she felt "a compulsion to get certain things in place in the living room, like seating." However, she had no "real dining room furniture." With the help and advice of an NBC set designer, she bought a piece of interim furniture—the sort of round folding table caterers use. She covered it with a pretty cloth that went down to the floor so the legs wouldn't betray its origin. "It gets us through the dinner party problem," she said.

But interim decorating doesn't get anyone off the hook. It's still just a delaying action. As long as there's a need to separate those who are truly committed to claiming their statuses from those who don't care at all, people will learn to distinguish the "real" tables from the interim solutions, even if they have to go around lifting tablecloths to do it.

Fear After Furnishing

Don't think that being fully furnished will allay decorating insecurity. After finally being cured of fear of furnishing and getting past the decorating interruptions, it is not unusual to contract a new malady. Fear *after* furnishing. Apparently, anxiety about one's home measuring up can be chronic. When a group of University of Chicago researchers did in-home interviews with eighty-two Chicago families, almost every woman of the house started the conversation by apologizing for the condition of her home. Even paragons of taste whose homes are picture perfect suffer from doubts about the rightness of their homes on certain occasions. Imagined imperfections start flashing "change me, polish me." Often the homemaker fixates on a particular area certain that the addition of one object or the refinishing of one surface—a new picture, plant, or shower curtain, a change of wallpaper—will restore his or her narcissistic illusions of perfection.

The living room walls in Vickie and Sam's Rhode Island home began to flash "paper me, paper me" a few days before they were to host a political fund-raiser in their home. "I wanted the house to be just so," said Vickie. She couldn't settle on a pattern, so Sam, a wallpaper dealer, chose a tree scene. "We have very high ceilings and I was worried about the design," said Vickie, "but Sam said it would look super. It would give the room character, with the trees around the windows, the outdoors coming in. I wasn't sure, but the party was in a few days, so Tony, my paperhanger, came and put the paper up that day. I took one look at it and said, 'Oh, my God. I cannot stand it. I find it offensive. It really bothers me.' Sam said, 'Wait a couple of weeks, if you still hate it you can take it down.' But the next morning, I looked at the paper and thought, 'I cannot have people here with this paper up.' I just started shaking, I was so upset. I called Tony and begged him to come right over. He was supposed to go to another job, but he took the paper down for me and painted the walls with some fast drying paint. I just could not live with that paper. The party went very well."

Sandra was absolutely certain her apartment was finished. Why else would she agree to open it to a house tour? Other than two switchplates that had to be covered with wallpaper, she was not planning to add one thing except fresh flowers for the tour. A week before the event, she swore she was totally relaxed about the prospect of 800 people trooping through her apartment. "I don't even know I'm having it," she said. No way was she going to be like her friend who went "stark raving mad" with decorating zeal before being featured on a house tour. "This woman," said

Sandra, "had the painters come in, she refinished chairs, she re-upholstered, and the house was only a few years old. She was frantic. Being on a tour makes some people crazy and that's so silly. I want my house to look pretty, but it's a home, after all."

The day before the tour, however, Sandra's veneer of self-assurance came loose. A wall started flashing, "Fill me, fill me," and her best intentions were overruled by total *insecurity*. Out she went, desperately searching for the one last item that would make her home right and reflect her perfection. "I found the most incredible mirror I ever saw in my life," she said. "I fainted, it was so gorgeous. Black cut glass. I got my workmen to come in. We worked for hours, but there was no way we could hang it because of the lousy five-eighth-inch walls in these luxury apartments. It killed me."

"The height of security is to not give a damn," said decorator Mario Buatta, who personally gives so much of a damn that for years he couldn't bring himself to invite his idol and mentor, Sister Parish, the doyenne of New York's decorating establishment, to his perfectly furnished and finished apartment. "I never felt the place was right enough. But now I realize it will probably never be right enough to my mind, and one should grow up. Any day now, I'll invite her."

10

The Status Merchants

SCENE ONE: *Town & Country*, March 1980. Full-page photo of dapper young man resembling actor Richard Chamberlain, dressed in black tie and those black velvet at-home slippers endemic to upper-class men and leprechauns. The young man is deployed debonairly on a Directoire divan in his "digs" surrounded by four long-stemmed postdebs, all dressed for pictorial purposes in shades of deep purple. Who is the gentleman and why are these women drawn to him? Is he Richard Chamberlain? An eligible bachelor? Their brother? Their dress designer? None of the above. He is James Ruddock, the decorator, and all of the women are his clients. "My clients always become friends," he was quoted as saying.

Scene Two: *Avenue* magazine (a controlled circulation monthly that is dropped off free of charge at the doors of apartment dwellers on Manhattan's Gold Coast, the Upper East Side), November 1981. Full-page photo of glitzy living room; several pale, quilted satin sofas; fireplace wall completely mirrored; elaborate moldings; in one corner stands one of those five-figure, six-panel antique Chinese screens, which are becoming as common in upper-class living rooms as reproduction *Last Suppers* are in the working-class's. In the center of the room there is a vast glass-topped coffee table, large enough to ice skate on and thick enough to warrant reinforcing the floor with steel beams; bud vases on the table are filled with orchids and esoteric blossoms street vendors don't sell.

In the foreground, facing the camera, is the lady of this house, an international beauty who, we are informed, speaks half a dozen languages and consults daily with "her talented florist" (Is he the one who wove the flowers into her braid?). She snuggles proprietarily into a corner of the sofa, an elbow on a plump satin cushion filled with no less than $200 worth of goosedown. If not to the manor born, she is certainly to the manner accustomed. But wait. Who are those two people standing in the shadows across the room—the gentleman in the Svengali beard and the businesslike woman? They are not snuggling into cushions or fingering the antiques possessively. Their body language says they don't own this house. They're not in uniform so they can't be the butler and the maid. Then who are they? Of course. They're the decorators. Lynn Jacobson and Richard Ohrbach.

Scene Three: The *New York Times* Home Section, February 18, 1982. Spacious, conservative, and costly looking living room; small patterned wool carpet on the floor that a crumb could disappear into like a thief in the Casbah; many brand-new and freshly puffed sofas and chairs covered in flowered, quilted chintz that a woman in a print dress could disappear into; many coffee tables defining conversation areas; many bibelots that we are told were gifts to the residents from "heads of state." The two well-groomed gentlemen standing stiffly in the background each resting a hand on a reproduction Louis XVI armchair seem too ill at ease to be the occupants. Then who are they? Of course, the decorators, John Cronin and Stephen Stempler, having their picture taken in the room they designed for Mr. and Mrs. Richard M. Nixon.

And what do these three scenes have in common? The decorator is in the picture.

Decorator as Celebrity

In case you've been on an anthropological dig for the past few years, this is the era of the decorator. No longer is the *design* the thing. Now the *designer* is the thing. The designer is not merely the coordinator of the craftsmen—the painters, paperhangers, upholsterers et al.—the designer is now an artist and high priest.

That's why in our publications, more and more decorators and designers (whatever their preferred designation) and architects can be seen posing *in situ* in rooms they designed. All this media attention is a boon to exercise clubs at which designers are shaping up for celebrity. Whether fame brings them their own TV shows, book contracts for their memoirs, agreements to design sheets or Formica patterns or to endorse a product, or just more pictures of themselves in clients' living rooms, the designers will be ready.

This is sweet revenge for many designers. Once upon a time when split philodendrons and zebra rugs were all the rage, the interior designer's pet peeve was the client who felt decorating was her wifely responsibility and claimed she did it all herself. The designer was lucky to be invited to the housewarming.

Well, those days are gone. When the designer is shot for posterity in the client's residence and the picture is published, there's no chance that the client's friends will ask one another: "Does she or doesn't she have an interior decorator?" Today the client isn't taking the credit. She is giving it. She is so anxious to give credit, in fact, that sometimes she gives it when it's not even deserved. The professional's *new* pet peeve is the client who hires him or her to do the breakfast room and then claims the decorator did the whole house.

In many circles having a decorator, the right decorator, is a status symbol. Why take credit for your decor when you can earn the envy and respect of your friends by saying you worked with a well-known designer. "If I did only a pillow for a client she'd make sure all her friends knew I did it," said Mario Buatta.

Status Passages

The decorator is a status symbol today because, as we've seen, the home is a major status symbol, not only in America but all over the world; not only with the upper classes but in all classes. In a mobile society where status is constantly in flux, large numbers of people are always engaged in "status passage"—the transit from one social level to another. The biggest job in an *up-*

ward status passage is to adjust one's home, style of living, and style of living room to the new position. Thus when "Hill Street Blues," the award-winning TV show, gave its star Daniel Travanti economic security, he turned in his modest Santa Monica cottage for a three-bedroom cliff house with a view of the ocean.

But buying the house is only the first part of claiming a status. Decorating it so that it speaks well of you is the next step, but that takes know-how. Making the house "stylistically acceptable" is important for many reasons. It's not just to impress old friends; not just because living well is the best revenge; and not just to feel superior to the people "below." Living in the accepted style of the new group serves "a bonding or unifying function," wrote economist C. Wright Mills. To be accepted as a member of a group means being invited to the group's consumption rituals—the dinner parties and tailgate picnics and charity balls. And offering hospitality in return. A suitable home helps.

Homes can be passports to new worlds. But passports are scrutinized carefully before admittance is granted. Every society has structures to maintain social boundaries and keep people in their places. The Yurok Indians of California needed great wealth in shells to enter the prestigious dance societies. In our culture good taste is the ticket. "Even when money is no object," said one critic, "the object is still to have a house that works, both beautifully and well." But just as army intelligence codes are changed daily to mystify the enemy, good taste is constantly being redefined by mutual agreement with fellow consumers. How does the newcomer keep up with the changing codes?

For the uninitiated, a move to another life-style segment can cause as much culture shock as resettlement in a foreign country. No matter how one attempts to assimilate, the natives can always detect one's accent. Taste is like language. It's the common property of groups of people. Every group has its verbal and visual codes—it's "we do not say *vaise* we say *vahse*"; "we do not call a sofa a couch, or draperies drapes"; "we do not frame pictures torn out of magazines; or use plastic flowers, or call our floral displays 'arrangements'"; "we do not eat cold asparagus with a fork, we eat them with our fingers; we do not serve Jell-O molds or twirl our pasta on a spoon; we do not have clear plastic slipcovers or cover the candy dish with Saran Wrap."

As one moves up through the class and taste cultures, the

rules get more and more complex. Manners and taste enable the insiders to spot the tourists; the entrenched to spot the novices; the seniors to spot the freshmen. It is almost impossible for a newcomer to get every gesture, nuance, fork, and throw pillow right without guidance. Just when the nouveau riche hostess thinks she has made it through dinner without a hitch, she hugs the butler and gives the guests she is trying to impress something to chuckle about for years to come.

Because of the burgeoning number of people in upward status passages, the etiquette advice business is flourishing. And apparently the earlier one starts learning the better. For children eight to fourteen years old, there is the new Emily Post Summer Camp in Palm Beach—$960 for two weeks. "Everyone wants to be upper crust today," said etiquette author Marjabelle Stewart. Not only in manners. In decor, too. Playing to these affiliative longings, the Levolor blind people advertise "How to decorate rich, rich, rich, when you're not, not, not." But any bona fide rich, rich, rich person can tell that the room in the ad, though pleasant, is not, not, not.

Even people who have been "passing" for years can make slips. Nancy Reagan took criticism from all sides for the déclassé use of antimacassars on the sofas and club chairs in the White House family quarters. If she didn't know better, one critic wanted his readers to realize, he did. But a status upholsterer in New York didn't mind the antimacassars—what he objected to was how poorly they were made. When they are made *properly,* the clients often accuse the upholsterer of forgetting them, he said. "But what can you expect of a West Coast upholsterer."

The least traumatic status ascents are *slow* ones that give aspirants enough time to make themselves "stylistically acceptable." Fast ascents call for some sort of status counselor who can save the aspirant from the sins of ostentation and bad taste. "There ought to be a school for new millionaires to teach them how to spend their money," suggested author James Fixx, who made a status leap from middle-class editor to millionaire writer of books on running. An interesting idea. Food consultant Barbara Kafka tried that a few years ago without success. She offered a course called "Upward Mobility Through Lifestyle" at New York's New School. Hardly anyone signed up. Not that there aren't enough upwardly mobile people. The status pole vault is the Odyssey of

American mythology. According to *Forbes* magazine, 300 of America's 400 wealthiest people are self-made—they did not inherit their money from their parents. But people in upward status passages are not eager to take group instruction. Their status yearnings embarrass them. One researcher after another in the social sciences has found that it is almost impossible to find anyone who will admit doing anything for status reasons. The closest people get to admitting status-seeking is to say, "I want quality"—the code word. If they need instruction, they prefer to read manuals in the privacy of their own homes, or better yet, have private tutors.

Status Guides

There is no shortage of instructors raring to restyle the upwardly mobile. Enter the status merchants—the decorators, designers, and architects, the florists, photographers, and art consultants, and the magazines that give instruction in taste.

In every century, in every culture, wherever there have been people moving up there have been style "agents" available to teach arrivistes the right way to walk, talk, dress, set the table, entertain, furnish, and collect. A status merchant serves as an instructor, guide, and tutor to a person in a status passage: teaching, preaching, prodding, demonstrating, role modeling, proselytizing to the heathens about the right way to live the good life, the ins and outs of which are constantly being refined and redefined. "I do missionary work among the rich," explained one status merchant, an art consultant who specializes in helping new collectors collect art.

The status merchants—the top designers and the shelter magazines who certify their work—are the gatekeepers of the world of taste, setting costly standards of style that are actually whopping admission fees for entrance into the upper reaches of society. A home done "right," according to standards illustrated in the media, is a costly home. It demands a lot of the client. "When you care enough to spend every cent you have," was the tongue-in-cheek yet deadly serious message used in a recent advertisement placed by Bray-Schaible, a New York interior design firm.

The average it would cost to have a room done "right" by a top decorator, said Paige Rense, editor-in-chief of *Architectural Di-*

gest, is $45,000. Not including art and *objets.* Many top-rated decorators have no qualms about announcing they will not take a job for less than $100,000. The exception might be an accommodation job for an old client. Designer Angelo Donghia, whose clients include new-money persons Ralph Lauren and Diana Ross, claims that 80 percent of his clients are millionaires and the rest are going to be. Being a millionaire does help when routine spending with the status merchants can involve sofas that cost as much as compact cars; *medium*-priced carpets and fabrics at upward of $80 per yard; decorative *objets* that run into the thousands; and appropriate flora and fauna to conform to a "look" rather than a predilection for living with nature.

Just when one catches on to the entrance requirements, new standards are embraced. High-pile carpets are out, flat-pile carpets are in; flowered bed linens are out; antique lace-trimmed linens are in. White walls are out, pastel walls are in. There is nothing worse than being told by your designer that your home looks just a bit, sigh, "dated." Go to the bank, go directly to the bank, do not pass Go. If you balk at shelling out for things that are necessary "to do the job right," the designer sulks. "The one thing you don't want is a penny-pinching client," said one interior designer.

Another way to control social boundaries is to refuse to transact. Designers do it all the time. "It's nicer to work with people who have money because it makes the job easier," said West Coast designer Sally Sirken Lewis, "but if I don't like the people, I don't care how much money they have. I will not work with them."

Suppliers also refuse to transact. The whole structure of the "designer" furnishings market is built on restriction of sales. Only people with the right credentials can purchase the special goods that are the "right" stuff. Certain workrooms whose products are in great demand will only sell to designers who are *old* clients. Exclusivity of sources gives high-status merchants hard-to-get products that keep the admission fees up. "If the public could go directly to my craftsmen what would they need me for?" said one designer.

"Doing it right" costs a bundle, but reflects positively on the client. Since you can't get a mortgage on decorating, decorating "right" symbolizes cash on hand. Money must be destroyed to yield its value. But people feel it is worth the sacrifice since things "have qualities that can't be expressed in money." People who know that a good velvet costs $96 a yard today can convert "decorating right" into dollars.

Extra status points come from the fact that most decorating costs are nonrecoupable: the renovation, the wiring, the built-ins cannot be sold at auction and you can't take them with you when you move. These costly expenses might not even be selling points when the real estate turns over. Future owners of the premises usually want to start from scratch because everything looks, sigh, "dated," or "not me."

Except for antiques, furniture has no trade-in value either. The conspicuousness of the waste that makes a $7,500 goose-down-filled sofa with hand-tied springs worth half as much the day after it is delivered is even more statusy. Perhaps to take the clients' minds off the depreciation to come, status upholsterers in New York name their floor samples after such former status clients as Mrs. Astor, Mrs. Paley, Mrs. Engelhard, Marshall Field, and such former and present status decorators as Elsie de Wolfe, Syrie Maugham, Billy Baldwin, Sister Parish, Albert Hadley, and Mario Buatta—capitalizing on the ever-so-seductive attraction of "status by association." Like riding to the hounds or vacationing in the Bahamas, decorating "right" is something the rich and famous do. Buying the same chair that Billy Baldwin sold to Mrs. So-and-so has the same cachet as dancing with the man who danced with the girl who danced with the Prince of Wales. The status trickles down.

Actually, decorating "right" qualifies on almost every count as a status symbol. It confers status by scarcity of objects and services. Most top decorators say they can't take more than ten or twenty clients a year, therefore a room designed by one of them is a rarity. Status merchants adore objects that are old and scarce like antiques, new and scarce because they're custom-made, and just plain scarce like rare fibers, woods, and marbles.

Then there is the status conferred by the deportment required to live in these rooms. To live a week in a room decorated "right" without destroying it certifies that one has the necessary restraint to keep feet off the lacquered coffee table; grace to walk on extra-thick carpets without tripping; and savoir faire to drink red wine without spilling it on the oyster-white sofa.

The only symbol of status that can't be provided by status

merchants is positive proof that the newly rich client has been a student of the fine and applied arts for some time. Decorators can supply instant collections, but points are deducted by those in the know for such shortcuts. The ultimate amount of status comes from having an ample set of status possessions and having been a user of status services for the longest possible time.

Today's new money, if it survives the test, will eventually become tomorrow's old money. But there is no microwave culture oven to speed up the process. The best that new money people can do is to keep decorating until they get it almost "right." If that doesn't make them Old Money, it will at least make them Old Clients, which qualifies them to pass judgment on newer money and taste and use their newly acquired "consumption finesse" to rise in the social system. As the inscription on a needlepoint pillow in Cristina and John DeLorean's Fifth Avenue apartment said: "Nouveau is better than not Riche at all."

The Solid Gold Status Chain

The magazines, the designers, and the clients—what a symbiotic system. Like a food chain or a Gucci bracelet, each link is dependent on the others. Interior design may be a service business but the service is reciprocal. The client commissions a setting; the setting becomes the vehicle for the designer's featured appearance in a shelter magazine; the magazine uses the setting to fill its chrome-coated pages; the designer uses the tear sheets to sell other clients more settings; which become still more vehicles and more chrome-coated pages.

These publications started out as advisers to their readers—service books purveying information on "how to" and "how much." But today the top design magazines have become accreditors, boards of certification,passing judgment on the worthiness of taste and life style. The magazines communicate their idealization of prevailing standards. Not necessarily *what is,* but *what ought to be.* Their role is to decide whose vision, which taste makers they will confirm, certify, and endorse, which ideas they will perpetuate. They control taste and set standards depending on whom they tap and whom they exclude from their pages. Designers say that to have their work published in *Architectural Digest,* the most successful of the status design magazines, is a guarantee of new commissions.

Paige Rense believes that decorating may well be "a work of art." And with few exceptions, only a professional decorator, designer, or architect can give you a magazine-certified artwork. How does she find the 150 or so residences she publishes each year? Suitable houses are to shelter magazines what blood is to vampires. There is a perpetual need for a fresh supply of virgin houses, never before published, to keep the readers renewing subscriptions and get the ads that pay the editors to outdo competing magazines. No wonder there is so much socializing of editors with designers.

The competition to publish the top designers' work is tastefully cutthroat. When one of her stable of designers gets out of line and diverts photos to a competing magazine, Miss Rense ever so firmly reminds the offender of the rules of her game. If an interior appears in any other magazine it cannot appear in hers. It doesn't matter if the designer is her favorite dinner partner. If the interior is the most important in the world. Nothing matters but exclusivity. And to assure it, she is now asking, like a movie mogul, that her star interior photographers sign exclusivity contracts.

Blessed are the beautiful homes. Many are viewed but few are chosen. Miss Rense says she rejects thousands of houses a year after seeing photos of them and making house calls. "I prefer the resident not to be home when I come looking," she said. "It's ghastly when the owners are there with tea and cakes and you can see it means so much to them."

Decorating done by loving hands is rarely published in the top magazines unless the hands belong to such celebrities as Edward Albee or Truman Capote. That's why "No matter how good your taste, decorating your own house or apartment without professional help is socially foolish," wrote the late Henry Post in *New York* magazine's guide to social climbing in the 1980s. Having a designer doesn't guarantee publication, but *not* having one almost guarantees it won't be published.

Publication benefits everyone in the design chain. It gives the designer credibility, prestige, ego massage—and exposure. Publication is like having a client with a million best friends. After all, how many people can see someone's living room in person? Two hundred and fifty people in a year, at most? Designers' first clients are usually themselves or a relative. The first job, if one has skill and charisma, leads to small commissions, which lead to larger commissions from clients well-heeled and pliable enough to afford and approve the designer's best ideas. With a little luck, by year eight in business, the designer will never have to suffer the word "budget" again.

"Budget" is almost as jarring to the designer's ear as a client saying, "I can't decide." No one wants a vacillating client. If clients are unsure of their taste, there's always the chance that they won't complete the job, won't move into the finished setting, and, worst of all, won't allow photographs. Work unlived in, unseen, unpublished, unacknowledged is worse than no work.

Clients care about publication as much as designers do. Yes, they appreciate what beauty and comfort can contribute to better living, but respect is important, too. One of New York's busiest and most frequently published interior designers estimates that more than half of his clients come to him for status design. They want a home that will intimidate their peers, make them "drop dead" with envy and humiliation. Such are the clients who commission the jobs that designers can sink their teeth into. Residential architecture in America has always depended on people moving up financially. "Respect my house, respect me." The ultimate sign of respect is for a magazine to pay tribute to the house by publishing it. The desire for authentication of their taste drives countless people each year to submit snapshots of their homes to design magazines. Publication in a magazine read by the right people will certify the taste, discrimination, and affluence of the owner. It will also confirm for clients that they picked the right designer. "Even the most secure clients are afraid of looking foolish," observed one architect. "It's like being on stage. You're always afraid you'll be booed and hissed off."

Many clients pretend they want their home published to enhance its resale value (which it does) when actually they have "respect" on their minds. People who have skipped through status passages like a genius skips grades in school are especially prone to seek confirmation of their taste in the press. But not in the *National Enquirer,* for goodness' sake. Stars are willing to publicize their films in any and every medium—the bigger the audience the better—but for their homes, they only want publicity in periodicals read by their "reference group," the people from whom

they get their values, standards, and attitudes. Thus, when asked
by his decorator in what style he wanted his New York townhouse,
comedian David Brenner is said to have responded, "I don't care
what style it's in so long as they put it in *Architectural Digest.*" To
accomplish his goal, he has to let someone else paint his residential
portrait.

Shooting Stars

If the room is a portrait of the client in the designer's style,
the interior photograph is a portrait of the room in the photographer's style, which suggests an idealized moment in time before
the room is polluted by living, living, living. The interior photographer's job, on one level, is to document the work, but that doesn't
mean *cinéma vérité.*

Beyond mere documentation, the top photographers are *in-
terpreters* of the design, ac-cent-u-ating the positive, elim-i-nating
the negative, augmenting the lighting, adjusting the furnishings—
making the mundane seem more heroic, warming up the cool, and
cooling off the frantic, and most of all creating layers of illusion.

When the augmentations and adjustments are excessive, the
idealized room in the picture may be a totally different entity from
the real room. How often do most of us see a space through the
arm of a sculpture or the fringe of a fern, or crouched in a corner
with our eyes at dining table level?

Photography is the clasp in the status design chain. In the
early days of the century when Elsie de Wolfe was doing her first
big job, designing the Colony Club, techniques for documenting
interiors were primitive. Photos were shot on glass plates without
light meters. Except for the awkward practice of having an assistant hold a light and "pan" around the room during a time exposure,
photographers were totally dependent on natural light. The best
one could hope for was a record of an interior. But, as the technology improved, so did appetites for consumer goods. Shelter magazines educated the public while hyping demand for a wide range of
products.

How are you going to keep them *down* after they see how the
other half lives? With improved photography and speeded-up printing, it now takes less than a year for an item to go from innovation

to fad. In a typical scenario that's not too far from the truth, you see the Ionic capital used as a coffee table base in a young man's apartment pictured in a January issue of *Interior Design* magazine. "That's interesting," say a couple of dozen readers, who start scouring junkyards for Ionic capitals. In May the *New York Times Magazine* shows a house in Massachusetts with a toaster on an Ionic pedestal; in August *House Beautiful* uses an Ionic capital as a dining table pedestal in their feature "Decorating at Retail"; by October there is a mail-order ad for Ionic capitals in every shelter book, and Vantage cigarettes has a capital as a wall decoration in their ads; by December, *Metropolitan Home* does a cover story on columns, and Paige Rense instructs her photographers to remove all columns in pictures or she won't publish the photos. The next month, twenty new clients pull pictures of Ionic capital coffee tables out of their folders marked "Dreamhouse" in meetings with their designers and twenty designers say, "Isn't that a bit," sigh, "dated?"

Actually, the young man whose apartment was originally photographed with the Ionic capital didn't own it. The coffee table he had ordered was tied up in a dock strike. The photographer pulled the capital out of his prop closet for the picture.

Photography also hypes the market for interior design services. "A designer could perpetuate his work through the judicious use of photography," said one of the foremost architectural photographers. Pictures are invaluable as a sales tool to show the next client. And when they are published in the right magazines, it's immortality—the next best thing to children. Nothing is more disheartening for a designer than not having pictures of the completed environment. "If all our photos were destroyed," said one designer, "I would feel cut in half. A major part of my life would be lost."

For this reason, it is imperative that pictures be taken as soon as possible once the job is complete. Decorating, after all, is an ephemeral art. There are more things to shorten the shelf life of an interior than sun rot. Things such as divorce, bankruptcy, death, losing an election, boredom, moving up, moving down. Even going down. Probably the fastest dissolution of a design job was Roy Cohn's yacht. His yacht sank the day after its interior was completed. There were no pictures. Designers know they have to get the pictures before the dispute over the final bill; before a newspaper account of kidnapping frightens the client back into anonymity; before the cigarette burns of the housewarming; before the unacceptable house gifts arrive, the plants droop, the dog leaves scent marks, and the vacuum cleaner scrapes the baseboards.

Designers would rather die than admit it, but the photos take on more reality to them than the reality of the room. Photos capture the room at its peak. And if the peak is cloudy the photographer can fake it and take the pictures from the best angle. "If the public could only see how much we remove for the picture," laughed one editor. And how much they add. If the client stinted on accessories, accessories are borrowed—for the picture. If the room has anything the client or designer is ashamed of, out it goes—for the picture.

Four months later the pictures appear in a shelter magazine; one million readers see a pluperfect room; a borrowed $750 orchid plant with a one-month life expectancy outside of a hothouse adorns an end table; three magnificent vases that the reader doesn't know are "on loan" in return for caption credit grace the niches; a mink throw belonging to the designer is tossed over a club chair. Inflated standards of consumption are reinforced. Another half-million people "moving on up" are intimidated. In homes all over the country, the picture is torn out and put in a folder marked "Dreamhouse," while readers vow that one day they will have a home as beautiful as that.

Implicit is the notion that life could be beautiful in such a home. Readers get the feeling that when the physical environment is under control, life will be under control. A dreamhouse couldn't be a heartbreak house, could it? "People have a fantasy about how their lives will be when their home is done," said Paige Rense. "Usually the fantasy is just that, and when the home is done, it doesn't work for them."

Still, design and home magazines aren't above a little deception to protect the reputation of the Good Life. In the blue sky, perfect rosebud, spotless crystal, retouched reality of the shelter magazine, life appears to be Scotchguarded against bad news. Unpleasantness is stuffed into the closet with the less photogenic possessions and the accompanying story isn't necessarily the whole story.

House Beautiful gave no hint to its readers that all was not hunky-dory in a handsome Long Island sandcastle featured recently. As succulent as an ear of local corn, the house had been photographed at the height of seasonal perfection. Cooked lobsters were lying on the kitchen counter ready to be cracked. A bathrobe was tossed casually on the bed, ready to be donned. "Just imagine a house so fine-tuned . . . there's nothing to do but enjoy yourself," the article began. Nothing to do, that is, but be alive and well. While her grass looked greener, the woman of the house lay in the hospital in a coma. She had been in a coma for some months before the pictures were taken and subsequently died without regaining consciousness. The image of domestic tranquillity was a deception—a gesture from the family who understood the absolute necessity for architects to have photographs of their work.

There is a popular misconception that houses are easily read. To believe you know much about a person because you have seen the inside of his or her house is the same as thinking you know a stripteaser intimately because you have seen her nude. Her blank expression is like "a fig leaf on her face," said anthropologist J. R. Silber; "in seeing all you have seen nothing." With pictures of houses, too, fig leaves of impeccability protect privacy. Pretense stands between the reader's desire to know as much as possible and the resident's desire not to tell too much. As Ortega y Gassett said, "The person portrayed and the portrait are two entirely different things." Interior design photographs are always deceitful. Perhaps they cover up bad housekeeping, discrepancies of taste, cut corners, design gaffes—or the truth about private lives. But that is to be expected. Masquerades "are part of good role performance," said Barry Schwartz. "Daily life is a constant tension between sincerity and guile. . . . We have to deceive others to be true to ourselves." And the photographer is always a coconspirator in the deception.

Flower Power

It's hard to picture a Babylonian orgy, a Delacroix still life, or a contemporary interior by a top designer without flowers galore. Flowers are so important today that on the first cover of the new, improved *House & Garden* the focal point was not a piece of furniture or an objet d'art but an abundant floral display. Elsie de Wolfe was content to accessorize with a small bowl of flowers in the center of the dining table and another on the mantel, but today's designers would say, "That's a little," sigh, "dated."

Flowers can compensate for weaknesses in a room's design and they are absolutely essential to fill in empty spaces in wide-angled photos. Where one-dozen flowers might look fine in a room in real life, five dozen are needed to make an impact in a photo. When readers see the extravagant profusion of flowers in interior photos in magazines, they sense flowers are the fashion, fashion fuels more desire, flowers become as important in real homes as in the pictures, and the whole system reverberates with the escalating quantity of flowers. Before one realizes how it happened, rooms begin to look *naked* without flowers.

But who does the flowers? Not the interior designer. A major link in the status merchant chain is the status florist. Floral designers are now status merchants, too, as important to interior design as hairdressers and makeup artists are to fashion. They are credited in captions and celebrated in feature articles. Admitted one flower star, "I couldn't survive without the magazines."

In the humid world of high fashion horticulture, the status flower designer does not stock gladioli; sell carnations in a box; have green ripple vases; use Oasis, the foam flower arranging material; decorate with tulle or ribbon; have prices marked, and definitely does not supply note cards with sentimental sayings. These artists operate from *intime* flower boutiques or work by appointment only.

You don't go to flower powers for a bunch of daisies; you go for their ideas, their compositions, their unique selection of containers, and the confidence you get from knowing the names of their customers, many of whom have their own greenhouses but use flower artists because good ideas don't grow on trees.

When everyone was selling bunches of cut tulips, flower designers sold uncut tulips in rough crates fresh from the nursery; when every florist was putting tall tapers in their centerpieces, the boutique florists were using votive candles and holders from religious supply houses. When commercial florists were selling big bouquets, floral designers reversed gears and advocated one precious stem in a chemical flask; when every caterer mastered that trick, the innovators moved on to ever more recherché flowers— perhaps cornering the market on nasturtium or cosmos, common garden flowers that don't ship very well, or ordering a carload of *Corylus contortus,* a rare corkscrew willow from Holland.

Recently, the flower leaders have returned to big bouquets —with a vengeance. The state of the art in flowers today is *abundanza*—armloads of flowers, truckloads of flowers, the $800 agglomeration. She never counts flowers, said one exclusive floral designer whose wealthy clients don't burden her with budgets. "We just plop in what looks right," she said. But this contestant in the *interior* tournament of roses does not do floralia displays that look like floats in the Rose Bowl Parade. Flowers should look like they were always sitting there. This takes artistry, finesse, and renouncement of cliché. And patrons of the art.

There are enough style-conscious clients to support these artists. But the hook seems to be more than esthetic sensibility. There is a status factor at work here. The art collection may be the Mount Everest of conspicuous consumption, but flowers are the Matterhorn. Invest in a Picasso and it will be worth a lot more in ten years. Monetarily, flowers are dead on arrival. They are consumables for the eye. They have the shortest life expectancy of any decorative artifact except candles. Which makes flowers perfect status symbols. Better even than food. After all, your guests can only consume so many viands and legumes. But what you say when you say it with flowers is how much money you can afford to destroy for the pleasure of your guests. Who says the potlatch is obsolete?

The legend on the New York flower circuit is the wedding that consumed $250,000 worth of flowers. However, this sort of one-time extravagance pales beside the information that it is not unusual for some affluent patrons of the floriculture arts to repeatedly spend $10,000 on exotic buds for a dinner party. These clients don't see the outlay as a flower expense—it's the creation of an experience.

Lavish expenditures on flowers are also self-advertisements for the hosts. Like precious jewels, flowers shine in the observer's direction, while at the same time setting the owner apart. Because only certain people can afford these adornments, they enable one to be, as Georg Simmel put it, "a representative of one's group with whose whole significance one is 'adorned.'"

Since "the average U.S. consumer spent $15 on cut flowers" in 1982, according to *Newsweek,* it's not difficult to be an above-average flower consumer. But with today's retail flower prices running $1 to $15 for one exotic stem, keeping up with the escalating flower standards certainly marks one as a member of a special affluent group, and makes it hard for competitors to keep level.

Which is the idea, of course.

Whose House Is It Anyway?

"There is no such thing as a well-designed
space that 'looks like the client.'"
—Richard Ohrbach and Lynn Jacobson

The status merchant system works well when no one disputes the authority of the priest designers. Ours is not to question why we can't have what we want. One client was in a twit when the sofa came. The designer had talked her into a sofa without arms. Not the most comfortable configuration for a seating piece in a one-sofa apartment, she learned too late. But it would look great in a photo.

Another client was angry because she wanted a door on her dressing room but the famous architect said a door would spoil the Design. In retaliation the client spoiled the designer's chance for recognition with the job. She refused to give him permission to photograph it.

Another client and his designer had their tense moments over windows. The client wanted an air-conditioned bedroom in his house in the tropics. But the designer thought the arched openings would look so much better *without* glass. He didn't think air conditioning was a good enough reason to spoil the Design. It wasn't until the client said glass was a must to keep *bats* out that the designer grudgingly gave in. Yet another designer complained that the client was spoiling his Design by cluttering it up with magazines. The designer believes in "centers of clutter." He wants the papers all stacked in one place.

It takes a lot of courage to disagree with the designer now that interior design is capital-A art—"art that you sit in rather than look at," as one designer considers his work. A home that's a work of art sounds like a nice place to *visit* but a hard place to *live in*. "Esthetic quality is no guarantee of livableness," wrote British architect James Scott in an article on psychological needs and housing. "It may, however, deceive everybody, including the designer but more seriously his client, as to the apparent excellence of what turns out to be qualitatively unlivable." Clients of famous designers have often been made to feel like desecrators for rearranging the master's work in an effort to make the designs conform to their living habits. The Littles of Minnesota, the original owners of the Frank Lloyd Wright room installed at New York's Metropolitan Museum, did not keep their furniture arranged the way Wright designed it in 1913, except when he came to visit and rearranged it. But after his death, the designer got his way. When the room was reconstructed, the museum chose to arrange things Wright's way, not the clients' way. Official taste is contemptuous of users' taste. And because of that, the nonprofessional gets the idea, said psychologist Norbett Mintz, "that only the expert has the right to esthetic opinion."

One reason that designers are so often in conflict with what would seem like basic human needs for privacy, security, and comfort is that architecture and design have been traditionally taught as visual arts. Only recently has there been research on how buildings function. In her 1970 book *With Man in Mind,* a plea for more humanistic architecture, city planner Constance Perin noted that out of forty-five criteria used in judging architectural design for awards, only two were concerned with human needs. Today, according to Gary T. Moore, director of architecture and urban planning research at the University of Wisconsin, the figure has increased to four or five.

Homes must be appreciated as "live-in" rather than "look-at" experiences, said one theoretician. Fine art objects are "fine-tuned and static," while living is "action-based. It's not possible for people to dwell authentically in art objects." Living is a messy business. People want things that aren't always esthetic: bulky armrests, footrests that spring out of hidden recesses of chairs, displays of trophies, children's paintings, and other unsightly personal objects. They often want more privacy than a designer thinks necessary. And they insist on being warm in the winter and cool in the summer and keeping insects out even if it spoils the Design.

Designers are caught in a bind. They know people have to live, but they themselves have spent so much of their own lives hiding newspapers under beds, folding towels immediately after using them, putting the attractive magazine covers on the top of the heap and "editing" (a favorite word which means *ruthlessly* de-accessioning) their possessions that they feel a client owes them the same dedication to appearances. Only servants and immediate family know that the real living room in many a perfectly designed residence is the little den off the master bedroom, which is furnished with the "old shoe" things that have been in the family for years.

Designers proclaim loudly that they serve the needs of the client but in unguarded moments they talk about their own needs. "The client often holds you back," said one decorator. "Peer approval is the highest thing to aim for," said one architect, "but it happens the least." If film people have their sights set on Academy Awards, designers are often working with one eye on the press, which is the vehicle that conveys their work to their peers. And because of this, they have to keep their work uncontaminated by the client. The wall of equestrian prints in the living room of New York newscaster Chuck Scarborough and his wife, the former Anne Ford Uzielli, "was the decorator's idea: neither Chuck nor Anne is especially enamored of horses," said *People*. A house in Easthampton, New York, said *New York* magazine, "fulfilled [the architect's] dream" of designing a house dedicated to outdoor living. No mention of the client's dream.

One designer admitted that the project that satisfied her client the best helped her career the least. "I did a room for a woman who was a fabric designer," she said. "Although I personally would not have chosen the fabrics we used, I never tried to discourage her from using them. But I wouldn't want my colleagues to think I had chosen them. When a home magazine came to look at the job, I told the editor, I don't think you'll like it, and I was right."

Designers value their peers' opinions because, very often, only their peers can appreciate what they are doing. Studies have shown that the more designers are educated in design, the further away they move from popular taste.

A British study done in the early 1970s showed that twenty-seven architects specializing in housing could not easily predict how 232 apartment dwellers would want their furniture arranged.

When the architects tried to predict how middle-class families would live in an apartment project, most of the designers referred to their own preferences and experiences to make judgments. In fact, almost one-quarter of them said the *only* way to design was to use their own behavior to predict other people's behavior.

One architect assumed, incorrectly, that most of the tenants would prefer to dine in the kitchen and not in the living room because *he* found it inconvenient to dine in the living room; another architect assumed that the tenants would have footstools because he liked having one. The architects assumed that, like themselves, the tenants would value ease of circulation and would divide living room space into activity zones; but circulation and zoning did not prove to be high priorities with the real-life tenants who were much more concerned with making a "pleasing display" of their furniture.

American researchers have also noticed that designers work hard to create free space, which middle-class families tend to fill with furnishings, abhorring the vacuum. Nondesigners can't resist filling voids; they have been known to put things in spaces it would never occur to designers to fill, lining things up on windowsills, smothering tabletops.

If designers have prejudices, they might as well recognize them, said Clare Cooper Marcus, who has accused the male architecture establishment of viewing humanistic concerns as "effeminate." "Just as an analyst must go through psychoanalysis [so as] not to lay his emotional trip on his patients, designers must understand their own biases and values and where they've come from in order not to lay them on their clients." In Marcus's "Environmental Autobiography" course at Berkeley, students are asked to describe their lives in terms of the very first environment they can remember through their current ones—writing about significant spaces and places. Then she asks the students if they can see a connection between past experiences and current design preferences. They often can.

One young woman recalled "an early attraction to high and secluded spaces." It was a theme repeated in many of her designs and in a house she did for herself, said Marcus. An Iranian student realized he was holding on to his roots by doing designs for courtyard houses; an only child saw a tendency in her work to design housing areas in which each resident would be isolated; and a young man raised by a blind parent recognized his desire for orderly spaces was a reaction to the "disorder and lack of visual coherence which characterized his childhood home."

Getting in touch with the roots of one's design ideas doesn't assure that designers won't "act out" their needs in designs for others. One New York architect had no qualms about stating his reason for giving his clients a partially open bathroom: "Frankly, I get lonely in a closed-off bath."

Altered Ego

With reputed earnings of $14 million a year, Kenny Rogers and his wife Marianne may be America's nouveau riche first family. Rogers, our leading country and western singer, celebrated his upward trajectory recently with a $12.5 million home in Los Angeles' tony Bel Aire section and spent another $1 million decorating it *himself,* not in Okefenokee country style but semifine French furniture—the odds-on favorite of new millionaires for decades. But the brute force of big bucks spent on high price-tag stuff is not enough. Unprocessed money is out. Discrimination is in. If good taste is the ultimate status symbol then you need the "total look." It's not just what you buy but the way you assemble it—the backgrounds, the built-ins, the moldings, the doorways. When Rogers saw entertainer Cher's Holmby Hills house with its crypto-Egyptian slant-sided doorways that had been "done" by Ron Wilson—decorator to Mike Douglas and Don Rickles—he realized what a status merchant could do and signed Wilson up for what eventually escalated to a multiple-vehicle-and-dwelling contract, three jets, one yacht, a beach cottage, a Georgia farm which boasts the largest barn in America, and a $14.5 million house, said to be the most expensive private home in America.

Wilson's first words after inspecting Rogers's furniture inventory were the five most favorite words in the decorating world: "Let's get rid of everything." Naturally, if there was something special . . . but no one wants to have to work with the impulse purchases from the client's first Gold Record period.

"How do you tell a potential client that absolutely everything has to go?" asked Robin Jacobsen, a New York designer, while discussing how he took a client in a taste passage from "Louis to less." He and his partner, architect Scott Bromley, admit they "love to gut" spaces and start from scratch. But clients must be ready. You know they're ready when they say these code words, "I want a change." Well, if you want a change, "Let's get rid of everything." However, few clients on the Up escalator are as frank as the wife of movie star James Garner who told San Francisco designer Anthony Hail when she hired him, "I'm nouveau riche, I don't want any of that to show and that's why I hired you."

The magnitude of a person's status jump can be calculated by the number of objects saved from the former life. The rule of thumb is—*less equals more.* The less they keep, the more they've moved up. Certainly the last thing most people in a status pole vault want is a home that looks like the old self. Until a new self is decided upon there is a sense of vulnerability. It's impossible to go back but one can't move forward either. Like a caterpillar shedding its chrysalis and reassembling its tissue into a butterfly, the person is in the process of becoming. The only decision to be made is whose markings to don, which design guru to follow.

"It's difficult for them to choose, and even after they've decided they worry that they've made the wrong decision," explained one designer with the weariness of a man who has navigated many people through the rough waters of status passage. "Their maid or lawyer or next-door neighbor can put a doubt in their mind about something they've ordered. You don't have to sell your plan *once*— you have to sell it half a dozen times."

No matter how exciting it seems to be starting over, there's always some ambivalence. The urge to maintain the status quo is a force of the same magnitude as the desire to obtain higher status. There will always be some grieving for the old selves when clients are buying a new way of life. And panic. Suppose they don't like the results? The process is as frightening as plastic surgery.

The inherent tension of this situation makes the Total Transformation the razzle-dazzle of the design world. This type of job is not the five-year plan, it's a six-month metamorphosis: rhinoplasty, depilation, everything. "It's a $2 million gamble. I'll know in six months if I made a mistake," said one client when he signed on with his decorators.

The space in question must be gutted and rebuilt; floors refinished; walls padded, papered, or striated; marble baths, skylights, and all new electronic light switches installed. But it is still unlivable. The custom rugs, hundreds of low-voltage spotlights, made-to-measure sofas, occasional tables covered with python and lacquer, obelisk collection, assorted cloisonné boxes, and one-ton coffee tables are collected over the months at a warehouse—waiting there for Installation Day. The day the bandages come off.

The clients who may have been camping out all these months in the attic or living with relatives or in a hotel are sent out for the day—to a double feature, a friend's house, or shopping. The suspense is as heavy as the coffee table. The client hopes it won't be a fiasco but can't really imagine what it will all look like. "They can't dream in technicolor," said designer Richard Ohrbach. Up until this point the clients have been writing checks on blind faith and the feeling of security that they got from seeing the designer's work in a magazine. If they were truly honest with themselves, there have been many moments when they wondered if they should have hired one of the other designers they interviewed.

Meanwhile, the design team and installation people go to work. The quadruple window treatments are hung—the blackout shades; the perforated scrim, accordion-pleated, pull-up shades; the lacquered goat-skin vertical blinds; and the satin side panels shirred on fat rods—the hand-painted reversible canvas area rugs laid; enough low-voltage spotlights with magenta, red, lemon, and aqua gels to stage *A Chorus Line* clipped on their tracks and focused; the Venetian mirrors hung on the mirrored walls; the twenty-five pounds of assorted jelly beans and $75 worth of Hershey's kisses poured into giant crystal jars; the master bed and its nine pillows (two king, two regular, two European, two neck-rolls, one baby) made up with Pratesi linens; the mohair throw thrown casually across the eiderdown quilt; and stacked in pyramids in the bathrooms, boldly monogrammed ice-cream-colored towels, each one folded and then rolled in the trendy mode of the day.

Nothing is forgotten. Not the spicy Brown Windsor soap in His bathroom or the Devon Violet soap in Hers or the sackfuls of Agraria potpourri that gives the living room the sweet smell of excess. The aluminum ladder is folded and stored, and the extravagant Cristal champagne is placed in the square steel-and-brass Cartier cooler—a house gift from the decorators. While the caterer heats up the dinner that will start with a soup in brioche, the dining table is set in a Sparkle Plenty scheme—clear crystal plates, goblets, saltcellars, candelabra with white candles (never colored), and a mammoth rough-cut glass boulder centerpiece as big as the Ritz. As the sun sets, one of the designers places an *amusant* little sterling silver Buccellati mouse under the coffee table and the other one picks up the cordless, remote control light wand and runs through the various preprogrammed computer lighting scenarios from Party Light to Cleaning Light, Watching the Snow Light, Going to Kitchen for Midnight Snack Light, and Dinner Light, finally settling on an ambience of Romantic Living Light.

As laser beams of colored light highlight and shadow the rooms, the disco beat of the *Flashdance* soundtrack emanating from six minispeakers deployed at different levels gives the sense that the room is one giant headphone. Places everybody. The $2 million moment of truth is at hand.

The doorbell rings. It's the clients. "Can we come in now?" they ask sheepishly. The decorators are as nervous and excited as they are. The surgeon has taken off the bandages. The nurse hands the patient the mirror. "Here's your new face, dear. How do you like it?"

How do you spell relief? Aaaauuueeeeaaaawwwwooo. The clients run through the rooms. They scream with joy. They feel like Dorothy in Oz. Cinderella. Queen for a Day. The Prince of Wales. Then why are they crying? Because they're so happy.

Living Up to the Image

The designers waved their wand and transformed this place into an enchanted castle. It must follow that these ordinary mortals are likewise transformed into royalty. Over and over again, said one designer, the clients say, "Am I worthy of this?" Then they rush to the phone to call Mother—or a best friend. "You must come over this minute. You must see this." Transactions between a person and an object usually involve a third party. What good is all the beauty if there is no audience, no critic to give what anthropologists call "marking services"? Someone to pronounce the social worthiness of the consumption.

The designers are delirious, too. The clients wanted a change, and change they got. The clients' gratitude is intoxicating. "You almost feel like you are curing cancer," said Richard Ohrbach.

But there's a letdown the morning after. When the change in

life style is drastic, the client may feel intimidated at first. "Can I live up to this place?" There have been clients who have been so uncomfortable they moved out immediately. But that's the minority. "It takes about a week before they begin to feel at home," said Ohrbach, who has gone through this enough times to see a pattern. "And then they start changing themselves to conform more to the image of their home. Some clients will get a chauffeur and a limousine; they may start buying their clothes in Paris; shopping for jewelry at David Webb instead of in the jewelry district."

Wait a minute. Dressing better was not what sociologist Eugene Rochberg-Halton had in mind when he said, "Optimistically, a person who buys a whole environment will live up to his new possessions, grow into them, find that they have an educative significance for him." Becoming more educated in the uses of status symbols was not what he meant. "People think culture is a technique you can buy like a how-to book. As if you can buy this advice and put it on. It has no connection to living. It reduces life to a cookbook. Taste," said Rochberg-Halton, "is earned, not just worn, it is a life lived in flesh and blood."

Yes, yes, but can we think about that tomorrow? Right now, it's time to think about the photographs. The magazines are calling. The designer needs their marking services and so does the client, who hates to admit it. But the editors' approval is no guarantee of social approval. Postpartum depression may result from publicity backlash. Instead of invitations to the best tables, there may be snide remarks in the gossip columns. "Where did we go wrong?" the clients wonder. They turn over the keys to the house and a line of credit to the decorator, then they take a long trip. They were sure that if they didn't do it themselves it had to be right.

Unfortunately, the very publicity social newcomers seek in order to establish their claim to membership in the upper class can work against them. Even when one has hired an experienced coach, gotten rid of everything, and done the job "right," there is always the chance that members of the "aspired to" group will refuse to acknowledge that the newcomers have made it to their level because the newcomer has committed the sin of "perfection." The place looks too new, too self-conscious.

People who demand the most perfection and harmony of their surroundings are often running from feelings of inferiority, said W.

Lloyd Warner in *Yankee City.* "Old family tradition demands under-statement about outward forms, particularly personal posses-sions. . . . The 'ideal' is to be avoided because it is often the mark of the parvenu driven by his feelings of anxiety that he won't do it right."

If acceptance into the aspired-to social group doesn't come as fast as the total transformation, there may be animosity toward the decorator. Decorators talk about backlash and resentment. "You don't want the authority figure around who knew you when," said one designer. The hostility and contempt that is often directed toward decorators is similar to the feelings people have for under-takers, said Warner. Both preside over the burial of the remains of former selves. When the difference between the old self and the reborn self is the most pronounced, the anger at the decorator may be the greatest. To complete their status leaps, therefore, people often must leave behind the decorator and friends who knew them when.

There is always the chance, however, that a ghost of the self laid to rest by a status decorator will come back to haunt the new self. In the process of becoming part of a new group one has to loosen connections to the old group. Initiates must guard against taste relapses; they can still betray their former selves with hold-over objects and attitudes from their former lives—the telephone dialer topped with a rhinestone poodle; the Have a Nice Day mug on the sideboard; the Lifebuoy soap they use so they won't waste the good soap. Vigilance is necessary. Newcomers are on trial for some time. More than the opening performance is reviewed. A grand home isn't a *symbol* of upper-class status, it is merely a *claim* to it until, as Warner said, "its inner way of life has been recognized and accepted through the intimate participation of the owners with the top group."

The sign of successful passage is when the clients and their children are invited to join the right clubs and attend the right pri-vate parties (not charity functions), when the right people accept their second invitation, return their phone calls—and ask them for the name of their decorator.

EPILOGUE
Surviving the System

O N JULY 14, 1983, Jimmy
and Rosalynn Carter's log cabin in the Blue Ridge Mountains was
featured in the *New York Times*. The three-room, two-bath hideaway with sleeping loft for guests was built from a kit for use as a
retreat, a place for Mrs. Carter to work on her memoirs, for family
to come with their sleeping bags, and for Mr. Carter to fish and
read and work on such hobbies as weaving bark chair seats; a place
where he can display his bottle collection and put the furniture he
builds in his Plains workshop to use.

Mrs. Carter loves the house, said journalist Enid Nemy, because it takes only a half-hour to clean. But beyond efficiency, the
cabin is a material expression of everything the Carters believe in.
It embodies simplicity, self-restraint, self-sufficiency, honest-as-
Abe materials, homespun charm, echoes of frontier courage, and
family ties—the hickory used to make the chairs comes from a
150-year-old family grove. If ever a home appeared to be personal
and unselfconscious, it was this one.

Yet, since a decorator, Carleton Varney (pictured in the article), assisted the Carters in decorating the cabin, the reader assumes there was some anxiety, some desire for approval, for

getting it right, for showing the Eastern establishment, which so often derided the Carters for their taste, that they can do it with style—their own style. One wonders what Henry David Thoreau, the author Jimmy Carter was reading so symbolically when he was photographed in his old reliable rocking chair, would say about the use of a decorator to coordinate the furnishings of a cabin in the woods? This is not exactly Thoreau's life lived "near the bone where it is the sweetest."

If you believe in simplifying, in getting back to essentials in a log cabin—a symbol of American virtue if ever there was one—if, like Mr. Carter, you can make your own furniture as competently as any Shaker craftsman, if you have excellent taste, as Mrs. Carter is said to have by Mr. Varney, you can certainly pick your own curtain fabric. Surely if Rosalynn Carter were not in the public eye she would have decorated her cabin on her own, as did her cousins Betty and John Pope who co-own the Carter cabin and live in their own log structure nearby. But in or out of the Oval Office, the Carters are being scrutinized. And you can't go home again when the secret service is camped on your frontier.

Whether you're redecorating the White house or giving a three-room log cabin an image suitable for an elder statesman, every element speaks for you, and getting it right is essential. If it's okay to use aides to brief you, and to get your props right for a political debate, why not a decorator for your backwoods backdrops? The home is a complicated symbol system and in the war of symbols, we are all on the line. The Carters, in character, are still espousing democratic simplicity in response to republican elitism, and all their decorative slogans work in unison: the Colonial colors, the American Heritage curtains and upholstery, the ruffled lampshade, the folksy stenciled stairs, the cozy pine table with removable lazy Susan, the flowery china pattern designed especially for Mrs. Carter by her decorator, all convey a patriotic litany that's as clear as the Pledge of Allegiance.

And if the Carters, like most of us, are aware of the messages they are communicating, we have to forgive them. Making an effort to create a certain impression and being conscious of the effects is only natural. People make judgments of us from whatever clues they can find, and who wouldn't want those to be favorable? You don't have to be a sociologist to observe, as Erving Goffman did, that "there is no way to say nothing with home furnishings. In a conversation with four people, you can pass your turn to talk, but you can't be silent with your house."

Not that these communications are telling all. Just as individuals have their public and private personas, the house has both a public façade and a private core. For the inhabitants, the objects of the home are transmuted by use. They become invested with meaning and personal history. The design of the table becomes less important than the memories of the meals shared around it. The silver bowl is filled with the significance of the occasion it commemorated. The rug is a reminder of the trip on which it was acquired. And all of them may symbolize the ability to provide for one's own or one's family's needs, which ranks among the most satisfying achievements of a human being.

It's important to understand and accept that the home in our society serves a dual function, personal and social. As more and more people leave the protection of closely knit communities and move into neighborhoods of strangers, the house becomes a credential as well as a haven. Just as we need the intimate relationships that a house can shelter, we need the respect and esteem provided by a home we create in our own image. And we must forgive ourselves for caring about the opinions of others and trying to influence them. Whether the stand we take is on old pegged wood floors, a well-worn Oriental rug, or Rosso Levanto marble, we all use material things to stand for us. That's the system. Surviving the system is finding a balance between the social and personal meanings of the home. To survive the system is to find the pleasure and satisfaction that can reside in every home.

NOTES

PREFACE:
Beyond Style

XV she laced into women for reading: Gloria Emerson "No News Is Bad News," *Savvy,* February 1980, pp. 12–13.

XVI "I read . . . all those frivolous sections . . .": In "Susan Sheehan often works 14 hours a day. She thinks she's very lucky . . ." Promotional insert for advertisers, *The New Yorker,* February 22, 1982.

XVI there are "more house-shrines in America . . .": Jan Cohn, *The Palace or the Poorhouse: The American House as a Cultural Symbol* (East Lansing, MI: Michigan State University Press, 1979), p.x.

XVII common stock of knowledge: E. Jean Callander, "The Contextual Meaning of Home: As Manifested by Objects Used to Personalize Space." Ph.D. Dissertation, Graduate School of Cornell University, August 1980, p. 59.

INTRODUCTION:
Guilt and Desire on the Home Front

2 his loft and his life style: Jane Geniesse, "When Nothing But the Best Will Do," *New York Times,* June 7, 1979, p. C1 ff.

3 "I live the American dream": Ibid.

3 "If someone looks at my census form they'll think . . .": Author's interview with Martin Davidson.

3 "All the Martin Davidsons in New York . . .": Richard Moseson, "Letters: Crossroads of Decadence and Destitution," *New York Times,* June 14, 1979, p. A28.

3 "How can one man embody so many of the ills . . .": Letter to the Editor, *New York Times,* June 14, 1979, p. C9.

3 "Thank you for your clever spoof": Letter to the Editor, ibid.

3 "While simultaneously consuming yesterday's paper . . .": Russell Baker, "Observer: Incompleat Consumer," *New York Times,* June 9, 1979, p. 25.

4 "People were objecting to my life style": Author's interview with Martin Davidson.

4 "It's not very fashionable to be an overt consumer . . .": Author's interview with Dawn Bennett.

4 "He designs dresses, she runs the house": Francesca Stanfill, "Living Well Is the Best Revenge," *New York Times Magazine,* December 21, 1980, pp. 20–25 ff., citation p. 20.

4 "infallibly fashionable interiors": Ibid.

4 "Rooms are constantly rearranged . . .": Ibid., p. 75.

4 "A great thing is made about linen. . .": Ibid., p. 76.

4 "By my book, I'm not extravagant . . .": Ibid., p. 76.

4 Calvin Trillin did a satirical "tap dance": Calvin Trillin, "Variations," *Nation,* January 17, 1981.

5 "no fear of ostentation, nor are they inhibited . . .": Stanfill, "Living Well," p. 56.

5 gave his wife carte blanche to refurbish: Steven R. Weisman, "Reagan Orders Cut in Federal Travel and Consultant Use," *New York Times,* January 23, 1981, p. 15.

5 the controversial family dining room wallpaper: Melinda Beck, Jane Whitmore, and Eleanor Clift, "Upstairs, Downstairs," *Newsweek,* January 12, 1981, p. 31.

5 This bride did not have to wait very long: Lynn Rosellini, "First Lady's China Makes Its Debut," *New York Times,* February 4, 1982, p. C3.

6 "The new White House china has become the single most . . .": Martin Filler, "Upstairs with Nancy and Ronnie," *Skyline,* March 1982, pp. 24–25.

6 "heedless of the plight of the ragged peasants . . .": Rosalind H. Williams, "High Life in the Opal Office," *New York Times,* February 25, 1981, Op-Ed page.

6 "a rise in materialism amid economic gloom": "Study Finds Rise in Materialism Amid Economic Gloom," *New York Times,* March 4, 1979.

6 as Tom Wolfe detailed in: Tom Wolfe, "The 'Me' Decade and the Third Great Awakening," *New York,* August 23, 1976, pp. 26–40.

6 "For the overwhelming majority of Americans . . .": Daniel Yankelovich, *New Rules: Searching for Fulfillment in a World Turned Upside Down* (New York: Random House, 1981), p. 176. See also William Looft, "The Psychology of More," *American Psychologist,* No. 26, 1971, pp. 561–65.

6 In 1975 people said a good job: "Study Finds Rise in Materialism."

6 "The egalitarian spirit is gone": Florence Skelly, "Life-Style 1980." Transcript of presentation given to National Conference American Society of Interior Designers, at Industry Foundation Luncheon, Washington, D.C., 1978.

7 In September 1981 the untrendy *U.S. News:* Susanna McBee, "Flaunting Wealth: It's Back in Style," *U.S. News & World Report,* September 21, 1981, pp. 61–64.

7 "The Success of Luxury": Carrie Donovan, "The Success of Luxury," *New*

York Times Magazine, November 15, 1981, pp. 140 ff. "It seems the more luxurious the design, the more desirable it is," said Donovan of the latest trend in women's clothing.

7 "It is now acceptable to show off one's wealth": Alison Lurie, quoted in John Duka, "Fashion Notes," *New York Times,* December 8, 1981.

7 "It's no longer chic to be poor": Craig Unger, "Attitude," *New York,* July 26, 1982, p. 24.

7 "You don't have to hide your ambition anymore . . .": Advertisement for *Fortune,* 1983.

7 Detroit noticed *big* cars were inching back: John Holusha, "Detroit Stressing Luxury Cars," *New York Times,* August 24, 1983, p. D1.

7 "Even If You Can't Have the Best of Everything . . .": Mitsubishi advertisement, *The Dial,* September 1982, pp. 2–3.

7 "the most expensive apartment house ever built . . .": Howard Rubenstein, public relations counsellor, held a champagne reception on March 10, 1983, to make this announcement at the sales office, 500 Park Avenue, New York City.

8 "materialism" lives on the wrong side of the page: *Roget's Thesaurus* (New York: St. Martin's Press, 1962).

8 "the tendency to be more concerned . . .": *Webster's New World Dictionary* (New York: World Publishing Co., 1970).

8 "chains binding them": Rosalind Williams, *Dream Worlds: Mass Consumption in Late Nineteenth Century France* (Berkeley, CA: University of California Press, 1982), p. 43.

8 The Protestant ethic promised eternal salvation: Max Weber, *The Protestant Ethic and the Spirit of Capitalism,* trans. Talcott Parson (New York: Charles Scribner's Sons [1958], 1976).

8 "conspicuous consumption," "pecuniary emulation . . .": Thorstein Veblen, *Theory of the Leisure Class* (New York: Mentor Books, 1953).

8 grass-roots philosopher Richard Gregg: Richard Gregg, *The Value of Voluntary Simplicity* (Pendle Hill, 1936). Also, "Voluntary Simplicity (1)," *CoEvolution Quarterly,* Summer 1977, pp. 20–27. (This is a condensed version of the article that first appeared in *Visva-Bharati Quarterly,* August 1936.)

9 "fully and wholeheartedly live a life of . . .": Duane Elgin and Arnold Mitchell, "Voluntary Simplicity (3)," *CoEvolution Quarterly,* Summer 1977, pp. 4–19, citation p. 10. But another article in the same journal disagreed with Elgin and Mitchell. In "SRI Is Wrong About Voluntary Simplicity," Spring 1977, pp. 32–34, Mike Phillips wrote, "I would put the number at 50,000 people who are involved in a NEW movement."

9 if "emphasis were put on *learning to appreciate human* . . .": "Flash! New Harris Poll on VS: *Washington Post,* 23 May 1977." Reprinted in *CoEvolution Quarterly,* Summer 1977, p. 34.

9 "I like this stuff": Anne Herbert, "Researcher's note," *CoEvolution Quarterly,* Summer 1977, p. 34.

9 "People are conflicted . . .": Author's interview with Barbara Caplan.

10 Even Maine homesteaders Scott and Helen Nearing: Kristin McMurran, "Couples: A Jug of Carrot Juice, a Loaf of Bread and One Another in the Wilderness

Give the Nearings Paradise Now," *People,* August 23, 1982, pp. 77–79.

10 Tolstoy said there were only two questions: Looft, "Psychology of More," p. 562.

11 Every society has ways of controlling consumption: Williams, *Dream Worlds,* pp. 213–275.

11 only a small percentage of people want to take: Richard Coleman and Lee Rainwater, *Social Standing in America: New Dimensions of Class* (New York: Basic Books, 1978), p. 303. Said the authors of this book: "Only a few respondents wanted to take substantial amounts of money away from the rich. . . . A mere 2 percent went so far as to urge near-total equalization of income."

11 "Sweetness here wanted it": Suzanne Daley, "A Year Later, Lottery Prize Still a 'Fantasy,'" *New York Times,* November 15, 1982, pp. B1 ff.

11 The economy depends on "the endless inculcation . . .": "Notes and Comments," *The New Yorker,* March 9, 1981, p. 31.

11 Sumptuary laws have been used throughout history: Lawrence Langner, *The Importance of Wearing Clothes* (New York: Hastings House, 1959); James Laver, *The Concise History of Costume and Fashion* (New York: Harry N. Abrams, undated).

11 Feudal Japan probably had the most detailed: Stephen Gardiner, *Evolution of the House: From Caves to Co-ops* (New York: Macmillan, 1974); Bernard Rudofsky, *The Kimono Mind: An Informal Guide to Japan and the Japanese* (Rutland, VT: Charles E. Tuttle Co. [1971], 1979).

12 "they do not have the right to have more . . .": Emile Durkheim, *Suicide: A Study in Sociology* (New York: Free Press [1897], 1951), quoted in Williams, *Dream Worlds,* p. 330.

13 misreading "normal class differences . . .": Herbert Gans, "Effects of the Move from City to Suburb," in Leonard J. Duhl, *The Urban Condition: People and Policy in the Metropolis* (New York: Basic Books, 1963), pp. 184–98, citation p. 190.

13 "It's a preoccupation with possessions . . .": Author's interview with Myra Bluebond-Langner.

13 "smaller is smarter . . . those energy-wasting gadgets . . .": Linda Flayton, "Great Expectations? Not Quite," *New York Times,* Long Island Section, August 8, 1982, p. 22.

13 a "great fan of electronic games . . .": James E. Braham, "Management/Personal Time: You Don't Have a Computer?" *Progressive Architecture,* August 1982, p. 134.

13 E.T.'s friend in the film, must stop spending his $5: Jim Calio, "Director Steven Spielberg Takes the Wraps Off E.T., Revealing His Secrets at Last," *People,* August 23, 1982, pp. 81–88, citation p. 83.

14 In Victorian England there was an agreed-upon standard: Leonore Davidoff, *The Best Circles: Society, Etiquette and the Season* (London: Croom Helm, 1973), p. 39. Said Davidoff: "It was the duty of the middle- and upper-class family to maintain an establishment on the most elaborate scale they could afford."

14 where to buy $1,000 clocks that only a Ph.D: Joseph Giovannini, "In the New Clocks, Design, Not Time, Is of the Essence," *New York Times,* March 24, 1983, p. C1.

14 The American dream of "individual elitism": Williams, "High Life," Op-Ed page.

15 "It is extraordinary to discover that no one knows . . .": Mary Douglas and Baron Isherwood, *The World of Goods* (New York: Basic Books, 1979), p. 15. A number of other social scientists have mentioned in recent works the lack of attention paid to the human relationship to possessions: See Coleman and Rainwater, *Social Standing*, p. 310. The authors observed that "the role of income in providing a wide range of rewards—consumption—has not received sufficient attention from sociologists." See Carl F. Graumann, "Psychology and the World of Things," *Journal of Phenomenological Psychology*, Vol. 4, 1974–75, pp. 389–404. Graumann accused the field of sociology of being thing-blind.

15 If it's *not mine*, it's *not me*: Lita Furby, "Possessions: Toward a Theory of Their Meaning and Function Throughout the Life Cycle," in Paul B. Baltes (ed.), *Life-Span Development and Behavior*, Vol. 1 (New York: Academic Press, 1978), pp. 297–336.

15 stabbed him to death with a paring knife: "'Touch That Dial and You're Dead,'" *New York Post*, March 30, 1983, p. 5.

15 the Kwakiutl Indian chiefs of the Pacific: Ruth Benedict, *Patterns of Culture* (Boston: Houghton Mifflin [1934], 1959); Frederick V. Grunfeld, "Homecoming: The Story of Cultural Outrage," *Connoisseur*, February 1983, pp. 100–106; and Lewis Hyde, *The Gift* (New York: Vintage Books, [1979, 1980], 1983) pp. 25–39.

16 "Every member of society . . . must learn . . .": Edmund Leach, *Claude Levi-Strauss* (New York: Penguin Books, 1980), p. 39.

16 "Status symbols provide the cue . . .": Erving Goffman, "Symbols of Class Status," *British Journal of Sociology*, Vol. 2, December 1951, pp. 294–304.

16 who is invited to share "bed, board, and cult": Douglas and Isherwood, *World of Goods*, p. 88.

16 "people tend to roost on the same branch as birds . . .": Michael J. Weiss, "By Their Numbers Ye Shall Know Them," *American Way*, February 1983, pp. 102–106 ff. "You tell me someone's zip code," said Jonathan Robbin, "and I can predict what they eat, drink, drive, buy, even think."

16 When *Forbes* profiled the 400 richest Americans: "The Forbes 400," *Forbes*, September 13, 1982, pp. 99–186.

16 "Only one bowl will bloom this year": Steuben Glass advertisement, *The New Yorker*, April 4, 1983, p. 3.

17 buy one yard of the tiger-patterned silk velvet: Paige Rense, "Lee Radziwill," *Celebrity Homes* (New York: Penguin Books, 1979), pp. 172–81.

17 "look like a . . . countess on a commoner's salary": *Synchronics* catalog, Hanover, Pennsylvania, Fall 1982.

17 "Signs of status are important symbols of self . . .": Mihaly Csikszentmihalyi and Eugene Rochberg-Halton, *The Meaning of Things: Domestic Symbols and the Self* (New York: Cambridge University Press, 1981), p. 18.

18 "It is clear that between what a man calls *me* . . .": William James, *Principles of Psychology*, Vol. 1 (New York: Macmillan, 1890), p. 291.

18 "Every possession is an extension of the self": Georg Simmel, *The Philosophy of Money*, trans. Tom Bottomore and

David Frisby (Boston: Routledge & Kegan Paul, 1978), p. 331.

18 "Humans tend to integrate their selves . . .": Ernest Beaglehole, *Property: A Study in Social Psychology* (New York: Macmillan, 1932).

18 Eskimos used to *lick*: Ibid. p. 134.

18 "things are cherished not because of the material comfort . . .": Csikszentmihalyi and Rochberg-Halton, p. 239.

18 "What's amazing is how few of these things . . .": Author's interview with Mihaly Csikszentmihalyi.

18 "How else should one relate to the Joneses . . .": Douglas and Isherwood, *World of Goods,* p. 125. Also see Jean Baudrillard, *For a Critique of the Political Economy of the Sign,* trans. Charles Levin (St. Louis, MO: Telos Press, 1981), p. 81. Said Baudrillard: "No one is free to live on raw roots and fresh water. . . . The vital minimum today . . . is the standard package. Beneath this level, you are an outcast." Two classic novels on consumption are (1). Georges Perec, *Les Choses,* (New York: Grove Press, [1965], 1967). (2). J. K. Huysmans, *Against the Grain (A Rebours)* (New York: Dover Publications, [1931], 1969).

18 The principle of reciprocity requires: Douglas and Isherwood, *World of Goods,* p. 124.

18 "the hardware and the software . . .": Ibid, p. 72.

19 "I think my father's belongings . . .": Maria Wilhelm, "Things Aren't Rosy in the Crosby Clan as Kathryn Sells Bing's Things (and not for a Song)," *People,* May 31, 1982, pp. 31–33.

19 "pure rank markers . . .": Douglas and Isherwood, *World of Goods,* p. 118.

19 One of the pleasures of goods is "sharing names": Ibid., p. 75.

19 "Next to actually eating food . . .": Mimi Sheraton, "More on Joys of Dining Past," *New York Times,* April 9, 1983, p. 48.

19 "Wouldn't you be mad if you had to eat green beans . . .": "Green Beans Stir Bad Blood," *New York Times,* March 26, 1983, p. 6.

19 If every meal were the same: Douglas and Isherwood, *World of Goods,* p. 66.

1. *What Is Home?*

22 "E.T. phone home": *E.T. The Extraterrestrial,* Universal Pictures, 1982.

23 data on whether Mom and Dad sit side by side: Irwin Altman and Patricia Nelson, *The Ecology of Home Environments.* Project No. 0-0502 U.S. Department of Health, Education and Welfare, January 1972, p. 37.

23 what percentage of people knock on bathroom doors: Ibid, p. 53.

23 how long it takes before Levittowners convert: Saim Nalkaya, "The Personalization of a Housing Environment." Ph.D. dissertation in architecture, University of Pennsylvania, 1980.

23 differences between the things people store in attics: Perla Korosec-Serfaty, "The Home, From Attic to Cellar," in D. Seamon and R. Mungerauer (eds.), *Place, Dwelling, and the Environments* (The Hague: Martinus-Nijhoff. In press).

23 "Home is our corner of the world . . .": Gaston Bachelard, *The Poet-*

ics of Space, trans. Maria Jolas (Boston: Beacon Press [1958], 1969), p. 4.

23 "Home is an ordering principle in space . . .": Kimberly Dovey, "Home: An Ordering Principle in Space," *Landscape,* Spring 1978, pp. 27–30.

23 Home is "the territorial core": J. Douglas Porteus, "Home: The Territorial Core," *Geographical Review,* October 1976, pp. 383–90.

23 Home "is the presence of children . . .": Robert M. Rakoff, "Ideology in Everyday Life: The Meaning of the House," *Politics & Society,* Vol. 7, 1977, pp. 85–104, citation p. 93.

24 Only 50 percent of Americans own their own homes: "Study Charts Century of Progress to the 'Good Life,'" *New York Times,* November 25, 1979.

24 "What is home?" he wondered: D. Geoffrey Hayward, "Housing Research and the Concept of Home," *Housing Educators Journal,* Vol. 4, No. 3, 1977, pp. 7–11, citation p. 9.

24 Hayward isolated nine dimensions of home: Ibid, p. 10. See also Hayward, "Home as an Environmental and Psychological Concept," *Landscape,* October 1975, pp. 2–9; and Hayward, "Psychological Concepts of Home Among Urban Middle-Class Families with Young Children." Ph.D. dissertation, Psychology Department, City University of New York, 1977.

24 "It really is a joy to have something . . .": Lee A. Daniels, "12 Win City Brownstones in Harlem," *New York Times,* February 10, 1982, p. B3.

24 "It means I'm a homeowner, a property owner . . .": Ibid.

25 Leaving "home" accelerates their

death rates: Leon A. Pastalan, "Environmental Displacement: A Literature Reflecting Old-Person–Environment Transactions," in Graham D. Rowles and Russell J. Ohta (eds.), *Aging and Milieu: Environmental Perspectives on Growing Old* (New York: Academic Press, 1983), pp. 189–203.

25 "We thought, well, if we have to die . . .": "Beirut Goes up in Flames," *Time,* August 16, 1982, p. 16.

25 "When I dropped my toothbrush . . .": ABC-TV interview with Barbara Walters, January 20, 1981.

25 "There I was standing in the bedroom . . .": "Looking Back in Anger," *Time,* February 9, 1981, p. 18.

25 "this is a real homecoming day . . .": Joseph B. Treaster, "Hometowns Give Freed Americans Hero's Welcome," *New York Times,* January 29, 1981, pp. A1 ff.

25–26 Moorhead C. Kennedy, Jr., "ran his fingers over the objects . . .": Ibid., p. B8.

26 "The first twenty-four hours . . .": ABC-TV interview with Barbara Walters, January 20, 1981.

26 "Whenever I moved," said Richard Queen: Richard Queen with Patricia Hass, *Inside and Out* (New York: G. P. Putnam's Sons, 1981), p. 137.

26 "I felt so good, so safe . . ." Ibid., p. 230.

26 "I can't describe the feeling I had . . .": Ibid., p. 273.

26 human motivations psychologist Abraham Maslow: Abraham Maslow, *Motivation and Personality,* 2nd edition (New York: Harper & Row, 1954).

26 its value had "never been explored": Robert Ardrey, *The Territorial Imperative* (New York: Dell Publishing [1966], 1973), p. 149.

27 "The ability to control and regulate privacy is essential . . .": Author's interview with Irwin Altman. See also Altman, "Privacy: A Conceptual Analysis," in *Environment and Behavior,* vol. 8, No. 1, March 1976, pp. 7–29.

27 "If you have no boundaries, no secrets . . .": Author's interview with Irwin Altman.

27 We need varying degrees of privacy for sharing secrets: Material on the functions of privacy based on Alan Westin, *Privacy and Freedom* (New York: Atheneum, 1967), pp. 32–39.

27 something Elizabeth Taylor's lawyers fought for: Tamar Lewin, "Whose Life Is It, Anyway? Legally, It's Hard to Tell," *New York Times,* November 21, 1982, Section 2, p. 1.

27 96 percent of the respondents said they closed: Altman and Nelson, *Ecology of Home Environments,* p. 53.

27 husbands and wives often "draw the line": Alexander Kira, *The Bathroom* (New York: Viking Press [1966], 1976), p. 169.

27 "not as a token of deference to nudity": Barry Schwartz, "The Social Psychology of Privacy," *American Journal of Sociology,* No. 73. 1968, pp. 741–52, citation p. 749.

28 yet without "distances and intermissions": Georg Simmel, "Knowledge, Truth, and Falsehood in Human Relations," in Kurt Wolff (ed. and trans.), *The Sociology of Georg Simmel* (New York: Free Press [1950] 1964), p. 315.

28 In a study of "cluster housing" in Australia: W. H. Foddy, "The Use of Common Residential Area Open Space in Australia," *Ekistics,* 255, February 1977, pp. 81–83. See also Sasha R. Weitman, "Intimacies: Notes Toward a Theory of Social Inclusion and Exclusion," in Arnold Birenbaum and Edward Sagarin, *People in Places: The Sociology of the Familiar* (New York: Praeger, 1973), pp. 217–38. According to Weitman, there is a universal tendency to engage in intimacies in private "in order to spare [others] the experience of feeling excluded."

28 privacy is not . . . a one-way "keep out" situation: Irwin Altman and Martin M. Chemers, *Culture and the Environment* (Monterey, CA: Brooks/Cole Publishing, 1980), p. 99.

28 "ability to hold back as well as to affiliate": Schwartz, "Social Psychology of Privacy," p. 752.

28 a privacy *system*: words, gestures, body language: This theory of privacy comes from author's discussions with Irwin Altman, as well as from Altman's *The Environment and Social Behavior: Privacy, Personal Space, Territoriality, and Crowding* (Monterey, CA: Brooks/Cole Publishing, 1975); and Altman and Chemers's *Culture and Environment.*

29 Berbers rub a little tarry secretion: H. Hediger, *The Psychology and Behaviour of Animals in Zoos and Circuses,* trans. Geoffrey Sircom (New York: Dover Press [1955], 1968), p. 23.

30 The Iroquois Indians used a slanted stick: In Irwin Altman, "A Cross-Cultural and Dialectic Analysis of Homes," in L. Liben, A. Patterson, and N. Newcombe (eds.), *Spatial Representation and Behavior Across Life Span* (New York: Academic Press, 1981), pp. 283–320, citation p. 311.

30 Lauren Bacall and Humphrey Bogart: Lauren Bacall, *By Myself* (New York: Ballantine [1978], 1980), p. 294.

30 pygmies . . . force their guests to leave: Altman and Chemers, *Culture and Environment,* p. 94.

30 In Java . . . privacy is a "general lack of candor in speech . . .": Clifford Geertz, cited in Westin, *Privacy and Freedom,* pp. 16–17.

30 In rural Ireland where neighbors come and go: Derek S. B. Davis, "At Home With Henry Glassie," *Pennsylvania Gazette,* December 1981, pp. 36–40. Henry Glassie, folklore professor at the University of Pennsylvania, said, "Since the [Irish] house is totally vulnerable to anyone coming into it, the householder has the complete right not to even acknowledge the presence of the other person. . . ."

31 Knowing your place, socially, was a substitute for walls: Philippe Ariès, *Centuries of Childhood: A Social History of Family Life,* trans. Robert Baldick (New York: Vintage Books [1960], 1962), p. 414.

31 For the Puritans, privacy was a diary: Gwendolyn Wright, *Building the Dream: A Social History of Housing in America* (New York: Pantheon, 1981), p. 15.

31 The English, unaccustomed as children: Edward Hall, *The Silent Language* (New York: Anchor Books [1959], 1973), p. 139.

31 When Arabs need to withdraw: Ibid., p. 159.

31 couples have been forced to patronize "love hotels." Robert C. Christopher, "Changing Face of Japan," *New York Times Magazine,* March 27, 1983, pp. 40–100, citation p. 83.

31 The Mehinacu of Brazil . . . have no spatial privacy: Altman, *Environment and Social Behavior,* p. 13.

31 "Stardom is a house without shades": Julie Baumgold, "Best Bets: Candy Darling Remembered: Oceans of Love, Tons of Kisses," *New York,* May 31, 1982, p. 83.

32 Cher considered installing: Hank Grant, "Rambling Reporter," *Hollywood Reporter,* September 20, 1982.

32 Victoria Principal was forced: Jeff Jarvis, reported by David Wallace, "Victoria Principal," *People,* May 23, 1983, p. 96.

32 Extroverts have a *low* arousal level: Author's interview with psychologist Rikard Küller, University of Lund, Lund, Sweden.

32 Judging by the results of one study: Nancy J. Marshall, "Environmental Components of Orientations Toward Privacy," in John Archea and Charles Eastman, *EDRA II* (Stroudsburg, PA: Dowden, Hutchinson, and Ross, 1975).

33 "No one dreams of fastening a door . . .": Wayne Andrews, *Architecture, Ambition, and Americans* (New York: Free Press, 1964), p. xxi.

33 "An American has no sense of privacy . . .": George Bernard Shaw, Speech, April 11, 1933. Cited in John Bartlett, *Bartlett's Familiar Quotations,* 14th edition (Boston: Little Brown [1855], 1968), p. 838.

33 The Crystal House, an all-glass house: Nory Miller, "Fred Keck at 81, 'Hit of the Show' After 56 Years," *Inland Architect,* May 1976, pp. 6–8 ff.

33 Philip Johnson gave openness a lot of visibility: Mary Jane Pool (ed.), *20th Century Decorating, Architecture, & Gardens:*

80 Years of Ideas & Pleasure from House & Garden (New York: Holt, Rinehart and Winston, 1980), pp. 158–61.

33 Or head for his pied-à-terre: Charlotte Curtis, "Philip Johnson's Home," *New York Times,* August 24, 1982, p. C8.

34 "Togetherness sought to resolve the opposing demands . . .": Ardrey, *Territorial Imperative,* p. 150.

34 "peace and quiet without the television . . .": Wright, *Building the Dream,* p. 257.

35 "It almost seems like a joke": Suzanne Slesin, "The New Lofts: Privacy Instead of Open Space," *New York Times,* March 27, 1980, pp. C1 ff.

35–36 "People today seem to be tired . . .": Carol Vogel, "Partial Walls: New Ways to Shape Space," *New York Times,* November 18, 1982, pp. C1 ff.

36 For decades government, savings and loan: See Lizabeth A. Cohen, "Embellishing a Life of Labor: An Interpretation of the Material Culture of American Working-Class Homes, 1885–1915," in Thomas J. Schlereth (ed.), *Material Culture Studies in America* (Nashville, TN: American Association for State and Local History, 1981), pp. 289–305. According to Cohen (p. 298), "some reformers felt a home-owning working class would be more dependable and less revolutionary"; "others hoped that meeting mortgage payments in America might discourage immigrants from sending money home, and hence stem the tide of further immigration." See also Nancy G. Duncan, "Home Ownership and Social Theory," in James S. Duncan (ed.), *Housing and Identity: Cross-Cultural Perspectives* (London: Croom Helm, 1981), pp. 98–134. According to Duncan (p. 113), "multi-family dwellings were seen [by the U.S. Savings and Loan League] as a psychologically unhealthy and unnatural living environment."

36 "A nation that can no longer . . .": Linda Flayton, "Great Expectations," *New York Times,* Long Island Section, August 8, 1982, p. 22.

36 "all those folks in the Eisenhower years . . .": Lance Morrow, "Downsizing the American Dream," *Time,* October 5, 1981, pp. 95–96.

37 In the 1970s a typical first house: Peter Kerr, "House Trend: Downsized," *New York Times,* September 23, 1982, pp. C1 ff. And James Delson, "The Marketplace: Real Estate Fact," *Psychology Today,* December 1982, p. 16.

37 social workers' nightmare, *taking in boarders*: Cohen, "Embellishing a Life of Labor," pp. 289–305. According to Cohen (p. 296), industries were involved in "setting standards for workers' homes through company housing [and] promoted the specialization of rooms in an effort to discourage the taking in of boarders. . . ."

37 A peek under the roofs in most communities: Andree Brooks, "When Several Generations Share a Home," *New York Times,* October 21, 1982, Home Section.

37 "I knew if I went back I'd have a room . . .": "Imprisoned Slayer, 93, Prefers Room of Her Own to Freedom," *New York Times,* August 19, 1982, p. A12.

37 in Melanesia's Dobu Island: Ruth Benedict, *Patterns of Culture* (Boston: Houghton Mifflin [1934], 1959), pp. 133–137.

38 Not only must we satisfy our biological drives: Harold M. Proshansky, William H. Ittelson, and Leanne G. Rivlin, "Freedom of Choice and Behavior in a Physical Setting," in Proshansky et al., *Environmental Psychology: People and Their Physical Set-*

tings, 2nd edition (New York: Holt, Rinehart and Winston [1970], 1976), pp. 170–81, citation pp. 177–78.

38 "without sacrificing individual privacy": Kenneth Lelen, "The Once and Future House," *Metropolis,* November 1982, pp. 9–13, citation p. 12.

38 even children who had to share rooms with siblings: Rachel Sebba and Arza Churchman, "Territories and Territoriality in the Home," *Environment and Behavior,* Vol. 15, No. 2, March 1983, pp. 191–210. According to the researchers, "adults seem to consider a place as representing them if they are responsible for its care or if it is designed or decorated according to their tastes and carries their personal signature. For most of the children, a place was considered to represent them if they were able to act freely there . . . family members who did not control any area stated that no place served them as a primary territory." Children who felt they had the least control and jurisdiction were the ones who shared rooms.

2. What Is Decorating?

43 In 1980 *House & Garden* reported: *A Report on the House & Garden Market for Decorating and Home Furnishings.* Research Report #8437 (New York: Scarborough Research Corporation, April 1980).

43 *Architectural Digest* stated that 51 percent: "A Profile of Subscribers." Simmons Market Research Bureau, July 1981.

44 *Better Homes and Gardens* claimed that 70 percent: "Inquiry: A Study on Home Furnishings from the Better Homes and Gardens Consumer Panel 1982" (New York: Meredith Corporation, 1982).

44 Americans spend $50 billion a year on furnishings: Statistics from author's interview with Wallace W. Epperson, Jr., senior vice-president, Wheat First Securities, specialists in the home furnishings industry.

44 "without meaning and without goals": Leonore Davidoff, *The Best Circles: Society, Etiquette, and the Season* (London: Croom Helm, 1973), p. 14.

44 social scientists call personalizing: Irwin Altman and Martin M. Chemers, *Culture and Environment* (Monterey, CA: Brooks/Cole Publishing, 1980), p. 137. See also Cheryl B. Coniglio, "The Meaning of Personalization and Freedom of Choice Within Residential Interiors." Master of Science Thesis, Graduate School of Cornell University, June 1974.

45 one, to regulate the social system: Ibid., Altman and Chemers, p. 143.

45 two, to express identity: Ibid., p. 143.

45 "Settling in a territory is equivalent . . .": Mircea Eliade, *The Sacred and the Profane,* trans. Willard R. Trask (New York: Harcourt Brace Jovanovitch [1957], 1959), p. 47.

46 "imago mundi": Ibid, p. 43.

46 We do not bury slaves alive in the postholes: Lord Raglan, *The Temple and the House* (London: Routledge & Kegan Paul, 1964), p. 20.

46 sacrifice the mason's wife: Eliade, *Sacred and the Profane,* p. 56.

46 build the walls of our houses on the bodies: Raglan, *Temple and the House,* p. 20.

46 the chimney . . . is no longer considered the ladder to heaven: Eliade, *Sacred and the Profane,* p. 26.

46 "Settings have plans for their inhabi-

tants' . . .": Roger Barker, "On the Nature of the Environment," in Harold M. Proshansky, William H. Ittelson, and Leanne G. Rivlin, *Environmental Psychology: People in Their Physical Settings,* 2nd edition (New York: Holt, Rinehart and Winston, 1976), pp. 12–26, citation p. 25.

46 The geography of the house is based on a whole range: Roderick J. Lawrence, "The Social Classification of Domestic Space: A Cross-Cultural Case Study," *Anthropos,* No. 76, 1981, pp. 649–64.

47 But the more technological a society: Author's interview with Irwin Altman.

47 "Around here," said Joe Duncan: Joan Kron, "Home on the Range: The Real South Fork," *Washington Star,* June 19, 1980, pp. C-1 ff.

47 "It's the face of the house, which speaks . . ." Mary Douglas, *Natural Symbols: Explorations in Cosmology* (New York: Penguin Books [1970], 1973), p. 191.

47 The Gauls and many other early peoples: Philippe Ariès, *Centuries of Childhood: A Social History of Family Life,* trans. Robert Baldick (New York: Vintage Books [1960], 1962), pp. 365–66.

47 an industry newsletter warns manufacturers: "1982 Home Furnishings Compendium" (Richmond, VA: Wheat First Securities, 1982), p. 482.

48 "No cooking in the house" and "no death . . .": Raglan, *Temple and the House,* pp. 42–49, 67–74.

48 Some societies still remove the dying: Ibid., pp. 67–74.

48 The kitchen is not supposed to be visible: Author's interview with psychologist Sandra Howell of MIT.

48 The kitchen in the French house: Susan G. Carlisle, "French Homes and French Character," *Landscape,* Vol. 26, No. 3, 1982, pp. 13–23, citation p. 20.

48 In a study comparing the English and the Australian: Lawrence, "Social Classification," pp. 649–64.

48 "it's the hub of our family": Television interview, NBC Nightly News, January 1983.

49 The custom of the connubial bed being the woman's place: Raglan, *Temple and the House,* p. 131. See also Edward Hall, *The Hidden Dimension* (New York: Anchor Books [1966], 1969), p. 133. Hall believes the English bedroom belongs to the husband.

49 the President of the United States: Russell Lynes and Sam Burchell, *"Architectural Digest* Visits: President and Mrs. Ronald Reagan at the White House," *Architectural Digest,* December 1981, pp. 104–21, citation pp. 112–13.

49 slept in "a peach and flowered bedroom: "Queens Neighbors Tour the Cuomos' New Home," *New York Times,* January 2, 1983, p. 24.

49 Only the Chinese see the left as honorable: Yi-Fu Tuan, *Space and Place* (Minneapolis, MN: University of Minnesota Press, 1977).

50 "It takes a while to settle in . . .": L. Langway et al. "Upstairs at the White House," *Newsweek,* January 5, 1981, pp. 61 ff.

50 In isolation studies done for the U.S. Navy: I. Altman and W. W. Haythorn, "The Ecology of Isolated Groups," *Behavioral Science,* No. 12, 1967, pp. 169–82. And I. Altman, D. A. Taylor, and L. Wheeler, "Ecological Aspects of Group Behavior in Social Isolation," *Journal of*

Applied Psychology, No. 1, 1971, pp. 76–100.

51 "The self can only be known . . ." Eugene Rochberg-Halton, "Where Is the Self: A Semiotic and Pragmatic Theory of Self and the Environment." Paper presented at the 1980 American Sociological Meeting, New York City, 1980, p. 3.

51 "He didn't like sleeping in strange beds:" Dora Jane Hamblin, "Brief Record of a Gentle Pope," *Life,* November 1978, p. 103.

52 "Returning each night to my silent, pictureless apartment . . .": D. M. Thomas, "On Literary Celebrity," *New York Times Magazine,* June 13, 1982, pp. 24–38, citation p. 27.

52 Robert Kennedy, Jr.'s bride Emily: "Back Home Again in Indiana Emily Black Picks Up a Freighted Name: Mrs. Robert F. Kennedy, Jr.," *People,* April 12, 1982, pp. 121–23, citation p. 123.

52 the five-year-long University of Chicago study: Eugene Rochberg-Halton, "Cultural Signs and Urban Adaptation: The Meaning of Cherished Household Possessions." Ph.D. dissertation, Department of Behavioral Science, Committee on Human Development, University of Chicago, August 1979; and Mihaly Csikszentmihalyi and Eugene Rochberg-Halton, *The Meaning of Things: Domestic Symbols of the Self* (New York: Cambridge University Press, 1981).

52 "I learned that things can embody self": Author's interview with Eugene Rochberg-Halton.

52 seemed to be "scripted by the culture": Csikszentmihalyi and Rochberg-Halton, *Meaning of Things,* p. 105.

52 "it is remarkable how influential sex-stereotyped goals . . .": Ibid, p. 112.

52 "pay attention to different things . . .": Ibid, p. 106.

53 since music "seems to act as a modulator . . .": Ibid., p. 72.

53 "ecological consciousness . . .": Ibid., p. 79.

53 "built environments": Amos Rapoport, "Identity and Environment," in James S. Duncan (ed.), *Housing and Identity: Cross-Cultural Perspectives* (London: Croom Helm, 1981), pp. 6–35, citation p. 18.

53 "This is where I live": Leonard Buder, "Berkowitz Is Described as 'Quiet' and as a Loner," *New York Times,* August 12, 1977, p. 10.

54 When John Warner was chairman of the Bicentennial: "Page Six: When Walters said No to John Warner," *New York Post,* October 26, 1982, p. 6.

54 Don Henley, the Texas-born country: Sandy Gibson, "At Your Service," *Beverly Hills People,* November 10, 1982, p. 16.

54 A prominent architect wrote his mentors large: John Duka, "Contradiction and Complexity Create a Home," *New York Times,* October 28, 1982, pp. C1 ff., an article featuring the home of architects Robert Venturi and Denise Scott Brown.

54 The hallways in Yoko Ono's apartment: David Sheff, "Yoko and Sean: Starting Over," *People,* December 13, 1982, pp. 42–45.

54 a decorative identity that was "truly me . . .": Suzanne Slesin, "On Redesigning a Loft with Energy and Ego," *New York Times,* November 11, 1982, pp. C1 ff.

54 "Every housewife of every taste culture who can afford . . .": Herbert Gans,

Popular Culture and High Culture: An Analysis and Evaluation of Taste (New York: Basic Books, 1974), p. 118.

54 photojournalist Barbara Pfeffer photographed: Joan Kron and Barbara Pfeffer, "The Whole Line: Different Faces of Identical Spaces," *New York,* August 30, 1976, pp. 53–57.

55 "I couldn't imagine hiring an interior decorator": Author's interview with Clare Cooper Marcus.

55 Classic paper on the house as a symbol of the self: Clare Cooper "The House as Symbol of the Self," in Proshansky et al., *Environmental Psychology,* pp. 435–48.

55 "I like to make my own mistakes": Hathaway Hardy, "*Architectural Digest* Visits: Edward Albee," *Architectural Digest,* March 1982, pp. 150–55, citation p. 153.

56 "will be considered a twentieth-century classic . . .": Peter Carlsen, "Minimalism in Manhattan," *Architectural Digest,* July 1982, pp. 60–67, citation p. 67.

56 "My settings support me, help me play my roles": Author's interview with Harold Proshansky.

56 "habitable and personally significant": Mary Carleton Miller, "Perceptual Foundations of Interior Design." Ph.D. dissertation, Columbia University, Environmental Sciences, 1971, p. 148.

56 "It's better than a photograph album": France Michele Adler, "A View from 1790, with Rustic Charm to Spare," *New York Post,* April 7, 1983, p. 41.

57 "Formative periods . . . are marked by the magic . . .": Barry Schwartz, "The Social Context of Commemoration: A Study in Collective Memory," *Social Forces,*

Vol. 61, No. 2, December 1982, pp. 374–402, citation p. 375–76.

59 "Mr. Tetlow feels he couldn't live . . .": George Price, *The New Yorker,* July 12, 1982, p. 39.

59 "I honestly don't think it could work out . . .": Ed Arno, *The New Yorker,* August 23, 1982, p. 40.

59 "I told the construction worker if my mother . . .": "Queens Neighbors," p. 24.

59 More than 96 percent said they would wait: "Inquiry: A Study on Home Furnishings from the Better Homes and Gardens Consumer Panel, 1982" (New York: Meredith Corporation, 1982), p. 12.

59 "Finally, Charlene," says the bug-eyed gent: Advertisement, AT&T Co., 1982.

59 "I knew instantly it was what I wanted . . .": "*Architectural Digest* Visits: Burt Lancaster," *Architectural Digest,* October 1982, pp. 138–43.

60 "A person's identity is not necessarily coherent or stable . . .": Donald Appleyard, "Home," *Architectural Association Quarterly,* Vol. II, No. 3, 1979, pp. 4–20, citation p. 5.

60 "to satisfy a passion I once had for . . .": Wendy Murphy, "A Rural Setting for Jewelry Designer Angela Cummings," *Architectural Digest,* April 1982, pp. 78–85, citation p. 84.

60 Regine, the nightclub impresario: Charlotte Aillaud, "*Architectural Digest* Visits: Regine," *Architectural Digest,* September 1981, pp. 120–23.

60 "I feel quite different in each place . . .": Eugenia Sheppard, "Around the Town with Eugenia Sheppard," *New York Post,* December 8, 1982, p. H–39.

60 Why else would 1,200 readers of *Metropolitan Home:* Dorothy Kalins, "Awards: A Triumph of Personal Style," *Metropolitan Home,* January 1983, p. 19.

61 Studies show that bicycle racers: Robert Sommer, *Personal Space: The Behavioral Basis of Design* (Englewood Cliffs, NJ: Prentice-Hall, 1969), pp. 58–59.

61 Psychologists call this the "social influence": Ibid., pp. 58–59.

61 "He had plastic plants in his waiting room": Rochelle Semmel Albin, "Therapists Choosing Therapists: What They Look For," *New York Times,* September 15, 1981, p. C3.

61 "Her personality, like her office . . .": Ibid.

61 "To furnish a house so it will express . . .": Erving Goffman, *Presentation of Self in Everyday Life* (New York: Anchor Books, 1959), p. 32.

61 "I want my house and office to convey the impression . . .": Paul Goldberger, "The Last Town House: On Gramercy Park Benjamin Sonnenberg Created a Great Showplace the Likes of Which Will Never Be Seen Again. His Collection Will Be Auctioned June 5," *Esquire,* March 13, 1979, pp. 35–40, citation p. 40.

62 Prince Charles recently remarked: Andrea Chambers, Fred Hauptfuhrer, and Jerene Jones, "Mum's the Word," *People,* March 7, 1983, pp. 95–98.

63 "cues being noticed and the meaning understood": Rapoport, "Identity and Environment," p. 28.

64 fish-bird decorations on a chief's house: Colin Duly, *The Houses of Mankind* (London: Thames and Hudson, 1979), p. 79.

3. *The Creative Imperative*

66 They convened on a Saturday morning: A breakfast at Tiffany's, New York, for brides, March 6, 1982.

66 the three most "important esthetic decisions . . .": *Tiffany & Co. Bridal Registry Guide,* 1982.

66 "When you choose your place settings . . .": Lecture by Donna Ferrari, *Bride's* magazine's tabletop, food, and wine editor, on "Serving with Style," Tiffany's, New York, March 6, 1982.

67 dinner parties which "we believe in . . .": Lecture by Lorraine Miller, Bridal Registrar, Tiffany's, New York, March 6, 1982. Ms. Miller also stated that "formal dinner parties are very much a part of Tiffany's."

67 *"You've got to make that personality . . .":* Lecture by Donna Ferrari, March 6, 1982.

67 "There is a great deal of pressure . . .": Author's interview with Stanley Barrows.

67 "Personality Decorating . . .": Laurel Lund, "Personality Decorating—How to Make Your Home Say You," *Better Homes and Gardens,* August 1980, pp. 77–85.

67 "What You Can Do to Develop . . .": *House & Garden,* August 1980, pp. 67–69.

68 including an article on Picasso: "Remembering Picasso: How Don Pablo Lived," ibid., pp. 102–103 ff.

68 "A house is who you are . . .": Leslie Garis, "A House Is Who You Are," ibid., pp. 104–107 ff.

68 "We're proud of our house . . ." "Architectural Surprise: Throwing a Curve," ibid., pp. 96–101.

68 "Style is not a roomful . . .": Ibid. p. 68.

68 "pull it out, fine-tune itt . . .": Ibid, p. 67.

68 See . . . how cartoonist Charles Addams: Glenn Collins, "Charles Addams's Idiosyncratic 'Heap,'" *New York Times,* June 11, 1981, pp. C1 ff.

68 how Sylvester Stallone personalized: "*Architectural Digest* Visits: Sylvester Stallone," *Architectural Digest,* February 1982, pp. 92–97.

68 how Robert Redford put his point of view: Michael Rogers, "If Robert Redford Rides Again as an 'Electric Horseman' Does Stellar Power Exceed Solar?," *People,* February 18, 1980, pp. 96–100.

69 as little place for originality . . . "as in the dress of a man . . .": Hermann Muthesius, *The English House* (New York: Rizzoli, 1979), p. 149. (Originally published, Berlin: Wasmuth, 1904, 1905.) In this description of the English turn-of-the-century house, Muthesius said: "There is nothing extravagant, no desire to impress about its conception, no flights of fancy in ornament or jumbles of forms; it does not . . . try to be artistic. . . . To the Englishman, to parade whatever advantages of position or breeding he may have smacks of the parvenu. . . . Fancifulness, originality (the self-conscious kind!), display, architectonic window-dressing, decorative forms—the English find them as little in place in the house as in the dress of the man who inhabits it. . . ."

69 "the cheap originality": Edith Wharton and Ogden Codman, Jr. Introductory notes: John Barrington Bayley and William Coles, *The Decoration of Houses* (New

York: W. W. Norton, 1978), p. 17. (Reprint of Scribner's 1902 edition.)

70 "Homemakers are determined to have their houses . . .": Elsie de Wolfe, *The House in Good Taste* (New York: Century Co., 1913), pp. 3–4.

70 would not make for "drab uniformity": Helen Appleton Read, "Harmonized Rooms," *Creative-Art,* Vol. IV, No. 6, June 1929, p. xviii. Cited in Robert Koch (ed.), *Chase Chrome* (Privately published in Stamford, CT: Gladys Koch Antiques, 1978), p. 4.

70 "To be happily livable . . .": "Latest Developments in Modern Design," in Mary Jane Pool (ed.), *20th Century Decorating, Architecture & Gardens: 80 Years of Ideas & Pleasure from House & Garden*(New York: Holt, Rinehart and Winston, 1980), p. 120.

70 "should unmistakably suggest *you*": Emily Post, *The Personality of a House* (New York: Funk & Wagnalls, 1948), p. 2.

70 "If you choose to live in a palace . . .": Ibid., p. 6.

70 "Two chairs or carpets . . .": Ibid., p. 10.

71 spoke to the "soul rather than . . . the dictates . . .": Norma Skurka and Oberto Gili, *Underground Interiors* (New York: Quadrangle Books, 1972), back cover blurb.

71 Tom Wolfe: "The 'Me' Decade: Reports on America's New Great Awakening," *New York,* August 23, 1976, pp. 26–40.

72 "It's me"; "It's me"; "It's me"; "It's *moi*": Generic TV commercial shown in Charlotte, North Carolina, and Kansas

City, Missouri, in 1982. Sponsored by the Wallcovering Information Bureau.

72 "I believe absolutely in a house being . . .": Author's interview with Paula.

72 "Nobody on the Main Line . . .": Author's interview with Binky.

73 It is now very fashionable: Author's interview with James Duncan.

73 Duncan . . . created a furor in Bedford: James S. Duncan, Jr., "Landscape Taste as a Symbol of Group Identity: A Westchester County Village," *Geographical Review*, Vol. 63, No. 3, July 1973, pp. 334–55.

73 the home . . . is not always a symbol of one's personality: James S. Duncan, "From Container of Women to Status Symbol: The Impact of Social Structure on the Meaning of the House." In James S. Duncan (ed.), *Housing and Identity: Cross-Cultural Perspectives* (London: Croom Helm, 1981), pp. 36–59.

73 Duncan believes that most societies: Ibid. In the same paper, Duncan stated that "the shift from collectivism to individualism [is] one of the most fundamental social transformations in history."

74 "The more individual a society, the greater dependence . . .": Author's interview with James Duncan.

74 In 1979 Gerry Pratt: Gerry Pratt, "The House as an Expression of Social Worlds," in Duncan, *Housing and Identity*, pp. 135–79.

77 In a study comparing the houses of the old elite . . .: James S. Duncan and Nancy G. Duncan, "Residential Landscapes and Social Worlds: A Case Study in Hyderabad, Andhra Pradesh," in D. Sopher (ed), *An Exploration of India* (Ithaca, NY: Cornell University Press,

1980), pp. 271–86. Also see their "Housing as Presentation of Self and the Structure of Social Networks," in G. T. Moore and R. G. Golledge, *Environmental Knowing* (Stroudsburg, PA: Dowden, Hutchinson & Ross, 1976), pp. 247–53; and their "Social Worlds, Status Passage, and Environmental Perspectives," in Moore and Golledge, *Environmental Knowing*, pp. 206–13.

78 The Zapotecs of southern Mexico: B. L. Chinas, *The Isthmus Zapotecs: Women's Roles in Cultural Context* (New York: Holt, Rinehart and Winston, 1973). Cited in Duncan, "From Container of Women to Status Symbol," pp. 36–57, citation p. 52.

78 "the community, the ancestors, and the saints": Ibid., p. 52.

78 how they would spend a "windfall profit": Ibid., pp. 52–53.

78 "Most replied they would fix up their house": Ibid., p. 53.

79 "the house, the address, and its façade . . .": Author's interview with James Duncan.

79 "Most human interaction is structured in terms of judgments . . .": Thomas Hoult, "Experimental Measurement of Clothing as a Factor in Some Social Ratings of Selected Men," *American Sociological Review*, Vol. 19, June 1954, pp. 324–28.

79 "both sheets on every bed . . .": Enid Nemy, "Harry Platt of Tiffany's: The Urbane New Yorker," *New York Times*, February 1, l981, p. 49. The full quote is: "'I also remember that both sheets on every bed were changed every day,' [Mr. Platt] said."

80 But he lives modestly: Ibid.

80 "a group of people that belong to the setting": Harry Platt quote, ibid.

80 Tiffany's will not sell: Author's interview with Duane Garrison, public relations director of Tiffany's.

80 It didn't get exercised when socialite: Marilyn Bethany, "Tales of Tables at Tiffany's," *New York Times Magazine,* August 30, 1981, pp. 56–60.

4. Who Am I?
The Living Room
and Class Connection

84 *What Do You Say to a Naked Room?*: Catherine Crane, *What Do You Say to a Naked Room?* (New York: Dial Press, 1979).

84 ho-hum rooms with no sense of style: Catherine C. Crane, *Personal Places: How to Make Your Home Your Own* (New York: Whitney Library of Design, 1982).

85 one writer confessed recently to "furniture flings": Elane Feldman, "Promises, Promises," *New York Daily News,* December 31, 1980, p. 27.

85 "I want a place where a ten-year-old boy can eat . . .": Advertisement for *Architectural Digest, Vogue,* October 1982, p. 195.

86 Low, middle, and highbrow: Arnold Mitchell, "Social Change: Implications of Trends in Values and Lifestyles" (Menlo Park, CA: SRI International, 1979), p. 5. (Some Social and Market Topologies.)

86 personality is determined by internal needs: Paul Good and the Editors of Time-Life Books, *The Individual.* Human Behavior Series (New York: Time-Life Books, 1974), p. 141. See also Richard A. Kalish, *The Psychology of Human Behavior,* 4th edition (Monterey, CA:

Brooks/Cole Publishing [1966], 1977); and Edwin S. Shneidman (ed.), *Endeavors in Psychology: Selections from the Personology of Henry A. Murray* (New York: Harper & Row, 1981).

86 "the world is full of invisible forces . . .": Kai T. Erikson, "On Teaching Sociology," *Yale Alumni Magazine,* November 1978, pp. 34–36.

86 But social class "is a cultural reality": James H. S. Bossard and Eleanor S. Boll, "Ritual in Family Living," *American Sociological Review,* Vol. 14, No. 4, August 1949, pp. 463–69, citation p. 466.

86 "people live and work and play and think": Ibid.

87 The term "life style" irritates newspaper copy editors: The *New York Times Manual of Usage and Style* (1976) advised reporters: "*life style.* Do not overuse; there are other ways of saying it."

87 to sociologists, "life style" is what Max Weber: Alvin L. Bertrand, *Basic Sociology: An Introduction to Theory and Method* (New York: Appleton-Century-Crofts, 1967), pp. 173, 178.

87 /"Finally, a copier for the most important person . . .": Advertisement for Canon PC-10/20, *Wall Street Journal,* January 19, 1983, p. 32.

87 According to Daniel Yankelovich, 20 percent: Daniel Yankelovich, *New Rules: Searching for Self-Fulfillment in a World Turned Upside Down* (New York: Random House, 1981).

88 Fashion in material things is "a product of class . . .": Georg Simmel, *On Individuality and Social Forms,* (ed.) Donald N. Levine (Chicago: University of Chicago Press, 1971), p. 297.

88 Psychological studies have shown the

more difficult: Michael Argyle, Adrian Furnham, and Jean Ann Graham, *Social Situations* (New York: Cambridge University Press, 1981), pp. 55–56.

88 "a group that has had a past history of success . . .": Ibid., p. 56.

88 the $37,000 English country drawing room in pink: Donald Vining and Carol Helms, "War of the Roses," *Metropolitan Home*, February 1983, pp. 63–69.

88 "What your home could have in common with the Met . . .": Advertisement for Original Print Collectors Group, Ltd., 215 Lexington Ave, New York, NY, *New York Times Book Review*, 1981.

88 two successful entertainment figures, record mogul: Jane Glassman, "Word of Mouth," *Beverly Hills World*, Vol. 1, No. 2, November 1982, p. 12.

89 "the costliest sheets in the world . . .": Dale Kern, "Pratesi," *Beverly Hills World*, Vol. 1, No. 3, December 1982, pp. 42–44.

89 Old Guard New England families who had fallen: W. Lloyd Warner, *Yankee City* (New Haven: Yale University Press [1963], 1975), p. 66. Said Warner: "Mrs. T, an upper-upper who had fallen into straitened circumstances, sold her antiques to a Boston dealer with the proviso that he come to collect them at night . . . selling these objects to an outsider for purely economic reasons lessens the likelihood that the spiritual value of the family heirlooms will be transferred to the purchaser."

89 "magazine of privileged information": "Your essential Spring Wardrobe is Now Ready in the February *Town & Country*." Advertisement, *New York Times*, February 1, 1983, p. D20.

89 "desire for beauty . . . through sanc-

tioned form": Melville J. Herskovits, *Cultural Anthropology: An Abridged Version of Man and His Works* (New York: Alfred A. Knopf, 1955), pp. 234, 266.

90 "People who like eighteenth-century [English] antiques . . .": "Antiques Notebook: Reflections on the English Style," *Architectural Digest*, March 1982, p. 192.

90 "The people who buy French eighteenth-century . . .": Author's interview with Leon Dalva.

90 "The person who collects Victoriana . . .": Author's interview with Hervé Aaron.

90 Gans divided Americans into five "taste cultures": Herbert J. Gans, *Popular Culture and High Culture: An Analysis and Evaluation of Taste* (New York: Basic Books, 1974).

91 *La Distinction,* a monumental study: Pierre Bourdieu, *La Distinction: Critique Sociale du Jugement* (Paris: Les Editions de Minuit, 1979).

92 Whistler's Mother was considered *highbrow*: Russell Lynes, *The Tastemakers: The Shaping of Popular American Taste* (New York: Dover Publications [1949], 1980), pp. 326–27.

92 "the culture that is closest to family and home . . .": Herbert J. Gans, "American Popular Culture and High Culture in a Changing Class Structure" (New York: Sociology Department, Columbia University, 1983), p. 18.

92 "Performances for guests are most often given": Erving Goffman, *Presentation of Self in Everyday Life* (Garden City, NY: Anchor Books, 1959).

92 "The living room stands for how it should be . . .": Harold Alexander, *De-*

sign: Criteria for Decisions (New York: Macmillan, 1976), p. 131.

92 "the living room is as close to being a sacred place . . .": Irwin Altman and Martin M. Chemers, *Culture and Environment* (Monterey, CA: Brooks/Cole Publishing, 1980), p. 198.

92 "a symbol of the family's status and values": Ibid.

93 "taste exchanging": David Reisman, with Nathan Glazer and Revel Denney, *The Lonely Crowd* (New Haven: Yale University Press [1950], 1971), p. 297.

93 "A living room . . . confronts . . .": W. H. Auden, "The Common Life," *About the House* (New York: Random House, 1965), p. 36.

93 Who wouldn't set aside: See Enid Nemy, "A Living Room: We Can't Do Without It," *New York Times*, Home Section, May 8, 1980.

94 Sixty-nine percent of *Better Homes and Gardens* consumer: "Inquiry: A Study on Home Furnishings From the Better Homes and Gardens Consumer Panel, 1982" (New York: Meredith Corporation, 1982).

94 *House & Garden* subscribers were planning to redecorate: *A Report on the House & Garden Market for Decorating and Home Furnishings.* Research Report #8437 (New York: Scarborough Research Corporation, April 1980), p. 14.

94 *Architectural Digest* subscribers had done more recent: Simmons Research Bureau, "*Architectural Digest:* A Profile of Subscribers," July 1981 (New York: Simmons Market Research Bureau, July 1981).

94 its average subscriber entertains sixty-five people: "Affluence America."

Promotional Literature and advertisement (Los Angeles: Knapp Communications Corporation, 1981).

96 "There appears to be a continuing need . . .": Philip Langdon, "Design Notebook: The Family Room and How It Has Changed," *New York Times,* January 6, 1983, p. C10.

96 Graff believes it's important: Charlan Graff, "Alienation or Identification: A Function of Space in the Home," in Perla Korosec-Serfaty (ed.), *Appropriation of Space: Proceedings of the Strasbourg Conference* (Strasbourg, France: Louis Pasteur University, 1976), pp. 291–334.

96 "Street life is not a choice but a necessity . . .": Herbert J. Gans, "Toward a Human Architecture: A Sociologist's View of the Profession," *Journal of Architectural Education,* Vol. XXXI, No. 2, 1978, pp. 26–31, citation p. 30.

97 "we feel obliged to sweep away the smell of dinner . . .": Marjorie Gelfond, "New Jersey Opinion: The Meaning of Home," *New York Times,* New Jersey Edition, August 22, 1982.

97 "There is no zero point in . . . human development": Norbert Elias, *The History of Manners: The Civilizing Process,* trans. Edmund Jephcott (New York: Pantheon [1939], 1978), p. 160.

98 "In times when life is threatening . . .": Patricia Leigh Brown, "Gimme Shelters," *Metropolis,* January/February 1983.

98 "Almost everyone is jealous of his social status . . .": F. Stuart Chapin, *Contemporary American Institutions: A Sociological Analysis* (New York: Harper & Brothers, 1935), p. 373.

99 "The Living Room Status Scale": Ibid., p. 378.

99 "to determine its social position in the community": Ibid., p. 375.

100 to an upper-middle class 149 points: Ibid., p. 378. (Chapin's scale gave no score for "upper-class.")

100 it "would have had to be constantly revised": Richard P. Coleman and Lee Rainwater, with Kent A. McClelland, *Social Standing in America: New Dimensions of Class* (New York: Basic Books, 1978), p. 320.

100 "It is well known that objects tell a great deal . . .": Jean Baudrillard, *For a Critique of the Political Economy of the Sign,* trans. Charles Levin (St. Louis: Telos Press, 1981), p. 35.

100 Some things denote "factual status": Ibid., p. 37.

101 the seminal study of status in Newburyport: Warner, *Yankee City.*

101 the house is "the very heart of the technical . . .": Ibid., p. 234.

101 James Davis in the 1950s asked Cambridge housewives: James Allan Davis, "Living Rooms as Symbols of Status: A Study in Social Judgment." Ph.D. dissertation, Department of Sociology, Harvard University, January 1955.

102 Edward Laumann and James House took the living room: Edward O. Laumann and James S. House, *Living Room Styles and Social Attributes: The Patterning of Material Artifacts in a Modern Urban Community.* Reprint Series #41 (Ann Arbor, MI: Center for Research on Social Organization: Department of Sociology, University of Michigan, 1970).

102 Veblen in his send-up of leisure class: Thorstein Veblen, *The Theory of the Leisure Class* (New York: Mentor, 1953).

103 "There is a strong acceleration of furniture spending . . .": Wallace W. Epperson, Jr., *1982 Home Furnishings Compendium* (Richmond, VA: Wheat First Securities, 1982), p. 531.

103 People judge other people by their standard of living: Coleman et al., *Social Standing in America.*

105 One of these studies is called "The Home": Dustin Macgregor, *The Home: VALS Analytical Report, Values and Lifestyle Program* (Menlo Park, CA: SRI International, December 1979).

106 the Inner Directed and the Outer Directed: David Reisman et al., *Lonely Crowd.* Reisman defined three types of individuals; *tradition-directed* people who operate in a tightly knit web of kin and family, and whose values are bound by tradition; *inner-directed* individuals who belong to the "old" middle class and get their values from their elders; and *other-directed* people, the new middle class who get their values from friends and the mass media.

107 Jacqueline Onassis's hideaway in Martha's Vineyard: "Mrs. Onassis' Hideaway is Nearing Completion," *New York Times,* October 1, 1981, p. C7.

108 a recent study of California homes: Thomas S. Weisner and Joan C. Weibel, "Home Environments and Family Lifestyles in California," *Environment and Behavior,* Vol. 13, No. 4, July 1981. Said the authors, "The higher the value placed by both parents on conventional achievement and materialism, the less disordered the home." Materialists have more "decoratively complex" homes, color coordinated and filled, *in an organized way,* with posters, maps, prints, pillows, plants, antiques, and knickknacks. The counterculture or antimaterialist home, on the contrary, has more books and more "disorder and functional complexity."

109 "rank must be marked": Mary Douglas and Baron Isherwood, *The World of Goods* (New York: Basic Books, 1979), p. 118.

5. *Sex Role and Decorating Role*

112 "They just assumed it would be a woman at home . . .": Author's interview with psychologist Jerome Tognoli of C. W. Post College.

113 "the home is the core aspect of human experience": Jerome Tognoli, "The Flight from Domestic Space: Men's Roles in the Household," *The Family Coordinator,* October 1979, pp. 599–607, citation p. 599. See also Susan Saegert and Gary Winkel, "The Home: A Critical Problem for Changing Sex Roles." Paper presented at the American Sociological Association meetings, San Francisco, September 1978.

113 "Men typically do not invite men friends . . .": Tognoli, "The Flight from Domestic Space," p. 604.

113 In Barry Goldwater's Washington, D.C., condominium: Susan Watters, "Barry Goldwater: Crusty and Cantankerous," *W,* April 8–15, 1983, p. 50.

113 consider the gender segregation experiment: John Ofrias and Jerome Tognoli, "Women's and Men's Responses Toward the Home in Heterosexual and Same Sex Households: A Case Study," in A. D. Seidel and S. Danfords (eds.), *Environmental Design: Theory, Research and Application* (Washington, D.C.: Environmental Design Research Association, 1979).

114 "Is it an experiment to find out their compatibility . . .": Ibid.

115 judging from the ads run by bookstores before Father's: Waldenbooks advertisement, *New York Times,* June 12, 1981, p. A14.

115 the thirteen TV shows most popular with children: Jerome Tognoli and J. L. Storch, "Inside and Out: Setting Locations of Female and Male Characters in Children's Television," in R. Stough and A. Wandersmann (eds.), *Optimizing Environments: Research, Practice and Policy* (Washington, D.C.: Environmental Design Research Association, 1980).

116 "Man is the lamp of the outside and woman the lamp . . .": Pierre Bourdieu, "The Berber House," in Mary Douglas (ed.), *Rules and Meanings* (New York: Penguin Books, 1973), pp. 98–110, citation p. 110.

116 "The man who stays too long in the house . . .": Ibid., p. 103. See also Thomas Gregor, "No Girls Allowed," *Science 82,* December 1982, pp. 26–31. According to Gregor, among the Mehinaku (sometimes spelled Mehinacu) Indians of Brazil, "a man who spends too much time in the house with his wife and family is called a trashyard person . . . or a woman."

116 "'A woman's place is in the home' is a relatively new . . .": Nona Glazer-Malbin, "Housework," *Signs: Journal of Women in Culture and Society* (University of Chicago), Vol. 1, No. 4, Summer 1976, pp. 905–22, citation p. 912.

116 It "was never shaken up and smoothed . . .": Joseph Gies and Frances Gies, *Women in the Middle Ages* (New York: Barnes & Noble Books [1978], 1980), p. 34.

116 "Details of housekeeping he should commit entirely . . .": Ibid., p. 229.

117 "Pray let it be neat and fashionable or send none": Edgar deN. Mayhew and Minor Meyers, Jr., *A Documentary His-*

tory of American Interiors from the Colonial Era to 1915 (New York: Charles Scribner's Sons, 1980), p. 51. Also Susan Gray Detweiler, *George Washington's Chinaware* (New York: Harry N. Abrams, Inc., 1982). Detweiler described Washington's interest in matters of taste: "Born into the Tidewater, Virginia gentry whose men found architecture, interiors, and the dining table appropriate pursuits in the art of 'genteel' living, he deliberated and corresponded about these matters as early as age twenty-five and as late as 1798, the year before his death."

In the author's conversation with Detweiler, she said, "It is hard to determine if women had a say in the home decoration in that period. In Virginia, the landed gentry were interested in interior decoration as part of architecture."

117 "these were my fancy": Mayhew and Meyers, *Documentary History of American Interiors,* p. 64.

117 no real evidence that upper-class: Edgar deN. Mayhew, Professor of Art History at Connecticut College, believes there "is not much evidence of women getting involved in the eighteenth century. . . . Maintenance was the woman's job. . . . It was the men who were competitive with their homes." Jane Nylander, curator of the re-created New England village at Sturbridge, Massachusetts, told the author: "You're in good company" if you are confused about the American women's role in decoration in the eighteenth century. The documentation of the period," she said, "shows men were doing the purchasing; it was popular to talk of the men as the tastemakers. . . . Wealthy women did do decorative work that was displayed in the home, but their work did not survive." Men even wrote the advice books. Women got power in the home about the same time that a household advice book was written by a woman. The first was the immensely successful 1825 book on domestic duties, including deco-

rating hints, by Frances Byerly Parkes (Mrs. William Parkes).

117 in 1845, when historic records show: Author's discussion with Jane Nylander.

117 symbol of "the man who earned it": Jan Cohn, *The Palace or the Poorhouse: The American House as a Cultural Symbol* (East Lansing, MI: Michigan State University Press, 1979), p. 224.

117 Man's house, woman's home: Ibid.

117 it was "man's business to earn money . . .": Albert Hayes, M.D., *Physiology of Women and her Diseases* (Boston: Peabody Medical Institute, 1869) p. 56. In Sarah Stage, *Female Complaints* (New York: W. W. Norton, 1979), p. 66.

117 advice books churned out to teach women: Catharine Beecher, *A Treatise on Domestic Economy* (New York: Schocken Books [1841 edition], 1977); Catharine Beecher and Harriet Beecher Stowe, *The American Woman's Home* (New York, 1869); Edith Wharton and Ogden Codman, Jr., *The Decoration of Houses* (W. W. Norton, New York [1897] 1978). The following books and articles illuminate the history of advice to women: Barbara Ehrenreich and Deirdre English, *For Her Own Good: 150 Years of the Experts' Advice to Women* (Garden City, NY: Anchor Books, 1979); Jane Davison, *The Fall of a Doll's House* (New York: Holt, Rinehart and Winston, 1980); Sheila Levant de Bretteville, "The 'Parlorization' of Our Homes and Ourselves," *Chrysalis,* No. 9, Fall 1979; Betty Friedan, *The Feminine Mystique* (New York: Dell Publishing [1963] 1974); Ruth Schwartz Cowan, "The 'Industrial Revolution' in the Home: Household Technology and Social Change in the 20th Century," *Journal of Technology and Culture,* No. 17, 1976, pp. 1–23; Joann Vanek, "Household Technology and Social Status: Rising Living Standards and Status and Residence Differences in

Housework," *Journal of Technology and Culture,* July 1978, pp. 361–75.

117 including not picking teeth at the table: *Decorum: A Practical Treatise on Etiquette and Dress of the Best American Society* (New York: Union Publishing House, 1881), p. 98.

117 a new stereotype . . . the frivolous woman: "The stereotype of the vain and giddy woman, ambitious for a fashionable house, appears as early as the 1840s," said historian Jan Cohn in *Palace or the Poorhouse,* p. 227. See also Florine B. Livson, "Changing Sex Roles in the Social Environment of Later Life," in Graham D. Rowles and Russell J. Ohta (eds.), *Aging and Milieu* (New York: Academic Press, 1983). According to Livson, two stereotypes were born in the nineteenth century: "the good provider" and "the dependent woman."

118 "Our whole social fabric would be better for it . . .": Ehrenreich and English, *For Her Own Good,* p. 148.

118 Erik Erikson . . . said . . . women were innately inner-oriented: Erik H. Erikson, "Genital Modes and Spatial Modalities," *Childhood and Society* (New York: W. W. Norton [1950], 1963), pp. 97–108.

118 "Spatial relationships are anathema to most women . . .": John N. Miller, "Sex and the Design Scene," *Washington Star Home-Life Magazine,* November 4, 1979, pp. 14–15.

118 "Has the female a characteristic way . . .": Yi-Fu Tuan, *Topophilia: A Study of Environmental Perception, Attitudes and Values* (Englewood Cliffs, NJ: Prentice-Hall, 1974), p. 53.

119 Woman's attachment to the home: Carol Gilligan, *In a Different Voice: Psychological Theory and Women's*

Development (Cambridge, MA: Harvard University Press, 1982).

119 the sexual division of space is culturally ingrained: Roger Hart, *Children's Experience of Place* (New York: Irvington Press, 1978). See also Marie Nordstrom, "This Is How I Would Like to Live," *Childhood City Newsletter,* No. 19, January 1980. Center for Human Environments, Graduate School of City University, New York. In a study of fifteen-year-olds' attitudes Nordstrom found that boys "regard the home as something one achieves, as well as something one leaves and returns to . . . the girls were looking upon the home as a place for being and living."

120 A content analysis of the rooms of children under six: Harriet L. Rheingold and Kaye V. Cook, "The Contents of Boys' and Girls' Rooms as an Index of Parents' Behavior," *Child Development,* No. 46, 1975, pp. 459–63.

120 In a study of dorm decor it was found that women spent: David R. Mandel, Reuben M. Baron, and Jeffrey D. Fisher, "Room Utilization and Dimensions of Density," *Environment & Behavior,* Vol. 12, No. 3, September 1980, pp. 308–19.

120 These attitudes carry over into marriage: Saegert and Winkel, "The Home," pp. 50–51.

120 Women consider the home: Ibid.

120 Men . . . aren't nearly as wrapped up: Ibid.

120 Keller found that 39 percent of the women: Suzanne Keller, *Women in a Planned Community,* pamphlet (Cambridge, MA: Lincoln Institute of Land Policy, 1978), p. 6.

120 men were consistently less emotionally involved: Saegert and Winkel, "The

Home." See also Susan Saegert, "House and Home in the Lives of Women" (New York: Center for Human Environments, City University of New York Graduate Center, 1978).

120 "unconscious desire . . . to assure that their home: Ibid.

120 British husbands . . . take pride in their neighborhood: Kathy Rees and David Canter, "Comparing Married Couples' Satisfaction with Their Housing Environment." Paper presented at the International Conference on Environmental Psychology, University of Surrey, Guildford, England, July 16–20, 1979.

121 satisfaction with the home: Ibid.

121 from their "role perspectives": Ibid. See also Mihaly Csikszentmihalyi and Eugene Rochberg-Halton, *The Meaning of Things: Domestic Symbols and the Self* (New York: Cambridge University Press, 1981). These authors found that men and women value different things in the home and value the same things for different reasons.

121 in an *Esquire* fashion spread we saw a liberated daddy: *Esquire,* March 1983, pp. 34–35.

121 a young man mastering the art of French cooking: Ibid., pp. 92–99.

121 TV's Ted Koppel is probably America's: Letty Cottin Pogrebin, "Househusbands," *Ladies' Home Journal,* November 1977, pp. 30–32 ff.

121 One man in three cooks one meal a week: Author's interview with Barbara Tober, Editor of *Bride's.*

121 But study after study shows men are masters: Saegert and Winkel, "The Home." According to Saegert and Winkel, there is "little movement in the direction

of greater equality either in activity or in symbolic involvement" in the home between men and women. They found that, on questioning, respondents in their survey "tend to present themselves as more egalitarian than might actually be the case." And that except for taking out the garbage, "most of the household tasks that must be performed on a regular basis are performed by women." See also Philip Shenon, "A Woman's Work Is Never Done," *New York Times,* March 6, 1983, p. F29. According to Shenon, in a study of dual-career couples, Wanda Brewster-O'Reilly of Stanford University's School of Education found that when it came to equality, working husbands and wives were "not very" equal. "If a couple had children . . . the wife took charge of them. . . . the mothers spent 31 hours a week on average for housework and child care. Their husbands . . . just 23 hours." "If somebody had to give up something, it was almost always the wife" who made the sacrifice. And see Julie A. Matthaei, *An Economic History of Women in America* (New York: Schocken Books, 1982). Matthaei, on the other hand, believes "a new conception of marriage and family life is clearly emerging" with more shared responsibility between mates.

121 "one parent should stay home with preschool children . . .": Louis Harris & Associates, *Families at Work: Strengths and Strains* (Minneapolis, MN: The General Mills American Family Report, 1980–81), p. 61.

121 "one of those cultural definitions enshrined in myth . . .": Bonnie Loyd, "Woman's Place, Man's Place," *Landscape,* October 1975, pp. 10–13, citation p. 11.

122 Marrying the house: I am *not* using this term to mean agoraphobia. A new book on that subject is Karen DeCrow and Robert Seidenberg's *Women Who Marry Houses* (New York: McGraw-Hill, 1983).

122 she wanted to "grow up and get married and have a house . . .": Thomas Thompson, "Private Thoughts of a Former Washingtonian," *Life,* March 1982, pp. 87–90, citation p. 90.

122 Marilyn Monroe, at the height of her celebrity: Margaret Parton, "A Revealing Last Interview with Marilyn Monroe," *Look,* February 19, 1979, pp. 23–26, citation p. 25.

122 Revlon's Charlie agrees it's time to settle down: Bill Abrams, "Why Revlon's Charlie Seems to Be Ready to Settle Down," *Wall Street Journal,* December 23, 1982, p. 11.

122 the Cosmo girl dropped the bombshell that she was buying: "I can't believe what I'm doing tomorrow . . . buying a house!" Advertisement for *Cosmopolitan, New York Times,* April 12, 1983, p. C18.

122 "It means being an artist on your own planet . . .": Nancy Collins, "Bette Midler: The Cheese-Bomb American Crapola Dream," *Rolling Stone,* December 9, 1982, pp. 15–21, citation p. 15.

122 In lovebirds . . . hormones trigger nest-building: Niko Tinbergen and the Editors of Time-Life Books, *Animal Behavior* (New York: Time-Life Books, 1965), pp. 87–88.

122 Until recently brides were marched: In fact, they still are. See Kim Wright Wiley, "A Bride by Any Other Name: Planning a Wedding Can Transform the Most Level-headed Executive into a Dithering Idiot," *Savvy,* August 1983, pp. 74–77.

124 "It's the beautiful accessories on your table . . .": "Nuances," *Bride's,* April/May 1983, pp. 252–253.

126 Caring for the house-as-status-symbol: Bonnie Loyd, "Women, Home and Status," in James S. Duncan (ed.), *Housing & Identity: Cross-Cultural Perspectives* (London: Croom Helm, 1981), pp. 181–97. The connection between woman and home is "a social ideal," wrote Loyd, a geographer and editor of *Landscape* magazine in Berkeley, CA. "Biology originally anchored women in the home. Their childbearing and child care kept them close to the hearth." But today, said Loyd, only a few years are spent as a full-time mother. As child-rearing responsibilities decrease, homemaking responsibilities increase—in proportion to income. "None of the schemes for reducing [housework] recognize that one of its functions is maintaining the icon of the family's status, the home," said Loyd.

126 "Decorating . . . is a major task for American homemakers . . .": Loyd, "Woman's Place, Man's Place," p. 11.

127 "A 'nice' home reflects a good homemaker . . .": Ibid. See also Theodore Caplow, *The Sociology of Work* (New York: McGraw Hill, 1964), p. 268. To avoid the "menial identification" of housework, said Caplow, "it is necessary to attach great importance to the difference in emotional quality between the work of the housewife and that of the servant."

127 the wife is still the purchase instigator: "Wife Has a Big Say in Buying Decisions," *Home Furnishings Daily,* February 11, 1975; "Straight Talk About the Potential Male Market," June 23, 1980. According to this article, the wife was still the purchase instigator on most items. Explaining why he pitched his advertising to women for his furniture accounts, Sandy Gaines of Levinstein & Gaines, an ad agency, said, "we advertise to the instigator." By 1983, according to the author's interview with Carl Levine of Bloomingdale's, women were still the major purchase influencers, even though men were an increasingly important market. At Conran's in mid-1983, however, according to store president Pauline Dora, men and women were shopping together: "I don't think women are the purchase influence anymore."

127 Take Chris Evert Lloyd: Andrea Feld, "A Perfect Match," *Bride's,* April/May 1983, p. 80.

127 "I leave it to my little lady to choose . . .": Ibid.

127 the lady of leisure: Suzanne Keller, "The Female Role: Constants and Change," in Violet Franks and Vasanti Burtle (eds.), *Women in Therapy* (New York: Brunner/Mazel, 1974), pp. 411–34, citation p. 423.

127 "First . . . she always dresses beautifully . . .": Cornelius Vanderbilt Whitney, "Live Six Months With a Millionaire," *Harper's,* May 1982, pp. 37–45, citation p. 37.

129 "All my life I wanted a canopy bed": Jeff Jarvis, reported by Fred Bernstein, "Mr. T.," *People,* May 30, 1983, pp. 108–112, citation p. 111.

129 she "discovered she had moved into a way of life . . .": Barbara Goldsmith, *Little Gloria . . . Happy at Last* (New York: Dell Publishing [1980], 1981), p. 132.

129 "he understands me," and "I would like conditions . . .": Ibid.

130 "he had very strong views . . .": Mary Lutyens, *Edwin Lutyens, By His Daughter* (London: John Murray Publishers, 1980), p. 46.

131 Judith Langer distinguishes the Old-Fashioned Man: Judith Langer, "Looking at Men: Change and Tradition." Speech delivered to the Advertising Research Foundation, March 9, 1983 (New York: Judith Langer Associates, 1983), p. 5.

131 "Men in long-term relationships resist change": Ibid., p. 14.

132 *Home Furnishings Daily* has dubbed them the "New Target": "Field's Setting the Table for the Contemporary Man," *HFD—Retailing Home Furnishings,* June 23, 1980, p. 16. "Inside Furniture: Probing the Male Shopper: What Will He Buy," ibid., p. 24. See also Sandra Salmans, "Advertising: The Male Consumer Market," *New York Times,* August 11, 1982.

133 Jean Harris . . . testified that she had a chair reupholstered: Diana Trilling, *Mrs. Harris: Death of the Scarsdale Diet Doctor* (New York: Harcourt Brace Jovanovich, 1981), p. 95.

134 But many men feel hurt by this image: Author's interview with Judith Langer. See "The Male Homemaker" (New York: Judith Langer Associates, June 1982). In this report, Langer divides the male homemaker into two categories: the "Settlers," who see their homes as reflections of themselves, and the "Pup-Tenters," who use their homes as hotels. But no matter which type they are, men view the home differently from women, said Langer; they have no guilt about housekeeping lapses and no ego-involvement in "cooking-cleaning-shopping."

134 men view their homes more as functional objects: Langer, "Looking at Men."

134 Carl Levine says the single male furniture customer: Author's interview with Carl Levine.

135 it is not unusual for her clients to spend one-quarter: Author's interview with Susan Shins.

135 A cartoon by Charles Saxon: Charles Saxon, "Sony customers don't buy different products. They buy different Sonys." Sony advertisement, *HFD,* July 28, 1980, p. 45.

135 "The only difference between men and boys . . .": Rebecca Bricker, "In the Image and Spirit of Terry Fox, Amputee Eric Fryer Runs to Stardom," *People,* May 30, 1983, pp. 46–48, citation p. 48.

135 The male fascination with equipment: Langer, "Looking at Men."

135 the best market for the $250 pasta machines: Speech by Barbara Kafka for American Institute of Kitchen Dealers. New York, Princeton Club, February 26, 1982.

135 an aftershave lotion that is "soft . . .": Langer, "Looking at Men."

136 "That any normal man should be repelled . . .": Emily Post, *The Personality of a House* (New York: Funk & Wagnalls, 1930), p. 405.

137 "Every open-beamed doorless barewalled room . . .": Ibid., 1948, p. 413.

137 "It was all brown, very boring male furniture . . .": "Page Six: David Stockman, Domestic Pussycat," *New York Post,* circa June 2, 1983, p. 6.

137 Male living rooms are being dressed: According to Bloomingdale's Carl Levine, the recent fashion for pastels did not sell at all well to men. See also Steven Woodward Naifeh and Gregory White Smith, *Playboy's Moving Up in Style* (New York: Playboy Paperbacks [1980], 1982). Readers of this book are advised: "You may think furniture is something only women need worry about. Not so. You may not have a woman around to guide the furniture selection or interior design. But whether you do or not, you should know enough about the subject to help yourself." Furniture budgets are suggested for various income levels along with color advice that is stereotypical: "Brown corduroy sleeper . . . white bunching tables . . . natural color armchairs . . . gray sofa . . . black leather Wassily chairs . . . medium gray carpet." Men are advised to avoid any color in a strong hue "except possibly deep blue." And they are advised to stick to the Bauhaus look—white walls and neutral colors—otherwise the whole variety of choices could be "overwhelming." "Too much of a good color is too much. . . . Geometric patterns are safest." And watch out for decorators, say the authors, or the reader will end up being "too tasteful for your own good." Other advice is "avoid knickknacks" and things that are "too personal or sentimental."

137 "everything was flowers and lace . . .": John Duka, "Notes on Fashion," *New York Times,* May 24, 1983. In the author's interview with Ed Newman, a creative director for Dan River, a manufacturer of bed linens, Newman said, "Blue-collar men who do dirty work enjoy going home and sleeping on pretty sheets." Just as long as everyone knows the man didn't pick the flowers, he enjoys the feeling of being a guest in the boudoir. A similar finding was reported in Joan Kron's "Sheets: The New Security Blanket," *New York,* March 24, 1975.

137 if Prince Charles were living alone his sitting room: Gwen Robyns, "Diana: When a Princess becomes a Superstar," *Ladies' Home Journal,* June 1983, pp. 85–88 ff.

137 "People say . . . 'You'll make someone . . .'": Author's interview with Judith Langer. Also in Langer, "Looking at Men."

137 "I'm not very houseproud," insisted one bachelor: Suzanne Slesin, "A Gentleman's Quarters, Made to Order," *New York Times,* November 25, 1982, pp. C1 ff.

138 using the kitchen to clean his motorcycle: Author's interview with Judith Langer.

138 "the androgynous personality": Livson, "Changing Sex Roles," p. 148.

138 "equally at home with masculine instrumentality . . .": Ibid.

6. Home Cycles: What Time of Life Is This Place?

140 memorialized on a needlepoint pillow: Anthony Haden-Guest, "Pia Zadora," *New York,* January 25, 1982.

140 "Uh, oh, cushions on the floor": Donald Reilly, *The New Yorker,* May 23, 1977, p. 32.

141 behavior "can be shown to relate to [chronological] age": David Canter, *Psychology for Architects* (London: Applied Science Publishers, 1974), p. 63. For a correlation of changing privacy needs to different times of life see Maxine Wolfe, "Childhood and Privacy," in Irwin Altman and Joachim F. Wohlwill, *Childhood and the Environment* (New York: Plenum Press, 1978), pp. 353–72.

141 life cycle is "the universal escalator on which everyone rides": Barney G. Glaser and Anselm L. Strauss, *Status Passage: A Formal Theory* (Chicago: Aldine, 1971), p. 171.

141 Are we students, workers, or retirees: freshman wives: Arnold Mitchell, "Social Change: Implications of Trends in Values and Lifestyles" (Menlo Park, CA:

SRI International, January 1979), p. 5. (Some Market and Social Typologies.)

141 Bloomingdale's Carl Levine divides old taste from young: Author's interview with Carl Levine, senior vice-president of Bloomingdale's. See also Mihaly Csikszentmihalyi and Eugene Rochberg-Halton, *The Meaning of Things: Domestic Symbols of the Self* (New York: Cambridge University Press, 1981).

142 Only the Manus of New Guinea have been able: Lita Furby, "Possessions: Toward a Theory of Their Meaning and Function Throughout the Life Cycle," in Paul B. Baltes (ed.), *Life-Span Development and Behavior,* Vol. 1 (New York: Academic Press, 1978), pp. 297–336, citation pp. 306–307. Furby quotes Margaret Mead (*Growing Up in New Guinea* [New York: Morrow, 1930]), who said that among the Manus, "a good baby is a baby which never touches anything; a good child is one who never touches anything and never asks for anything not its own."

142 "The place wasn't designed to hide the wires of two of them": Tom Stites, "Computers Come Home but Where Do They Go?" *New York Times,* March 31, 1983, p. C8. This was a temporary problem for Toffler while he was trying out a new computer.

143 almost 18 percent of the population moving each year: John Herbers, "Poll Find Mobility Varies by Region," *New York Times,* March 2, 1983, p. B6.

143 three basic reasons for moving are all related to life cycle: Housing Research Unit, Department of Psychology, University of Surrey, England. "Reasons for Moving," Report #9, May 1980.

143 William Agee and Mary Cunningham bought a house: "Take One," *People,* May 16, 1983, p. 33.

143 Roxanne Pulitzer had to vacate her $1.5 million Palm Beach: Margot Dougherty, "Life Visits Palm Beach," *Life,* March 1983, pp. 93–98, citation p. 95.

143 Robert Wagner moved the kids: Jeff Jarvis, reported by David Wallace, "Superdad Wagner," *People,* July 4, 1983, pp. 96–100.

143 Patty Hearst's husband, Bernard Shaw, is leaving: Sharon Churcher, "Intelligencer," *New York,* June 27, 1983, p. 9.

143 his wife Sheila wrote a first-person piece: Sheila Foster, "The Rigors and Rewards of Marriage to a Star," *New York Times,* July 25, 1982, Sports Section, p. 2.

143 Judi "was not at all happy at the prospect . . .": "New New Yorker," *New York Times,* July 20, 1982.

143 Mike Deaver had to leave his grand piano behind: John Duka, "Arriving Washington Wives: Moving and Settling In," *New York Times,* May 28, 1981, pp. C1 ff.

143 the Caspar Weinbergers left their California rose garden: Ibid.

143 Alexander Haig couldn't find a house: "Land Rush in Washington," *Time,* February 9, 1981, p. 28.

143 People generally upgrade to bring "their residences": Peter H. Rossi, *Why Families Move,* 2nd edition (Beverly Hills: Sage Publications, 1980), p. 227.

144 and look at more houses when they are upgrading: "Reasons for Moving," Report #9.

144 three things in a residence: Nikke Finke Greenberg, "People in Class Houses," *Ultra,* May 1983, p. 83.

144 give them Park Avenue addresses: Randall Smith, "A Fancy Address in New York May Be Just Fanciful," *Wall Street Journal,* May 27, 1983, p. 1.

144 north of Beverly Hills use a tony Beverly Hills address: Ibid.

144 "The Browns are really excited about moving . . .": Quotes from "Buyer Profiles: Woodbridge Cottage Homes," supplied by the Irvine Company, Newport Beach, California.

145 if you're young, you want your fireplace: Author's interview with Donald Moe, Irvine's director of marketing.

145 Irvine builds for thirteen market segments: "How the Irvine Company Decides What to Build (November 1981)." Press material supplied by the Irvine Company.

145 600 communities around the country geared to older adults: Marianne Constantinou, "For Empty-Nesters, the Adult Village," *New York Times,* May 15, 1983, Section 8, pp. 1 ff.

146 Solon, the early Greek poet: Daniel J. Levinson, *The Seasons of a Man's Life* (New York: Ballantine, 1978), pp. 28–29.

146 "to lose and find oneself in another": Erik H. Erikson, *Identity and the Life Cycle* (New York: W. W. Norton [1959], 1980), p. 178.

146 today's life-cycle theorists generally agree: Roger Gould, M.D., *Transformation: Growth and Change in Adult Life* (New York: Touchstone, 1978); Levinson, *Seasons of a Man's Life;* Bernice L. Neugarten (ed.), *Middle Age and Aging* (Chicago: University of Chicago Press, 1968); Gail Sheehy, *Passages: Predictable Crises of Adult Life* (New York: E. P. Dutton [1974], 1976); George E. Vaillant, *Adaptation to Life: How the Best and the*

Brightest Came of Age (Boston: Little, Brown, 1977).

146 must transfer to gerontologists who will tell you: Nancy Datan, "Star-Crossed Love: The Developmental Phenomenologies of the Life Cycle," in Graham D. Rowles and Russell J. Ohta (eds.), *Aging and Milieu: Environmental Perspectives on Growing Old* (New York: Academic Press, 1983), pp. 29–38.

147 "If the commune prevents loneliness before thirty . . .": Vaillant, *Adaptation to Life*, p. 215.

147 "A person's residence is in part a place to sleep . . .": All the quotes in this paragraph are from the author's interview with Daniel J. Levinson.

147 a major study of the male life cycle: Levinson, *Seasons of a Man's Life.*

147 Even Andy Warhol's factory headquarters: John Richardson, "Andy on the Move: The Factory Factor," *House & Garden,* July 1983, pp. 90–97 ff.

148 "establish the Factory socially as well as artistically": Ibid., p. 148.

148 "To mature we all have to 'die' . . .": Victor Turner, "Rites of Passage," *Celebration: A World of Art and Ritual* (Washington, D.C.: Smithsonian Institution Press, 1982), p. 107. See also Mircea Eliade, *The Sacred and the Profane: The Nature of Religion,* trans. Willard R. Trask (New York: Harcourt Brace Jovanovich/Harvest [1957], 1959), p. 184.

148 ending one stage involves evaluating the past: Levinson, *Seasons of a Man's Life,* p. 51.

148 "Throwing away any possession, however useless . . .": Perla Korosec-Serfaty, "The Home, From Attic to Cellar." Paper presented at the 2nd Annual University of California at Irvine Symposium on Environmental Psychology, 1982, p. 13. See also Harold Searles, *The Nonhuman Environment* (New York: International Universities Press, 1960), p.389. According to Searles, people who repeatedly discard material possessions for more prestigious ones could be inflicting emotional impoverishment on themselves and on their families.

148 Leaving home is a crucial time in one's life . . .": Daniel Goleman, "Leaving Home," *Psychology Today,* August 1980, pp. 52–61.

149 "I was dredging out my son's room . . .": Barbara Thwaites, "Letters: Destroying Childhood," *New York Times,* October 21, 1982, p. C7.

149 "once away the children won't want to come home": Suzanne Slesin, "Three Suburban Couples Start Over Again in City Apartments," *New York Times,* February 17, 1983, pp. C1 ff., citation p. C6.

149 "they really need the feeling of having a home . . .": Author's interview with Jay Haley.

149 "Our daughter is in college . . .": Ibid.

149 Feeling at home in a place: Jerome Tognoli and Jaime Horwitz, "Development of a Home of One's Own: Individuals Living Alone Describe Their Residential Histories." Paper presented at the 12th Environmental Design Research Association Conference, Ames, Iowa, April 1981.

150 the first home as "a perch, not a nest": Florence C. Ladd and Kathryn J. Allott, "First Marriage and First Home," in Perla Korosec-Serfaty, *Appropriation of Space: Proceedings of the Strasbourg Conference* (Strasbourg, France: Louis

Pasteur University, June 21–25, 1976), pp. 553–75.

151 decorating can be one of the most trying experiences: Milton Sapirstein, "More Stately Mansions: The Paradox of Decorating a Home," in Milton R. Sapirstein, *Paradoxes of Everyday Life: A Psychoanalyst's Interpretations* (New York: Random House, 1955), pp. 120–45.

151 "The need to imitate one's mother is a strong, deep force . . .": Gould, *Transformation*, p. 129. See also Nancy Friday, *My Mother/My Self: The Search for a Daughter's Identity* (Dell Publishing, 1977).

151 Averil Meyer . . . asked her decorator for a bedroom: "At Home," *Town & Country,* March 1980, pp. 133–39, citation p. 137.

151 "more likely to rebel and want something different": *Home Furnishings Daily,* May 21, 1975. According to this study, the higher the social class and income, "the more the mother's influence. The daughters of blue collar families, the rich bricklayers and electricians, are more likely to rebel and want something different."

155 "If I ever could afford it . . .": Quoted in William G. Blair, "Luxury Is Boundless for Some in Hotels," *New York Times,* May 11, 1980, Real Estate Section 8, p. 1.

156 "This is my final resting place . . .": Anne-Marie Schiro, "Trying the Loft Life After Years Uptown," *New York Times,* June 10, 1982, Home Section.

156 "I never have felt and never will feel connected out there": Ron Cohen, "Arts & People: Peter Falk Shuffling Back on Stage," *Women's Wear Daily,* April 26, 1983, p. 22.

156 threw "snowballs at the single family house . . .": Jane Davison, *The Fall of a Doll's House* (New York: Holt, Rinehart and Winston, 1980), p. 225.

156 "When the home-as-object threatens to dominate . . .": Ibid.

156 women, who must deal with the loss of attractiveness: Suzanne Keller, "The Female Role: Constants and Change," in Violet Franks and Vasanti Burtle (eds.), *Women and Therapy* (New York: Brunner/Mazel, 1974), pp. 411–34, citation p. 431.

156 "It is an extremely common phenomenon of middle-class . . .": Author's interview with Daniel J. Levinson.

156 A recent survey by the American Society: Peter Kerr, "Computers Affect Decorator's Plans," *New York Times,* June 9, 1983, p. C3.

157 the "life review": Robert N. Butler, "The Life Review: An Interpretation of Reminiscence in the Aged," in Neugarten, *Middle Age and Aging,* pp. 486–96. According to Butler, older people universally go through a mental process of reviewing their lives. It involves "increased reminiscence, mild nostalgia, mild regret," sometimes "anxiety, guilt, despair, and depression," and often involves "mirror-gazing."

158 Small rooms filled with many things: Ernst D. Lantermann, "Environmental Competence as an Important Concept for Designing for the Elderly," in Korosec-Serfaty, *Appropriation of Space,* pp. 543–52, citation p. 549.

158 For people with reduced vision glare on surfaces: Lorraine G. Hiatt et al., *What Are Friends For? Groups for Older Persons With Sensory Loss—the U.S.E. Program* (New York: American Foundation for the Blind, 1982). This is an excellent handbook dealing with the environmental problems of the elderly and those with sight and hearing impairments.

158 Painting her brown kitchen chairs white: Jessica Finch, "Making Things Easier to See" in Hiatt, *What Are Friends For?*, pp. 67–69.

158 "I like to live in a place that I know blindfolded . . .": George Christy, "*Architectural Digest* Visits: George Burns," *Architectural Digest*, August 1982, pp. 64–69, citation p. 68.

159 the pieces of furniture most symbolic of self to widows: Sandra C. Howell, "The Elderly and the Architect: Interpreting Life Style Research in Design Guidelines," in H. Orimo et al., *Recent Advances in Gerontology*. Proceeding of the XI International Conference of Gerontology, Tokyo, August 20–25, 1978, pp. 412–19, citation p. 413. See also Sandra C. Howell, "The Meaning of Place in Old Age," in Rowles and Ohta, *Aging and Milieu*, pp. 97–107. And see Mary Kalymun, "Factors Influencing Elderly Women's Decisions Concerning Living-Room Items During Relocation," in Doug Amadeo et al., *EDRA 1983*, Proceedings of the Fourteenth International Conference of the Environmental Design Research Association, University of Nebraska, Lincoln, pp. 75–83.

159 Older people also need familiarity: Sarah H. Matthews, *The Social World of Old Women: Management of Self-Identity* (Beverly Hills: Sage Publications, 1979), p. 107.

159 "Transplantation shock" can result in higher mortality: Leon A. Pastalan, "Environmental Displacement: A Literature Reflecting Old-Person–Environment Transactions," in Rowles and Ohta, *Aging and Milieu*, pp. 189–203, citation pp. 198–201.

160 to "establish a new life style *apart and separate* . . .": Eva Kahana and Boaz Kahana, "Environmental Continuity and Adaptation of the Aged," in Rowles and Ohta, *Aging and Milieu*, pp. 205–39, citation p. 216. See also M. Powell Lawton, "Competence, Environmental Press, and the Adaptation of Older People," in M. Powell Lawton, Paul G. Windley and Thomas O. Byerts (eds.), *Aging and the Environment: Theoretical Approaches* (New York: Springer Publishing, 1982), pp. 33–59. Also Edward T. Hall, *The Dance of Life: The Other Dimension of Time* (Garden City, NY: Anchor Press/Doubleday, 1983).

160 relocators can be divided into four types: Kahana and Kahana, "Environmental Continuity," p. 220.

7. Making It You: Preference and Personality

162 appointed to the staff of the Harvard: Norbett Mintz is also a staff psychologist at McLean Hospital, and an associate professor at Boston University School of Social Work

163 The first experiment Maslow and Mintz undertook: Abraham H. Maslow and Norbett L. Mintz, "The Effects of Esthetic Surroundings: I. Initial Effects of Three Esthetic Conditions Upon Perceiving 'Energy' and 'Well-being' in Faces," *Journal of Psychology*, Vol. 41, 1956, April 1956, pp. 247–54.

164 In a follow-up experiment, Mintz examined the long-term: Norbett L. Mintz, "The Effects of Esthetic Surroundings: II. Prolonged and Repeated Experience in a 'Beautiful' and 'Ugly' Room," *Journal of Psychology*, Vol. 41, 1956, April 1956, pp. 459–66.

165 skepticism about the benefits of beauty: Norbett L. Mintz, "Reflections on the Psychology of Esthetics with Applica-

tion to the Human Habitat," in David
Canter (ed.), *What Is Environmental Psychology?* (Tokyo: Shokokusha, 1972), pp.
13–50. See also Mintz, "Studies Extending Schactel's Developmental Theories'
Problematic Aspects of Esthetic Encounters," in *Contemporary Psychoanalysis*,
Vol. 13, No. 2, 1977, pp. 261–86, citation
pp. 266–67. Some years ago, according to
Mintz, thousands of Americans in a variety of occupations as well as many student
groups were polled on how much they valued a variety of intellectual pursuits,
including esthetics. In all but one group,
esthetics ranked last behind the meat and
potatoes of economics and politics. Those
who gave high marks to esthetics were
Midwest college women. However, a subsequent poll revealed that esthetic
appreciation was not a value these women
felt they *ought* to have.

165 probably no coincidence that . . .
"good taste": Mintz, "Reflections on the
Psychology of Esthetics," pp. 13–50.

165 "Ugly rooms are like a bad meal":
The author's interview with decorator
Mario Buatta.

165 "Some rooms have so much color I
could gag": The author's interview with
designer John Saladino.

165 "Psychic satisfaction is related to
physiological well-being": James Marston
Fitch, "The Aesthetics of Function," in
Robert Gutman (ed.), *People and Buildings* (New York: Basic Books, 1972), pp.
3–16, citation p. 9.

166 Human habitats are almost uterine:
Ibid., p. 5.

166 gibbering incoherence: Ibid., p. 7.

166 the appreciation of beauty has
evolved: Peter F. Smith, "Urban Esthetics," in Byron Mikellides (ed.),
Architecture for People (New York: Holt,

Rinehart and Winston, 1980), pp. 74–86,
citation p. 74. Also Nicholas K.
Humphrey, "Natural Esthetics," in
Mikellides, *Architecture for People*, pp.
59–73, citation p. 67.

166 Decisions have to be made: Author's
interview with Rikard Küller, University
of Lund, Lund, Sweden.

166 It involves recognizing balance, harmony, complexity: Peter F. Smith,
Architecture and the Human Dimension
(Westfield, NJ: Eastview Editions, 1979).
Also Smith, "Urban Esthetics," pp. 74–
86.

166 the likeness tempered with difference: Humphrey, "Natural Esthetics," p.
65.

166 Just as there is pleasure in sex *without* procreation: Ibid., p. 67.

167 We leave more packages on the bus:
Rudolph H. Moos, "Conceptualizations of
Human Environments," in Harold M.
Proshansky, William H. Ittelson, and
Leanne G. Rivlin, *Environmental Psychology: People and Their Physical Settings*,
2nd edition (New York: Holt, Rinehart and
Winston, 1976), pp. 37–51, citation p. 39.

167 under noisy conditions and in hot
weather: Frank W. Schneider, Wayne A.
Lesko, and William A. Garrett, "Helping
Behavior in Hot, Comfortable, and Cold
Temperatures: A Field Study," *Environment and Behavior*, Vol. 12, No. 2, June
1980, pp. 231–40; Sherry Ahrentzen,
"Student Responses to Openness, Softness, and Seclusion in Elementary School
Classrooms," *Journal of Man-Environment Relations*, Vol. 1, No. 3, Spring
1982, pp. 42–53, citation p. 51.

167 a request for a salary increase in a
noisy room: Franklin Becker, *The Successful Office* (Reading, MA: AddisonWesley Publishing, 1982), pp. 95–96.

167 we tend to disclose less to our therapists: Alan L. Chaiken, Valerian J. Derlega, and Sarah Jane Miller, "Effects of Room Environment of Self-Disclosure in a Counseling Analogue," *Journal of Counseling Psychology,* Vol. 23, No. 5, 1976, pp. 479–81.

167 "An organism must prefer those environments . . .": Stephen Kaplan and Rachel Kaplan, *Humanscape: Environments for People* (Ann Arbor, MI: Ulrich's Books, Inc. [1978], 1982), p. 147.

168 Fashion is a perpetual game of Us against Them: Georg Simmel, "Fashion," in Donald Levine (ed.), *Georg Simmel: On Individuality and Social Forms* (Chicago: University of Chicago Press, 1971), pp. 294–323. This essay, originally published in 1904, is a *classic* among analyses of fashion. According to Simmel, fashion "satisfies the demand for social adaptation" and "the need for differentiation." It "signifies union with those in the same class . . . and . . . the exclusion of all other groups."

168 there is no agreement on whether traits remain: Author's interview with psychologist Brian Little of Canada's Carleton University.

169 a disposition is a behavioral tend: Henry Murray, "Proposals for Theory of Personality," in Edwin Shneidman (ed.), *Endeavors in Psychology: Selections from the Personology of Henry A. Murray* (New York: Harper & Row, 1981). "Disposition" and "behavioral trend" are terms used by Murray.

169 *"You are what you prefer to do"*: Author's interview with Brian Little.

169 "I built my house myself": Author's interview with Paul Windley.

169 an Oregon housewife, built herself a Rube Goldberg-type: Francis Gabe, a

Newberg, Oregon, woman and her self-cleaning house were featured on Metromedia's "PM Magazine," March 25, 1983.

169 "The more competent you are in a domain . . .": Author's interview with Brian Little.

170 Selecting and acquiring; arranging and organizing: This section was inspired by two works: (1.) Nicole Haumont, "Some Appropriation Practices," in Perla Korosec-Serfaty (ed.), *Appropriation of Space: Proceedings of the Strasbourg Conference* (Strasbourg, France: Louis Pasteur University, June 21–25, 1976), pp. 226–31. Haumont said that we mark our spaces by furnishing, arranging, handiwork, and upkeep. (2.) Henry Murray, "Proposals for Theory of Personality," in Shneidman, *Endeavors in Psychology,* p. 157. Murray theorized that among the secondary human needs (needs that are not basic biological drives), there are five needs "that pertain chiefly to actions associated with inanimate objects": Acquisition, Conservance, Order, Retention, and Construction.

170 "If her shoes are cleaned, she wants them put back . . .": "While Baby William Grows, Diana Shrinks—But She'll Never Be a Shrinking Violet," *People,* November 29, 1982, p. 47.

170 Colonel Jack Lousma likes to build things: "Men in the News: Jack R. Lousma," *New York Times,* March 23, 1982, p. C4. "I like to build things. I built a garage and converted a garage into a room for the house. I even built a house one time."

170 Joyce Ride, mother of astronaut Sally Ride: Michael Ryan, "A Ride in Space," *People,* June 20, 1983, pp. 83–88, citation p. 84.

170 Elsie found houses and furniture "a happier adventure": Jane S. Smith, *Elsie*

de Wolfe: A Life in High Style (New York: Atheneum, 1982), p. 121.

171 "more comfortable expressing her passion . . .": Ibid.

171 infants can be classified as either thing- or people-oriented: Samuel Abrams and Peter Neubauer, "Object Oriented-ness: the Person or the Thing," *Psychoanalytic Quarterly,* Vol. XLV, No. 1, 1976, pp. 73–99.

171 He has isolated four types of "specialists . . .": Brian Little, "Personal Systems and Specialization." Ph.D. dissertation, University of California, Berkeley, 1976.

171 "You'd want your designer to be a generalist . . .": Author's interview with Brian Little.

171 the majority of people "*select* rather than create": Donald Appleyard, "Home," *Architectural Association Quarterly,* Vol. II, No. 3, 1979, pp. 4–20, citation p. 4.

171 one is constantly assessing whether an item: Stephen Kaplan and Rachel Kaplan, *Cognition and Environment: Functioning in an Uncertain World* (New York: Praeger, 1982), p. 88. According to the Kaplans, this is the concept of "affordance"—What can I do with this object?

172 "It's my color": Smith, *Elsie de Wolfe.*

172 "I always pick blue gingham, if available . . .": Phyllis Theroux, "The Pursuit of Individuality: How to Find the Joy of Being Yourself," *House & Garden,* February 1978, pp. 104–5, ff., citation p. 105.

172 "as telling as body language, as revealing as psychology . . .": Faber Birren, *Color Your World* (New York: Collier Books [1962], 1978).

173 "a highly developed conscience . . .": Margaret H. Harmon, *Psycho-Decorating* (New York: Wyden Books, distributed by Simon & Schuster, 1977).

173 Mr. Schauss admitted there have been no controlled: In response to a request for proof of his theory, Mr. Schauss insisted the author take a $10 annual subscription to his "journal." The first issue was Alexander G. Schauss, *Biosocial: The Journal of Behavioral Ecology,* November Special Edition, 1980, and it was apparently the premier issue of his journal. In this four-page newsletter which was prepared, wrote Schauss, "due to the considerable amount of inquiries received" after articles appeared in the "*Los Angeles Times . . . Time . . . Next, Omni,*" Schauss recognized "the need for a long term study. This study, yet to begin . . ."

173 "Pink affects muscle strength and the penis is a muscle . . .": Author's interview with Alexander Schauss. Schauss believes color preference can fluctuate with blood sugar changes. If you have a craving for a purple potholder, he said, "it may just be a potassium imbalance." Does that mean you should take your vitamins before shopping for something you expect to live with for some years? "Say, that's a good question," answered Schauss, whose own home is done in yellows and greens, reds and oranges.

173 "some sadistic individual might use it . . .": Author's interview with Alexander Schauss.

173 "More nonsense has been written about color effects . . .": Corwin Bennett, *Spaces for People: Human Factors in Design* (Englewood Cliffs, NJ: Prentice-Hall, 1977), p. 104.

174 "Some people wish for colors that *contrast* . . .": Author's interview with Norbett Mintz. See R. W. Burnham, R. M. Hanes and C. James Bartleson, *Color:*

A Guide to Basic Facts and Concepts (New York: John Wiley & Sons, 1963). This is an excellent no-nonsense book about color. In a recent rereview praising this book (*EDRA Design Research News*, Vol. XII, No. 6, November 1981, p. 7), it was said: "The notion that there is a specific human affective response to color is a very popular one. Empirically, however, it has not been possible to demonstrate that preference for or exposure to a particular color has any strong or potent affect . . . it is difficult to believe that the situation has changed [since the publication of this book]."

174 "I believe in color vibrations": Audrey Farolino, "Ken Page Doesn't Pussyfoot Around With Color," *New York Post,* June 9, 1983, p. 29.

174 the residents were up in arms when the Methodist Church: William E. Geist, "In Litchfield, Hue and Cry for 'Tradition,'" *New York Times,* December 3, 1982, pp. B1 ff.

174 when the Art Commission tried to paint: Anna Quindlen, "Art Commission Raises Cry Over Hues in Picking Colors for Bridges," *New York Times,* November 20, 1979, pp. B1 ff.

174 colors had powers and their meanings: Amos Rapoport, *The Meaning of the Built Environment* (Beverly Hills: Sage Publications, 1982).

174 white walls and kitchens signaled "sanitary awareness": Gwendolyn Wright, *Building the Dream: A Social History of Housing in America* (New York: Pantheon, 1981), p. 162.

174 inspired by the wife of a wealthy British coal merchant: Cecil Beaton, *The Glass of Fashion* (Garden City, NY: Doubleday, 1954), pp. 246–47.

174 between a red bus and a red breast:

David Canter, *Psychology for Architects* (London: Applied Science Publishers, 1974), p. 43.

175 they usually choose their style: See Leonard B. Meyer, "Toward a Theory of Style," in Berel Lang (ed.), *The Concept of Style* (Philadelphia: University of Pennsylvania Press, 1979), pp. 3–44.

175 who "don't live in the past, they just visit": Advertisement for *Colonial Homes* magazine. New York, Hearst Corporation, 1980.

175 "had 'sincerity,' a nail did not": Russell Lynes, *The Tastemakers* (New York: Dover Publications [1949], 1980), p. 103.

176 "unselfish devotion of our forefathers: Jane Davison, *The Fall of a Doll's House* (New York: Holt, Rinehart and Winston, 1980), p. 129.

176 NASA have furnished its Houston lunar reception area: Rapoport, *Meaning of the Built Environment,* p. 16.

176 Daughters of the American Revolution: Lizabeth A. Cohen, "Embellishing a Life of Labor: An Interpretation of the Material Culture of American Working-Class Homes, 1885–1915," in Thomas J. Schlereth (ed.). *Material Culture Studies in America* (Nashville, TN: American Association for State and Local History, 1982), pp. 289–305, citation pp. 292–95.

176 Symbols of tradition link people to ancestors: Maryann Jacobi and Daniel Stokols, "The Role of Tradition in Group-Environment Relations," in N. R. Feimer and E. S. Geller (eds.), *Environmental Psychology: Directions and Perspectives* (New York: Praeger. In press).

176 "Kinship is so entwined with social class": Anselm Strauss, *Mirrors and Masks: The Search for Identity* (San Francisco: Sociology Press, 1969), p. 166.

176 Rooms "must not look new": Elaine Greene, "A Very Personal Luxury," *House & Garden,* January 1983, pp. 116–25, citation p. 119.

176 "Newness is something I generally find disagreeable": Marilyn Bethany, "Discreet Charm of Decoration," *New York Times Magazine,* May 9, 1983, pp. 75–79, citation p. 78.

176 the whole concept of antique is modern: Yi-Fu Tuan, *Space and Place* (Minneapolis: University of Minnesota Press, 1977), p. 193.

177 "nostalgia for the idyllic past waxes strong": Ibid, p. 195. See also Carl Shear Werthman, "The Social Meaning of the Environment." Ph.D. dissertation in Sociology, University of California, Berkeley, 1968. In this study of five housing developments, Werthman, a sociologist, found that house style predicted social type. There were correlations among people who bought either Gingerbread (a style influenced by illustrations in children's books), Display style (neo-Colonial), Ranch style (conservative), or Distinctly Modern. "Each of these styles tends to attract people with a different socioeconomic status," said Werthman. Gingerbread people had more education than money, but they were the lowest economically. Display style people had more money than education—they were risk takers. Ranch house people had equal money and education and a "mood of modest contentment, stability and security." Ranch house people criticized the Gingerbread houses, calling them "cute." People who liked Modern—mostly young professionals—had a great deal more education than income. Their homes symbolized the epitome of "progressive 'good taste,'" said Werthman.

177 the home of astronaut Sally Ride: William J. Broad, "Cool, Versatile Astro-naut: Sally Kristen Ride," *New York Times,* June 19, 1983, p. 1 ff.

177 readers preferred new furniture to "secondhand": Better Homes and Gardens Consumer Panel Report #6, Home Furnishings (New York: Meredith Corporation, 1977), p. 9. (This question was not posed in the 1982 panel report.)

177 he wanted to "make new, not buy old": Joseph Alsop, *The Rare Art Traditions* (New York: Harper & Row, 1982), p. 160.

177 declaring torn draperies beautiful: Suzanne Slesin, "Spareness Gains New Meaning in a Quartet of City Apartments," *New York Times,* March 24, 1983, pp. C1 ff.

177 "a process of breaking unwritten design laws": Dinah Prince, "Scavengers of Style," *New York Daily News,* March 10, 1983, p. 45.

178 "My main project this fall is getting rid of things": "Things," *The New Yorker,* October 23, 1978, p. 32.

178 "It all seems so simple, it looks as if we didn't . . .": Bernadine Morris, "Clutter to Minimal: A Couple Simplifies," *New York Times,* July 17, 1980, pp. C1 ff., citation p. C8.

178 Minimalism is actually "conspicuous austerity": Jean Baudrillard, "Sign-Function and Class Logic," *For a Critique of the Political Economy of the Sign,* trans. Charles Levin (St. Louis: Telos Press, 1981), pp. 29–62, citation pp. 77–78. Baudrillard believes there is no difference between conspicuous luxury and conspicuous austerity: "You pay through the nose to eat practically nothing. To deny oneself is a luxury. This is the sophistry of consumption."

179 "Man's feeling about being properly

oriented . . .": Edward T. Hall, *The Hidden Dimension* (New York: Anchor Books [1966], 1969), p. 105.

179 How far chairs are from one another: See Hall, *Hidden Dimension.* Hall's book contains his seminal analysis on cross-cultural attitudes about space and the distance people like to be from one another. See also Irwin Altman and Anne M. Vinsel, "Personal Space: An Analysis of E. T. Hall's Proxemics Framework," in Irwin Altman and Joachim F. Wohlwill, *Human Behavior and Environment: Advances in Theory and Research,* Vol. 2 (New York: Plenum Press, 1977), pp. 181–259.

179 people who rearranged their furniture: Cheryl B. Coniglio, "The Meaning of Personalization and Freedom of Choice Within Residential Interiors." Master of Science Degree thesis, Graduate School of Cornell University, June 1974, p. 36.

180 accessories "can make or break rooms": Marilyn Bethany, "Accessories: They Can Make or Break a Room," *New York Times,* March 10, 1983, pp. C1 ff.

180 "tabletops should have a composition . . .": Ibid.

180 To ensure that "no home in America is ever dull . . .": Anne Bagamery,"Please Make me Feel Special," *Forbes,* March 28, 1983, pp. 88–89.

181 Styles of arrangement are grammatical: Jurgen Ruesch and Weldon Kees, *Nonverbal Communication* (Berkeley: University of California Press, 1969), p. 136.

181 supposed to be a sign of schizophrenia: Ibid.

181 "I think of symmetry as comfortable, asymmetry as not": Suzanne Slesin, "The Improvisers, with More Dash than Cash,"

New York Times, May 7, 1981, pp. C1 ff., citation p. C6.

181 "I get ulcers if anything is crooked": Valentine Lawford, Foreword by Diana Vreeland, *Vogue's Book of Houses, Gardens, People* (New York: Viking Press, 1968), p. 193.

181 "naked contact": Ruesch and Kees, *Nonverbal Communication,* p. 143.

181 "vertical orientation" and "horizontal orientation": Ibid.

182 "Dirt is matter out of place": Mary Douglas, *Purity and Danger: An Analysis of the Concepts of Pollution and Taboo* (Boston: Routledge & Kegan Paul [1966], 1979), p. 35.

182 "Dirt offends against order": Ibid., p. 2.

182 he opened a cleaning service to capitalize: Jane Wollman, "A Dancer's Style in Cleaning," *New York Times,* March 10, 1983, p. C11.

182 Dorothy Parker in her own house: "Swifty Lazar: The Artful Pitchman," *New York Times,* November 2, 1980, p. 78.

182 Cleanliness is also "conspicuous morality": Jean Baudrillard, "Sign-Function and Class Logic," p. 45. In discussing "the moral fanaticism of housekeeping," Baudrillard compares objects that must be polished and varnished to "children in whom one must instill good manners, who must be 'civilized' . . ."

182 It is assumed the resident has some control over it: Appleyard, "Home," p. 18.

182 "So they think at least I'm a decent housekeeper": Coniglio, "The Meaning of Personalization," p. 47.

183 Estée Lauder "is pleased that her hardwood floors . . .": "Estée and Joe," *Women's Wear Daily,* January 7, 1983, pp. 4–5.

183 Mary Lopez, mother of one of the hostages: "For Families of Hostages, the Worrying Never Ends," *New York Times,* November 2, 1980, p. 1 ff.

183 Joan Gould kept her house from going to pieces: Joan Gould, "Hers," *New York Times,* November 13, 1980, p. C2.

184 The urge to preserve, rescue, and reconstruct: Murray, "Proposals for Theory of Personality," pp. 125–203, citation p. 157.

184 "After thirty years of married life": Author's interview with psychologist Harold Proshansky.

184 "I love seeing something really depressing . . .": Elizabeth Lambert, "Along Pelham Crescent," *Architectural Digest,* June 1981, pp. 67–69, citation p. 67.

184 a three-step process of "birth, death, and redemption": John B. Jackson, "The Necessity for Ruins," *The Necessity for Ruins and Other Topics* (Amherst: University of Massachusetts Press, 1980), pp. 89–102, citation pp. 101–102.

185 You have to "rehab" right: Helaine Kaplan and Blair Prentice, *Rehab Right: How to Rehabilitate Your Oakland House Without Sacrificing Architectural Assets* (Oakland, CA: City of Oakland Planning Department, 1979).

185 blue-collar people have had their fill: Author's interview with Nat Hendricks, founder and president of the Brooklyn Brownstone Conference.

185 Rehabing *wrong* means gift wrapping: Ken Jackson, David Halle, and Lisa Vergara, *Transformed Houses.* Text for

traveling exhibition, sponsored by Smithsonian Institution, 1981. Exhibited were houses that had been altered by succeeding owners. The thrust was "not to restore the past but to improve upon it."

185 "The fellow that owns his own home . . .": Frank McKinney Hubbard ("Kin Hubbard"), in Lawrence J. Peter, *Peter's Quotations: Ideas for Our Times* (New York: William Morrow, 1977).

185 more than four out of five Do-It-Yourselfers: "Analysis '82: Second Annual Investment Community Seminar on the Do-It-Yourself Industry, March 31, 1982, The Waldorf-Astoria Hotel, New York, NY." Handbook. (Indianapolis: DIY Research Institute, 1982.) Do-It-Yourself statistics come from the above handbook.

186 mirrors on "the women's side": Author's interview with Robert Strickland, chairman of Lowe's.

186 "some tangible accomplishment in a world . . .": Barbara Caplan (of Yankelovich, Skelly and White). Presentation to Wallcovering Manufacturers Association, May 11, 1981, Boca Raton, Florida.

186 "but the conscious—or unconscious—payoff . . .": Author's interview with Clare Cooper Marcus, a geographer and planner at the University of California, Berkeley.

187 Americans spend more time gardening than making love: Nadine Brozan, "Family Is Focus of Leisure Time, Study Finds," *New York Times,* December 15, 1982, pp. C1 ff.

188 the attraction of plants is almost primordial: Robert L. Thayer and Brian G. Atwood, "Plants, Complexity, and Pleasure in Urban and Suburban Environments," *Environmental Psychology and Nonverbal Behavior,* Vol. 3, No.

2, Winter 1978, pp. 67–76. Said the authors: "It is not inconceivable that humans find plants highly complex and pleasurable due to the genetic development of human consciousness in environments where plants played an essential role in human behavior."

188 Most people find green things: Stephen Kaplan and Rachel Kaplan, *Humanscape: Environments for People* (Ann Arbor, MI: Ulrich's Books, Inc: [1978], 1982), pp. 88–89.

188 only since the seventeenth century: John B. Jackson, "Gardens to Decipher and Gardens to Admire," *The Necessity for Ruins and Other Topics* (Amherst: University of Massachusetts Press, 1980), pp. 37–53, citation p. 39. In this essay, Jackson, the renowned geographer, said: "The pure flower-garden, the garden of absolute pleasure, the garden altogether divided from utility, is a very late fancy of the human mind."

188 "I think of my garden as a *place, not an activity*": Author's interview with Rachel Kaplan.

188 Nature fascination accounts in large measure: Rachel Kaplan, "Some Psychological Benefits of Gardening," *Environment and Behavior*, Vol. 5, No. 2, June 1973. Also Rachel Kaplan, "The Role of Nature in the Urban Context," in Irwin Altman and Joachim F. Wohlwill (eds.), *Behavior and the Natural Environment* (New York: Plenum Press. In press).

189 "Keeping a garden makes you aware . . .": Arthur Miller, "After the Spring," *House & Garden*, April 1983, pp. 104–105 ff, citation p. 104.

189 "The question is the same each year": Ibid.

189 People who use *chemical* fertilizers: See Kaplan, "Role of Nature."

189 "You simply have to face the moment . . .": Miller, "After the Spring," p. 183.

189 the interest that neighbors take in one another's lawns: See Jon Keller, "Trouble: A Man's Home is His Castle, But Does His Backyard Have to be an Overgrown Eyesore?" *People*, June 28, 1982, pp. 82–83. See also William Geist, "Blue-Collar Revolt Against Suburban Esthetics," *New York Times*, March 8, 1982, pp. B1 ff.

189 Veblen, who called it a glorified cow pasture: Thorstein Veblen, *The Theory of the Leisure Class*. (New York: Mentor, 1953), pp. 98–99.

189 Chemcare, a major lawn care company: Philip H. Dougherty, "Advertising: Chemlawn Campaign Spreading," *New York Times*, March 1, 1983, p. D21.

189 a front yard is a "national institution": John B. Jackson, "Front Yards," in Kaplan and Kaplan, *Humanscape*, p. 176.

189 "an index of the taste and enterprise . . .": Ibid. See also John B. Jackson, "Fences and Hedges," in Kaplan and Kaplan, *Humanscape*, pp. 270–273. And John B. Jackson, "After the Forest Came the Pasture," in Kaplan and Kaplan, *Humanscape*, pp. 347–351. And see Bayard Webster, "Man and Lawn—a Long Love Story," *New York Times*, April 12, 1983, p. C3. According to Webster, John H. Falk, an ecologist at the Smithsonian Institution's Chesapeake Bay Center for Environmental Studies at Edgewater, MD, found four reasons for lawn interest: conditioning, peer pressure, sense of power in subduing nature, and an innate preference for the landscape of the savannah.

190 "Since other people are needed to confer status . . .": Werthman, "Social Meaning of the Environment," p. 68. See also Herbert Gans, *The Levittowners: Ways of Life and Politics in a New Suburban Community* (Vintage Books, 1967), p. 48. Gans found that both lawn underachievers and overachievers "were brought into line by wisecracks." One neighbor said he would have to move out if Gans (who had moved into the community in order to study it) was going to have such a fancy lawn.

8. *Psyching Out Collecting*

193 one out of three Americans collects something: George O'Brien, "Living with Collections," *New York Times Magazine, Part 2, Home Design,* April 26, 1981, p. 25.

193 A collector is not the same as an accumulator: Jens Jensen, "Collector's Mania," *Acta Psychiat Scandinavia,* Vol. 39, No. 4, 1963, pp. 606–18.

193 "three of anything is a collection": Author's discussion with Leo Lerman.

194 "I'm a compulsive saver; it must stem from . . .": Kathy A. MegYeri, "The Collecting Craze," Letter to the Editor, *New York Times Magazine,* August 31, 1980, p. 46.

194 "Most of us collect for profit": Fred Ferretti, "The Collecting Compulsion," *New York Times Magazine,* July 27, 1980, pp. 24–25.

194 "Money is out, things are in": Linda Bird Francke, "Auctions for Everybody," *New York,* March 30, 1981, pp. 22–26, citation p. 23.

194 "There are just three reasons for collecting . . .": Russell Lynes, "Russell Lynes Observes: The Romance of Collecting," *Architectural Digest,* June 1980, pp. 36–42, citation p. 36.

194 Lita Furby . . . has done a major sur-

vey of the literature: Lita Furby, "Possessions: Toward a Theory of Their Meaning and Function Throughout the Life Cycle," in Paul B. Baltes (ed.), *Life-Span Development and Behavior,* Vol. 1 (New York: Academic Press, 1978), pp. 297–336.

194 One of the problems in studying colecting: Author's interview with Lita Furby.

194 leaned heavily on an "instinct for acquisition: Furby, "Possessions," p. 298.

194 [Darwin] concluded his leaning was "innate": Ernest Beaglehole, *Property: A Study in Social Psychology* (New York: Macmillan, 1932), p. 254.

195 how could the mania for stamp collecting: "Hobbies," *Encyclopedia Britannica, Macropaedia,* Volume 8 (Chicago: University of Chicago, 1976), p. 977.

195 a leopard hanging a carcass in a tree for a month: Niko Tinbergen and the Editors of Time-Life Books (New York: Time-Life Books [1965], 1971), p. 191.

195 the ad placed in *The Times* of London in 1841: "Hobbies," p. 977.

195 the *impulse to construct* that is found: Beaglehole, p. 281. Beaglehole attributed the idea of collecting as the instinct to construct to K. Groos, *The Play of Man* (New York: Appleton, 1901).

195 Bowerbirds may be the most prodigious and tasteful: Ibid., pp. 74–76. Also Joseph Alsop, *The Rare Art Traditions: The History of Art Collecting and its Linked Phenomena Wherever These Have Appeared* (New York: Harper & Row, 1982), p. 422.

195 In 1900, Caroline Burk, an educational psychologist: Beaglehole, p. 255.

195 the instinct for collecting debunked: Ibid., p. 257.

196 In the Freudian view, a child moves from the pleasure: "Anal-Erotic Character Traits," Ernest Jones, M.D., *Papers on Psycho-analysis,* 5th edition (Baltimore: Williams & Wilkins Co., 1948), pp. 413–37; Bela Grunberger, "Study of Anal Object Relations," *International Review of Psycho-analysis,* Vol. 4, Part 1, pp. 99–110; Sigmund Freud, "On the Transformation of Instincts with Special Reference to Anal Erotism (1917)," *Character and Culture* (New York: Collier Books, 1963), pp. 27–33. A popular subsequent theory that misers use things as a substitute for people, as well as a defense against the loss of love, was based on Freud.

196 "all collectors are anal erotics . . .": Beaglehole, pp. 266–72.

196 Very interesting, said Ernest Beaglehole: Ibid, p. 278.

196 "Growing curiosity and interest lead the child . . .": Ibid., p. 280. On grasping, Beaglehole refers to Groos, *Play of Man.*

196 "by rivalry, by the desire for that admiration . . .": Ibid., p. 280.

196 "we taste the joys of superiority . . .": Ibid., p. 281. See also Susan Isaacs, "Property and Possessiveness," in T. Talbot (ed.), *The World of the Child* (Garden City, NY: Doubleday [1949], 1967), p. 256. Isaacs says, "it is always a triangular relation between at least *two* people and the thing in question."

196 "Blind love seems to be the tie that binds . . .": Marilyn Bethany, "Stalking the Wild Collector," *New York Times Magazine, Part 2, Home Design,* April 26, 1981, pp. 12 ff, citation p. 38.

196 "It's like, well, having a love affair":

Paula Rice Jackson, "Collections," *House Beautiful,* February 1982, p. 67.

197 Saying that love is what draws collectors: Nicholas K. Humphrey, "The Biological Basis of Collecting," *Human Nature,* February 1979, pp. 44–47, citation, p. 46.

197 "Biologists generally assume that most behavior patterns . . .": Ibid., p. 44.

197 "Animals that devised precise methods . . .": Ibid., p. 47.

197 "Collectors of objects as well as collectors . . .": Ibid., p. 44.

197 "My eye, uncontrollable, is constantly reconnoitering . . .": Bernard Kalb, "Some Detours in Pursuit of Porcelain," *New York Times,* April 10, 1983, Travel Section, p. 9.

198 like infants who delight in discovering stimuli: Humphrey, "Biological Basis of Collecting," citation p. 47.

198 By using the same highly developed discriminatory powers: Information about animal food preferences comes from Niko Tinbergen and the Editors of Time-Life Books, *Animal Behavior* (New York: Time-Life Books [1965], 1971).

198 "the 'empty' landscape becomes very rich": Amos Rapoport, "Nomadism as a Man-Environment System," *Environment and Behavior,* June 1978, pp. 215–46, citation p. 226.

198 a study of young collectors showed: Walter Nelson Durost, "Children's Collecting Activity Related to Social Factors." Ph.D. dissertation, Columbia University, 1932, p. 88.

198 Armand Hammer . . . used his educated eye to outwit: Milton Esterow, "Armand Hammer Talks About Daumier,

Lenin, van Gogh, Brezhnev, Renoir & Reagan," *Art News,* December 1982, pp. 68–76, citation p. 72.

199 "one of the great Lawrences of all time": *Ibid,* citation p. 73.

199 Francis Garvan, one of the great Americana: Alden Whitman, "We Bought Not for Ourselves Alone, But for the Whole Country . . ." *Antiques World,* Summer 1980, pp. 53–58, citation p. 58.

199 "the most phenomenal collection of stamps . . .": Author's interview with psychologist Robert Bechtel. In the author's interview, New York philatelist Abbot Lutz said that Ishakawa has won many important medals in stamp collecting, usually sells his collections after completing them, and recently sold his U.S. one-cent stamp collection.

199 "I felt right dejected," said the man: William Borders, "The British Treasure Hunt For Jeweled Rabbit is Over," *New York Times,* March 15, 1982, pp. A1 ff., citation p. A6.

199 "Let us congratulate the person . . .": Jean Baudrillard, "Le Systeme Marginal: La Collection," *Le Systeme Des Objets: La Consommation des Signes* (Paris: Editions Gallimard, 1968), pp. 103–28.

200 "the master of the secret seraglio": Ibid.

200 "I'm a compulsive buyer": Author's interview with Robert Metzger.

200 "have lied and cheated to throw a competitor off . . .": Bernard Kalb, "Me and My Porcelain," *Antiques World,* Summer 1980, pp. 74–76, citation p. 76.

201 "Everyone tries to develop programs . . .": Author's interview with

Rikard Küller, University of Lund, Lund, Sweden.

201 "central defining dimension of possession": Furby, "Possessions," p. 298.

201 "You feel insecure, you don't have control . . .": Author's interview with Lita Furby.

202 Du Pont had a valued adviser: Alden Whitman, "The Passion of Henry Francis du Pont, *Antiques World,* March 1980, pp. 50–55, citation p. 55.

203 "It got to the point where it was sickening": Enid Nemy, "New Yorkers, etc: They Collect Mice and Turtles and Frogs and Owls. But Why?" *New York Times,* February 13, 1980.

203 "involuntary collectors": Ibid.

203 "It's a good time to call it quits": Ibid.

205 "Spend your initial funds . . . on books and travel": Frank Donegan, "American Art Pottery," *The Club Member,* March/April 1983, pp. 20–25, citation p. 25.

205 "Collecting is a richer context for travel": Author's interview with Holly Solomon.

206 The "decorating factor": Alsop, *Rare Art Traditions,* p. 422.

206 a long tradition of using collections as decor: Ibid., pp. 422–24.

206 choosing sculpture according to the size: Ibid.

206 the obsession with housing the collection: Mark Girouard, *Life in the English Country House* (New Haven: Yale University Press, 1978), pp. 173–80. Also see Yi-Fu Tuan, *Space and Place* (Minneapolis: University of Minnesota Press,

1977), p. 193. Tuan noted that the "interest in the past waxed with the desire to collect and possess material objects and with the growing prestige of disciplined curiosity."

207 The Bob Newharts had cabinets designed: Paige Rense (ed.), "Bob Newhart," *Celebrity Homes* (New York: Penguin Books, 1977), p. 139.

207 the Manheim Galleries has created: Author's interview with salesperson at Manheim Galleries.

208 "I designed the proportions of the house . . .": Joseph Giovannini, "Architecture: Barry A. Berkus," *Architectural Digest*, May 1983, pp. 152–59, citation p. 156.

208 "A museum of one's own," said *Town & Country*: "The Personal Museum," *Town & Country*, March 1982, pp. 109–21 ff., citation p. 109.

208 *The Meaning of Things* found that upper-middle class: Mihaly Csikszentmihalyi and Eugene Rochberg-Halton, *The Meaning of Things: Domestic Symbols and the Self* (New York: Cambridge University Press, 1981), p. 64.

209 "attested to the buying power of the owner": "The Fascination of the Ornate," *Sotheby's Newsletter*, June 1981, p. 13.

209 "to admit that it may also serve other uses": Durost, "Children's Collecting Activity," p. 88.

210 "These bowls have become the most important status symbol . . .": Abner Cohen, *Custom & Politics in Urban Africa: A Study of Hausa Migrants in Yoruba Towns* (Berkeley: University of California Press, 1969), pp. 67–68."In 1963," said Cohen, "a woman with five hundred bowls gave a dowry of fifty bowls to a foster daughter." The system "serves to stabilize marriage"

and attract young women from other communities to Sabo.

210 Whistler went bankrupt buying Chinese porcelains: Mario Amaya, "Antiques: K'ank Hsi Porcelain," *Architectural Digest*, July/August 1979, p. 66.

211 "By and large, today's collectors do not choose . . .": O'Brien, "Living with Collections," p. 25.

211 "I don't *want* to sell it—do you sell your dog?": Malcolm N. Carter, "A Collector Who Can't Say No," *Saturday Review*, May 1981 (Copyright © 1980), pp. 62–65, citation p. 65.

212 "Occasionally, I look at that vase and wonder . . .": Kalb, "Me and My Porcelain," p. 76.

212 "the equal of the canvas itself": . . . Jean Baudrillard, "The Art Auction: Sign Exchange and Sumptuary Value," *For a Critique of the Political Economy of the Sign*, trans. Charles Levin (St. Louis: Telos Press, 1981), p. 118.

9. Fear of Furnishing

216 The personally conducted tour of the house: Some of the ideas and phrases in this chapter appeared originally in Joan Kron, "I'd Love to Have You Over for Dinner . . . But the House Isn't Finished," *New York Times*, March 17, 1977, p. C16.

216 meaning is part of function: Amos Rapoport, *The Meaning of the Built Environment* (Beverly Hills: Sage Publications, 1982), p. 15.

217 performances "will tend to incorporate . . .": Erving Goffman, *Presentation of Self in Everyday Life* (Garden City, NY: Doubleday, 1959), p. 35.

217 in England a prince need not apply:

Martin Wenglinsky, "Errands," in Arnold Birenbaum and Edward Sagarin (eds.), *People in Places: The Sociology of the Familiar* (New York: Praeger, 1973), p. 93.

217 "give a clue that the status is being maintained": Ibid.

218 Two psychologists hypothesized recently: William B. Hansen and Irwin Altman, "Decorating Personal Places: A Descriptive Analysis," *Environment & Behavior*, Vol. 8, 1976, pp. 491–504.

218 marking is symbolic of "ownership . . .": Ibid., p. 503.

219 "Since my future at the company . . .": Aljean Harmetz, "New Head of Fox Planning for New Technologies," *New York Times*, August 16, 1981, p. C16.

221 Commune members finesse the communal identity issue: Clare Cooper Marcus, "The House as Symbol of Self," in Jon Lang et al. (eds.). *Designing for Human Behavior: Architecture and the Behavioral Sciences* (Stroudsburg, PA: Dowden, Hutchinson & Ross, 1974), pp. 130–46, citation p. 135.

222 "who decorated the apartment": Catherine Warren, "Eye View: A Set Piece," *Women's Wear Daily*, October 26, 1976, p. 17.

222 According to a study of first homes: Florence C. Ladd and Kathryn J. Allott, "First Marriage and First Home," in Perla Korosec-Serfaty (ed.), *Appropriation of Space: Proceedings of the Strasbourg Conference* (Strasbourg, France: Louis Pasteur University, June 21–25, 1976), pp. 553–78.

223 Money is the number one cause of arguments: "Pollsters Report on American Consumers and Businessmen."

Hearing before the Joint Economic Committee, Congress of the United States, Ninety-Fourth Congress, First Session, Part 2, October 30, 1975 (Washington, D.C: U.S. Government Printing Office, 1976), p. 203.

223 the first stage is the *possession of the money*: Georg Simmel, *The Philosophy of Money,* trans. Tom Bottomore and David Frisby (Boston: Routledge & Kegan Paul, 1978), p. 248 (see also pp. 242, 310).

224 the Queen of England turns off lights: Neil Blincow and Martin Ralbovsky, "Queen Elizabeth's Strange Secret Life," *National Enquirer,* March 8, 1983, pp. 32–33 ff.

225 information can be gleaned in the simplest face-to-face: Erving Goffman, "Role Distance," in Arnold Birenbaum and Edward Sagarin (eds.), *People in Places: The Sociology of the Familiar* (New York: Praeger, 1973), pp. 121–38, citation p. 126. Originally published in Erving Goffman, *Encounters* (Indianapolis: Bobbs-Merrill, 1961).

225 information that is "ego-alien": Ibid., p. 127.

225 They must act to "control the implications": Ibid., p. 128.

225 Through the apology "the individual begs . . .": Ibid., p. 128.

225 "I don't like my house," said actress Angie Dickinson: Peter Lester, "Redress or Undress: Feminists Fume While Angie Scores a Thriller," *People,* September 15, 1980, pp. 70–72 ff., citation p. 81.

226 The famed Southern hospitality: Joe Gray Taylor, *Eating, Drinking, and Visiting in the South: An Informal History* (Baton Rouge: Louisiana State University Press, 1982), pp. 62–63.

226 It's too time-consuming: Judy Klemesrud, "Sissela Bok: A View of Life and Ethics," *New York Times,* March 6, 1983, p. 66.

227 "I hate it, all these people coming here to judge me": Author's interview with John Saladino.

227 "This place is like a blank canvas . . .": Marilyn Bethany, "Two Top Talents Seeing Eye to Eye," *New York Times Magazine,* June 29, 1980, pp. 50–54, citation p. 54.

227 what Goffman called the "unserious style": Erving Goffman, "Role Distance," p. 128.

228 calling his decor "Upper East Side Poverty": Michael deCourcey Hinds, "The Personal Taste of Four Curators," *New York Times,* December 25, 1980, pp. C1 ff.

228 "It's half finished, the other half is in my mind": Ibid.

228 Governor Edmund G. (Jerry) Brown, Jr., made a mistake: Wayne King, "Brown Image: Chief Problem," *New York Times,* January 8, 1980, p. 16.

228 "The image is all wrong," he said: Terence Smith, "Rafshoon Downplays Role in White House," *New York Times,* November 27, 1977, p. A1.

229 "Presumably because Fran thinks it bad form": C. Heimel, "Fran Leibowitz Isn't Kidding," *New York,* September 14, 1981, pp. 39–42.

230 "We never stayed in California or Washington long enough . . .": Author's interview with Meredith Brokaw.

231 almost every woman of the house started the conversation: Author's interview with the University of Chicago's Professor Mihaly Csikszentmihalyi, co-author with Eugene Rochberg-Halton of *The Meaning of Things: Domestic Symbols of the Self* (New York: Cambridge University Press, 1981).

232 "The height of security is to not give a damn": Joan Kron, "I'd Love to Have You Over," p. C16.

10. *The Status Merchants*

234 "My clients always become friends": "At Home," *Town & Country,* March 1980, p. 133.

234 Scene Two: *Avenue* magazine: "A Home That Mirrors Her Every Mood," *Avenue,* November 1981.

235 consults daily with "her talented florist": Ibid.

235 Scene Three . . . The *New York Times* Home Section: John Duka, "Decorating for Traditionalists: When Details Count," *New York Times,* February 18, 1982, pp. C1 ff.

236 "If I did only a pillow . . .": Author's interview with Mario Buatta.

236 the home is a major status symbol: See James S. Duncan and Nancy G. Duncan, "Residential Landscapes and Social Worlds: A Case Study in Hyderabad, Andhra Pradesh," in D. Sopher (ed.), *An Exploration of India* (Ithaca: Cornell University Press, 1980), pp. 271–86; and James S. Duncan, "From Container of Women to Status Symbol: the Impact of Social Structure on the Meaning of the House," in James S. Duncan (ed.), *Housing and Identity: Cross-Cultural Perspectives* (London: Croom Helm, 1981), pp. 36–59.

236 people are always engaged in "status passage": Anselm L. Strauss, *Mirrors and Masks: The Search for Identity* (San Francisco: Sociology Press, 1969), p. 125.

237 he turned in his modest Santa Monica cottage: David Gritten, "'Hill Street Blues.' The Cop Show That Couldn't Get Arrested, Hits with a Sexy Trio," *People*, February 22, 1982, pp. 88–92.

237 Making the house "stylistically acceptable": Barney Glaser and Anselm L. Strauss, *Status Passage: A Formal Theory* (Chicago: Aldine, 1971), p. 169.

237 serves "a bonding or unifying function": C. Wright Mills, Introduction to Thorstein Veblen, *The Theory of the Leisure Class* (New York: Mentor, 1953).

237 The Yurok Indians of California: Mary Douglas and Baron Isherwood, *The World of Goods* (New York: Basic Books, 1979), p. 140.

237 "Even when money is no object . . .": Martin Filler, "Luminous Luxury," *House & Garden*, March 1983, pp. 54–62.

237 "we do not eat cold asparagus with a fork . . .": See Walter Hoving, *Tiffany's Table Manners for Teen-Agers* (New York: Ives Washburn, 1961), pp. 56–57.

238 the new Emily Post Summer Camp: "Lifeline," *USA Today*, June 6, 1983.

238 "Everyone wants to be upper crust today": Ron Alexander, "Once Again, Etiquette Is a Popular Topic," *New York Times*, June 2, 1982, p. C1.

238 "How to decorate rich, rich, rich . . .": Advertisement for Levolor, *People*, May 2, 1983.

238 If she didn't know better, one critic: Martin Filler, "The Taste of Power: Upstairs with Nancy and Ronnie," *Skyline*, March 1982, pp. 24–25, citation p. 24.

238 "There ought to be a school for new millionaires . . .": James Fixx, on ABC's "Good Morning America," March 8, 1982. In fact *D* magazine produced "A Millionaires Handbook," February 1981, pp. 104–37.

238 Food consultant Barbara Kafka tried that: Barbara Kafka, "Upward Mobility Through Lifestyle," Parson's School of Design of the New School, Extension course brochure, Fall 1979.

239 According to *Forbes* magazine: N. R. Kleinfeld, "Forbes's Hunt for Richest 400," *New York Times*, September 11, 1982.

239 there have been style "agents" available to teach: On coaching and coaches, see Strauss, *Mirrors and Masks*, pp. 109–18.

239 "When you care enough to spend every cent you have": Advertisement for Bray-Schaible Design, Inc., *Manhattan* catalog, Summer 1979.

239 The average it would cost to have it done "right": Paige Rense, *Decorating for Celebrities: Interviews with Twenty of the World's Best Designers* (New York, Doubleday, 1980), p. xv.

240 refuse to transact: Douglas and Isherwood, *World of Goods*, p. 140.

240 "It's nicer to work with people who have money . . .": Rense, *Decorating for Celebrities*, p. 128.

240 "If the public could go directly to my craftsmen . . .": Deborah Haber, "Top-

Drawer Spring Cleaning: Experts the Decorators Call On," *New York Times,* March 11, 1982, pp. C1 ff.

240 decorating "right" symbolizes cash on hand: Author's interview with sociologist Barry Schwartz of the University of Georgia.

241 "have qualities that can't be expressed in money": Georg Simmel, *The Philosophy of Money,* trans. Tom Bottomore and David Frisby (Boston: Routledge & Kegan Paul, 1978), p. 404.

241 "status by association": Erving Goffman, "Symbols of Class Status," *British Journal of Sociology,* Vol. 2, 1951, pp. 294–304, citation p. 299.

241 decorating "right" qualifies on almost every count: Ibid.

242 "Nouveau is better than not Riche . . .": Charlotte Curtis, "De-Lorean's Tastes Required Flow of Big Money," *New York Times,* November 9, 1982, p. A20.

243 decorating may well be "a work of art": Paige Rense, *Architectural Digest,* February 1982, p. 20.

243 "I prefer the resident not to be home when I come looking": Joan Kron, "The House and Garden Blues," *New York,* April 28, 1975, pp. 53–56, citation p. 56.

243 "No mattter how good your taste, decorating your own house . . .": Henry Post, "Social Climbing in the '80s," *New York,* December 29, 1980–January 5, 1981, pp. 22–34, citation p. 28.

244 "Even the most secure clients are afraid of looking foolish": Author's interview with Alan Buchsbaum.

244 in periodicals read by their "reference group": Strauss, *Mirrors and Masks,* p. 151. Strauss says that social scientists distinguish between a membership group "in which an individual 'is an actual member'" and a reference group— one "from which the individual's standards, attitudes and status aspirations stem."

245 "I don't care what style it's in . . .": "Page Six: David's Style," *New York Post,* November 17, 1982, p. 6.

247 "People have a fantasy about how their lives . . .": Anne Gilbar, "The Interior World of Paige Rense," *Prime Time,* July 1980, pp. 62–68, citation p. 66.

248 "Just imagine a house so fine-tuned . . . there's nothing . . .": "A Super Sandcastle," *House Beautiful,* August 1980, pp. 72–74.

248 like "a fig-leaf on her face": J. R. Silber, "Masks and Fig Leaves," quoted in Irwin Altman, *The Environment and Social Behavior* (Monterey, CA: Brooks/Cole Publishing, 1975), p. 16.

248 "The person portrayed and the portrait . . .": Jose Ortega y Gasset, *Dehumanization of Art; and Notes on the Novel,* trans. Helene Weyl (Princeton: Princeton University Press, 1948).

248 Masquerades "are part of good role performance": Barry Schwartz, "The Social Psychology of Privacy," *American Journal of Sociology,* Vol. 73, 1968, pp. 741–52, citation p. 752.

248 the focal point was not a piece of furniture: *House & Garden,* January 1983, front cover.

249 does not stock gladioli: Certain phrases and ideas in this section appeared originally in Joan Kron, "The Flower

Powers," *New York Times,* April 7, 1977, pp. C1 ff.

250 "We just plop in what looks right": Suzanne Slesin, "Floral Displays for the Custom Client," *New York Times,* April 3, 1983, p. 37.

250 "a representative of one's group . . .": Georg Simmel, "Secrecy," in Kurt H. Wolff (trans.), *The Sociology of Georg Simmel* (New York: Free Press, 1950), pp. 330–44, citation p. 343.

250 "the average U.S. consumer spent $15 on cut flowers": "Do-It-Yourself Nosegays," *Newsweek,* February 14, 1983, p. 83.

251 "There is no such thing as a well-designed space . . .": "Flair and Fantasy," *Interior Design,* October 1981, pp. 290–95, citation p. 290.

251 had their tense moments over windows: Marilyn Bethany, "Carefree Luxury in Acapulco," *New York Times Magazine,* February 1, 1981, pp. 58–59.

251 The designer believes in "centers of clutter": Jane Geniesse, "A '60's Echo in an '80's Loft: The Conversation Pit," *New York Times,* August 13, 1981, p. C6.

251 "art that you sit in rather than look at": Barbaralee Diamonstein, "John Saladino on Designing a Room," *House Beautiful,* September 1981, pp. 28 ff.

252 "Esthetic quality is no guarantee of livableness": James Scott, "Psychological Need and Housing Design," in *Proceedings of the Architectural Psychology Conference at Kingston Polytechnic,* September 4, 1970, pp. 79–81, citation p. 80.

252 the museum chose to arrange things Wright's way: Paul Goldberger, "Making

Room for Wright," *New York Times Magazine,* December 5, 1982, pp. 162–63 ff.

252 Constance Perin noted that out of forty-five criteria: Constance Perin, *With Man in Mind: An Interdisciplinary Prospectus for Environmental Design* (Cambridge, MA: MIT Press, 1970), pp. 120–21.

252 Today according to Gary T. Moore: Author's interview with Gary T. Moore. Moore believes that there has been some progress in the past decade in making architecture more responsive to human needs: there are numerous guidelines on the design of *public* buildings; the United Kingdom's Department of the Environment has issued design guidelines for the single family house; and *Progressive Architecture* magazine now gives awards in design research. "It's a struggle, but I'm encouraged," he said.

252 Homes must be appreciated as "live-in": Kimberly Dovey, "Participatory Design and the Dwelling Experience," University of Melbourne, Faculty of Architecture and Building. Research Paper, 1979. In the author's interview with Dovey, he said, "You can't have somebody else interpret the place that mirrors yourself. People need to be authentically engaged in creating their own places, and I think people are capable of it, and if they believe they're not, they've been misled. You can't expect people to live in art objects, because they need change as they grow."

253 "the client often holds you back": Jesse Kornbluth, "The Chintziest Decorator in New York," *Metropolitan Home,* June 1983, pp. 47–54 ff, citation p. 98.

253 "was the decorator's idea: neither Chuck nor Anne . . .": Richard Lemon, "Couples: Married Life Begins at Prime Time for Anne Ford and the TV Anchor who Snagged Her, Chuck Scarborough," *People,* March 7, 1983, pp. 83–87.

253 "fulfilled [the architect's] dream": Anna Wintour, "Peach House," *New York,* July 25, 1983, pp. 51–52. The full quote is: "The owners have fulfilled Chapell's dream of outdoor living: they have left the interior very simply furnished . . ."

253 twenty-seven architects specializing in housing: Michael Edwards, "Comparison of Some Expectations of a Sample of Housing Architects With Known Data," in David Canter and Terence Lee (eds.), *Psychology and the Built Environment* (London: Architectural Press, Ltd., 1974), pp. 38–47.

254 American researchers have also noticed: Irving Rosow, "The Social Effects of the Physical Environment," *Journal of the American Institute of Planners,* no. 27, 1961, pp. 127–33.

254 viewing humanistic concerns as "effeminate": Clare Cooper Marcus, "The Gender Gap: Does it Exist in Environmental Design Research?" in Doug Amadeo, James B. Griffin, and James J. Potter, *EDRA, 1983,* Proceedings of the Fourteenth International Conference of the Environmental Design Research Association, University of Nebraska—Lincoln, p. 184.

254 "an early attraction to high and secluded spaces": Clare Cooper Marcus, *Environmental Autobiography.* Working paper 301. University of California, Berkeley: Institute of Urban & Regional Development, January 1979, p. 8.

254 "An Iranian student realized he was holding on: Ibid.

255 "disorder and lack of visual coherence . . .": Ibid., p. 9.

255 "Frankly, I get lonely in a closed-off bath": Marilyn Bethany, "Us Generation Bathroom," *New York Times Magazine,* August 24, 1980, pp. 60–63.

255 Rogers, our leading country and western singer: Suzy Kalter, "For Kenny Rogers and Cher, a House is not a Home—Unless Ron Wilson Decorates it," *People,* June 29, 1981, pp. 35–39.

255 "Let's get rid of everything": Ibid., p. 36.

255 "How do you tell a potential client . . .": Suzanne Slesin, "The Apartment of the Future: A Luxurious Design for Today," *New York Times,* February 11, 1982, pp. C1 ff.

256 "I'm nouveau riche, I don't want any of that to show . . .": Rense, *Decorating for Celebrities,* p. 108.

256 The urge to maintain the status quo: Rikard Küller, "Architecture and Emotions," in Byron Mikellides (ed.), *Architecture for People* (New York: Holt, Rinehart and Winston, 1980), pp. 87–100, citation p. 96.

257 "They can't dream in technicolor": Author's interview with Richard Ohrbach.

258 "Marking services": Douglas and Isherwood, *World of Goods,* p. 74.

259 "Optimistically, a person who buys a whole environment . . .": Author's interview with Eugene Rochberg-Halton.

260 "Old family tradition demands understatement . . .": W. Lloyd Warner, *Yankee City,* Vol. 1, abridged edition (New Haven: Yale University Press [1963], 1975), p. 236.

260 similar to the feelings people have for undertakers: Ibid.

260 A grand home isn't a *symbol* of upper-class status: Ibid.

EPILOGUE:
Surviving the System

261 Mrs. Carter loves the house: Enid Nemy, "A Small Blue Ridge Pine Cabin Is the Carter's Rustic Retreat," *New York Times,* July 14, 1983, pp. C1 ff.

262 "there is no way to say nothing . . .": The author's conversation with Erving Goffman, 1980.

INDEX